D0804955

Second Edition

Invitation to the Psychology of Religion

Raymond F. Paloutzian

Westmont College

Allyn and Bacon

Boston • London • Toronto • Sydney • Tokyo • Singapore

Vice President, Publisher, Social Sciences: Susan Badger
Series Editor: Sean W. Wakely
Executive Marketing Manager: Joyce Nilsen
Production Administrator: Marjorie Payne
Editorial Assistant: Jennifer Normandin
Cover Administrator: Suzanne Harbison
Composition/Prepress Buyer: Linda Cox
Manufacturing Buyer: Aloka Ratham
Editorial-Production Service: Chestnut Hill Enterprises, Inc.

Copyright 1996 by Allyn & Bacon
A Simon & Schuster Company
Needham Heights, Massachusetts 02194

Library of Congress Cataloging-in-Publication Data

Paloutzian, Raymond F., (date)
    Invitation to the psychology of religion / Raymond F. Paloutzian.
    —2nd ed.
        p. cm.
    Includes bibliographical references and indexes.
    ISBN 0–205–14840–9 (pbk.)
    1. Psychology, Religious. I. Title.
BL53.P19 1996
200'.1'9—dc20   95-36563
                                                                CIP

Printed in the United States of America
10 9 8 7 6 5 4 3 2 1   00 99 98 97 96

Contents

Preface to the Second Edition

Since the publication of the first edition of *Invitation to the Psychology of Religion*, the field of the psychology of religion has expanded greatly and has increased in importance and visibility. The scientific study of religious belief and behavior has a greater role in psychological circles and in the American Psychological Association. Psychological research material contributes even more to the allied disciplines of religious studies, philosophy, theology, and cross-cultural studies. Several excellent books have been published and the research has moved in important, crucial new directions. I am gratified that this book has been one of the key contributors and stimuli to this progress. This new, second *Invitation* is equally as timely and important as the first. It promises to accurately reflect psychology of religion research, to illustrate how such research is done, and to stretch the reader's mind and the discipline further.

Most important, I have designed this new edition specifically with the student and teacher in mind. It is intended to be the best teaching tool possible for a course in the psychology of religion and related courses. As in the first edition, the key questions and lines of research are explored in a way that engages the student's mind in the thought processes of the research in the area. The student learns how one does scientific research on a topic as nebulous as religion and learns to recognize and appreciate the contributions to knowledge and practical implications that a psychological research approach can and cannot offer.

Also, this book offers the perspective of what the empirical, data-based lines of scholarship have to say in a way that is accessible to most students. Although it is clear that this scientific approach is not the only legitimate way to study religion, it is certainly an important, essential, and powerful one. It offers its special set of methodological and intellectual tools designed to answer certain types of questions. It is the unique contribution of this book to the general scholarship in this area to present this empirical focus as one key approach among several. It is in addition to, not in place of, the other approaches of religious studies, theology, sociology, anthropology, literature, and the rest. Therefore, this approach complements others, and our knowledge is not complete without it.

This book can be used in several types of courses in which an empirical, research-oriented, psychological contribution is needed. It can serve as a stand-alone text or can be used as the anchor text supplemented with other materials. It is also short enough to serve as a supplement in other standard courses such as social psychology or other topics.

New Features

I have taken care, in response to the advice of a wonderful team of reviewers, to make sure that this new edition is not merely a matter of new additions. This book is reorganized and longer than its predecessor, and some new space was needed in order to do justice to the new lines of research.

Some of the new material and new organization are as follows. The introductory chapter has been reorganized in order to provide a more logical flow of the ideas fundamental to the rest of the book. Also, the first chapter introduces a more cross-cultural perspective that better conveys the vastness of the topic, and this perspective is woven throughout the rest of the book where appropriate and where sufficient material is available. The research methods section in the third chapter includes an updated treatment of how we measure psychology of religion variables. Most important, it also includes treatment of our scientific approach in light of recent philosophy-of-science discussions in the postmodern movement. This places the entire discussion in current context. The first edition's chapter on religious development has now become two chapters, focusing on children and on a lifespan perspective that reflects the latest scholarship on religion in adolescence and adulthood. The chapter on religious conversion and persuasion has been reorganized to present a clearer picture of the material on how people come to a religion and hold on to it. A new chapter dealing with the relation between religion and conscious experience has been added. The material on religious orientation, prejudice, and socially relevant behavior is considerably updated in light of new research on religion as a quest and exciting new studies of authoritarianism and fundamentalism. The chapter on religion, personality, and health and well-being reflects the latest scholarship on religion and various health measures (including mental and physical health), plus work on religion and coping and on spirituality. Overall, this material represents the most recent advances in the most important lines of work in the area.

Regarding organization and flow of chapters: the chapters have been written in a way that allows considerable flexibility in the order in which they are read. Although the material tends to build from beginning to end, the sections are crafted to allow them to be read in any order without undue loss. Also, some teachers might prefer to treat the historical and methodological material (Chapters 2 and 3) separately from the central content chapters (e.g., at the end of the course). The book allows such flexibility.

Acknowledgments

Four people from my new publisher, Allyn and Bacon, must be thanked. My gratitude and admiration go to Ms. Susan Badger for inviting me to Allyn and Bacon and for her thoughtful, in-depth guidance. Appreciation goes to Ms. Laura Pearson for her cordial oversight as developmental editor. Thank you to Ms. Jennifer Normandin and Ms. Marjorie Payne for skillfully carrying me through the revision process. My thanks also to Cynthia Newby of Chestnut Hill Enterprises who turned my manuscript into a bound book.

Many scholarly reviewers provided expert evaluations during various phases of the revision process. Space does not allow me to elaborate on the contributions of each one, but they are much appreciated and are listed here in alphabetical order: Jeffrey Adams, Allen Bergin, Terry Darling, Michael Donahue, Jennifer Gould, Joseph Hayden, Ralph Hood, Jr., Bruce Hunsberger, Richard Kahoe, Lee Kirkpatrick, Susan Kwilecki, H. Newton Malony, Beverly (Macy) McCallister, Susan McFadden, Mike Nielsen, Dolores Nieratka, Lawrence Nixon, Kenneth Pargament, Jack Shaffer, Bernard Spilka, and John Tisdale. Their critiques and contributions were excellent.

Westmont College funded part of the preparation of the book with a faculty development grant, and such support is acknowledged. Karen Cheng assisted with a variety of final details. Susan Kaufman, my skillful secretary, did her magic in preparing the final copy.

From the Preface to the First Edition

In order to put this revised edition in temporal context and convey the continuity and same teaching orientation as the first edition, portions of the preface to the first edition are reprinted below.

Goals

This book is an outgrowth of my course taught at Stanford University and the University of Idaho. While teaching at these two universities, I encountered an excessive amount of student demand for a quality introductory book. This book is meant to fill that void.

The goals for the book are several: First, I want to create interest in the psychology of religion within an academic framework. Serious scholars, when asked, will readily agree that this field is very important and grossly neglected in mainline psychology—but few seem to be willing to study it. Serious scholarship in the psychology of religion is something much needed in modern psychology.

Second, fluent verbal quality has been a goal. Other books exist which overlap in content, but are stiff to read. I wanted to write a book in which the verbal quality pulled the reader along in an engaging, pleasurable manner.

Third, this book is an invitation to the psychology of religion, not an encyclopedia of it. I made no attempt to review every possible study. Such excessive coverage is desirable in a comprehensive reference work, but not in a short book that undergraduates are supposed to read and enjoy. Instead, I have opted to treat fewer studies and issues in more depth, rather than try to surface-review everything. In this way, the central questions that students have in mind are addressed, while adequate depth and representation are still given to the key studies and areas of research.

Finally, the book is about research in the psychology of religion, as opposed to being about religion per se or any particular religion. As such, it adopts a nonsectarian approach and should be compatible for use within a variety of religious and academic contexts.

Features

A word about book construction: I employ several integrating themes which appear across several chapters. These help to knit the material together and provide a sense of coherency. In order to facilitate the student's conceptual organization of the material, outlines appear at the beginning of each chapter. To facilitate the book's use as a teaching tool and research stimulant, suggestions for research projects and further reading are included at the close of appropriate chapters. Finally, to let the reader know "early on" what are my orientations to the field and the limitations of the book, these are specifically stated at the close of Chapter 1. You are welcome to send me your evaluation of the book's strengths and weaknesses plus suggestions for improvement, so that I can make the next edition even better.

About the Author

Photo, Brad Elliott

Raymond F. Paloutzian received his Ph.D. in 1972 from Claremont Graduate School and has been a professor of experimental and social psychology at Westmont College in Santa Barbara, California since 1981. He previously was on the faculty of the University of Idaho and has been a visiting professor teaching Psychology of Religion at Stanford University. He is a Fellow of the American Psychological Association, the American Psychological Society, and the Western Psychological Association. In 1992–93 Paloutzian was honored to serve as president of APA Division 36 (Psychology of Religion). An active contributor to teaching and scholarship, he co-edited a special issue of the *Journal of Social Issues* on the topic "Religious Influences on Personal and Societal Well-Being."

Foundations

1

Religion In Psychological Perspective

Probably nothing in human history has sparked more controversy and debate than religion. It is obvious that religious questions, experiences, and religiously motivated behavior are alive and well in Eastern and Western cultures. A small glance at the prevalence, scope, and effects of religion reveals how sweeping are its influences and how important it is to learn what psychological research has to say about it.

The Prevalence and Scope of Religion

A recent Gallup poll indicates that 94 percent of the adult American population believe in God, 88 percent pray, and 65 percent claim to be members of a church or synagogue (Gallup & Jones, 1989). Fifty-three percent of the people say that religion is a "very important" part of their lives; an additional 31 percent say it is "fairly important." A high proportion (84 percent) believe that God is personal and is a "Heavenly father who can be reached by prayers." These and similar statistics have been stable for many years. In addition, religious experiences are among the most profound and perplexing in human life, and mystical experiences may occur in up to 35 percent of the American population (Greeley, 1974).

Religion is also pervasive and influential worldwide. In Poland and Italy, over 85 percent of the people are Catholic (*Encyclopaedia Britannica*). In post-Soviet Russia, the Russian Orthodox Church has shown remarkable resurgence and prominence with a reported 60 million believers (Associated Press, 1993). In Latin America, various forms of charismatic religion are reported to be on the rise (*Time*, 1987). In addition, some countries are officially religious.

For example, Iran is formally an Islamic country, Israel is officially a Jewish state, and the United Kingdom is Christian as expressed in the Church of England. Globally, we can predict that over 3 billion people out of the world's 5.5 billion total population are religious or have their lives affected by religion in important ways.

All countries of the world are affected in profound ways by the religious beliefs and practices of their citizens. Examples in both Western and Eastern cultures are easy to find. For example, fundamental religious differences that date back several centuries are part of the hatred, bloodshed, and wars between the Orthodox Serbs and the Muslims in Bosnia-Herzegovina, between the Christian Armenians and Muslim Azeris in Nagorno-Karabagh, and countless other conflicts around the globe. In the United States, certain forms of religion appear to be a major force in political and social affairs, as is illustrated by the "pro-life" movement and the "religious right" of the 1980s and 1990s. Furthermore, people turn to religion for help in coping with personal or social crises, as occurred in the aftermath of the 1992 Los Angeles riots and the 1995 Oklahoma City bombing. Victims of the riots depended on the African Methodist Episcopal Church for help, and victims of the bombing received personal comfort, hope, and physical aid through religious services and agencies. Overall, it is clear that some of religion's influences are undeniably positive and some are undeniably negative.

Although religious events seem prominent now, religion is not a mere fad reserved for the youth and celebrities of the late twentieth century nor is it only in the West. Religion is worldwide and for all time. A quick look at the past reveals that religion has affected the lives of many of the central figures of history, who, due to religious motivation, became pivotal influences in their world—for good or evil. Because of religious motivation, both conservative and revolutionary events have occurred. This is true in both the personal and social sense. Religion may represent a profound revolution in the life of the individual. It may also motivate people toward social revolution—social revolution either in the sense of effecting change in some facet of society such as church function, health care, or race relations; or in the sense of changing the entire social structure. On the other hand, religious motivation can stimulate people to maintain the status quo and hold onto existing forms and consequently resist change. In either case, religious influences on behavior can be potent.

Even today many people claim to have special religious experiences or to be special religious people, and other people turn to them as new messiahs. In 1979, 913 members of the People's Temple church in San Francisco followed their leader, Jim Jones, to their deaths by apparent mass murder-suicide by drinking poisoned Kool-Aid at the Guyana camp they had built with their own sweat and labor (*Time*, 1978). The general population was stunned to the point of disbelief that religious people could follow their leader so totally. Just over a decade later, in 1993, David Koresh led a sect called the Branch Davidians, an offshoot of the Seventh Day Adventist Church, to its destruction in a blaze in their Waco, Texas compound after months of siege by the U.S. Department of Alcohol, Tobacco, and Firearms (*Time,* 1993a, 1993b). Eighty-seven people died, including children, rather than surrender. The group members reportedly believed that they were God's special people who had the Truth and who would gain eternal rewards by following Koresh, even to a cataclysmic death. The general population was again stunned. What motivates people to hold religious beliefs such as these, and to act upon them—beliefs so powerful as to be held "unto death?"

Finally, religion in America has become a substantial media enterprise with a large publishing, television, radio, and educational industry. Religion is big business. A paradox is that while American society seems to have become more secular and less tied to its religious traditions, people seem to be becoming more religious.

Religion in Action

In this book we shall explore religious belief and behavior from the point of view of empirical psychological research. But just what is this "religion" we are talking about? How is it best characterized? Or, is it an "it"—a thing—at all? And what do we mean by "psychology of religion," and what is its role in aiding our understanding of religion and its role in psychology?

Consider the following true instances of religious belief and behavior, and see whether you can then define the nature and scope of the psychology of religion:

1. A small religious group is formed and begins to increase in size. Its leader claims to be a prophet, teaches about her contact with deity, and predicts that the earth will end on a specific date by a great flood. The flood does not happen, but her followers continue to believe (Festinger, Riecken, & Schachter, 1956).

2. A church meets in the rural South. In obedience to God's commands, live, poisonous rattlesnakes are brought out. During one phase of the service, members of the congregation dance in a frenzy to loud music while handling the snakes. During the service, one man is bitten. The congregation prays through the night for his healing. He lives. This man has been similarly bitten 68 times during the past 20 years (*Jolo Serpent Handlers;* see also La Barre, 1962; Hood & Kimbrough, 1995).

3. A group of four young, single professional women meets weekly for bible study and prayer. They report that the fellowship with like-minded believers during these meetings and the communication with God through prayer are the most meaningful times during their busy weekly schedule.

4. A Muslim conscientiously practices the Five Pillars of Islam—confession of faith, ritual prayer, the prescribed alms, fasting during the month of Ramadan, and the pilgrimage to Mecca (Woodberry, 1992).

5. Forty thousand followers of Reverend Sun Myung Moon of the Unification Church get married in the Olympic Stadium in Seoul, Korea. Several of the couples do not speak the same language and have never met each other (*Today* program, Aug. 25, 1992). This follows a similar mass wedding of 4200 people in New York's Madison Square Garden a decade earlier.

6. Even though with advancing age it is becoming more difficult to do, an elderly woman with multiple chronic health problems still manages to attend weekly religious services. For her, doing so has become more spiritually meaningful as it has become more difficult.

7. Augustine of Hippo, while still a young man, goes through a period of anguish. One day he is in a garden in Milan, and while meditating he hears a child's voice saying "Take and read." He opens his Bible to the first place that he finds, the Epistle to the Romans 13:13, and reads "Not in reveling and drunkenness, not in debauchery and licentiousness, not in quarreling and jealousy: but put on the Lord Jesus Christ, and make no provision for the flesh to gratify its desires (NIV)." He instantly feels a serenity in his heart and the darkness and doubt that he felt vanishes away (Augustine, 397/1960). He then becomes one of the most influential Christian writers of all time.

8. Malcolm Little is in an American prison for armed robbery. While there, he is introduced to Black Muslim teachings, which he accepts and which transform his life. He changes his name to Malcolm X and becomes a follower of Allah. He also becomes a Black Muslim minister who teaches racial segregation. His religious quest leads him on a pilgrimage to visit Mecca, where he communes and feels a complete unity with the other "white" Muslims. This experience convinces him of the unity of all people and he subsequently speaks out for the oneness of people of all races (Malcolm X, 1964).

9. While travelling down the road on the way to Damascus, Saul of Tarsus sees a bright light that stops him in his path. He hears a voice saying "Saul, Saul, Why do you persecute me?" Saul is convinced that this is the voice of Jesus. Although he used to track down and persecute Christians, he changes his name to Paul and becomes the most forceful of the Apostles and writes much of the New Testament.

10. A religious rite-festival is held on a rural island in the Aegean Sea. The people gather at dusk at the site of an isolated Greek Orthodox church. During the evening festival a large bull is auctioned and goes to a senior man of the village. This man has the privilege of cutting the bull's throat. The bull's meat is then cooked all night, along with three goats and a barrel of onions in a large stew. The people use the blood of the bull to make the sign of the cross on their foreheads. Believing that this increases their fertility, the people consume the bull the next day.

How can so many behaviors and events with such variety all be called by one name—*religious*? If you have tried to grapple with this question, "What is religion?," you know that trying to define religion is like trying to take something that has endless variation and talking about it as if it were one thing. This is difficult to do. It is no simple task to identify the essential threads that tie together those things referred to as religious. Although there is no one universally accepted definition of religion, it is nevertheless useful and necessary to describe the field in order to give us an idea of what this field comprises. Various ways of conceiving religion are illustrated in this chapter, along with alternative perspectives that psychologists may take toward conceptualizing and interpreting it.

Psychological Questions about Religion

There are a variety of questions to be asked about the psychology of religion. In this first chapter we are concerned with outlining the nature and scope of the field: How do psychologists approach the task of analyzing and conceptualizing religion in meaningful psychological terms? In subsequent chapters we take up a series of more typically focused issues: What is the field's history? Where has it been and where is it going? What are the important theories, methods of study, and conflicts in the area? What is the course of religious development from childhood through old age? How are religious change and conversion best conceptualized and interpreted? What is the process and experience of conversion? What are the consequences of religion in life? What is the difference, psychologically, between genuine and phony religion in someone? Why are some people fanatics and others rather mellow about their religion? What is the process of religious doubt? Does religion promote or retard human compassion and individual health? Is there a particular type of personality, normal or abnormal, that is prone to adopt religion? Finally, what direction should the field take; what types of work need to be done? Along the way, we shall explore the factors that contribute to religiousness in the individual (i.e., religion as a consequence), as well as how individual religiousness influences other attitudes and behaviors (i.e., religion as a cause).

In order to deal with such issues, it will be useful for us to do three separate things in this chapter: (1) present different uses of the concept of religion and the research psychologist's response to them; (2) break down religiousness into its conceptual parts, the dimensions of religious commitment; (3) sketch the approaches psychologists may take to understand religiosity—where they can look to find the psychological cause of religious belief and action. Although these three things are interconnected, we can expect this interconnectedness to become clearer only as we get further into the topic. Each of these alternative ways of thinking about religion provides a set of conceptual tools, like building blocks, with which to build our understanding. After examining them, we will be better prepared to think in terms of psychological research about religion. We will also be better able to differentiate between the psychological and philosophical questions about religion.

What Is Religion?

A glance at the variety of religions in the world and at the examples of religious experience and behavior presented earlier in this chapter may impress you with the subtleties involved in defining religion. The *Encyclopedia of American Religions* (Melton, 1993) lists 1,730 primary religious bodies in America alone. By "primary religious body" is meant a "church, denomination, sect, or cult." If we add to this the full scope of world religions including the varieties of Buddhism, Hinduism, New Age religions, Spiritualist, Wisdom religions and others, the list becomes very long (Eliade, 1987; Smart, 1989).

In addition, scholars have defined religion in a variety of ways. Religious behavior has been defined at the individual, group, or societal levels. Religion has been conceived of as being either whatever fulfills religious functions for the person or group or a partiuclar content or substance which the person or group expounds and to which they adhere. In either case, the diversity of religious behaviors, which can be thought of as one expression of religion, is very great.

Do research psychologists think there is a common element running through all of these, one essence that makes them all "truly religious?" Let's draw the distinctions between the personal versus social level of analysis of religion, on the one hand, and between the psychological function it serves versus the content or substance of what is believed, on the other, and then see how psychologists respond to the question of what is "essentially religious."

Religion as a Reconnection

The etymology of the word *religion* may be revealing. It is related to the Latin word *legare,* which means to bind or to connect. The English word ligament, which comes from the same root, means connection. "Religion," then, refers somehow to the process of rebinding or reconnecting. An assumption is that unconnecting must have happened, and that, as a consequence, reconnecting is necessary. But reconnecting to what? Unfortunately, it is not clear from the word itself whether people are supposed to be reconnected to God, Nature, a state of mind, a cosmic force, each other as individuals, or their communities. Wulff (1991) also notes that the term *religio* may have connoted reference to a great power, or to people's feelings or acts in response to that power. Nevertheless, the universality of religion suggests that the need to repair some kind of basic brokenness is present among all peoples. An etymological look at *religion*, therefore, would lead one to the idea that religion involves peoples' striving for a sense of wholeness or completeness or to that which has a claim on one's commitment. But is this something that is personal, social, or both?

Personal and Social Religion

The examples of religion-in-action noted above and the notion that religion involves some human need for connectedness imply what is now made explicit: Religion can be understood at both the personal and social levels of analysis. Examine the following statement by Kenneth Pargament:

> *Religion can be found in every dimension of personal and social life. We can speak of religion as a way of feeling, a way of thinking, a way of acting, and a way of relating."* (Pargament, 1992, p. 206.)

Religion at the personal level refers to how it operates in the individual's life. It may supply the individual's life with meaning, create ecstatic states of consciousness, provide a code of conduct, make one feel guilty or free, or clarify the truth to be believed. This is partly what William James (1902) must have had in mind when he said that personal religion is concerned with "the inner disposition of man himself, his conscience, his deserts, his helplessness, his incompleteness." The key question at this level of analysis is: What do you personally believe and how does your religion function in your life; what does it do to, for, or against you; how does it affect what you do, your attitudes on social issues, your mental and physical health, your well-being and your ability to cope with crises?

At the social and societal levels, religion refers to specialized social groups (e.g., Melton's primary religious bodies), or religion as a social institution. This may refer to churches, synagogues, and other groups such as independent sects, together with their collective beliefs and practices. Here the emphasis is on how religion interacts with other parts of society and on how group processes operate in religious organizations.

This difference between religion in the individual person (you personally) and in religious organizations and society-in-general matters because the content of people's beliefs and the psychological processes that function to sustain or change them are not necessarily the same for individuals and groups. As a simple example of how they may differ, you as an individual may not believe exactly the same thing as your religious group does about the doctrine that "God answers prayer." Or, the psychological processes for why you hold your own beliefs (e.g., logical analysis) may not be the same as those for the group or religious institution as a whole (e.g., tradition).

Thus, both conceptual clarity and methodological precision require that we grasp the difference between personal and social religion. Also, this "levels of analysis" argument can be extended to include the biological level of understanding of religious belief or experience (e.g., Jaynes, 1976; Liddon, 1989; Waller et al., 1990) at the micro end, and the sociological and cultural anthropological level at the macro end. In real life, of course, both the psychological function that religion serves and the content and substance of what is believed are the result of the *interaction* between individuals and their social context.

3. Religious Function and Religious Substance

a. Religious Function

Both functional and substantive definitions of religion have been offered. Functional definitions are those that define religion in terms of what it does for a person or the society (Figure 1.1). For example, Emile Durkheim (1915)

Conceptualization of Religion

Level of Analysis		Function	Substance
	Personal	Whatever serves a religious purpose for the individual; e.g., supplies meaning, reduces guilt, increases guilt, supplies moral guidelines, assists in facing death, etc.	Unique belief of individual Personal awareness of sacred, transcendent, or divine
	Social	Whatever performs a religious function for society Operation of group processes in religious groups	Formal creed and deity it represents Group consensus on belief and practice Public stance of church, synagogue, denomination, sect, etc.

FIGURE 1.1   Conceptualizing religion in terms of its psychological function versus its substance, at both the personal and social levels of analysis

saw religion as a positive social institution that helped to bring people together and stabilize society. This was accomplished by religion functioning as that which contained and perpetuated necessary social and moral codes and that which made it possible for people to overcome "anomie" or isolation. Anything that did these things could be said to serve a religious function.

The functional approach is also represented at a more personal level of analysis. Milton Yinger (1970), for example, noted that religion in the life of individuals concerns the manner in which they cope with ultimate problems, such as the inevitability of death, the meaning of life, the absoluteness versus relativity of morality, and the quest to overcome existential aloneness. In a similar way, theologian Paul Tillich (1952, 1963) argued that religion involves a person's relationship to some "ultimate concern." Whatever is of ultimate concern to someone is filling a religious role for that person.

There is one obvious strength to emphasizing the function of religion: religion is seen as a process, not as a doctrinal content. Because of this, the functional approach is very tolerant. Almost anything can serve a religious function. It can be theistic (e.g., Judaism) or atheistic (e.g., Buddhism); it can include one god or several; it can be a stick, a stone, or an idea. As Malony (1980) put it, "religion can be God, Country or Yale!"

However, this very tolerance also embodies the most important weakness of the functional emphasis. If anything can be religion, then just what is religion? There is the built-in danger that the definition will become so broad as to include everything—at which point it becomes impossible to differentiate religion from something else. In other words, it is difficult to avoid the pitfall that "everybody is religious." Note also that the functional approach includes the logical dilemma of answering the question "Functional for what?" and hence implies a definition in terms of substance that it attempts to avoid.

Religious Substance

Definitions of religion in terms of substance place the emphasis on the belief, doctrine, creed, or practice of the religion; these reflect and point to the essence of what is believed. Often this is stated in terms relating to the sacred, holy, numinous, transcendent, or divine. The key for the substantive approach is that it is *what* is believed or done that matters, not the psychological function it serves. Substantive definitions range from the very specific (e.g., belief in the God of Biblical Christianity) to the broad (e.g., belief in a universal spirit or in general human community) (Eliade, 1987; Smart, 1989).

As with the functional approach, the substantive approach can be differentiated into the personal and social levels (Figure 1.1). At the social level it is reflected in the common creed that is given assent by the social unit (e g., congregation, denomination, order). It may also include practices performed as part of the religion.

At the personal level, religion-as-substance refers to belief in the sacred, transcendent, or divine as seen by the individual. The individual's religious belief may be very similar to that of the group, but it does not have to be. It is entirely possible, psychologically speaking, for your religious belief to be unique to you.

Conceptualizing religion in terms of substance has its merits as well as its drawbacks. The primary advantage to the substantive approach is that it is simple. It is relatively easy to categorize a group as religious if it essentially identifies itself as such. Religion becomes easy to see and label. This approach also avoids the potential error of considering as religious those who attempt to deal with life's problems but who would not label themselves as religious (e.g., self-help groups, health faddists, social action groups, political groups). It circumvents the simplistic overgeneralization that "everyone is religious."

The problem with the religion-as-substance approach, however, is that it might exclude an apparently "nonreligious" force in the life of a person or group even though such influence is fulfilling a religious function. For example, politics has no formal religious content, but participation in a political party can do the same thing for one person that an established religion does for another. Overall, we can say functional approaches refer to *how* something is essentially religious, whereas substantive approaches indicate *what* is essentially religious.

4. The Variety of Religious Behaviors

The complexities involved in clarifying what religion is can be made more vivid by making one final point. With all the different ways of conceptualizing religion mentioned above, one would predict an almost endless variety of behaviors labeled "religious." This point has been made clear by James Dittes (1969, p. 607) of Yale University:

> The diversity of phenomena within religion has been catalogued dramatically by Paul Johnson (1959, pp. 47–48):
>
> In the name of religion what deed has not been done? For the sake of religion men have earnestly affirmed and contradicted almost every idea and form of conduct. In the long history of religion appear chastity and sacred prostitution, feasting and fasting, intoxication and prohibition, dancing and sobriety, human sacrifice and the saving of life in orphanages and hospitals, superstition and education, poverty and wealthy endowments, prayer wheels and silent worship, gods and demons, one God and many gods, attempts to escape and to reform the world. How can such diametrical oppositions all be religious?
>
> Johnson's catalog of contradictions could easily be extended. Even within the relatively homogeneous Judeo-Christian tradition, one finds firm insistence

on the importance of obedience to regulation and on freedom from regulation, on inculcation of guilt feelings and on freedom from guilt feelings, on autonomy and on "absolute dependence," on the conservation of social values and on the overthrow of social values, on individual mystical aloofness and on the interdependence and responsibilities of group membership, on fear and on trust, on intellect and on emotion, on salvation by passively received "justification" and on salvation by energetically pursued "good works." The catalog is almost endless.

Therefore, with this diverse set of behaviors carrying a single label "religious," it is important that whenever we discuss religious behavior, we specify the precise behaviors in question. Actions, however diverse, can be considered religious to the extent to which they can be related to one's conception of religion. Even though they are diverse, focusing on religious actions can be useful in part because actions form the basis of two of the dimensions of religious commitment that are presented below.

Defining Religion in Psychological Research

It is now no surprise to say that there is no agreed-upon definition of religion either in religious studies and philosophy nor in psychology (c.f., Eliade, 1987; Otto, 1923). One important psychological book uses a functional approach by stating that religion is what one does to come to grips with existential questions (Batson, Schoenrade, & Ventis, 1993), but that is limited in scope and focuses on only one aspect of the general phenomenon of human religiousness. Another important book avoids a strict psychological definition of religion and offers an alternative and useful distinction between "cumulative tradition" and "faith," and lets what is meant by "religion" to be apparent from the context in which it is used (Wulff, 1991). Another definition emphasizes the substantive aspect of religious growth and development, "personal attentiveness to realities perceived as having qualities that make them 'supernatural'" (Kwilecki, 1990, 1991). Yet another approach attempts to combine both substantive and functional aspects into one definition: "Religiousness is more or less conscious dependency on a deity/God and the transcendent. This dependency or commitment is evident in one's personality—experiences, beliefs and thinking—and motivates one's devotional practice and moral behavior and other activity" (Tamminen, 1991). The substantive aspects (God) and the functional aspects (conscious dependency, motivation) are evident in this definition. But it breaks down immediately when confronting criticisms of it by psychologists who do not adopt this approach. For example, some psychodynamically oriented psychologists would emphasize the unconscious rather than the conscious, most would allow for nontheistic religion rather than only belief in deity, and some of the research data on the correspondence between belief and behavior would seriously question whether religion actually motivates one's moral behavior. The lesson I have learned from this was bluntly stated by an earlier scholar: "Any definition of religion is likely to be satisfactory only to its author" (Yinger, 1967, p. 18).

My own approach, consistent with that stated by Spilka, Hood, and Gorsuch (1985), is that for psychological research purposes there has not been much benefit to adhering to one strict definition of religion because such efforts do not seem to have pushed scientific research forward. For the purposes of psychological understanding, religion at least includes the notion that it is a generalized, abstract orientation through which people see the world; it defines their reality, provides a sense of significance, and receives their fundamental allegiance and commitment. In light of this and the conceptual distinctions discussed above, for research purposes it is a multidimensional variable that includes facets such as what people believe, feel, do, know, and how they respond to their beliefs. Such facets are explained below and are called dimensions of religious commitment.

It is not our purpose as psychologists to state what is the essence of "true religion" in a philosophical or theological sense (though trying to do so might be important for other purposes). Instead, it is our task to learn how it works in people's lives. But now you might ask "How can you learn how it works in people's lives if you do not first know exactly what it is?" The answer is that for the purposes of a psychological study religion is represented by a variety of procedures. Many of these procedures reflect the conceptual properties of religion discussed above.

The scientific methodology that we use means that research psychologists of religion are not "essentialists" (Popper, 1972; Stanovich, 1992). That is, we do not continually try to define a concept until we are satisfied that we know what it "truly is"—its essential properties, its essence—before we do research on it. Rather, we do our studies (experiments, surveys, behavioral observation, interviews) the best we can using the most precise methods available at the time for measuring and manipulating the religious variables we are trying to study. These measures and manipulations are called *operational definitions* of religious variables because they are defined by the operations, or procedures, used to assess them. This methodology assumes that across a cumulative set of studies using many operational definitions, a more complete picture of the general concept of religion will emerge—as an outgrowth, not a precursor, of our investigations.

A corollary of this is that the results that you get from doing one study are technique-tied, dependent upon the specific procedures and measures of religion that you use. Therefore, if you do a second study and use a different technique to test the same general question, your results may be different. Such differences in results based on differences in technique make you refine your measures of religious variables and force you to state more clearly the general religious concept you are attempting to study. Thus, our conceptual under-standing of religion evolves out of our empirical investigations that use many operational definitions of it.

The bulk of this book will reveal that researchers have used multiple approaches. These are discussed more fully in the second half of Chapter 3 and are illustrated throughout the book.

Dimensions of Religious Commitment

As is the case in the progress of any science, the science of the psychology of religion begins with descriptions of the events to be explained. After the descriptions are reasonably clear, researchers create more refined techniques for measuring the key variables. These subsequent measures both stimulate ideas for theory and are used to test for predictions derived from theory. In the case of our psychological understanding of religion, the best place to start is with a good "psychography" (Deconchy, 1991) of religion that describes plainly and objectively what it is in terms of people's thoughts, feelings, and actions.

A simple and often-used technique to accomplish this (in addition to the previous definitional distinctions) is to recast religion as a series of dimensions that describe how people can or do function in it. Have you ever known people who did not "practice what they preach," that is, who believed in their religion's teaching on some moral issue (say, sexual or economic behavior) but who nevertheless acted in the opposite way? Or, have you known someone who had strong religious beliefs but who had very little knowledge about the basis for those beliefs? This would be a classic instance of "blind faith." These examples illustrate how religion is made up of a variety of facets called dimensions of religious commitment (Glock & Stark 1965; Stark & Bainbridge, 1985). They also illustrate how these facets (belief, knowledge, effects, etc.) can occur in various combinations. Figure 1.2 illustrates various combinations of religious belief with religious knowledge and with the practical effects of religion in life.

 Implicit in what has been said so far is a conceptually rich schema for mapping out some logically distinct dimensions of religiosity. This schema, developed by Glock (1962), is a useful way of organizing the field. He made explicit the distinction between what people believe as religious truth, what they do as part of the practice of their faith, how emotion or conscious experience is involved in their religion, what they know about their beliefs, and how their everyday lives are affected by their religion. Glock summarized this analysis of religious commitment in terms of five dimensions: beliefs, practice, feelings, knowledge, and effects. Religion was seen as a multidimen-sional variable composed of at least these five factors, and they are implied by

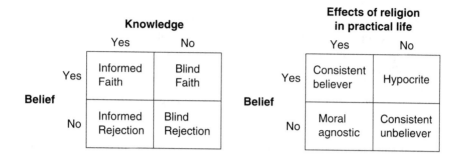

FIGURE 1.2 **Combinations of religious belief with religious knowledge and with the effects of religion in life**

the more recent characterization of religion by Pargament (1992; see quote above).

I have found this and similar schemas useful because they conveniently enable me to describe different religions. Ninian Smart (1989) clearly illustrated the differences among the world's major religions by distinguishing them along such lines. For example, certain religions are long on practice and ritual (e.g., an Armenian Apostolic mass can last an hour and a half), other religions or religious individuals place heavy emphasis on feelings and emotions (e.g., Otto, 1923/1950, emphasized a sense of the "numinous" and awe), whereas others put the emphasis on a specific doctrine to be believed (e.g., the doctrine of the Trinity). Thinking of religiousness as being made up of a combination of these facets also makes it easy for me to ask questions about the relation among cognitive variables (religious belief and knowledge), emotional variables (religious feelings), and behavioral variables (religious practice and effects). Similarly, much research and several modern, refined measures in the psychology of religion (see Chapter 3) are designed with the relations among such facets of religion in mind.

These five factors are not completely independent of each other—a methodological issue to be discussed later. They correlate with each other to a moderate degree (Clayton, 1971; Faulkner & DeJong, 1966); that is, people who have strong beliefs may also (but not necessarily) have religious feelings, display religious practice, etc. Nevertheless, due to its logical clarity and its potential for wide application, this schema gives us a good descriptive language that we can use as a starting point to talk psychologically about religion.

Religious Belief (the Ideological Dimension)

The belief dimension refers to what is believed as part of a religion, how strongly the belief is held, the bases for the intellectual assent, and how salient that belief is in the person's life. For example, belief in the existence of God is a religious ideology. In nontraditional religions, this dimension could correspond to a deep commitment to a set of values. Or, in primitive religions, it could refer to the belief that spirits inhabit physical objects.

It is the content of the belief, or doctrine, that is the most basic dimension along which religions differ. It can even be said that it is the belief variable that defines different religions. Untold numbers of religious groups have divided over the question of what is believed to be the truth—that is, over issues of doctrine.

Different categories of belief exist. One type of belief essentially warrants the existence of the religion: it amounts to a bottom-line assumption that serves as the basis for the religion. For example, the belief in the common foundation of all religion serves as justification of the Baha'i faith. In an analogous way, belief in specific teachings about God, Christ, and salvation serves to warrant the existence of the Roman Catholic Church. Such beliefs embody the essential "ground" upon which the religion rests.

A second type of belief refers to purpose, i.e., belief about what is the divine purpose of humankind. For example, an ethically oriented religion might teach that God's purpose is for people to behave kindly toward each other. The purpose of human beings, then, might be to obey God by treating each other kindly.

A third type of belief refers to how to best implement the divine purpose. For example, if one of God's purposes is for people to behave kindly toward each other, then this type of belief would be concerned with specific ways in which kindness should be expressed. Believing that it is good to obey the Ten Commandments and belief that one should follow the example of the Good Samaritan would be beliefs of this type.

Personal religious beliefs can be held with varying degrees of strength. They can also hold either central or peripheral roles in a person's life. Clearly, the more central the beliefs and the more strongly they are held, the more pervasive will be the effects of religion in the person's life and the more "religious" the person will appear to others.

2. *Religious Practice (the Ritualistic Dimension)*

The religious practice dimension refers to the set of behaviors that are expected of a person who declares belief in a certain religion. The emphasis is not on the effect the religion may have on the "nonreligious" aspects of the person's daily life, but on the specific acts that are part of the religion itself. This includes such acts as attendance at worship services, the format of worship services, prayer, baptism, tithing, confession, observance of special holidays or days of the week as sacred, fasting, and participation in sacraments. For example, devout religious practice might mean facing the East and bowing in prayer

The religious practice of taking communion, illustrated by these people receiving the Eucharist from the priest, is a ritual that defines part of the behavioral dimension of Roman Catholicism. Various religions teach that specific behaviors should be performed, both as a visible evidence of belief and as a stimulant to faith and commitment.

three times a day or not eating taboo foods. Examine the examples of religion in action listed early in this chapter and identify those which constitute or involve religious practice.

The "rules" of religious practice may vary from group to group and depend upon the degree to which the religion is institutionalized and regimented. The more a religion becomes organizationally structured, the more specific will be the codes of conduct, codes of dress, format of confession, and line of authority.

Most religions include as part of religious practice some ethical code that members of the group are expected to observe. In the Hebrew Bible, for example, the code was given in the Law of Moses and was stated in the Ten

Muslims engaged in ritual prayer perform behavior prescribed by Islam. What rituals are considered essential in other religions? What psychological functions do they serve, and why?

Commandments. In the New Testament, the same principle is summarized as the command to love one's neighbor as oneself. Scobie (1975) notes that the degree to which a person adheres to the code in daily life is frequently used by others as a measure of the sincerity and depth of a person's commitment. The more your practice corresponds to your stated belief, the more likely it is that you will be looked upon as being devout.

Religious Feeling (the Experiential Dimension)

The religious feeling dimension is concerned with the inner mental and emotional world of the individual. In addition to experiential events that people may label "religious experiences," the feeling dimension includes such things as the desire to believe in some religion, the fear of not being religious, the sense of physical, psychological, and spiritual well-being that derives from belief, and the like. Inner experiences can be perceived directly only by the experiencing person and can only be inferred by outside observers. Research on the nature of religious mysticism (Greeley, 1974; Hood, 1975, 1977) and intense religious experience (Hay, 1985; Hay & Morisy, 1978; Hood, 1973) focuses on this dimension.

Different religious groups place varying degrees of emphasis on inner experiences. Transcendental Meditation, for example, places a great deal of emphasis on the individual's learning how to do a special type of meditation designed to produce an altered state of consciousness. Mystical states are important to some Eastern religions. Certain forms of ecstatic utterances, glossolalia or "speaking in tongues," are important to some Western religious groups, especially Pentecostals (Malony & Lovekin, 1985). Other religions deemphasize feelings because such religions are primarily ethical systems serving to regulate overt behavior.

Feeling states serve a variety of functions in religious life. One function is motivational. The absence of desired feelings can be perceived as a deprivation and can therefore motivate people to pursue religion in order to fill in the feelings gap. For example, lack of perceived meaning in life may move people toward religion, with the hope that in religion the desired meaning will be found. This "deprivation hypothesis" will appear in different forms in later chapters.

Dramatic changes in feelings may accompany or be central to the crucial turning points in a person's religious life. Profound conversion experiences, for example, are frequently described as involving deep emotional crises or uplifts (James, 1902). Following such dramatic conversions, people frequently report feelings of wholeness, fulfillment, joy, absence of guilt, and meaning in life. Prior to conversion, people sometimes report feelings of incompleteness, guilt, or existential anxiety. The experiences associated with conversion may be radically different for people who grew up in a church and were converted over a period of many years, as compared with people who undergo very sudden conversions such as that of Apostle Paul. Sudden converts may report "peak experiences" (Maslow, 1964) that influence them for the rest of their lives. Gradual converts are less likely to report such experiences.

Feelings are sometimes used as a test of the validity of one's faith. For example, people who feel close to God may conclude that their faith is genuine. Feelings are also used as an indication of the presence or absence of a divine spirit. People who feel fearful and anxious may conclude that they are out of step with God, that they have sinned, or that God has left them.

Religious Knowledge (the Intellectual Dimension)

The religious knowledge dimension refers to the information one has about one's faith, as compared to belief in the faith. Obviously, all religions have an origin and a history, but not all followers of a religion are well informed about them. In the case of Christianity, for example, the knowledge dimension refers to what the believer knows about the first-century setting in which Jesus appeared, the roots of Christianity in Judaism, the history of manuscripts, and other similar information both in agreement with and in opposition to the teaching of that religion. Also part of this dimension is one's attitude, open or closed, toward evaluating material contrary to one's faith. Highly dogmatic religious persons may not be open to literature that is critical of their own tradition. Finally, religious knowledge can vary in degree of importance. As is illustrated in Figure 1.2, it is entirely possible that a person could be committed to a set of beliefs (thus score high along the belief dimension), yet know very little about them (thus score low along the knowledge dimension).

Religious Effects (the Consequential Dimension)

The effects dimension refers to behavior, but not behavior that is a formal part of religious practice itself. Rather, the reference here is to the effect one's religion has on the other "nonreligious" facets of the person's life. An example would be an alcoholic who stops drinking shortly after a religious conversion. The drinking or nondrinking behavior is not in itself a religious act, but one consequence of the conversion may be that the person stops drinking. In general, a person's pattern of moral behavior or personal habits may be guided by religious beliefs, although such actions are not aspects of religious practice itself.

Religious effects can be positive or negative at both the personal and social levels. The Reverend Martin Luther King, Jr., promoted racial equality in the American South, a prosocial act that was in part an effect of his religious beliefs. In contrast, Jim Jones invoked a religious guise in entrapping his followers in the Jonestown, Guyana camp, eventually leading to their deaths (*Time*, 1978). At an individual level there are claims of positive effects of certain types of religion in the form of greater mental health and personal growth (Cox, 1973; Kilbourne & Richardson, 1984; Richardson, 1985b). On the other hand, some professional observers such as Albert Ellis (1960, 1962, 1977) argue that religions, especially those incorporating concepts such as sin and guilt, can only make people worse off than they would be without them.

It is often the effects of a religion by which the religion is evaluated. William James, in the classic *Varieties of Religious Experience* (1902), reemphasizes a common claim that a religion should be judged by its "fruits" (i.e., effects) rather than its "roots" (i.e., specifics of doctrine or psychological sources). Note also, however, that in drawing upon the Biblical concept of "fruits," James implies the substantive problem of defining the criteria for "fruits": Which effects are the good ones, and why?

The Dimensions in Combination

The chief advantage of conceptualizing religion along these five dimensions is that it forces our minds to dismiss the simple idea that religion is something that some people "have" and others "don't have." It is this simple idea that is often conveyed in popular language (e.g., "Joe Goodman has 'got' religion"). Instead, we see religion as a multidimensional variable composed of several facets, and we assume that these are interrelated. Furthermore, we can find out through empirical studies to what degree and under what circumstances they are related, for whom, and how much they do or do not predict other psychological and behavioral variables such as mental health and social compassion. It is also possible to combine aspects of them in specialized ways to create new measures of psychologically functional dimensions of religiousness. Some of these are illustrated toward the end of Chapter 3.

These facets can be teased apart in order to see how the different aspects of religiosity work in combination. For example, when we see someone who has strong belief but little knowledge, or one for whom knowledge is unimportant, we think of this person as having "blind faith." Such a believer is in effect saying "Don't confuse me with the facts." When we observe someone with strong belief and who engages in religious practice, but who displays none of the expected effects, we tend to consider that person a hypocrite. In popular terms, such a person does not practice what he or she preaches. When the expected effects are present, we see the person as devout. A similar analysis shows that performing religious practices without belief or feelings amounts to little more than dryly "going through the motions." It would be misleading to say, however, that such a person is not religious. It would be more correct to say that the person performs religious behavior without the corresponding belief.

In some religions this five-dimension schema breaks down—but even this breakdown helps us understand the nature of that religion. A case in point is Orthodox Judaism. Here the distinction between practice and effects all but vanishes. A reading of the Mosaic law in the Hebrew Bible reveals that obedience to the civil law and rituals of everyday life for the Orthodox Jew are in essence both religious practice and religious effects. In this instance, the effect is the practice. In other words, displaying the appropriate behaviors in everyday life is part of the practice of that religion.

Status and Utility of the Multidimensional Schema

Other schemas for separating religiousness into its component parts have been offered (cf. Spilka, Hood, & Gorsuch, 1985). But some of them are very similar to the one presented above—refinements or extensions of it, really—so that there is no particular benefit to our presenting every variation on the general theme. For example, the intellectual dimension might be called "cognitive," or the consequential dimension might be broken down into two subcategories: personal and social. Although these descriptive approaches are useful, what they amount to is a "psychography" (descriptive account) of religion. But our goal is to go from "—graphy" to "—ology" (Deconchy, 1991).

We want to move from description of religion to scientific research on psychological explanations of it, to understanding the "invariants" (constants; fundamental psychological processes) that underlie religious belief and behavior (Deconchy, 1991).

Chapter 3 will show how there is a debate in the literature as to whether the above five dimensions are only conceptual, logical distinctions or whether they are statistically uncorrelated also. For example, Stark and Bainbridge (1985) have said, "Research has found that, empirically, there is much independence among these different dimensions of religious commitment. People who are high on one are not necessarily high on any others (Stark & Glock, 1968)." But others say the opposite (cf., Spilka et al., 1985). The latter observe that often four of the five dimensions intercorrelate positively (belief, feeling, practice, and knowledge); the effects dimension is apparently independent of the other four. The studies use a complex statistical technique called *factor analysis* to show that there seems to be one basic psychological process underlying this set of intercorrelations, and they suggest that this is a general religious factor. This methodological issue will lead us to see how some psychologically functional religiousness measures combine aspects of belief, behavior, etc., in order to tap what the researchers think is the underlying psychological process. It will also help us to see how some researchers frame their questions about religion with these concepts.

Overall, the language we have so far serves as a starting point for talking about facets of religion and "keeps the conceptual field more open" (Hargrove, 1973). The next step is to briefly sketch where psychologists might possibly look for the answer to the question, "What psychological processes underlie religion?"

Psychological Approaches to Religion

One crucial point to appreciate and keep in mind about psychology and its application to the study of religion is that psychologists look in many different places to find the causes and consequences of religiousness. Most of them have a flexible mental perspective that allows them to focus on multiple and complementary processes that influence religious behavior. They prefer to think in terms of not only one but many causal mechanisms operating simultaneously (interacting) to cause religiousness in someone. By learning to think in terms of such complementarity and by learning where it is possible to look for the processes that might underlie religiousness, we move closer to thinking like research psychologists about it, and we are better able to design the complicated types of research needed to explore the multiple causes and consequences of religion.

⁞ *Complementary Viewpoints within Psychology*

The roots of the word *psychology* are found in the Greek words *psyche* and *logos*. *Psyche* is variously translated as "soul," "spirit," "breath;" *logos* has been translated as "word," "meaning," "account," or "study of." Thus roughly translated, psychology means the understanding of the soul. Being defined in this way, psychology used to be one branch of philosophy. But around one hundred years ago, with the introduction of the more objective methods of modern science, psychologists began to realize that any understanding of the soul, mind, or psyche had to be based upon inferences drawn from observable behavior or verbal reports. As a consequence, we now have psychology typically defined as the science of behavior and mental processes.

Even though today the emphasis is on behavior and mental processes, psychologists are still intensely interested in knowing more about what determines our experience. The problem is simply that we can't see our experience and feelings directly. They must always be inferred from some type of overt behavior, even verbal reporting. This point can be illustrated by looking at an example of religious experience: Suppose you say "I feel close to God." Your verbal statement describing your feelings can be seen from two different perspectives, the inside and the outside. You and only you are in the unique position of being able to directly perceive the experience that you describe. All other people must be content to perceive your experience from the outside—as you describe it. Besides observing your verbal statement of your experience, they may also observe other changes in your behavior: for example, you may attend church more frequently, read religious literature more often, behave more morally, etc. What other people may observe, however, is not the same as your own private experience, even though it may be an outward expression of it. This illustrates that you and the psychologist each have a unique and complementary perspective on your religious experience.

In addition, the field of psychology does not have one single perspective from which to view religious behavior or experience. Rather, it has a mixture of several perspectives that may shed complementary light on any single piece of religiousness and that may all be partially correct at the same time. Consider praying, for example. The act of getting down on one's knees and vocalizing a prayer may be seen from several different angles at the same time. Figure 1.3 illustrates multiple antecedent causes that could influence the specific prayer act. Figure 1.3 also identifies the mediating process that corresponds to each type of antecedent influence. First, you might explain the prayer behavior by pointing out that it has been learned, that is, by noting that the act of praying has been taught, and that the person has been rewarded either personally or socially whenever he or she has prayed in the past. Technically, we would say that you are viewing the act as a function of past learning or reinforcement. Second, you might note that the praying person has a motive for praying, that

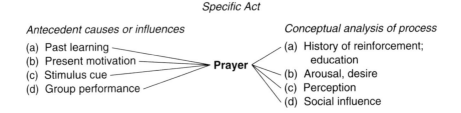

FIGURE 1.3 **Complementary psychological angles from which the same instances of religious behavior can be analyzed**

Note: An antecedent cause and a conceptual analysis of process identified by the same letter correspond to each other.

he or she wants to do so. In this case, you would explain the act by attributing to the person a certain desire, which we call motivation. Third, you might note that the person prays only when the proper signal is given by the pastor, such as in a church service, and that the signal is the cue that tells the individual that it is time to pray. In this case, you would be viewing the prayer act as a function of the perceptual variable of the signal. Fourth, you could point out that every time this particular person prays, every other person in the congregation prays also, so that the entire group is doing it together. You might infer that the individual would feel too conspicuous if he or she did not pray like everybody else and consequently would explain the praying behavior as a function of group conformity pressure. There may be other ways of viewing praying behavior besides the possibilities just discussed. It is important that you realize that no single explanation or viewpoint necessarily negates or discounts the rest. Indeed, by taking all of the possible viewpoints into account, we have a more complete picture of the whole set of reasons behind the specific prayer act than we would have if we relied on only one perspective.

2. *Where Can We Look for the Processes Underlying Religiousness?*

It is possible for psychologists to look in several locations to find the causes of religiousness. These are summarized below in abbreviated form for the purpose of either simple introduction or review. The following is but a small sketch of the vast, rich, and complex nature of these ideas.

Psychology is not a unified field of research or theory. It is a heterogeneous field with many diverse ways of thinking about human functioning. Each of these interpretations, or perspectives, on how best to understand people includes fundamental assumptions about the root causes of behavior. And each perspective points our attention to look for the basis of religiousness in a different place. We can appreciate each perspective on its own, as was historically done, but current theory is to combine aspects of them all in order to have a more complete picture of how various psychological factors in religion work. In other words, religious beliefs, behaviors, and experiences are multiply determined. Five psychological locations where we can begin to look for the bases of religiousness are:

Location 1: Unconscious Mental Processes and Personality. Perhaps the most well known of the possible psychological views is based on the psychodynamic approach whose origin is in the thought of Sigmund Freud (1900). There are variations of this approach in the writings of Adler, Jung, Erikson, and others. The fundamental proposition in this approach is that people are seldom aware of the true determinants of their own feelings and actions because the true causes of action are unconscious. That is, the energy out of which our actions spring and the true motives that propel us to do whatever we do lie hidden in the unconscious mind. Seldom do we ever get in touch with these hidden motives. Instead, we usually must be content only with knowledge of our perceived, surface motives. It is these unconscious processes that are the "real" determiners of religious motivation. If we want to understand human religiousness, the unconscious mind is where to look.

Different types of psychodynamic theory interpret the psychological function served by religion to be either positive or negative. Freud's theory, for example, as represented in *The Future of an Illusion* (1927), was that religion is a type of group neurosis and that God is a fantasized substitute father figure. His rationale was that religious people are basically infantile, insecure, and unstable. (Actually, Freud believed this to be the case for everyone, not just religious people.) Consequently, they need religious doctrine, rules of conduct, and religious social support in addition to the other aspects of civilization in order to maintain a stable life. According to Freud, therefore, the religion that he observed was essentially a crutch for weak people, a protection against anxiety. Not surprisingly, this idea was offensive to many people in the religious community. In contrast, Jung's (1933, 1938) psychodynamic view was that religion served a more positive role in the personality. Jung taught that people had an unconscious need to look for and find God. This motive for God as a psychic reality was believed to be a natural part of human psychological makeup.

Looking ahead, there are several newer approaches to both the application of psychodynamic ideas (e.g., Rizzuto, 1979, 1991) and concepts of personality traits and structure to understanding people's religion, and these will be touched upon in Chapter 2 and elsewhere when they are related to our research-oriented discussion. Some views of the role of religion in conversion (Chapter 6) and of the relation between religion and mental health, well-being, and authoritarianism (Chapters 8 and 9) have their roots in such theory.

Location 2: People's Behavior as Conditioned by Rewards, Punishments, and Modeling Influences. In the classical behavioristic approach, represented historically in the works of Watson (1925), Skinner (1953, 1972), and the earlier writings of Bandura (1977), people behave the way they do because they have been conditioned to behave that way. Virtually all behavior, except simple reflexes, is learned and can be changed by the procedures of classical conditioning, instrumental or operant conditioning, or modeling and imitation. When religiousness is seen as learned behavior, as contrasted with seeing it as the fulfillment of deep needs, there is no interest in unconscious processes nor other needs that might exist inside people's personalities. Rather, we look for specific stimulus cues that trigger religious responses, the religious responses to those stimuli, and the basic conditioning processes that link the two.

A good analogy for this approach is that of a machine or complex computer. The computer is empty in its beginning, but it has the capacity to be programmed in many different ways. The specific way that it eventually becomes programmed—with either simple connections or complex (intelligent) ones, prosocially or antisocially, or religious or nonreligious—depends upon what is learned through life's training.

Strict behaviorists have tended to reject religion, but not because doing so is inherent in their position. It is simply that, historically speaking, behaviorists have been unconcerned with things they think cannot be observed. For them, supernatural influences would be in this category. Because they consider that all behavior, including all religious behavior, is learned via basic processes of reward, punishment, association, and imitation, there has been no reason for them to look for an alternate perspective such as a supernatural or other religious one. Behaviorists can bring their powerful conceptual framework and terminology to bear upon the analysis of religious behavior, but they do not offer a formal, clearly stated "psychology of religion."

Location 3: People's Values and Needs for Growth, Fulfillment, and Meaning. In this approach, one looks for the cause of religion in something that fulfills people's needs for fulfillment, growth, and meaning. The writings of Carl Rogers (1961), Abraham Maslow (1970), and Rollo May (1967) are representative of this basic outlook, sometimes called the "humanistic" or "fulfillment" views in psychology. Existentialistic variations of this approach are found in the provocative works of Frankl (1955, 1975). In the fulfillment view, people are generally thought to be born with positive potential for growth—an innate striving to continually become more fully human. The emphasis is on the purposive growth process—the process of becoming—rather than on attaining a static end state. "Self-actualization" is the term used to describe the direction of movement. By this term, it is meant that each person strives to unfold and fulfill the natural potential that is part of the self. In Frankl's view, each person has an innate striving for meaning, and religion is one thing that can fulfill this need.

If we look to this positive side of human nature to explain religion, how do we account for the existence of human problems? Humanistic psychologists generally believe that people's problems are a consequence of a repressive and disorganized world, rather than some defect in human nature. Thus, it is argued that as the more basic needs for food, shelter, and safety are satisfied, the more positive growth motives within people are free to guide behavior.

Those who posit growth and fulfillment needs as the basis of religion have been more likely than Freudians or behaviorists to be tolerant or positive regarding the value of religion (Allport, 1950; Maslow, 1964). They have pointed out that people have needs for fulfillment, and that having a mature faith is one way to meet these needs. They would also add that religion can take on both positive and negative expressions. In one case, religion might supply a sense of fulfillment and completeness for the individual; whereas in another case, religion might supply a rigid set of rules that restrict individual freedom and work against growth.

Locations 4 and 5: Social Forces, Cognitive Mechanisms, and the Interaction between the Two. This strategy places the emphasis on two observations: first, that human beings are social creatures, and second, that we respond to our experience of the world rather than to the world itself. The emphasis on the social dimension of human behavior (location 4) stems from research in social psychology. Work in this field has shown that most of our behavior, most of the time, is influenced by social forces of one type or another. Sometimes this influence is much more powerful than we would intuitively guess. Milgram's (1963, 1965) demonstration of people's willingness to obey destructive commands, Asch's (1952) demonstration of the power of conformity influence, and Zimbardo's (1973) simulated prison in which a social situation created very pathological behavior even in normal people, are all classic examples of this. It has even been demonstrated that social influence affects such "purely" biological responses as eating (Schachter & Rodin, 1974) and urinating (Middlemist et al., 1976).

The cognitive emphasis (location 5) stems from the idea that our minds process information before we respond to it. We respond to the meaning of a stimulus, that is, to our interpretation of it rather than to the stimulus itself. Also, our minds use special cognitive structures, called schemas, to plan and guide the sequence of our behaviors in accord with the circumstance. For example, if someone bows down and worships before a stone idol, that response is performed not because the person observes a piece of carved stone, but because that particular piece of carved stone carries a special religious meaning to the person, which activates a schema that regulates the appropriate bowing and worshiping behaviors.

Combining the social and cognitive emphases points out that much of the meaning we attribute to things and events in our world comes from our social environment. We learn meanings and schemas from other people, and our lives are molded by social influence processes. And it is this interplay between social and cognitive processes to which we respond.

Social-cognitive psychologists interpret religion in a fashion similar to the way they interpret any other piece of social behavior. Their "slant" is to see in religion good examples of social psychological processes operating in real life. Processes such as conformity to the norms set by the religious group or the dynamics underlying commitment to the belief and/or group are emphasized (Batson, Schoenrade, & Ventis, 1993; Festinger, Riecken, & Schachter, 1956; Lofland, 1977b).

3. *Relevance of the Possible Bases of Religion*

Each of the above potential bases of religion reflects fundamental assumptions about how to view human nature and to interpret religious behavior, and modern research psychologists of religion are likely to employ them synthetically, with parts of them knit together. Each approach is related to some form of research mentioned in the text. For example, the various classical theories noted in Chapter 2 are reflections of the fundamental approaches. Cognitive approaches to religious development are prevalent in Chapters 4 and 5. We will find psychodynamic, behavioristic, and cognitive interpretations of religious conversion in Chapter 6. Strong social influence processes will be found to operate in some religious groups, as noted in Chapter 6. A combination of humanistic influence with social and cognitive emphases is the basis for Allport's research on religious orientation, which appears in Chapter 8. Psychodynamic perspectives are related to research on the authoritarian personality in Chapter 9, where we examine whether a religious personality exists. Taken together, the overall list of approaches gives us a variety of perspectives that we can use to think with. We can combine them and apply them to those aspects of religious belief and behavior where they seem to fit. To do this, however, assumes that the psychology of religion is a valid enterprise.

Is the Psychology of Religion Valid?

The psychology of religion is the field that studies religious belief and behavior from a psychological perspective. This means that we attempt to understand the psychological processes affecting both religious behavior and religious experience, that we attempt to take into account the multiple influences, whether environmental, personal, or social, that determine religious belief and behavior, and that we may draw upon a variety of research and theory in order to help reveal the psychological processes mediating religiosity. Conceptualizing religion along a series of dimensions facilitates its analysis from a psychological perspective.

Now that we have examined the ways of defining religion and various schemas for conceptualizing it, we come to a question basic to the whole field. Is the psychology of religion possible? That is, to what degree can psychological analysis be validly applied to religious phenomena? One's answer to this question depends upon one's assumptions regarding the degree to which religion is unique among human activities.

Is Religion Unique?

The central question of the issue of the uniqueness of religion is whether religion is fundamentally different from other enterprises. Is it "essentially" unique? If so, then we need unique psychological principles to understand it. If not, then the principles from general psychology can more easily be applied to the understanding of religion. Below are Dittes's (1969) four steps along a continuum ranging from "religion is not unique" at one end, to "religion is unique" at the other. Each step in succession represents increasing contention for uniqueness and a decreasing amount of relevance of psychological concepts.

The first and most open position is that religious behavior is regarded as one example of behavior in general. The principles of general psychology are simply brought to bear upon the analysis of religious behavior. Those who adopt this position might point out, for example, that there are similarities between the religious concept of conversion and the social psychological concept of attitude change. They might even argue that conversion *is* attitude change. They then would propose that in order to understand the nature of religious conversion, one must first understand the nature of attitudes and then apply attitude change principles to the analysis of conversion. Consider a conversion that occurs at a large emotional, evangelistic meeting. If the preacher gives an emotional appeal and a person responds, then that conversion might be seen as a result of emotional persuasion. This type of attitude change tactic is commonly used to sell everything from toothpaste to presidential candidates. The basic point is that attitude change principles may be applied whether one is talking about changing political attitudes, religious attitudes, or any other attitude.

The second position is that religious phenomena contain uniquely prominent relationships. The basic position here is that religious behavior is governed by the same principles as any other behavior (so that the principles from general psychology should be applied), but that in the case of religion certain phenomena are more discernible than they are elsewhere. These phenomena may exist in other behavioral areas but they "stand out" more in the area of religion. An example of a behavior that might be uniquely prominent in religion is the phenomenon of emotional arousal in groups. Imagine a speaker giving an emotional appeal to a group for which emotional processes are important features of religious meetings, as is the case for some religious sects. The speaker might raise the emotional pitch with the audience responding increasingly over time. The result might include chanting, crying, fainting, or extreme arousal within a large proportion of the audience. Because this is a group phenomenon, those people who are part of the audience probably would not react in the same way if they were alone, not part of a large crowd. Considering such behavior to be uniquely prominent in religion means that, although such behavior may occur in other areas, it is more likely to be seen in the area of religion.

c. The third position holds that religious phenomena contain unique relationships. The assumption here is that the basic factors that operate to produce religious behavior are the same as those found in any behavior, but that due to the special nature of religion they work together in such a way that they generate forms of behavior and states of experience that are unlike those found elsewhere. In this case the explanations for religious phenomena are not unique to religion, but the phenomena themselves are. An example might be a feeling of freedom that follows absolute acceptance by God. One might argue that the principles that operate to produce this type of freedom are understandable enough, but that religion is the only place where it can be observed.

d. The fourth position is that religious phenomena contain basically unique variables. Those variables that operate in religion appear in religion alone. The assumption is that the factors that make religion what it is are part of its essence and thus cannot be found elsewhere. Any correspondence between religious and nonreligious behavior is either artifactual or illusory. As an illustration, some people might argue that religious commitment is unlike other types of commitment even though they would acknowledge that other commitments exist. They would say that the sentiment involved in commitment to one's religion is fundamentally different from the sentiment involved in commitment to a political party, a personal goal, a social institution, or another person.

2. Implications of the Various Positions

There are several aspects to the process of studying religion that may be related to one's position on the uniqueness of religion issue. First, your position on uniqueness of religion is likely to influence the methods with which you approach the study of religion. Those arguing strongly for uniqueness are more likely to use a phenomonological strategy for research because they do not believe that religion can be understood in terms of the same variables as other behaviors. They are more likely to be content with a complete descriptive account. They may be less intent on relating religious experiences to nonreligious behaviors. On the other hand, those who see religion as one instance of general behavior are more likely to employ quantitative measurement of religious variables. They will make an effort to discover relationships between those variables and other, nonreligious variables.

Second, an investigator's position on the uniqueness issue will influence the starting point from which his or her study of religion begins. One who sees religion as part of general behavior will begin with principles that come from general psychology. These could include principles of reward and punishment, unconscious motivation, or social influence. In any case, the strategy will be to come to the study of religion with a preconceived set of concepts, and possibly a theoretical framework. The researcher may analyze religion only within this set of concepts or framework, or perhaps even make the religious phenomena under investigation "fit" the preconceived way of viewing them. This approach has both strengths and weaknesses. Its strength is that it offers the investigator a powerful, pretested framework for understanding religion (if the theory is a good one, that is). Its weakness is that it may make the researcher narrow-minded, able to see things from only one point of view. Important discoveries could be missed because the "theoretical filter" screens out information inconsistent with the theory. In contrast, one who views religion as unique is more likely to begin investigating it by looking at the raw religious phenomena. Afterwards, building a coherent set of statements about religion might be attempted. This latter approach has less theoretical power than the former approach.

Third, a strong position that religion is unique is more likely to be adopted by those who believe that a scientific and religious or supernatural explanation of something cannot both be correct at the same time. They might say that if God does something (supernatural) then it can't be fully understood by human reason (science). In other words, naturalistic methods cannot yield explanations of such events. In contrast, the religion-as-general-behavior position is more consistent with the view that scientific and religious explanations can coexist. The latter approach might point out, for example, that a scientific explanation of conversion merely helps us understand more about how the supernatural works. The possibility of such influences may be fully granted.

Approach and Plan of the Book

We proceed on the premise that psychological methods, concepts, and perspectives can be validly applied to the understanding of religion (Paloutzian, 1986). But this does not mean that we believe psychology has any corner on truth about religion. A psychological way of looking at religion is only one of many possible ways. Before you move on through this text, therefore, it will be helpful to know the orientations, limitations, and organization of the book.

1. Orientations

There are some overall orientations or themes that are reflected throughout the book. The most fundamental of these is that the text attempts to invite both students and more seasoned researchers to the field. To facilitate this, appropriate chapters close with suggestions for studies or areas of work in which activity seems to be needed.

Another orientation is that psychological explanations of religious experience need not be feared by people in the religious community. If you are an average religious person, chances are that at one time or another you have feared scientific psychology as some kind of opponent of religion. You might believe that if psychologists can understand or explain some aspect of your religious experience (say, your conversion), then they are trying to "explain it away," and thereby negate a religious explanation of the same event. If you do think this, then you are operating on the assumption that a scientific and a religious account of your behavior or experience cannot coexist, or both be valid at the same time. Regarding psychological and religious explanations as mutually exclusive is unnecessary. In fact, as will be clarified in Chapter 3, it is opposed to a sound and modern philosophy of science. Psychology cannot explain away religion, and religion cannot explain away psychology. Clearly, some psychologists say some anti-religious things (as do some physicists, historians, and even theologians). Some psychological findings appear consistent with religious teaching and some do not. But there is nothing in psychological methodology that makes it inherently contradictory to nor supportive of religion.

Another orientation is that psychological concepts and method can help us understand religion in a way that is complementary to the contributions of other disciplines. Fields such as history, anthropology, and linguistics, for example, each offer a set of concepts, a perspective, and a method, which, when brought to the study of religion, add a special insight that cannot be gained in any other way. There are certain insights into religion that historians can gain because of their perspective, and there are other insights available to psychologists because of their perspective. The alternative approaches to understanding religion are not contradictory to each other, but instead are complementary. No single approach by itself can give you the whole truth, but each approach taken by itself can give you part of the truth.

2. Limitations

Because religious belief and behavior is a very broad topic, you won't learn everything there is to know about it by the end of this book. There are approximately 5.5 billion people on Earth as of 1995, and about two-thirds of them are affiliated in one way or another with some religion. Furthermore, we are just beginning to learn about the psychological factors involved in the various belief and behavior systems represented by the world's major religions.

This state of affairs may be unfortunate, but it is understandable and is the result of an historically culture-bound research phenomenon. Most knowledge that we gain about the various religious belief and behavior systems in the world is obtained via the methods of empirical social science. But the modern, empirical scientific tradition of which psychology is a part is primarily a Western phenomenon. Most empirical social scientists and psychologists are products of western culture and live in western countries. Hence, whenever they do study religious belief and behavior, they study those of the West, primarily those in the Judaic and Christian traditions. The latter fact occurs for two main reasons: First, it is the Judaic and Christian religions in which Western, empirical social scientists and psychologists have been most interested and with which they are most familiar. Second, it is simply more convenient for them to study things close to them. Thus, most of the research on religious belief and behavior that exists, and most of the content of this book, is based upon the study of religion in a Western context. Indeed, as Argyle and Beit-Hallahmi (1975) point out, the vast majority of research in this area has been done in England and the United States, and most of that since 1900. Nevertheless, we can attempt to extend our ideas as much as possible to other religious contexts. And fortunately, as will be noted in the next chapter, a new international perspective is on the rise.

You may be asking, "Well, if psychological knowledge about religious belief and behavior is so limited, then why read this book?" The answer is that we do have some knowledge and intriguing insights into this area of study, and we have the basic research and conceptual tools with which we can gain more. So in a sense, you are studying a topic that is in the middle of a journey from ignorance, partial but growing information, and weak understanding to knowledge, complete information, and insight. At present we have traveled only part way on that journey. From the looks of what has been seen so far, we are just now approaching the most interesting part of it.

Organization

The flow of the book is as follows: The first three chapters are foundational. Chapter 1 has mapped out the basic ways of construing religion and the psychological ways of approaching it. Chapter 2 sketches how the psychology of religion began, the major phases and conflicts in the history of the field, and the important theoretical questions that have come out of that history. Chapter 3 states an appropriate philosophy of science for the psychology of religion. It also illustrates the predominant research methods used in the field. These three chapters provide the conceptual, historical, theoretical, philosophical, and methodological tools that serve as the basis for the remainder of the book.

Chapters 4–6 deal with the acquisition and maintenance of religion. The focus is on how people become religious, what their religion means to them psychologically, what personal motives and social experiences are involved, and which factors help sustain the individual's religiousness. Chapters 4 and 5 trace the process of religious development from childhood through adulthood. Chapter 6 is an analysis of the psychological and social forces involved in religious conversion and persuasion. Change to both traditional and new religions is considered. Chapter 7 focuses on religious experiences. The discussion includes the relationships between religion, purpose in life and values, and the theory and research on unusual and mystical states of consciousness.

Chapters 8 and 9 examine the relation between different forms of religiousness and social and personal health. Here the overall question is "Does religion make any difference in people's social behavior, personality, and psychological well-being?" The first half of Chapter 8 details the main lines of research on intrinsic and extrinsic religious orientation and its relation to social attitudes, especially racial prejudice. The second half reports the equally important line of work on whether religion influences morally relevant behavior—prosocial and antisocial. New research on right-wing authoritarianism is related to the material on prejudice and behavior. Chapter 9 evaluates the as-yet-inconclusive line of research on whether religion is associated with certain types of personalities and measures of psychopathology, mental health, physical health, and well-being.

Chapter 10, the final chapter, provides review statements for the various topics. It also suggests future directions that researchers might take and closes with a note on the importance of the psychology of religion to general psychology.

Projects and Questions

1. Visit several churches or other similar religious bodies on occasions other than the one with which you are familiar. Analyze those according to the aspects of religion discussed in Chapter 1, such as Glock's scheme.

2. Read religious literature from traditions other than your own.

3. Take various scales that measure psychology of religion dimensions.

4. Do a computer literature search on a topic of interest to you in the psychology of religion.

5. Communicate via the Internet with people of other religions than your own and ask them questions based on the material in Chapter 1. You may also explore a religion discussion group on the Internet.

6. Explain why (or debate whether) defining the essence of religion is or is not necessary for psychology of religion research to advance.

7. For information about religions as such, examine reference sources such as encyclopedias of religion and books on comparative religions.

Further Reading

Argyle, M., & Beit-Hallahmi, B. *The social psychology of religion.* London: Routledge and Kegan Paul, 1975. A comprehensive report of findings in the psychology of religion from 1900 to 1975; contains many statistical summaries.

Batson, C. D., Schoenrade, P., & Ventis, W. L. *Religion and the individual.* New York, NY: Oxford University Press, 1993. A well-written book from a social psychological perspective that reviews much empirical research in view of Batson's model.

Hood, R. W., Jr., Spilka, B., Hunsberger, B., & Gorsuch, R. *The psychology of religion: An empirical approach,* 2nd ed. New York: Guilford, in press. A comprehensive survey of recent empirical literature across all areas of the psychology of religion.

Wulff, D. *Psychology of religion: Classic and contemporary views.* New York, NY: Wiley, 1991. An encyclopedic presentation of theoretical literature in the psychology of religion; includes presentations of international material.

2

⎡ History ⎤

Historical and Theoretical Developments

Understanding why the psychology of religion is currently reemerging requires that you be aware of the field's past. It would not make sense for me to invite you to the field without letting you know where the invitation has come from and why it is being given now. I believe that two key developments are responsible for the reemergence of the field: a modern philosophy of science and an emphasis on modern empirical research methods. These two developments are explained in Chapter 3. However, the basic issues of the appropriate philosophy of science for the psychology of religion and of the appropriate methods for studying it have their roots in the early history of the field.

In this chapter, I explain some of the conflict in the field's past, plus its progress and my perspective on whether we should consider this field to be unique. In the first part of the next chapter, I try to explain why this conflict is unnecessary—why religionists do not have to be suspicious about psychology and why psychology of religion is now fulfilling its potential in general psychology.

Historically speaking, the science of the psychology of religion did not have to wait until the twentieth century computer age to be born. It could have begun centuries before as soon as human beings were able to think, remember, communicate, and record events with pencil and paper (or stick and clay). Why, then, did it wait until now? The answer has to do with the rise of the scientific method and the scientific and naturalistic way of thinking and viewing the world. Only when people began to emphasize a naturalistic world view would religious belief and behavior be subject to naturalistic analysis. This includes the belief that natural laws determine events, including human religious events. We shall see how this perspective had both beneficial and tragic consequences. On the one hand, it set the stage for a modern psychology of religion. On the other hand, it led to an unnecessary split between the psychological and religious communities.

To begin: when the psychology of religion started around 1900, it was novel, important, creative, and adventurous, and it also contained the seeds of its own destruction. The self-contained barriers to growth were not logically inherent in the field. However, due to the "temper of the times," it is no surprise that this hybrid field did not last.

The Early Period: An Impressive Start

Imagine that you were part of the "hall of fame" of the science of psychology when it was in its infancy just over 100 years ago. Without having had any exposure to our modern research methods, how would you have studied the psychological aspects of religion? Remember that psychologists at that time had no computer, no sophisticated techniques of questionnaire design, scaling, or test construction, and limited statistical procedures compared with those of today. They didn't even have separate academic departments with a course in research methods. Add to this the difficulties in studying a topic such as religion, which by nature is difficult to study with laboratory experimental methods. One would guess that those researchers would forget it and study more measurable topics.

Yet, in the beginning of psychology, before there was much psychology to be written about, there were research articles (Leuba, 1896; Starbuck, 1897) followed by a book dealing with the psychology of religion. One of the first books to apply psychology to any topic was Edwin Starbuck's *Psychology of Religion* (1899). Starbuck was a young professor at Stanford University, and had previously been a student of William James at Harvard. In 1902, William James published his classic *The Varieties of Religious Experience*. Many of the ideas of current writers on this topic have roots in James' thought. Other notable pioneers in psychology and former presidents of the American Psychological Association, such as G. Stanley Hall, also published research on religion. Finally, one of the first psychological journals was entitled *The American Journal of Religious Psychology and Education* (1904–1911). Therefore, even though the psychology of religion was not the only predominant topic in psychology at that time, it did enjoy its share of attention from leaders in the field (Beit-Hallahmi, 1974, 1989; Dittes, 1969; Vande Kemp, 1992). It has been speculated that those early pioneers may have regarded it as a novelty which only the top leaders in the field could risk examining.

These pioneers used two basic approaches to their research, which represent early versions of some of the more modern procedures. I label these two approaches the *empirical-statistical* and *interpretive-analytic* approaches. Each of these contained subtleties that unnecessarily contributed to the downfall of the field.

Starbuck and the "Either/Or" Philosophy

Edwin Starbuck (1899) did the first well-known empirical-statistical investigation of the psychology of religious conversion. He began with a premise which he states unambiguously on page two of his classic work. (This statement also reflects a flaw that I call the "either/or" philosophy.)

> Let us understand each other in the beginning. We proceed on the assumption that this is a lawful universe; that there is no fraction of any part of it which is not entirely determined and conditioned by orderly sequence: that the laws which determine every event, *no matter how mysterious, are ascertainable and thinkable* . . . All things follow an irresistible sequence of cause and effect. [emphasis added]

This is a statement of the classical doctrine of naturalistic determinism. Starbuck clearly means to apply this doctrine to religious phenomena. He is saying that religion is non-unique and can be understood by the same princi-

William James (left) and his student Edwin Starbuck were among the early psychologists who studied the psychological factors involved in religiousness. James taught at Harvard University; Starbuck taught at Stanford University. Their theories and ways of doing research influence the discipline today.

ples as any other behavior. So right at the outset, he is involved with an issue that troubled people for years to come, that of appearing to pit religion and psychology against each other. This apparent opposition is more obvious when we want to explain how an event (say, a religious conversion) occurred. Either the religious explanation or the naturalistic explanation could be valid, but not both. It was an implicit assumption that somehow an explanation at one level violated the truth value of an explanation at the other level (e.g., if your conversion is determined by naturalistic processes then how could God do it?). This apparent opposition still causes misunderstanding on both sides today. It sounds as if science were a threat because it might "explain away" religion. The unnecessary splitting of the two camps was a natural consequence of this idea.

Starbuck also wrote, "Science has conquered one field after another, until it is now entering the most complex, the most inaccessible, and the most sacred domain—that of religion" (1899, p. 1). Notice his use of the word *conquered*, as if science and religion were inherently and necessarily in conflict with each other and only one of them could win. This is an unfortunate and incorrect idea.

The way Starbuck's statements were phrased—and the way others responded to that general idea—represent the historical context of that time.

Starbuck's statements were phrased in terms of a nineteenth century philosophy of science. Modern thinking about the nature and limits of science has advanced beyond this stage. A crucial point to be developed in the next chapter is that a sound philosophy of science does not include the either/or orientation.

You may be wondering what Starbuck did. His procedures were an early version of a questionnaire-interview approach. He made a list of twelve open-ended questions, printed them on paper, and asked people to write what amounted to a religious autobiography in response to the set of questions. Examples of his questions are

II. What force and motive led you to seek a higher and better life?
III. [What were the] circumstances and experiences preceding conversion . . .?
VI. What changes did you find that conversion had worked out in your life . . .? (Starbuck, 1899, p. 23)

These and the other questions indicate that Starbuck had on his mind many of the questions that we still have on our minds today. He tried to get at the "ripe-age" issue, the motives for conversion, the effects of conversion, the role of emotions, among others.

Starbuck then made large charts, on which he categorized the information contained in the autobiographies. His particular method allowed him to see both the important data for an individual subject as well as to observe the commonality and frequency of a certain response category across the whole group of subjects.

This method allowed two desirable features. First, it allowed him to see what a particular conversion in a particular person looked like (at least as it was reflected in the verbal report). Second, it allowed him to see a composite picture of conversion-in-general for the statistically average person. We still try to do both of these today, as is reflected by what are now called, respectively, the *ideographic* and *nomothetic* approaches to research.

2. James

Unlike his student, William James chose not to rely on statistical records for his research. Some writers have argued that the richness of the religious life of the individual is lost with a statistical-records approach. Instead, James used what we may call a *phenomenological* or *interpretive-analytic* strategy. Much of his book is filled with biographical or literary case study material; and much of that is in the form of personal descriptions of religious experiences. What James did was analyze these according to their psychological meanings and vividly use them to illustrate his points made via philosophical analysis.

James' strategy was different from Starbuck's in several ways. This difference reflects the different orientations from which they came and from which people come today. First, James' work was much more of a personal expression of himself. Whereas Starbuck attempted to stay closer to remaining "scientific," James interjected a sizeable dose of his own philosophy, such as his insistence that the test of the religious life of the individual must be found in its "fruits" rather than its "roots"—an obvious expression of his philosophy of pragmatism for which he was famous. Second, James attempted to illustrate via rich and vivid case study material the extreme forms of religious experience. The descriptions of conversion experiences that he cites are selected for their unusual vividness. Starbuck, on the other hand, was more interested in discovering the psychological laws that direct the lines of religious growth in the average person (rather than the extreme special case). Third, whereas James believed that the greatest insight could be gained via a blending of phenomenological description, logical analysis, and speculative analysis, Starbuck believed that statistical summaries would reveal the most important trends in religious life.

Even though your own personality style may lead you to prefer one of these two approaches over the other, the fact is that neither one is better than the other in any pure sense. They complement each other. Their differences indicate that they were developed in order to do different things—to answer different types of questions. People who have been trained to think critically sometimes fall into the trap of criticizing a study for not yielding information which that type of method was not intended to yield in the first place. It's like getting mad at an apple for not being an orange. For example, because I have the biases of an experimental social psychologist, I tend to criticize James for not being statistically oriented and for engaging in too much speculation. But such a response is unfair. His approach should be appreciated for what it does contribute, whether it's in line with my own inclinations or not.

The Middle Period: Factors Contributing to the Decline

The middle period, roughly between 1930 and 1950, was marked by an almost complete absence of systematic work on the psychological aspects of religion. There was an occasional essay or research report but no sustained program of research in which a series of projects was developed in a systematic, step-by-step way in order to answer parts of one general question. Sometimes a contribution was made to the field indirectly. For example, in 1929 Louis L. Thurstone was concerned with developing attitude scaling techniques. In his efforts to develop instruments that would measure social attitudes, Thurstone developed his first attitude scale by measuring attitudes toward the church (Thurstone & Chave, 1929).

Several factors worked together to bring about the decline of the field. Perhaps most pervasive was the either/or philosophy mentioned previously. During those early days there were people who, perhaps only at a subtle level, believed that somehow psychological and religious accounts of things had to be mutually exclusive. The creation versus evolution debate over the question of human origin no doubt contributed to this separation of science and religion, as it still does today in the minds of some people. With many on both sides operating on this presupposition, it is no surprise that, with some exceptions, there was little interchange between the fields.

Another factor concerned competition for clients. Religious professionals had understood that it was part of their role to "cure sick souls" to offer counsel to people who were hurting with personal problems. But about this time, along came the modern professional fields of psychiatry and psychology, appearing to proclaim a "new gospel." The job of helping disturbed people, they said, now belonged to the new mental health professionals and not to the church. This competition naturally fed division and misunderstanding.

Meanwhile, an analogous split was occurring in academic departments. Psychology had been part of philosophy, and most psychologists who worked as professors did so in philosophy departments. At that time, studying philosophical or religious questions was natural. However, during the 1920s and 1930s, psychologists were busy leaving philosophy departments and setting up departments of their own. Psychology was gaining recognition as an independent scientific field, modeling itself after physics, and in no way did it want to be confused with "speculative" fields such as philosophy. Hence, psychologists rejected the study of things that were "tainted" with philosophical or religious questions.

A poignant piece of evidence illustrates the force with which this split was felt. During the years just before and after 1920, psychologists were involved in the instinct-versus-behaviorism debate. William McDougall was presenting the case that human nature is governed by instincts. At the same time, the famous John B. Watson, whose influence permanently changed the course of psychology, was busy founding the doctrine of behaviorism—that all behavior is governed by the principle of conditioning. McDougall published a classic book entitled *Outline of Psychology* in which he argued the instinct view. In exchange, Watson published a devastating review of McDougall's book, which leaves no secret about his attitude toward religion. The title of the review was "Professor McDougall Returns to Religion" (Larson, 1979).

Even as late as 1959, this antagonistic sentiment prevailed. For example, the following quotation illustrates the problems one psychologist had in even getting a group of psychologists together to discuss the topic:

> *During the American Psychological Association Convention of 1959 in Cincinnati, a dozen or so psychologists gathered in a local bistro to plan an exploration in depth of the relation between religion and psychology. In spite*

of hesitancies over the professional hazards of such an undertaking, and some fumbling over the hazy distinction between the psychology of religion and an investigation of the mutual interrelations of the disciplines, there was considerable interest in pursuing the investigation. . . .

The difficulties confronting this undertaking were twofold: one, that we would be unable to find competent and thoughtful psychologists, with standing in their field who would be interested; two, that such men, even if they participated, would decline, for reasons of professional reputation, *to come to grips solidly and imaginatively with the issues. If psychologists are personally religious, they tend to keep this fact aseptically separate from their professional work. If they are not, religious phenomena usually appear irrelevant to them. In spite of its evident importance in human behavior and experience, the psychological study of religion has languished since the days of William James. Though this is not the place to analyze the reasons for this situation, one fact may be noted: psychology and the social sciences are today occupying the center of the stage in the conflict between science and religious faith—a position occupied by astronomy in the 17th century, physics in the 18th, and biology and physical anthropology in the 19th. It is likely that the complexity, subtlety, and touchiness of the issues are factors in the relative silence of psychology regarding religious phenomena.* [emphasis added]*

One other factor had essentially leveled the death blow to the field during the middle period. This was the publication of *The Future of an Illusion* in 1927 by Sigmund Freud, who was by training a neurologist, not a psychologist. According to Freud's theory, religion was a sign of grand-scale neurosis and insecurity that humankind would hopefully outgrow. Obviously, this idea was unlikely to be well received by people in the religious community. They may have assumed that all religion was under attack by all psychology and psychiatry due to the negative statement about religion made by Freud. The fact that Freud's theory was speculative and almost completely nontestable by empirical methods was probably not recognized by religious people. The tendency on their part was to simply discount all psychology as contrary to religious teaching.

Finally, even as late as three-fourths of the way through the twentieth century—when news media reported that extreme Islamic fundamentalists were killing people in the name of Allah, "cultic" and "new-age" religious experimenting was on the upsurge worldwide, and Western cultural dialogue included talk of the meaning of the "post-Christian era"—there was still a residue of bias as documented in the comment by the former editor of the prestigious *Journal of Personality and Social Psychology*, Robert Hogan:

*Havens, J. (Ed.). *Psychology and religion: A contemporary dialogue.* Van Nostrand, pp. 1–2. Reprinted by permission of Wadsworth Publishing Company.

Religion is the most important social force in the history of man: There is a legitimate field called sociology of religion. But in psychology, anyone who gets involved in or tries to talk in an analytic way about religion is immediately branded a meat-head; a mystic; an intuitive, touchy-feely sort of moron, despite the fact that William James' original book, The Varieties of Religious Experience, *is regarded, I think, by almost everyone as both a philosophical and a psychological classic. (Robert Hogan, 1979, p. 4).*

With the factors of the either/or philosophy, the competition for clients, the splitting of departments, and the forceful statement by Freud, it is no wonder that psychology and religion reduced cooperation, communication, and cross-fertilization. A parting of the ways could hardly be avoided. Douglas (1963) has noted the following factors involved in the decline of the field:

1. The psychology of religion failed to separate itself from theology, philosophy of religion, and the general dogmatic and evangelistic tasks of religious institutions.
2. In the desperate effort to be recognized as "scientific," there was an emphasis on collecting discrete facts, without integrating them into a comprehensive theory.
3. The use of data-collection methods and explanations was often uncritical and incompetent.
4. The climate of public opinion was changing, away from religion and toward a behavioristic and positivistic world view.
5. The study of religion was conflictual for both researcher and subject, because of their own personal investment in religion.
6. "Subjective" phenomena were avoided by developing social science, which tried to be "empirical" and "objective."

Additional summary points that help illuminate the split between religion and psychology have been offered by Narramore (1973). He lists several fears on the part of the conservative religious community and on the part of psychologists that blocked dialogue between the two fields. On the part of the conservative religious community, he lists:

1. The fear of naturalistic explanations for our behavior; i.e., the fear that a psychologist might "explain away" what we do and why we do it.
2. The fear of determinism and irresponsibility; i.e., the belief that if our behavior is caused by natural processes, then we cannot be held individually accountable for our own actions, and therefore, actions that religion seems to call sinful are instead seen as a result of sickness, mental illness, or improper conditioning.

3. The fear of humanistic views of human nature; i.e., opposition to the humanistic model of human nature, which seems to be at odds with religious statements about people's sinful nature.
4. The fear of sex; a reaction against the Freudian notion that many problems have their origin in a frustrated sex drive.
5. The fear of feelings; a possible overemphasis on a rational, cognitive type of faith with a corresponding reluctance to share one's true feelings with another person.

On the part of psychology, he lists the following set of factors that helped to alienate psychology from religion:

1. A superficial understanding of religious faith, the observation that most psychologists had a surface understanding of religious teachings.
2. The psychologists' identity problem; the idea that because psychology was becoming a "hard" science like physics, it should avoid "soft" topics such as religion.
3. Unclear perceptions; the notion that differences in world view between religious believer and nonbeliever lead to different perceptions of truth and reality.
4. Realities of time; the fact that it takes too many years of study for one person to become fully competent in one discipline such as psychology or theology, let alone both.

We can now add two additional details that help to complete this picture of this part of psychology of religion's past. The first has to do with the apparent religious motivations behind some subset of psychologies of religion. Pruyser (1987) has listed seven motives or aims in psychologies of religion, most of which are consistent with the comments I have made above. Number one on his list, however, is this: "Some psychologies of religion seek to buttress religion or to defend it apologetically by trying to describe, if not prove, its psychological necessity or inevitability." He is referring primarily to "subscholarly tracts of this ilk (p. 174)." I regard this as an inappropriate goal and believe that those few who have tried to use psychology for such a purpose have harmed rather than helped psychologists of religion in their efforts to contribute the knowledge from this field to the general discipline of psychology. Psychology cannot prove religion (or a particular religion) any more than it can disprove it, and those who try to use it to do so only help to tarnish the reputation of the legitimate, scientific psychology of religion.

The second detail has to do with the methods used in most psychology of religion research. Batson (1977, 1979, 1986) has strongly argued for more experimental and quasi-experimental behavioral studies to be done in the psychology of religion and proportionally less reliance on questionnaire and correlational methods. As Canadian psychologist Bruce Hunsberger (1991) has well stated: "Countless studies report thousands of weak correlational relationships between many aspects of religion and almost every other variable imaginable" (p. 498). However, as more research is done assessing what people do, rather than what they say they might do in attitude questionnaires, the field advances.

Theoretical Interlude

Let us pick up some theoretical threads that are part of the field's history. The role of theory in the development of the psychology of religion is somewhat mixed. There are classical theories that are sweeping in scope, such as those by Freud and Jung, but these do not seem to have much direct connection with the current empirical research. Rather, the current research seems to be derived from a set of new ideas, more narrowly focused mini-theories that are more readily put to the test of data. A glance at the classical ideas, the questions they posed, and a few of the new ideas that have stimulated research will set the stage for the new progress that is now occurring in the field.

Classical Theories and Their Questions

Various theories of religion rested upon different models of human nature, that is, they looked for the root cause of human religiousness in different psychological locations. Freud's (1927) psychodynamic view emphasized unconscious tendencies in the personality as key determinants of religion. The person's need for safety and security, and the relevance to these needs of religious symbols such as "Father," "heaven," and "forgiveness" were salient features of his views. In contrast to Freud's emphasis on the individual unconscious, Jung's (1933, 1938) psychodynamic view postulated a God archetype in the collective unconscious of the human race. He thought that finding God fulfills this natural psychic function. Arguing from a humanistic-existential view, Frankl (1947/1975) proposed that people have a "will to meaning" in life which can be satisfied by pursuing transcendent goals. Because religion focuses our attention on a transcendent god or spiritual goals, religion is said to satisfy the motive for meaning.

The above theories each made important contributions and postulated basic human needs met by religion but are best seen in historical context because they tend to be somewhat self-contained. Once stated, they were generally not significantly modified by subsequent research. Perhaps the reason why they have not been substantially changed is because they seem intuitively convincing—people have needs for safety, security, meaning, so the theories are each given some tolerance. One important reason for the lag in theoretical development is that none of them drives current research in a formal sense. We have theories and large amounts of data, but somehow the theories and data lack relevance to each other (Dittes, 1969). The inability to stimulate theory-testing empirical research seems to be a common element among most past theories of religion. Their contribution, with some exceptions, lies in their intuitive appeal, their use as a heuristic in interpreting some findings, and their ability to stimulate our thinking about religion.

Although these early theories of religion did not stimulate much empirical research, the questions with which they were concerned did do so. The questions typically came in three forms. The first was "Where does religion come from?" As it stands, this question is ambiguous because it contains many different questions at once. It can be rephrased with more precision, however, in the following forms: What was the origin of religion in society, for example, back in primitive, historical periods? Did it emerge out of a social need in small tribes? Is it an instinct? Did its development hurt or help the growth and maintenance of human society? Was it necessary for religion to exist in order for human society to develop?

The second question was typically "How does religion operate to affect people's lives?" Again, several sides to this question can be probed: What factors in religion help or hinder our progress toward living meaningful and moral lives? How do we become committed to our religion and how does it control us? To what degree is our religion a result of pressures from social groups and of our own individual commitment? How do religious attitudes change, and how can we influence others to adopt or resist certain beliefs?

The third question was a variation of the first and asked about religious development in children and adolescents. Some of the issues currently involved in this category are whether religious concepts develop gradually or in stages, whether certain personality types are more prone to accept religion than others, and whether there is a critical age when youth either accept some religious belief or not. Is it really true that "the earlier in life you get them, the better," or is adolescence the most effective disciple-making age group to reach? Such notions are now put in the context of a lifespan developmental perspective, so that new questions are being posed about developmental processes and changes in religiousness in young, middle-aged, and older adults.

Some Stimuli to Current Research

Some of the above questions are now receiving research attention that has been stimulated by more recent theoretical ideas. Each of these ideas, or mini-theories as I shall call them, seems to have at least one of two properties that makes them scientifically useful at this stage in the development of this discipline. These properties are (1) they tend to be more narrow in scope, stated or focused in a way that is concerned with only one or a few questions, not all of them at once, and (2) they are stated in terms that can be translated into testable research hypotheses, i.e., they are able to be evaluated against the criterion of data. Furthermore, consistent with the argument that the theoretical ideas and data base in the psychology of religion ought to be expressions of their counterparts in general psychology (Paloutzian, 1986, 1994), we can identify a link between the root of the idea from some area of general psychology and its application to psychology of religion questions.

The most influential of these ideas is that proposed by Gordon Allport (1950, 1966) that humans express either an intrinsic or an extrinsic form of religiousness. This was Allport's way of trying to describe the difference between faith that was internalized (motivated from within) and one that was utilitarian (motivated by external rewards), and it is obviously tied to the concepts of intrinsic and extrinsic motivation from general motivational theory (Deci, 1975). Part 2 of the book, especially Chapter 8, will show how much important research was stimulated by this idea and its modifications, including its relation to prejudice, discrimination, helping behavior, personality, mental health, and developmental variables.

Other ideas that are stimulating a portion of the current research include (a) the theoretical notions of right-wing authoritarianism (Altemeyer, 1988; Altemeyer & Hunsberger, 1992), which explores new associations of authoritarianism and fundamentalism; (b) attribution theory (Spilka, Shaver, & Kirkpatrick, 1985) borrowed from research on social cognition and an intellectual descendant of cognitive dissonance theory (Festinger, 1957), which is a convenient tool for predicting how religious believers might explain and interpret events; and (c) attachment theory (Kirkpatrick, 1992, 1995) which is both a general model of relationships (e.g., attachment to God) as well as a source of predictions regarding such things as stress, coping, and loneliness. A cognitive developmental model has also been a stimulus to recent research, such as studies of the development of religious understanding and the complexity of mental operations associated with different religious orientations. Finally, the concept of schema from cognitive psychology has stimulated new work on whether religion is a schema or involves schemas, and the implications this has for processes such as coping and religious experience (McCallister, 1995; McIntosh, 1995). These ideas will reappear in context with their corresponding lines of research.

The Contemporary Period: The Reemergence of the Field

During the past twenty-five years, there has been a dramatic increase in the study of psychology–religion relationships. The result has been more dialogue between the two than has ever occurred before. The current flurry of activity includes more research, theoretical papers, and books being published relating psychology to religion; more symposia and conventions in which researchers from both fields exchange ideas; increased discussion about integrating psychology and theology; the rise of the field of pastoral counseling; an increased emphasis on the field of psychology in religious colleges and theological seminaries; and a greater number of psychology of religion courses being taught at colleges and universities.

Indicators of the Trend

In addition to the above list, several other specific and interconnected signs reflect increased activity in the field. First, there are several journals and an annual series that have either been recently created or have increased in prominence that publish psychology of religion research. These publications include the following:[1]

> *The International Journal for the Psychology of Religion*
> *Journal for the Scientific Study of Religion*
> *Research in the Social Scientific Study of Religion* (annual series)
> *Journal of Psychology and Judaism*
> *Journal of Psychology and Theology*
> *Review of Religious Research*
> *Journal of Religion and Health*
> *Journal of Religious Gerontology*
> *Pastoral Psychology*

Second, during the past decade several psychology of religion texts were published by major houses in succession (Batson & Ventis, 1982; Meadow & Kahoe, 1984; Paloutzian, 1983; Spilka, Hood, & Gorsuch, 1985). These have been accompanied by Wulff's (1991) comprehensive treatise as well as books by scholars writing from several countries including Australia (Brown, 1985, 1987), Switzerland (Oser & Gmünder, 1991), and Israel (Beit-Hallahmi, 1989).

Third, chapters and articles on psychology of religion topics have recently appeared in important publication outlets. For example, the past decade has seen the first chapter on the psychology of religion in the coveted *Annual Review of Psychology* (Gorsuch, 1988), several articles in the *American Psychologist* (Bergin, 1991; Gorsuch, 1984; Jones, 1994; Kilbourne & Richardson, 1984; Vande Kemp, 1992; Weiner, 1993), articles in the new flagship journal of the American Psychological Society, *Psychological Science* (Sethi & Seligman, 1993; Waller et al., 1990), and the development of a special issue of the *Journal of Social Issues* on the topic of religious influences on personal and societal well-being (Paloutzian & Kirkpatrick, 1995). That these journals, books, and articles have been published is concrete evidence of the progress of the field.

Fourth, there are now several graduate programs that offer doctoral-level training in the psychology of religion. There are also many psychologists doing psychology of religion research within the framework of another doctoral area, such as clinical or social psychology. The opportunity for an entering student to do advanced work in this area has never been greater.

Fifth, professional organizations relevant to the psychology of religion have come into being. Important for students is that most of them have a special category for student members, with reduced fees. Thus students can enjoy the benefits of full participation in the organization—attendance at conventions, subscriptions to journals, receipt of newsletters—for only a portion of the cost charged to their professors! Among these organizations are Psychology of Religion (Division 36 of the American Psychological Association) with approximately 1,400 members and 1,000 student affiliates; the Society for the Scientific Study of Religion, which includes anthropologists, sociologists, and theologians as well as psychologists; the Religious Research Association; and the International Federation for the Psychology of Religion, with its secretariat in Belgium.

These signs are interconnected in the sense that they all reflect the same increase in activity in the psychology of religion. They are also forces that stimulate further activity.

2. *Is Psychology of Religion Influencing General Psychology?*

The above trend suggests that the psychology of religion is advancing as a self-contained field. A related and equally important question, however, is whether the psychology of religion is having any influence in general psychology. One would think that a field such as psychology, committed to being balanced, fair, objective, and relevant to human concerns would not neglect the psychological aspects of religious life in America in which over 90 percent of the people believe in God and over 40 percent claim attendance at regular religious services (Gallup & Jones, 1989) or in a multicultural world in which religious influences have historically been profound.

One source of evidence bearing upon this issue can be obtained from introductory psychology textbooks. Authors of textbooks in general psychology include in their books whatever material is the most important in psychology at the time they are writing. Therefore, by doing a content analysis of general psychology textbooks produced during any given period, we get an idea of the main lines of research in psychology at that time. Also, one gets an idea of the changes in psychology over time by examining those texts across a span of many years.

The oldest text for general psychology is *Psychology and Life.*[2] This book has been in general use for approximately 60 years. The interesting thing for our purposes is that across its many editions we have a history of the content of modern psychology from 1937 to present.

How is the psychology of religion represented in general psychology across this time period? In order to answer this question, we traced the references to religious content across the book's first ten editions (1937–1979).[3] Two measures were taken. One was a simple word count of the total number of words devoted to religious topics in each volume. The second was a proportional measure: the total number of words devoted to religious topics relative to the total number of words in the book. Thus, we had indices of the absolute amount of space given to the topic, as well as the relative space given to it. According to both measures, the psychology of religion received an upsurge of attention in the 9th and 10th editions of the text. This study suggests that the psychology of religion is being addressed more than in the past in general psychology. Is this conclusion valid?

If the psychology of religion is contributing fully, it should appear in all general psychology texts, not just one. How do other books fare on this question? Spilka, Comp, and Goldsmith (1981) surveyed 40 texts published during the 1950s and 160 texts published during the 1970s in order to find out. They report that the vast majority of books showed either a decrease or no change in religious content during that 20-year period. This study was extended by Lehr and Spilka (1989) who scored 98 general psychology textbooks published from 1980–1988 for religious content and compared those findings with the previous data for books published in the 1970s. They found that the percent of books with religious content increased significantly from 17.5 percent to 84.7 percent from the 1970s to the 1980s. The mean number of words per citation dropped for the same time period, however, going from 730 words to 231 words each. Thus, in the 1980s, more text authors mentioned religion but did so in a less complete way.

Therefore, the recent past shows that the psychology of religion has enjoyed some contribution to general psychology, and that a much greater contribution remains to be made. One positive sign is the publication of the first full chapter on the psychology of religion as part of a general psychology text (Paloutzian & Santrock, in press). This is the best way to invite people to this area, by introducing it to them early in their academic careers. It will be instructive during the next few years to see whether other authors follow this example.

Reasons for the Trend

Why would interest in the psychology of religion be on the upswing at the present time? Two kinds of factors can be identified that have helped create a climate conducive to the psychological study of religious life: situational factors and substantive reasons.

It is likely that several situational factors in contemporary America have worked together to bring this situation about. First, there seems to have been an increased interest in religion among people in general during the 1970s and 1980s. This may have been a consequence of the turbulent period of the 1960s, when many of the nation's youth began struggling with life's basic questions. A generalized increase in religion as a means of finding answers would result in a greater interest in religious phenomena on the part of psychologists. The controversial religious publicity in the news media has also contributed to this. Second, some psychologists have expressed interest in the relation between religion and mental health. Some of them have argued that rather than serving as a crutch, a mature faith can be a positive, integrating factor in a person's life. They point out that a mature faith gives life a sense of meaning, something which people need. Other researchers such as Gordon Allport have brought to the forefront some paradoxical relationships between religious orientation and racial prejudice (discussed in Chapter 8), findings that have sparked many research investigations in this area. Third, within the current generation of young professionals, there are a sufficient number of persons entering psychology who see religious belief and behavior as an important domain of study—analogous to studying the psychology of women, race relations, or organizations—for there to be a meaningful dialogue between psychology and religion. The rise of pastoral and religious counseling provides additional avenues where the dialogue can occur. As a result, there is a spin-off of interest in psychology on the part of the lay religious population. Finally, two reasons for contemporary interest in the psychology of religion stem from the needs of psychologists themselves. Many psychologists are now more interested than they used to be in relating their work to the central needs of people—an effect resulting from the cry for "relevance" of the recent past. Also, psychologists are beginning to realize that religious phenomena represent a potentially rich and varied source of behaviors and experience that can be studied scientifically in order to gain greater understanding of basic psychological processes.

The substantive reasons underlying the current trends are, I believe, more basic than the situational factors. The substantive reasons include recent developments in the philosophy of science and research methodology. These are the essential groundwork upon which any science rests. It is these developments that solve some of the problems, such as the either/or philosophy, that were at the root of the conflict during the earlier periods of the field. Therefore, a clear understanding of the philosophy of science is necessary to understand how psychology and religion can complement each other. Such understanding also illustrates how each method of exploring psychological questions about religion adds a unique piece of information about how religion works. It is to these points that we must now turn.

3

[Research Design]

Research in the Psychology of Religion

In addition to having a good idea to pursue, doing good research in the psychology of religion requires two things. The first requirement is an understanding of how the philosophy of science applies to this field. A careful analysis of the philosophy of science within the context of the psychology of religion will help clarify my view that psychology and religion are complementary and why I think the field is growing. The second requirement is skill at using the variety of research methods available. Each method enables us to create a unique piece of information about how religion works. Illustrations of several research methods will acquaint you with alternative strategies for testing a good idea.

Philosophy of Science for Psychology of Religion

Tensions between Psychology and Religion

As we saw in previous chapters, psychology and religion have experienced mutual tensions in the past. Part of the reason for this tension centers on two pivotal and interrelated issues regarding the relationship of the natural to the religious or supernatural. The first of these is the determinism-freedom issue and the corollary issue of whether people are responsible for their own actions. The second, closely linked to the first, is whether psychological accounts of religious experience are a threat to the religious or supernatural accounts; that is, whether a scientific explanation displaces a religious or supernatural one, making the latter invalid.

There is abundant evidence within psychology to indicate that much of our behavior can be understood in naturalistic terms—that it is determined by the operation of cause-effect laws. A primary source of this evidence comes from behavioristic psychologists. They have been able to show quite dramatically how overt actions can be manipulated and precisely controlled through giving rewards for desired behavior and punishment for undesirable behavior. B. F. Skinner, the most prominent spokesman for behaviorism during its heyday, wrote *Beyond Freedom and Dignity* (1972), which presupposes this machine-like model of human nature. Another source of support for the naturalistic approach to behavior comes from ethology, the study of animal behavior. Ethologists emphasize instincts and behavior patterns that are permanently "wired in" to the nervous system. Even in Freudian psychoanalysis, the underlying assumption is one of intrapsychic, unconscious determinism. For Freud, there were no accidents in mental life. Everything could eventually be explained by naturalistic principles.

One of the most impressive demonstrations of the power of naturalism as applied to behavior comes from the area of brain research. It has been shown, for example, that a normally dominant monkey can be made submissive when its amygdala, an area in the temporal lobe, is lesioned. Human behavior can be similarly changed by precisely located brain lesions. For example, Mark and Ervin (1970) report the case of a violent epileptic woman whose violence was reduced following surgical lesions in her right amygdala.

Taken as a whole, the evidence is clear that the scientific strategy is a powerful tool for understanding behavior. There is no necessary reason to suppose that it cannot be equally impressive when brought to the study of religion. The crucial question is "Is the scientific approach inconsistent with religion?"

The Nature of Psychological Science

As a science, psychology operates on the assumption that behavior, including religious behavior and the things we choose to do of our own free will, is the result of the operation of natural cause-effect laws. By this is meant that every act has antecedent causes that produced the behavior, and that would produce it again if the same conditions were repeated. At the outset it should be made clear that the notion that natural cause-effect laws exist and regulate what we do is not a fact of science. It is a working assumption that is inherent in the scientific method. The purpose of this section is to help you understand the nature of scientific inquiry and psychological "laws of behavior" so that the apparent disparity between psychology and religion might be more clearly understood and resolved.

Scientific Inquiry through Different "Worlds"

Part of the essential nature of science is the notion that there exist two different "worlds": the world of events and observations and the world of abstract ideas or concepts (Kemeny, 1959; Popper, 1972). Outside events occur and can be observed, but ideas cannot. An idea or abstract concept is something that we produce in our minds after noticing some common thread in a whole set of specific observations.

As a way of seeing the difference between an observation and an idea, consider the example of prayer, taken from Chapter 1, once again. We can observe and record a single instance of prayer behavior. Note, however, that when we do this we are not actually observing prayer in the general sense. Rather, we are observing someone kneel, fold her hands, bow her head, and talk to someone referred to as God or Lord. We are not observing the prayer; we are observing the behavior. In other words, the term *pray* is a general term that includes many specific acts that have key aspects in common. Not all of the specific acts within the general class called *prayer* are identical, since a person could pray while standing up, with open hands, and holding the head erect. Therefore, the specific instances of any type of religious behavior belong to the world of events or actual occurrences. The concepts, generalities, and abstract principles belong to the world of ideas.

It is important to understand that because scientific "laws" of behavior belong to the world of ideas, they are creations of our minds. They are generated by people who perceive common elements running through many particular instances of behavior.

Induction, Deduction, Verification/Falsification: The Research Cycle

Like all sciences, the science of religious behavior begins and ends in the world of "facts" (events plus our perception of them). But it cycles through the idea world of theory as a way of maintaining a common coherent framework in which to understand the facts. This is illustrated in Figure 3.1. We start by recording observations of some type. From these observations we make an inference about the common factors or relationships we think are operating through all of those particular events. These common elements become the theory that we use to guide the next investigation. It is from the theory that we arrive at a research hypothesis and deduce the predicted result from the next study. The process of developing the general theory from the particular observations is called *induction*. The process of predicting some results or relationships from a theory is called *deduction*, or going from the general case

Process of Scientific Inquiry: The Research Cycle

Abstract theories: T_1, T_2, T_3, etc.	Deduction $\longrightarrow$	Testable hypotheses and predictions
Induction and inference $\uparrow$	(World of Ideas) — — — — — — — — (World of Events or "Facts"*)	**Verification/ Falsification** $\downarrow$
Observations: O_1, O_2, O_3, etc. * An event + interpretation of it.	$\longleftarrow$ Comparison of predicted observations with previous observations	Observations: O_4, O_5, etc.

FIGURE 3.1 Process of scientific inquiry: The research cycle

Source: Kemeny, J. G. *A philosopher looks at science.* Copyright © 1959 by Litton Educational Publishing, Inc. Reprinted by permission of Wadsworth Publishing Company, Belmont, CA 94002.

to predicting the particular observations. The results, which are new observations at the end of the research cycle, are then checked against those which were predicted by the theory. If the obtained results correspond to the predictions, then the theory is supported; if they do not, then those predictions are falsified and the results function as new, additional observations that may themselves be fed into the beginnings of the research cycle. It is this last property of a theory, its ability to lead to predictions that can be shown to be false in order to eliminate inadequate explanatory ideas one at a time, that allows the research cycle to lead us closer to the truth (Popper, 1963). In this way the theory can be modified and adapted so as to take into account these new observations.

Through this research cycle, theories become more refined. If a theory stands for a long time and endures the test of much research, it is raised to a higher status and we begin to call it a "law." Note, however, that theories and "laws" are not necessarily out in nature waiting for us to discover them. Rather, they are our creations and must change in order to accommodate new emerging observations that challenge the "existing law."

An Example from Physics

This overall process can be illustrated by three examples. First, take an example from the physical realm: the "fact" that air, fuel, and heat produce fire. We might begin at the beginning of the research cycle, the observation stage, by pointing out O_1, one single instance in which we saw some combination of air, fuel, and heat being associated with fire. We might then notice O_2, a different instance of air, fuel, and heat occurring just before fire. Observations 3, 4, 5, etc., would each be another instance of this relationship. By seeing the common elements that link all of these specific cases together, we may develop the idea (theory) that air, fuel, and heat will result in fire when placed together in a specified way. At this point we have taken the inductive leap and moved from the world of observations to the world of ideas and theory. It is at this latter level where "laws" of behavior (including religious behavior) exist.

After we have developed our theory about air, fuel, and heat resulting in fire, we are then ready to deduce another specific instance of the fire-element relationship. In other words, we would predict that if we put air, fuel, and heat together in a new way, one that we had not observed before, then this new combination would also result in fire. If we did place the elements together in this new way and fire did occur, we would have generated a new observation that supports the theory. If we placed the elements together and fire did not occur, then we have generated new observations that falsify the theory. In this latter case, the theory must be revised, thrown out, or at least tested again. Note the cycle: the theories and "laws" emerge out of the common elements in the observations, and the theories then serve as the guide in our search for new observations.

An Example from Psychology of Religion

This same process, the cycle of research, can be illustrated in the area of religion also. The cycle may be less easily noticed because the observed relationships are much less obvious in religion than they are in physics. We might observe several instances in which "being raised in a loving home" and "adopting the creed of one's parents" go together. From this we might then develop the abstract theory that loving parents cause their offspring to adopt their own beliefs. From this abstract conception we would predict (deduce) that in other cases of loving homes the offspring will also adopt the parents' beliefs.

Although the logic of the research cycle in the psychology of religion is the same as that in physics, there are two important aspects of the psychology of religion that make it more complex. First, the physicist can define concepts operationally (i.e., in terms of specific, objective measuring procedures) much more easily than the psychologist of religion can. Physicists study a more limited sphere. For example, it is more difficult to be precise about what is meant by the term *loving home*, than it is about the term *fire*. This difficulty in defining concepts in operational terms means that it is harder to be sure whether an observation is actually an instance of one concept or another.

Second, in the psychology of religion our knowledge is so incomplete that it is possible to generate many "theories" to explain the observations. Because the theories are hard to test due to the complexity of religion, it is more difficult to eliminate the weak ones through falsification of hypotheses. In the case of the youth from a loving home adopting the same beliefs as the parents, for example, we can think of several possible "theories" that might account for it. One hypothetical explanation is that the children perceive that their parents genuinely care for them, and this makes the children feel secure and worthwhile. The feelings of security and worth may be psychologically linked to the religion of the parents via an associative learning process. This "theory" leads us to say that children from loving homes adopt beliefs because they have learned such beliefs make them feel secure and worthy. Another possible explanation is that children from loving homes are likely to internalize the personalities of their parents, and that these personalities are especially prone to that particular set of beliefs. A third possible explanation might rely on the concept of imitation. We could point out, for example, that all children tend to imitate their parents; so that just as a delinquent boy might imitate his delinquent parents, so also a loving, religious youth may be imitating loving, religious parents. It could also be that all of these explanations work in combination. The point is that in the psychology of religion many different explanations can be offered to try to account for the observed relationships. Clearly, it is not as likely that we would generate as many possible explanations for the relationship between air, fuel, heat, and fire. Nevertheless, the logic of the psychology of religion is the same as that of physics or any other science, although the content is different.

d *Illustration of Language Rules*

Another way of illustrating the relationship between the specific observation and the general principle is to use the rules of a language as an analogy. Let us take the French language as a case in point. If you have studied French (or any other language) you learned that there were rules of the language that you had to follow if you were going to learn French properly. The "rules" are generalities about how the nouns and verbs operate. These rules are derived from the language, not imposed upon it. In other words, the writers of French textbooks observe the French language and then describe the language to the student in general principles called "rules of French." There may also be exceptions to the rules. These exceptions must be explained on the basis of influences from other than the mainstream French.

To carry the analogy further, we can add that the rules of French were not always the same as they are today. The French language has been different in different periods of history. Each period had its own rules of the language that were correct for that period. None of them would be called the correct rules for all time, because, as the language undergoes natural changes, the "rules" (general descriptions) must change or else they will be out of date and no longer accurate.

The application of the language analogy to the psychology of religion is direct. The "laws" of religious behavior are not imposed upon people by nature, so that we are bound to obey them whether we like it or not. Rather, the "laws" are essentially descriptions of how people behave, together with the relationships between our behavior and environmental circumstances.

It is more correct to say that the "law" is caused by our behavior, than to say that our behavior is caused by the "law" (Kemeny, 1959). If we do something that the law of behavior does not predict, we are not "violating" the law. It is simply that the law is an incomplete description, and must be changed in order to account accurately for the behavior.

e *Determinism, Causality, Probability*

The process of theory building described above is closely linked to three other concepts that are inherent in the research cycle: the concepts of determinism, causality, and probability. Determinism refers to the assumption that there is an underlying order in nature. When we say our religious behavior is determined, we mean that it follows a pattern of regularity that is part of the natural order. Another way of saying this is to say that people behave according to a natural law of behavior. But in the preceding section we saw that natural laws of behavior are generalities created in our minds from the observation of common elements in many behaviors, rather than being "hard" rules that exist outside of behavior and merely direct it. Therefore, the principle of complete determinism must forever remain at the level of an assumption. It is not something that can be proved to be certain. A science of behavior must adopt some form of determinism as a working assumption, however.

The principle of causality is another thing that we must assume. Another way of stating the principle of determinism as applied to behavior is by saying that our behavior follows the principles of cause and effect. By this it is meant that each piece of behavior is the consequence of antecedent factors that brought it about. For example, in common language I might say that the sight of a barking dog causes me to feel afraid. In saying this, I mean that my fear is a consequence of my seeing and hearing the dog, and that whenever I do see a barking dog, the same symptoms of fear will follow. This can be put symbolically as follows:

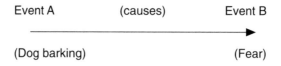

This analysis of causality must be carried one step further. When we say that one event (A) causes another event (B) we are too quick to assume that there is an essential, mechanical connection between the two. We too quickly believe that whenever A exists, B *must* follow. This is not the case. The concept of causality does not necessarily imply that one event must mechanically follow another, because we cannot see cause. The notion that one event causes another is an inferred link that we place between the observed events. We don't actually see causation; we do see the events and infer a causal link or association between them. To go back to an earlier illustration, when we see a loving home (event A) regularly preceding the children's espousing of parental religious beliefs (event B), we do not actually see the loving home *causing* the children to accept parental religious beliefs. What we do see are many instances of the two events associated with each other in some regular way; in this case the loving home preceding the belief acquisition. Any perception of a causal relation between the events, in the sense that the first event mechanically forces the second event to occur, is an inference and can never be known with absolute certainty.

These analyses of determinism and causality lead us to the next point, that scientific statements are probabilistic. Because we cannot know with complete assurance that one event causes the next (or that one determines the next), we can know with only partial assurance. We can say that a conclusion is true or that a principle about religious behavior holds only with some degree of probability, but not absolutely. If we have discovered that the adoption of parental beliefs reliably follows a loving home environment, we can say that children from loving homes are likely to (i.e., probably will) believe the same as their parents, but we cannot say for certain that they will do so.

Naturalism and Religion
A final point implicit in a science of behavior is that, like any science, it is concerned with processes of nature. We use the scientific method to try to understand events in nature, including the religious aspects of life, from a naturalistic perspective rather than from a religious or supernatural one. Nature is the focal realm of observation. This naturalistic assumption says nothing about who or what creates and sustains nature, just as the rules of a football game say nothing about who created the game or the rules. Professionals disagree over the role of supernatural assumptions in research on religion. However, the possibility that we might understand religious behavior from a natural perspective in no way detracts from nor adds to the validity of a religious or supernatural perspective. Both can be valid at the same time.[2]

Multiple Accounts of Religious Behavior

In our discussion of the process of generating theories, it was pointed out that many theories could be devised to account for the same religious behavior. At the strictly scientific level, each theory could be partially correct, yet none of them be totally correct on its own. If this were the case, then each theory would require that the others be added to it in order to account for all aspects of the behavior. In other words, in order to understand behavior more fully we need to be able to see it from many different perspectives at the same time.

Maps and Theories
Building several theories about religious behavior is like drawing different types of maps of a single area of ground. You could draw several different types of maps of California: a map of freeways and paved roads, a detailed map of population density, and a topographical map of the desert and mountain areas. Each map could be accurate, and each would provide you with some information about California. But none of them by itself would give you the complete picture. If you had only the topographical map you might read it correctly but still arrive at the erroneous conclusion that California has no roads and few people! Clearly, the whole set of maps taken together provides a more complete picture than any single one by itself.

Theories and maps are images of the things that they purport to represent. In the case of maps, a red line is not actually a freeway, but an image or "scale model" of the real thing. In the case of theories of religious behavior, the concept "Hindu" is not an actual Hindu person; and the concept "conversion experience" is not identical to the phenomenon of a person experiencing conversion. The theories are images or summary reflections of the actual events, and each particular theory is an image from only the point of view of the theory builder.

When building theories, it is a rule of thumb that we try to eliminate those that are incomplete (Popper, 1963). We gradually try to construct a single, encompassing theory that contains all phenomena of interest within its scope. As noted previously, however, the theories that we do develop are views only from the naturalistic perspective. In the final analysis, they leave open the question of the religious or supernatural account of the same event. Both can be correct at the same time, but from different viewpoints.

Multiple Viewpoints and the Fallacy of "Nothing But-ery"

This last point can be illustrated by examining a triangle from different points of view. Suppose we show a drawing of a triangle to two very different types of people: an artist and a physicist. If you show the triangle to an artist and ask him or her what it is, the response may be "It's nothing but a triangle, three straight lines that intersect forming three angles." This statement would be accurate but not complete. If you asked a physicist the same question, the answer might be "It is nothing but certain chemicals (ink) placed together upon some other matter (paper) in a certain way." This statement of the physicist may be just as correct as that made by the artist, but it also would be incomplete. We might get a third answer if we asked a geometrician. Each account requires the others in order for a complete account to be given. All accounts must be correct in order for the figure to be what it is. Each account can be said to embody the others (MacKay, 1974). It would not make sense to say that the triangle caused the chemical arrangement or that the chemical arrangement caused the triangle. It would make more sense to say that the chemical arrangement embodies the triangle and vice versa. This relationship is more intimate than cause and effect because one facet of the figure cannot be changed without also changing the other. If we alter the chemical arrangement, we alter the shape of the triangle and vice versa.

Illustrations such as the triangle analogy can be used to argue that both a psychological and a religious account of life, or some "spiritual" or "psychological" event, can be accurate at the same time but from different viewpoints (MacKay, 1974). It is a mistake to claim that one is "nothing but" the other, as if the truth of one necessarily negated the possible truth of the other.

Consider the following example: Suppose someone experiences a sudden religious conversion. The key question here would be whether a religious explanation for that conversion and a psychological explanation could both be correct at the same time. Suppose the religious explanation stated that a supernatural being was involved in the event. Suppose also that the psychological explanation said that the conversion occurred due to the operation of psychological processes such as the resolution of personal conflict, a cognitive need for closure, or imitative learning and reinforcement. Can these two types of accounts of the same event coexist, or must they be mutually exclusive? Is it possible that both types of things occurred as an integral part of the same conversion?

The answer to this last question is yes. The truth of one type of explanation does not necessarily rule out the possible truth of the other. If the person's conversion was genuine and if the religion to which the person is converting is true (for the sake of illustration, assume that it is true), then the religious explanation for that conversion would be valid—it could be correctly seen from the religious viewpoint. But this does not negate the possibility or accuracy of naturalistic accounts of the same conversion. There might be a number of natural accounts that could be equally correct—from their own viewpoints. One account could be an analysis from the standpoint of behaviorism. The person's behavior could be described as changing from a nonconvert behavior pattern to a convert behavior pattern. This description would include the antecedent stimuli that "caused" the change to the convert behavior pattern. A second natural account could come from a cognitive level of analysis. In it, the cognitive needs and processes involved in the conversion would be described. Just as the triangle may be correctly, but partially, understood from each viewpoint alone, so also the role of religion in life may be correctly but partially viewed from the psychological and religious viewpoints.

When all the explanations are taken together they provide complementary views of the conversion rather than competitive views. Thus, it is possible for a conversion to be seen accurately from a religious viewpoint and from the viewpoint of an outside psychological observer. Neither of these necessarily reduces the accuracy or validity of the other. It is like looking at different photographs of a building, each taken from a different side, the top, bottom, and the inside, and putting them all together to get a more complete picture of the building than you would have otherwise.

"Explaining" versus "Explaining Away"

The above sections on the cycle of research, theory building, causality, and multiple viewpoints all relate to an issue of basic concern. This is the difference between explaining or understanding how something works and "explaining it away"—judging it to be worthless or of no value. Psychologists may or may not understand much about the workings of religious behavior and experience. But even if we could offer a full psychological explanation, we still could not "explain away" religious life as "nothing but" psychological processes, as if to say extrapsychological influences were impossible. Another, equally plausible view would be that we have learned something about how religious influences work in and through nature. It would be just as much an error to say that conversion is "nothing but" a supernatural event. It may be that, but if so, it involves other things as well. In other words, the either/or philosophy that seemed to be a barrier in previous years is inadequate and unnecessary from the point of view of contemporary philosophy of science.

To explain behavior means to describe it with its functional relationships to other behaviors and environmental circumstances, pulling it together with some organizing framework called a theory. This does not negate nor prove the religious or the supernatural. To "explain away" behavior means to discount the possibility of other viewpoints being valid—to declare that the other explanations are of no value. This is something that scientific psychology and religion/theology, by their very nature, cannot do. The religious-theological and psychological-scientific approaches are on two different but noncontradictory planes. The psychological approach is on the natural plane, and leaves the question of other planes open.

The Role Psychology Can Fulfill

The role psychology can fulfill, then, is complementary to that of other approaches. It offers religious persons additional methodological and conceptual tools with which to understand their religion a little more fully. It offers a psychological level of analysis to complement rather than replace others. In another vein, it provides the means whereby we can begin to understand the "personal universe" just as physics allows us to understand something of the physical universe. Finally, it offers psychological concepts, perspectives, and methods to complement other disciplines such as history, anthropology, or linguistics as an aid in illuminating the richness of religious teachings.

Post-Modernism and the Psychology of Religion

The post-modernism movement has recently added a new twist, and challenge, to our picture of the nature of social scientific knowledge about religion. Our picture, which underlies the way a scientific approach to the psychology of religion has been presented in this chapter, assumes that either (a) there is a truth and our methods can help us get closer to it, (b) whether or not there is a truth, in order to play the game of science you have to pretend that there is one, (c) whether or not there is a truth or you pretend in your own mind that there is one, the methods of science proceed as if there were, or (d) you don't assume there is a truth but you create theories that pretend to be approximations of an imaginary truth. You can adopt any of these stances and legitimately do psychology of religion research.

Extreme versions of post-modernism will have none of this. According to this relatively recent school of thought, tied to the deconstructionist school of literature, "reality is pure illusion" (Rosenau, 1992, p. 23). The extension of this view leads to the idea that all progress in knowledge is illusory, all theories are "merely" mental constructions, and that all data have equal validity or no validity because there are no such things as valid rules for evaluating them. A softer version of this idea says that truth is personal and relative to personal and cultural context. There may be one truth for you and another truth for me; one truth may attain for a Buddhist and a different truth may attain for a Hebrew. Truths are relative to religion, culture, context, and time.

At one level, the post-modern argument for the relativity of truth makes sense. Certainly there are some things that are true in one religious culture that are not true in another. Roman Catholicism may affect its adherents in ways that are different from the ways in which Hare Krishna affects its adherents. However, it ought to be possibe for us to discover or create some principles of how religion works that are applicable across religions. For example, if the psychological processes that operate in conversion can be stated at a sufficient degree of abstraction, with a large enough degree of generality, then they ought to apply trans-religiously—i.e., the principles ought to be the same whether you are talking about conversion to a new religious movement or to a traditional religion. This is a researchable issue. Stating such principles is a goal inherent in doing psychology of religion; the discipline assumes that such statements can be meaningfully made.

Although the post-modernist argument raises questions that deserve serious attention, I believe that as it is carried from the humanities through the social sciences to the natural sciences, at some point it breaks down. It may be true that the data that one looks for are determined by the theory one brings to the task. However, there is something amiss with the premise that we must proceed as if scientific truth does not in principle exist. If one says that, one must also be willing to say, for example, that the statement $E = Mc^2$ has no meaning, that it is "merely" a "text" in a story. That may or may not be so according to some types of post-modernist analysis, but those who say so have also to be willing to say that the atomic bomb (an application of the statement $E = Mc^2$) did not explode at Hiroshima. They would have to be willing to say something like: There are different truths in the statement $E = Mc^2$, one for you and one for me, and they are both equally valid. That would be like saying that the bomb went off for you, but it did not go off for me.

Such reasoning breaks down because it is believed that there are principles that apply to people whether one wishes to "deconstruct" them or not. For example, the principle of gravity works. We do not have two different systems of physics—a gravity physics and a nongravity physics, i.e., one physics for people for whom gravity works and a different physics for people for whom gravity does not work. As far as is known, the principle is not relative to your belief in it. Even post-modernists themselves acknowledge this every day; when they go home from work, they do so on the assumption that their house is still sitting on the ground.

I think that the future will reveal that the post-modernist movement has made important contributions by pointing out our biases in interpreting data (espeically in the psychology of religion, a field with great bias potential), the relativity of knowledge, the contextual and tentative nature of truths that we propose. These are useful contributions. As a result, psychologists of religion will continue to do their work, but they will have a more healthy skepticism and caution about the assumptions and limits of their methods and the meaning of their data. This issue is being hotly debated (Gergen, 1994; Smith, 1994).

Methods of Researching Religion

The most convincing piece of evidence that researchers are accepting this invitation to the psychology of religion is the increased frequency of empirical research studies on the topic. What methods and strategies for research are available for you to use if you want to do a research project of your own? Several methods are frequently used, each providing a special type of information. The two basic methodological concerns for doing psychological research on religion are what general approach or procedure should you use (i.e., whom do you study, and how?) and how should you measure religion.

People sometimes think that there is only one best way to do something. When it comes to doing research, nothing could be further from the truth. Research means to re-search—to look again, to examine one more time and find out more. There are many procedures for doing this, each one having its special strength, each one complementary to the rest. Some allow us to answer questions about behavior, some about feelings, some about attitudes. With some, we examine ongoing action; with others, we examine the traces left by past action; with others, we study imagined future action.

The techniques sketched below are not mutually exclusive. They can overlap and be used effectively to explore a common question, even in the same study. Taken together and used effectively to study a central question, these can yield a rich mosaic of results that address a common theme. They feed into the research cycle and stimulate theory development.

Strategies and Methods

The Individual and People in General: The Ideographic and Nomothetic Approaches

Two broad classes of questions come to mind: do you want to learn about the religion in one person's life, like getting a psychological profile or biography of that person; or do you want to learn about the psychological aspects of religion from people in general? The former type of question illustrates the ideographic approach; the latter illustrates the nomothetic approach. Which of these approaches you adopt will determine the basic strategy of your study.

In the ideographic approach, one person is studied as much as possible and a psychological account of the person is constructed from all available information. For an ideographic study of religion, you might choose as a subject someone who is perceived as very religious. The attempt is to learn everything about that person in all his or her uniqueness. The assumption and hope is that if we can completely know one person, then we will be better able to have insight into other people also.

For example, suppose you wanted to study the religion of your friend. You might begin by following the person everywhere, making observations and taking notes on everything he or she does, when and how it is done, with whom, etc. You would record whether this person's religious behavior was related to other behaviors and in what way. You would follow your friend to church and record everything that occurred there. You might study any personal documents, such as letters or a diary, which might contain illuminating information. Several in-depth interviews would help clarify the meaning of your friend's religion from his or her own perspective. After you did all this, you might have a clear picture of this person, especially with regard to the unique features of his or her religious life.

How reliable are the conclusions drawn from studies using the ideographic orientation? Strictly speaking, the conclusions must normally be restricted to the individual who was studied. Learning everything about the religious life and conversion experience of one person (your friend) doesn't allow you to generalize too much about the religious lives and conversion experiences of other people. The high degree of emotionality in one person's conversion experience, for example, tells you little about other conversion experiences. Similarly, extending this argument to religions in different cultures, we would say that knowing a lot about the psychology of one Muslim in Turkey does not allow you to draw specific psychological conclusions about a particular member of the Church of England. This restriction of conclusions is one fundamental limitation of the ideographic approach.

Yet, the ideographic approach has two important contributions. First, to the extent to which people are similar, the results derived from an ideographic study are transferable to other people. Knowing this, a priest, rabbi, or counselor who attempts to help someone going through a religious crisis can validly draw upon his or her experience with former clients with similar problems. Second, the method yields many hypotheses and research questions that guide psychologists in constructing theories of religion and suggest specific studies that can be done to test the theories.

The nomothetic strategy contrasts with the ideographic strategy in an important respect: whereas the ideographic approach yields knowledge in depth about someone, the nomothetic approach yields knowledge in breadth about many people. In the nomothetic approach, one is less concerned about knowing all the facets of the religious life of one person and more interested in the principles that affect religion in people in general. The hypothetical average person is what you want to learn about. Usually a large sample of people is studied on the psychological or behavioral dimension in question, and conclusions are reached that pertain to the hypothetical average person. For example, if you wanted to know the average age of conversion for certain groups of Protestants, you might gather a large sample of people from such groups and ask how old they were when they were converted. Then, compute the average age, which you would infer to be representative of the larger population. Another example would your wanting to know the average frequency of church attendance per month for the members of your church. You could select a random sample of people from the church roster, find out how frequently they attend, and calculate the average church attendance. Thus you would know the attendance rate of the hypothetical average church member, based on your sample, but you could not predict with certainty the attendance rate of any specific individual.

Such a strategy reflects both the strength and the weakness of the nomothetic approach. The strength is that it enables us to begin to state generalities—tentative statements of natural normal processes that produce observed regularities in the phenomenon under study. (In terms of the research cycle these generalities are in the world of ideas.) Starbuck (1899) did a primitive version of this with his study of the age of conversion and its accompanying psychological components. He proposed that religious conversion is an adolescent crisis reaction that generally occurs around the age of sixteen. The nomothetic approach, therefore, is very powerful in the development of any science because it facilitates the development of theories. Its weakness is equally glaring, however: the strategy does not allow us to know anything specific about a particular person. Finally, general conclusions seem imprecise because we can always find exceptions to the mythical average person.

Phenomenology

"The heart of phenomenology is to go beyond bare facts to the level of facts-as-perceived" (Rambo & Reh, 1992). The basic approach of phenomenology is the accurate description of the perceptual field of the individual. By "perceptual field" we mean the totality of experience within a person's mind. The procedure may involve introspection—"looking inside our minds" and reporting what we see—as well as autobiographical or other information. In the case of religious experience, the attempt is made to describe fully the meaning of the experience from the perspective of the individual. Several analogies may be offered to describe the many meanings of the same event. Oates (1973), for example, presented four analogies to describe the phenomenology of conversion: rapid growth, the unification of a divided self, a change of direction, and an act of surrender. Also, various aspects of phenomenological methods have been identified. To illustrate, Rambo and Reh (1992) listed six facets of the process of phenomenology that emerged in interview dialogues with a woman, Esther, about her conversion. These included observation of the phenomena to be explored, description, empathy with the other person's experience, understanding, interpretation, and explanation. Because this method is used to study private, subjective experiences rather than public behavior, it is especially fruitful for answering ideographic-type questions.

Content Analysis

Content analysis is a set of procedures for scoring verbal material for various types of content. For example, suppose you have a reason to think that psychotics more often have religion "on their minds" than neurotics. One way to test this hypothesis would be with content analysis. You could go to your local mental health center and conduct interviews with people who have been diagnosed as neurotic or psychotic. Your assumption would be that what is "on people's minds" is expressed in their speech. The interviews would all be conducted in the same way so that you do not bias the results by artificially drawing out more religious material from one group over the other. After transcribing the interviews, you could have "blind" judges (who would be ignorant of the hypothesis and subject categories) score the subjects' verbal responses for amount of religious content. A simple coding procedure would be to count the number of times the patient used the words "God," "religion," "Christ," or other words with obvious religious meaning corresponding to his or her cultural context. You would then see which group scored greater on this measure. More imaginative types of content analysis might be to analyze works of art, music, or dance for religious content.

The content of something can be categorized by a content analysis. The psychological meaning behind that content is a separate issue—actually an inference made by the researcher. In our hypothetical neurotic-psychotic study, for example, a greater frequency of religious language in the psychotics could be the raw finding. But the psychological meaning of those results (i.e., whether religion caused the disorder or is helping the patient recover) is an inference that the investigator must make based upon some theory of what religion does to or for people.

An intriguing use of content analysis occurred in regard to disputed authorship of Paul's Epistles. Morton (1963) developed a method of scoring seven elements of writing style, which he thought would clearly distinguish authors. His style indicators included frequency of use of the words "in," "and," and "but," among other things. Using this system of scoring, he concluded that Paul's Epistles were written by six different people. Ellison (1965) then used Morton's scoring system to analyze the writings of James Joyce, finding them to be written by six different "authors." Ellison even scored Morton's initial report with Morton's methods, and "discovered" that different parts of that report were written by different people! This illustrates that content analysis is not foolproof, and that scientific findings must always be retested to see whether they are valid.

Questionnaires and Surveys

The most common form of research in contemporary psychology of religion is the questionnaire and survey. The word "survey" refers to the procedure for sampling the subjects for a particular study; "questionnaire" refers to the instrument itself. Questionnaire survey data can be collected from one person at a time, but a big advantage of this method is that data can be collected from many subjects at once. Subject sampling procedure can be random, representative, or biased, with several specialized techniques available for determining who should be in the sample.

Questionnaires do not measure overt behavior. Instead, they ask a series of structured questions about people's opinions on issues, judgments, and guesses as to how they might behave in a particular situation. For example, with a questionnaire you might be able to assess whether people claim that they actively participate in church work, but you cannot measure actual church-working behavior with a questionnaire.

A psychometric issue concerning the use of behavioral versus questionnaire measures of religiousness is applicable here. Whether a study is experimental or correlational in nature, it is highly desirable to include behavioral dependent variables (outcome measures). By doing this, knowledge is gained about what people actually do in response to their beliefs, rather than how they feel or what they say they might do on a paper-and-pencil questionnaire. This is important. However, this concern is softened somewhat in light of the work by Fishbein and Ajzen (1975). They have shown that when a questionnaire is designed to tap tendencies to act such that the range of religious behaviors sampled by the set of questions approximates the range of actions that comprise the behavioral measure, the correspondence between the questionnaire score and the behavioral outcome measure increases.

Questionnaires used to study religion come in two forms: the simple questionnaire and the formal scale. The simple questionnaire is composed of items designed for straightforward measurement. The respondent is asked for the raw information of interest to the investigator. An illustration would be a questionnaire asking for such things as denominational affiliation, agreement with Biblical statements, number of hours of work in the church, or opinion on some issue.

The formal scale is a multiple-item measuring device. It is different from the simple questionnaire in two respects. First the formal scale is designed to measure some psychologically meaningful dimension, as opposed to assessing opinion or demographic variables. Second, it is not always immediately apparent what a particular scale is measuring. A scale item that looks as though it measures one thing may actually be getting at something else. For example, a question that asks about how often you pray may be part of a scale that is really designed to measure the degree of genuineness of your faith, not simply how often you pray. Today we have many psycho-religious scales available. The list of dimensions measured by them includes religious funda-mentalism, dogmatism, purpose in life, intrinsic and extrinsic religious orien-tation, doubt, faith maturity, authoritarianism, mysticism, orthodoxy, religion as a quest, spiritual well-being, and others (Bassett et al., 1991; Butman, 1990; Robinson & Shaver, 1973; Van Wicklin, 1990).

Naturalistic Studies

In naturalistic studies the researcher takes advantage of naturally occurring circumstances in the real world. Rather than artificially constructing a situ-ation to test some hypothesis, as would be done with formal experimental procedures, the researcher uses the "natural laboratory" of real life. One advantage of naturalistic studies is that the results speak directly back to real-world events. Another advantage is that with naturalistic methods we can study actual, overt behavior directly—rather than measuring only opinions or psychological dimensions as is the case with questionnaires.

In one type of naturalistic method called *field observation*, the investigator develops coding categories appropriate to the behaviors under study and then observes and scores the subjects' behavior without interfering in any way. An example would be if you wanted to find out how religious denominations differ in the degree of vocalizing done by the congregation during church services. An outside, nonparticipating observer would visit the worship serv-ices of the various groups and record how often people in the audience spoke, what they said, whether the pastor or priest encouraged it, and so on.

Another type of naturalistic method called *participant observation* is used when it is necessary for the investigator to appear to be actively involved in the group whose behavior is being studied. In this case the investigator "joins" the group and acts like an average participant. A good participant observer takes care to be inconspicuous, in order to avoid drawing personal attention and distorting the situation. The necessary data are thus gathered from "in-side" the group, resulting in unique findings not obtainable by other methods. A classic example of the participant observation method appears in *When Prophecy Fails* by Festinger, Riecken, and Schachter (1956). These three infil-trated a "doomsday group" that predicted the end of the world. Their study of the formation, maintenance, and dissolution of the group, and of the activity of the members after the world was not destroyed on the expected date, became a milestone in the study of social forces operating in small religious groups.

Studying Deviant Groups

The approach of studying deviant groups has been used in conjunction with the methods listed above. It involves studying specialized groups or individuals, and generalizing the findings to the normal population as far as is valid. Studying deviant groups has both positive and negative aspects. A positive aspect of this approach is that it enables you to learn much about one special population, as is illustrated by the Festinger et al. study mentioned above. It could also illustrate especially potent forms of religiousness. But these good aspects set the stage for a possible negative side effect—overgeneralization. This is a difficulty for any approach that involves studying only a unique group and then drawing conclusions about the population as a whole. Freud, for example, studied neurotic patients and then applied his theory to normal individuals. Albert Ellis (1962) made the logical error of concluding that all religion is bad for mental health by basing his conclusions primarily on observations of his clients (who came to him because they had problems). Even James (1902) based his insights on the analysis of cases of extreme religious experience. In fact, many important contributions to understanding religiousness have come from studying extreme cases. Therefore, there is an important place for this approach. At the same time, it would be a mistake to rely exclusively on this approach because making global generalizations about religiousness based solely on highly specialized populations might not be valid. Instead, we should balance the study of specialized cases with its opposite, the study of religiousness in normal populations, from which we then generalize to and predict the deviations.

Experiments

The most precise form of research design is the laboratory experiment. This procedure allows you to come closest to a cause-effect conclusion of the form "changes in variable *A* reliably lead to changes in variable *B*." In the psychology of religion, such a statement might be "adopting a transcendental belief system reduces the fear of death." The laboratory experiment is the logical prototype for all empirical psychological research, even when actual experiments cannot be conducted. It is the criteria of precision and clarity of the experiment against which any research procedure or conclusion is judged.

In a true experiment, the investigator manipulates one variable, called the *independent variable,* to see whether changes in that variable bring about changes in a consequence variable called the *dependent variable.* Suppose, for example, you wanted to find out whether thinking about religious ideas causes people to feel emotional. You could show a list of religious words to one group of subjects (the experimental group) and a list of neutral words to another group of subjects (the control group). The independent variable in this case would be the religious content of the word list. The dependent variable could be the increase in skin conductance due to perspiration in the palms of the hands, one evidence of emotional response. You would determine whether the people who are shown religious words respond more, or less, emotionally (as measured by skin conductance) than the people who see neutral words. If the results show that the religious-word subjects have greater skin conductance responses than the neutral-word subjects, then one piece of evidence has been offered for the general proposition that seeing religious words or thinking religious thoughts causes emotional arousal.

Unfortunately, there have not been very many controlled experiments done in the psychology of religion. In fact, Warren (1976) found that from 1950 to 1970 only 2 percent of the studies were true experiments; most studies were corelational, in which variables are related to each other but are not manipulated. Hunsberger (1991) notes that subsequent calls for more experimental studies have had little effect. The advisability of doing true experiments in the psychology of religion is debated from time to time (Batson, 1977, 1979, 1986; Gorsuch, 1982; Yeatts & Asher, 1979). On the one hand, it is generally agreed that we should do experimental studies if it were practically and ethically possible. However, although we want to treat some aspects of religiosity as an independent variable, we often cannot manipulate that variable ourselves. For example, I am interested in the effects of conversion, but it is impossible to randomly assign people to the condition of being converts or nonconverts (nor would it be ethnical do do if it were possible). Doing more experimental studies constitutes one of the exciting possibilities for psychology of religion in the future.

Besides laboratory experiments and correlational procedures, two types of research designs should be fruitful for psychologists of religion: field experiments and natural experiments. Field experiments allow the researcher some degree of control over the independent variable, although this control will often not be as precise as it is in the laboratory experiment. However, field experiments do allow you to give a treatment to some people but not to others and, consequently, assess the effects of that treatment as compared to the control group. An example of this type of experiment was done by Pahnke (1970). The subjects were theology students attending a Good Friday service. Some of them were given the hallucinogenic drug Psilocybin before the service, while others were given a mild control drug that would not show "mind-expanding" properties. Results showed that those who took Psilocybin showed a significantly greater degree of having had a mystical religious experience at the Good Friday service, as compared to the control group. The key things about a field experiment that make it desirable are that (1) the investigator can exercise some control of the independent variable treatment and avoid too much confounding due to extraneous variables, and (2) the research is done in real-life settings, so that the results are generalizable to real-life situations.

Natural experiments share these features of field experiments, with one exception: in a natural experiment you do not manipulate the independent variable. Nature manipulates it for you, and you simply record its effects. You could not, for example, produce an experimental group of religious converts on your own; but naturally occurring events (e.g., a Billy Graham crusade; Newton & Mann, 1980) might produce them for you. You could collect pre-post data on converts and nonconverts as a function of such an event. In general, in order to use this method you must keep a prepared mind so that you can exploit the research possibilities imbedded in circumstances the occurrence of which is beyond your control.

2. *Measuring Religion*

The process of doing empirical research on religion requires that you measure it. This is an essential step in the research cycle. The problem is that measuring religion is about as easy as defining it conceptually: not at all simple, but educational to try. Measuring religion empirically is a useful endeavor because the process of developing measures of religion not only gives us tests we can use in research; it also forces us to clarify our conceptual definitions and distinctions. Our conceptual definitions and our operational definitions interact. We translate our conceptions into concrete procedures; then, refining these procedures enables us to rethink and possibly reconstruct our conceptions so as to make them reflect reality more accurately.

In Chapter 1, I argued that religion is fruitfully thought of as a multidimensional variable. Glock's five dimensions were presented for their intuitive appeal. The other way of conceiving of religion is as a set of yes-or-no, all-or-nothing categories: people either are religious or are not; they either believe in God or they do not.[3] Other ways of measuring religion exist that reflect either the categorical approach or the multidimensional approach. The categorical approach is based upon simple identification. The multidimensional approach is based upon factors and formal scales.

Simple Identification

The simple identification approach is straightforward. You ask people what they believe, what they do, or to what religious group they belong and then place the data for like subjects into one category. Although seemingly primitive, this approach has been used in many studies—especially before the modern period of the field. For example, numerous studies have made simple comparisons between Protestants, Catholics, and Jews on some dependent variable (Argyle & Beit-Hallahmi, 1975). Some of my work comparing Christian believers and nonbelievers is of this type (Paloutzian, 1981; Paloutzian, Jackson, & Crandall, 1978). Asking direct questions such as "Do you believe in God?," as is done by the Gallup polling organization (Gallup & Jones, 1989), also fits this category.

The simple identification approach is useful for several reasons. First, it is easy. You can simply ask people, usually via a paper-and-pencil questionnaire, for the information you desire. Second, it has intuitive appeal. For example, if you have reason to believe that Protestants, Catholics, and Jews differ on some dimension (say, attitudes toward abortion), then why not ask people straightforwardly what their religious affiliation is and what their attitudes are? Third, it is versatile. You can ask people about their beliefs (e.g., Do you believe in the Virgin Birth?), practice (e.g., How often do you attend church?), experience (e.g., Have you ever experienced the presence of a spirit or divine being?), and other of the dimensions of religious commitment (Chapter 1). Fourth, it fits in well with what we are likely to think are the important variables—and these are usually variables with which we are already familiar, such as religious grouping, doctrinal belief, type of practice, and frequency of ritual.

But simple identification has its drawbacks. The first drawback is that it can easily be misleading. For example, if you desire to compare "religious" persons with "nonreligious" persons, and you do so by using religious affiliation to operationally define a "religious person," you will be misled—because over half of those who claim an affiliation are not regularly active (Alston, 1971). A similar problem occurs when considering church membership. Some churches do not count children as members, some do not have formal membership at all, and in the past some did not count women (Argyle & Beit-Hallahmi, 1975). Add to this the fact that many people are active in religious groups but are not formal members, that others consider themselves to be religious but do not participate in religious services, and over 75 percent of the U.S. population thinks that "a person can be a good Christian or Jew if he or she doesn't attend church or synagogue" (Gallup & Jones, 1989), and it becomes clear that using simple identification as a means of identifying truly religious people can be very misleading.

A second drawback is that simple identification, because it puts people into imprecise and undifferentiated categories, can mask other key variables. Knowing whether you have a Protestant or Catholic affiliation reveals little about your deep religious attitudes. Why you hold your beliefs could determine more of your behavior than the beliefs themselves. For example, within limits, whether people have an intrinsic or extrinsic orientation to their faith is more important in predicting their racial attitudes than what their denominational affiliation happens to be (Allport & Ross, 1967; Gorsuch & Aleshire, 1974; Donahue, 1985). Extrinsics are more prejudiced than intrinsics, regardless of denomination. Simple denomination identification masks the finer distinction based on religious orientation. It will be these finer distinctions, which we assess with a variety of specialized scales, that are involved in the most interesting current research.

Factors and Scales

The above discussion highlights the need for refined ways of measuring religion. Once we have specified the criteria for devout religiousness, we need measuring instruments that will identify the genuinely religious person, as compared to one with only nominal religious affiliation. We also must be able to measure the degree of a person's religious belief, feeling, or practice. Fortunately, various multi-factor or multi-item scales have been designed to do this. Table 3.1 lists several of them.

These refined scales do several useful things. First, they enable us to measure someone on the various dimensions of religion. We can get a belief score, practice score, experience score, etc. We can measure the person on each factor, as well as assess the degree of consistency between these factors. Intuitively, we would expect a high degree of belief to correlate with a high degree of practice. With multidimensional tests we can explore such questions. The Dimensions of Religious Commitment test (Glock & Stark, 1966) is based on this idea.

Second, some of the scales help us assess the "inside" of a person's religious life, rather than the more visible religious practice or institutional

TABLE 3.1 Psychology of Religion Measures and their Locations

Measure	Location or source
Age-Universal Intrinsic-Extrinsic Religious Orientation	Gorsuch & Venable, 1983
Attributions of Responsibility to God	Gorsuch & Smith, 1983
Christian Orthodoxy Scale	Fullerton & Hunsberger, 1982
Death Transcendence	Hood & Morris, 1983
Dimensions of Religious Commitment	Glock & Stark, 1966
Dogmatism	Robinson, Shaver, & Wrightsman, 1991
	Rokeach, 1956
Doubts	Altemeyer, 1988
	Hunsberger et al., 1983
Faith Maturity Scale	Benson, Donahue, & Erickson, 1993
Indiscriminate Proreligious Scale	Pargament et al., 1987
Intrinsic-Extrinsic Religious Orientation (Allport & Ross, 1967)	Robinson & Shaver, 1973
Literal, Antiliteral, Mythological Scale	Hunt, 1972
Mysticism	Hood, 1975
Purpose in Life	Crumbaugh, 1968
	Crumbaugh & Maholick, 1969
	Robinson, Shaver, & Wrightsman, 1991
Quest	Altemeyer & Hunsberger, 1992
	Batson, Schoenrade, & Ventis, 1993
Religious Experience	Hood, 1970
Religious Fundamentalism	Altemeyer & Hunsberger, 1992
Right-Wing Authoritarianism	Altemeyer, 1988
Spiritual Well-Being Scale	Paloutzian & Ellison, 1982
	Ellison & Smith, 1991
Value Survey	Rokeach, 1973

affiliation. They help tap such things as the motives behind the religion (e.g., intrinsic and extrinsic motives) and the subjective experience of religion (e.g., degree of mystical experience). The Intrinsic-Extrinsic Religious Orientation Scale (Allport & Ross, 1967) and the Religious Experience Episodes Measure (Hood, 1970) are two well-known scales developed to do this. The former measures the extent to which someone "lives" their religion (intrinsic) versus "uses" their religion (extrinsic). The latter measures the extent to which someone has experienced vivid subjective religious experience. Additional scales include the Christian Orthodoxy Scale, Religious Fundamentalism Scale, Right-Wing Authoritarianism Scale, Quest Scale, Literal-Antiliteral-Mythological Scale, Spiritual Well-Being Scale, Faith Maturity Scale, a method for measuring religious doubt, a Value Survey, and others. Table 3.1 lists a reference and/or source where these instruments can be seen.

The overall advantage to the multiple scale approach is that it allows us more precision. We can measure finer distinctions along religious dimensions within the broader classifications. This notion has empirical support. With the aid of factor analysis (a statistical procedure that helps us see which dimensions are empirically real), we have learned that there exists a general religious factor and several religious dimensions of narrower focus that exist within the general religious factor (Gorsuch, 1980, 1984).

One limitation on the present state of the art of measuring religion is that most of the available scales were developed to study religion in a Judaic and Christian tradition. Such work needs to be extended to other religions and cultures. Some steps toward this end have begun. For example, the Religious Fundamentalism Scale of Altemeyer & Hunsberger (1992) was skillfully designed so that it does *not* focus on specifically Christian fundamentalism. Instead, they designed their scale to tap the sort of fundamentalistic mental process that might appear in any religion—Christian, Muslim, or other. Also, this general adaptation of scales to other contexts is beginning to occur across traditional age barriers: Gorsuch and Venable (1983) have developed an "age-universal" version of the Intrinsic-Extrinsic Religious Orientation Scale that is intended to be used for research with children.

Which Is Best?
Which procedure is best for you depends on what you want to know. The nature of your question will lead you to the procedures best suited to answer it. Creative ways of using several research methods are illustrated in the research presented in the following chapters.

Further Reading

Popper, K. R. *Objective knowledge: An evolutionary approach.* Oxford: Oxford University Press, 1972. An influential presentation of modern philosophy of science.

Lynn, M. & Moberg, D. (Eds.). *Research in the social scientific study of religion.* Vols. 1–6, 1989–1994. Greenwich, CT: JAI Press. This annual series of volumes publishes approximately a dozen articles a year on a variety of lines of research in the psychology of religion.

A number of textbooks on research methods in psychology or the behavioral sciences may be consulted for information about questionnaire design, experimental methods, etc.

The following are some "standard" psychology of religion journals that publish original research: *Journal for the Scientific Study of Religion, Review of Religious Research, Journal of Psychology and Theology, The International Journal for the Psychology of Religion.* Examine recent issues of these publications to see many kinds of research being done, using several different methods.

Notes

1. This discussion is concerned with the philosophy of science as reflected in an empirical research strategy. Therefore, "data" refers to the record of observable and recordable events. Other approaches to research exist that broaden the meaning of the concept of data to include additional sorts of information outside the domain of this discussion.

2. This and the following section are based on the idea that there is no automatic, essential conflict between religion and science. Psychology and religion may appear to be in conflict when each one tries to make statements that are within the domain of the other. An example of this would be when the Roman Church of the early 1600s taught that the earth was the center of the universe, in opposition to the findings of Galileo. Some contemporary "pop psychologies" promoted by certain religious authors make a similar error—that of "reading" their scriptures so as to make it "teach" a particular psychological model of human functioning.

3. It should be clarified that, in one sense, all people are religious when answering basic questions about life, such as "Does God exist?", "What is the meaning of life?", "What is the basis for right and wrong?", "What happens after death?" Because questions of this sort raise essentially religious issues, the answers of all, both "religious" and "nonreligious" persons, are fundamentally religious answers. They rest upon basic presuppositions that are accepted by faith. Some (the religious) happen to fit preformed groups, whereas others (the nonreligious) do not.

4

Acquisition + Maintenance

[Developmental]

Religious Development in Children

It has been said that religion is primarily an adult affair—that the questions with which religion tries to deal are too deep, complicated, or mystical for children to worry about. After all, who would expect little children to grapple with issues such as what life means, what happens after death, the rationale for morality, the purpose of existence, and other ultimate questions? Surely, such matters need not trouble children until they are old enough to cope with the basic uncertainties of life.

Nevertheless, children are involved in religion—sometimes in ways that have lifelong impact. Sunday schools, children's church services, religious instruction classes, parochial schools, and some religious television programs are all designed to teach, convert, and retain children as well as adults. A more potent influence, perhaps, is the role of religious parents in teaching, training, and modeling their religion for their offspring.

Psychological Research on Religious Development

It has also been tacitly assumed, in the history of psychological research on religious development, that a person's religious life doesn't change too much after young adulthood. It is known that after young adulthood, people's general beliefs and religious affiliations stay the same more often than they change. For example, if you are a Catholic by the time you are 25, chances are that you will remain one, at least in name. But what is not known, or at least not backed up with sufficient scientific studies, is the nature of religious development mechanisms that mediate changes in the way a person holds religious beliefs and responds to them in middle adulthood and old age (McFadden, 1995, in press). The available empirical studies on developmental processes that are part of religiousness across the lifespan have, for the most part, stopped at the end of adolescence. Part of this "invitation," therefore, is for you to extend this research.

With such potent and enduring influences on children, one would suppose that psychologists would be doing extensive research on religious development. However, the recent past reflects a gap in the research literature on this topic. The *Journal for the Scientific Study of Religion*, commonly regarded as the leading publisher of empirical research in the psychology of religion (Hunsberger, 1979), published over 275 articles in the decade from 1970 through 1979. Of these, only eight are concerned with developmental issues, and at best four are concerned with developmental issues as the primary focus. The decade from 1980 through 1989 was about the same: a total of approximately 325 papers were published; perhaps 10–12 concerned development. For the half-decade from 1990 through 1994: approximately 160 papers—five concerned development. This means that, at least as evidenced in this one journal, the rate of studies focusing particularly on religious development has been fairly constant and low. For 25 years the field has been dominated by a nondevelopmental approach.

We need research that focuses on questions such as: What does religion mean to a child? What changes take place over the process of religious development from childhood through old age? Certainly, religion cannot mean the same thing to people of diverse ages, can it? And what do we mean when we say that one person's religion is "more developed" than that of another person? How does this vary across different religions and different cultures? Fortunately, some excellent books have now been published (Hyde, 1990; Kimble, McFadden, Ellor, & Seeber, 1995; Oser & Scarlett, 1991; Tamminen, 1991) that place the relevant literature on children, adolescents, and adults into a developmental context in an effort to deal with such questions.

Our previous discussions of the dimensions of religious commitment and psychological orientations to interpreting religion can be brought into play in order to understand the interlocking network of factors involved in religious development from childhood to old age. Cognitive capacity and social environment both expand markedly over the course of development, and these changes in some ways stimulate and in some ways retard the religious commitment of the child. The process of maturity modifies the role of religion during adulthood. Whatever the final outcome, one thing is certain: the meaning of religion for the person changes over the course of development from childhood to old age.

This chapter is based on the following ideas: Religion for the young child is largely imitative in nature; beliefs are held uncritically. There is initially little concern for consistency between beliefs, practice, and effects. Children are first trained to follow a religious practice rather than to choose and internalize a belief. It is at this time that basic attachments are formed and social learning patterns are begun. As children grow older, their cognitive abilities and social environments prompt questions that move them to a deeper and more abstract level of questioning and hence understanding of the faith. In the final analysis, whether the older youth retains the religion of his or her upbringing (or whether the youth raised without a formal religion adopts one) depends upon his or her own inner choices and the perceived value of and rationale for the religion. As adulthood unfolds, new confrontations and life experiences may further modify the meaning of someone's religiousness. Finally, religious development can be understood in part as a process in which the degree or form of religiousness changes over a long period of time.

These fundamental points rest on the notion that children are different from adults. Let's first examine some of the ways children differ from adults psychologically. We will then be in a position to try to understand how children acquire religion, and how the meaning of religion changes during adolescence and adulthood.

The Nature of Childhood Religion

It is probably true that there can be no meaningful religion in young children (Kupky, 1928), if we are referring to a fully developed (mature or internalized) type of religious life. In order to have a "more developed" type of religious life, the individual must first be psychologically more developed. However, children are religious in some sense. Religion, like other facets of life, is developing from an early age.

Perception, Language, and the Meaning of Symbols: Cognitive Mechanisms

There have been a variety of theories put forth to account for developmental changes. Prominent among them is the cognitive developmental model introduced by Swiss psychologist Jean Piaget. Most of the several stage models of religious development that exist today are intellectual descendants of Piaget's notion of general human development; therefore, although some of his notions may be modified by subsequent research, it will help for you to have a general idea of how he did his studies and his view of the process of change from infancy to adulthood. A basic proposition of this view is that children develop through an invariant sequence of cognitive stages, each more complex than, and qualitatively different from, the preceding stages. Research within this framework suggests that children pass through stages of moral reasoning and religious development that are expressions of the general cognitive stages. While working within this framework, we will emphasize that our understanding of religious development requires an appreciation of how cognitive factors interact with the child's social context, particularly the family. Research derived from this approach suggests that as a child develops, critical changes occur in his or her perception, social context, ability to understand the meaning of symbols, language, and ability for conceptual thought.

One basic aspect of early childhood is that very young children lack *object permanence*. They behave as though an object exists only as long as they can see it. As soon as the object is placed out of sight, the child behaves as if it did not exist. This was Piaget's conclusion after he discovered that a child will pursue a desired object while it is visible, but when it is placed out of sight (e.g., under a pillow) the child no longer pursues it (Piaget & Inhelder, 1969). Adults, on the other hand, pursue many things that are not visible, having come to realize that objects continue to exist even though they are temporarily out of sight. The key point here is that young children perceive reality differently. Early in life, reality equals whatever the child senses at the moment. There is no time, no memory, no sense of past and future by which to anchor one's percepts. Whatever "is" at the moment is reality.

Intimately linked to the above aspects of child perception is the child's language. It is through words[1] that thoughts, percepts, and experiences become specific points of reference in our minds. Words are symbolic pegs on which we hang selected thoughts, and words gain meaning through experience. But unlike the adult, who has a large store of language and memory to draw on in order to understand (and even modify) the meaning of new words, the child must learn the meaning of every new word from scratch. A consequence of this is that words have only concrete, limited meanings. There is initially little abstraction to general classes and little ability to think in terms of general principles (such as kindness, goodness, etc.) or nonphysical entities (e.g., God, heaven). Children of necessity can understand a word to represent only concrete (experienced) things or acts.

Nowhere does this question of the meaning of children's language become more important than as it pertains to the question of religion (i.e., religious language and religious symbols). Because children think in concrete terms, religious language for them connotes concrete entities. Thus, the term *God* for a young child is likely to mean *big person.* If God is called *Father,* the child thinks in terms of an oversized, more powerful father who is basically similar to the child's actual father. Depending upon the language with which the child has heard God referred to and the child's perceptions of those purported to have God-like attributes (e.g., Santa Claus), the child may have the mental impression that God is a big old man in the sky.

Questions asked about God by children in grades K–3 reveal the way in which they think: "Does God die like everyone else? How does God pick up people that are dead?" They also ask about how God makes himself, how he gets up in the sky, and how he makes things, how and when he was born, how old he is, whether he is married, and whether he is Christian or Jewish (Zeligs, 1974).[2] Figure 4.1 illustrates how youngsters communicate with God, via letter, about the earth, friends, and religion. This same age group also tends to talk as though death were like a vacation. The nature of these questions illustrates the concrete mode of thinking in young children and how that age group tends

---

Dear God,
    Why did you give Jesus such a hard time? My dad is rough on me too. So I know what it's like. Maybe you both could ease up?

                              Mark [age 11]

Dear Ms. God:
    I believe that you are a woman. In fact I am sure for sure. I think that is why the rivers and sky and birds are so beautiful.
    If by some flook you are a boy please do not take it out on me. Boys should not hit girls.

                              Trisha [age 11]

FIGURE 4.1 Children's Letters to God

Source: Heller, D. (1987). *Dear God: Children's Letters to God.* New York: Doubleday.

to give very specific meaning to religious language. As children get older, the way they talk about God tends to change from the concrete mode of thinking illustrated above, to reflect more abstraction, conceptualization, and symbolization (Coles, 1990; Heller, 1986, 1987; Tamminen, 1991).

In addition to verbal symbols, visual symbols also carry different meanings for children. For example, a child has little special response to religious symbols such as a cross or religious art. It is only after the youth has been taught what these symbols represent, and that such objects are something of importance, that religious symbols acquire meaning for the child. Perhaps the strongest influence in teaching the child the meaning of these symbols is the family.

2. *Family, Social Context, and Personal Needs: Social Learning and Attachment Processes*

We can now add two additional theoretical notions to the cognitive approach illustrated above, in order to help round out our initial search of processes involved in children's religion. Particularly helpful for our understanding of the role of family and social context are the principles that come from social learning theory, mentioned in Chapter 1, and attachment theory, mentioned in Chapter 2.

Social learning principles are based on the ideas of reward, punishment, reinforcement, and imitation and modeling. Simply put, a child is more likely to remember and reproduce those behaviors for which he or she gets a reward and is less likely to perform those behaviors that are punished. According to modern versions of this theory, reinforced behaviors are stored as memory traces in a cognitive retrieval system so that, at a later time, the child can reconstruct those memories and enact the behaviors represented in them. The process of imitation and modeling works the same way. When a child sees an adult perform a behavior, a partial representation of that perception is stored as a memory trace in the child's cognitive system, and it is later reconstructed and implemented when the child is sufficiently motivated to perform that behavior. The applications of this type of understanding to the question of how children learn to perform religious behaviors is straightforward and is illustrated below.

Attachment theory can be drawn on in order to help us understand the nature of the emotional bond between the child and the family and how this relationship affects the child's religiousness. The essential notions of attachment theory are that the infant is by nature in a biosocial system in which he or she must stay in physical proximity to the parent or primary caregiver (Bowlby, 1969, 1973, 1980). This enables the child to get those things that are essential for survival, such as sustenance and protection from predators. According to the theory, the optimal relationship between the infant and the

Religious symbols such as words, visual art, and objects take on meanings as part of religious development during early childhood, especially due to family influence, as illustrated above.

primary caregiver, or attachment figure, is one in which the attachment figure provides two things: "(1) a *haven* of safety and comfort to which the infant can turn in times of distress or threat, and (2) a *secure base* for exploration of the environment in the absence of danger (Kirkpatrick & Shaver, 1990, p. 317. Emphasis in original.)." How optimally this is done leaves traces in an emotional-behavioral-cognitive system that are presumed to be active, or at least be available, as a schematic "working model" of the attachment relationship to influence behavior throughout the lifetime. Applications of this idea to the psychology of religion have been made by Lee Kirkpatrick (Kirkpatrick &

Shaver, 1992; Kirkpatrick, 1992), who has noted that in most theologies God is the ideal attachment figure: God is said to be like the perfect parent who, either literally or spiritually, is always there to provide you a sense of security and protect you from danger.

The interaction of social learning and attachment notions can help us describe religion in young children. The preschool age child's exposure to religious symbols, teachings, and practices is under almost the total control of the family. Hence, whatever sort of religion the parents have exposed the child to determines what religion means to him or her. The thought that other people believe and do things differently is simply not a live option in the mind of the young child. It is presumed that the way they do it is the way everybody does it. This can easily be seen as a result of social learning.

This single-mindedness of early childhood becomes apparent when children enter school. As children talk about things other than school, and as they are involved in play activities with each other outside of regular school hours, children from religious families sometimes express bewilderment at finding that other people don't believe and practice the same as themselves. For example, a child who is used to talking about God at home is puzzled to learn that it is not possible to do so with a school friend—not because of any antagonism, but simply because the concept "God" has no meaning to the friend. The friend's family has never used the concept, and hence there can be little meaningful discussion between the children regarding that concept.

Similar lessons emerge with regard to religious practice. One child learns to pray only in a kneeling position and with a memorized text, while another child learns to pray conversationally and with no particular posture. One child attends church on Sundays, another on Saturdays. Or, the unchurched child wonders why a friend cannot play on Sunday—because for the unchurched child having little experience with such restrictions it is difficult to understand why the friend's family would endorse such a policy. A consequence is that there may be genuine expressions of puzzlement over why people differ in these ways. For a cognitive developmentalist, such puzzles are normal confrontations to the child; they are problem-solving tasks that prompt the child to move from the present stage to the next one.

The child's social context can either promote or retard the child's religion. Family and church influences are obviously supportive. But the higher the child goes in school (except sectarian schools), the greater the likelihood of exposure to people and ideas different from those of his or her experience. One consequence is a greater tendency to realize that a variety of options exist in addition to those practiced by the family. This exposure, in combination with the developing cognitive abilities in older children, prompts the questioning and doubt during adolescence of what one has been taught during childhood. But how the adolescent responds to this may depend on the type of attachment relationship that is part of his or her past: Those with an insecure attachment relationship with their mothers or primary caregivers may become religious in order to compensate—use God as the secure attachment figure that is absent in their backgrounds. In contrast, those with a secure attachment relationship, at least those with nonreligious parents to serve as model, may be less likely to become religious for those reasons.

At the preschool stage, interacting with social context are the child's personal needs for belonging, love, and approval. Children will expend large amounts of energy to gain approval and affection. Because the main source of these rewards for the young child is the family, the child will display the religious practice that is modeled and approved by the family. This becomes the "reality" of religion for the preschool child. It seems clear that religion is held at this time of life as more of a practice than a belief.

3. *Practice versus Belief*

The question then emerges, "What does religion mean to the child?" The answer seems to be that religion means religious practice performed because that is what is approved. Even statements of belief in children appear to be verbal utterances performed in a more-or-less imitative fashion. This is apparent in young children's prayers said as "grace" before meals. The prayer is repeated, or mimicked after the parents' example, and it is difficult to tell whether there is any level of conceptual understanding. Depth of belief is questionable.

The meaning of prayer is also simple for young children. Often prayer is understood to be a tool used to get something—a kind of backup plan to be used when nothing else works. For example, I have observed 4-year-old boys playing a game. When one child did not get to make his desired move, he would say, "Next time I'm going to pray before I throw the dice!" In other words, prayer is seen as a type of concrete, mechanical force—a tool to be used to produce a desired outcome. Only when the child reaches a higher level of cognitive ability will this and other religious practices become infused with deeper meaning.

Prayer is seen in the same way by elementary school children also. For example, when Tamminen (1991) asked Finnish youngsters in the third grade to complete the sentence "I think prayer is . . ." and then assigned each answer to one of ten categories such as "praise and worship" or "conversation with God," he found that the category "asking something from God" was the most commonly used. This same pattern was robust over several years; it was obtained in an initial study of Finnish children in 1974 and replicated in a separate study with different children in 1986.

Actually, Tamminen asked children across several ages from third grade through high school to complete the "prayer question" and many others. Interesting and pertinent to our understanding of the nature of religious development, his conclusion was that there was a difference in the nature of the prayer requests made across the age span. Children in the lowest grades had a greater tendency to ask for concrete things, whereas those in the upper grades were more likely to mention spiritual things or present a request to God in general terms. This suggests that only when the child reaches a higher level of cognitive ability will prayer and other religious practices become infused with deeper meaning.

Cognitive Factors in Moral Development

With what we have seen of the cognitive differences between children and adults, we would predict developmental changes in such things as the process of arriving at moral judgments—a process that can tax one's cognitive ability. Therefore, let's look at what the cognitive-developmental approach has to say about the development of moral reasoning. We would expect what we learn about the development of moral judgments to have a parallel in the research on religious development, because these two areas, religious teaching and questions of right and wrong, have much in common. As in the preceding discussion, the findings seem to indicate that the primitive meaning of religion in young children is due not merely to a simple lack of learning, but also to special features of the nature of children. We shall see that there are stage models of moral reasoning, and stage models of religious development that are their direct intellectual descendants.

Piaget's Two Stages of Moral Reasoning

Piaget is responsible for introducing the cognitive stage model to the study of moral reasoning. Some of his classic demonstrations showing that children develop through different levels of cognitive ability are found in his *Moral Judgment of the Child* (1932/1965). He proposed that children develop through two stages of moral reasoning—the stage of moral realism and the stage of moral independence. Each stage is evidenced by a qualitatively different set of rules used to assess right and wrong. The different modes of thinking represented at these two stages are illustrated by the responses of children of different ages to Piaget's moral decision stories. Piaget tells the children stories and then asks them for a judgment of right and wrong. Two of his stories are about John and Henry:

> A.   *A little boy who is called John is in his room. He is called to dinner. He goes into the dining room. But behind the door there was a chair, and on the chair there was a tray with fifteen cups on it. John couldn't have known that there was all this behind the door. He goes in; the door knocks against the tray; bang go the fifteen cups and they all get broken!*
> B.   *Once there was a little boy whose name was Henry. One day when his mother was out he tried to get some jam out of the cupboard. He climbed onto*

a chair and stretched out his arm. But the jam was too high up, and he couldn't reach it and have any. While he was trying to get it, he knocked over a cup. The cup fell down and broke.

Piaget asks children to say which of the two boys, John or Henry, is the naughtier and why. Their answers reveal that younger children (those in the stage of moral realism) judge actions by their material consequences: John was naughtier because he broke fifteen cups. Older children who have reached the stage of moral independence take intentions into account: Henry was naughtier because he was trying to do something he presumably was not supposed to do. Piaget argues that it takes a more complicated type of mental ability to make moral judgments based upon intentions than the simple visible consequences of an act.

This type of cognitive stage model is applicable to religion. Young children interpret religion in concrete terms in the same way that they evaluate right and wrong in terms of concrete, material consequences. Older children are able to grasp more of the meaning of religion in a fashion similar to the way they evaluate morality—by reasoning at a more abstract level.

Piaget's Three Stages of Cognitive Development

In addition to his two stages of moral reasoning, Piaget also proposed a general theory of cognitive development (of which his two levels of moral reasoning are only a part) composed of three stages (Piaget & Inhelder, 1969). Ages 2–7 is the preoperational stage. During this period the child's mind does not think in terms of abstract logic. Rather, whatever the child perceives equals reality. Piaget's well-known demonstration in which a child who observes liquid being poured from a tall, thin glass into a short, fat glass believes that the volume of liquid changes in the process (because it looks different) illustrates preoperational thinking. Between the ages of 7 and 11 a child is in Piaget's stage of concrete operations. Here the child can use rules of logic and classification, but only as applied to concrete events and objects. Fully developed mental capabilities emerge after the age of 11, in Piaget's stage of formal operations. It is here that people develop the ability to abstract and conceptualize. As applied to religion, it is during this last stage that people are more able to understand the deeper meanings of religion, to assess the true value of what they have been taught, and make their own decisions about religion independently.

Kohlberg's Six Stages of Moral Judgment

With Piaget's two-stage model of moral development and three-stage model of cognitive development as a background, Lawrence Kohlberg (1964, 1969) created his influential six-stage model of the development of the complexity of moral reasoning. It is a direct extrapolation of Piagetian thinking and is composed of three overall stages with two substages of each. As with the views that came before his, Kohlberg's stages are presumed to be invariant in sequence and hierarchical, with each one seen as something like a layer on top of the previous ones.

Before you can appreciate the nature of Kohlberg's stages, you should be confronted with the same type of problems that he gave his subjects. He used an interview method in which he gave his subjects real-life dilemmas, and then he asked a series of questions abut them. Here is the most famous of the dilemmas, the story of Heinz and the drug.

> *In Europe, a woman was near death from a special kind of cancer. There was one drug that the doctors thought might save her. It was a form of radium that a druggist in the same town had recently discovered. The drug was expensive to make, but the druggist was charging ten times what the drug cost him to make. He paid $200 for the radium and charged $2000 for a small dose of the drug. The sick woman's husband, Heinz, went to everyone he knew to borrow the money, but could only get together about $1000, which was half of what it cost. He told the druggist that his wife was dying and asked him to sell it cheaper or let him pay later. But the druggist said, "No, I discovered the drug and I'm going to make money from it." So Heinz got desperate and broke into the man's store to steal the drug for his wife.*

In order to detect the level of moral reasoning with which a person would try to solve Heinz's problem, Kohlberg asked his subjects questions such as the following: Should he have stolen the drug? Why or why not? Should he have stolen the drug if the sick person was not his wife? Suppose the sick person was not his wife but was someone who was a stranger. Should he then steal it? How about if the sick person was an enemy? Should he steal the drug in order to save an enemy? Would a "good" person steal it or not steal it? Why? Would you steal it? Why or why not? (Kohlberg, 1964, 1969).

Look carefully at the genius behind Kohlberg's technique. He has created a moral dilemma that has obvious analogy to real life and into which we can easily project ourselves. More basic than that, he has pitted two ancient, universal, religious values against each other, values that go back at least to Moses: the value of property (thou shalt not steal; Exodus 20:15) and the value of life (thou shalt not kill; Exodus 20:13). Real-life dilemmas are often like this; would you steal to save someone's life, or let the person die but not steal?

Kohlberg's system was supposed to be direction-neutral with respect to the answer the subject gave. That is, a person's score on the scale of moral development should not be based on whether the person decided in favor of or against stealing the drug but rather on the complexity of the mental operations behind the decision—whichever direction it was in. He concluded that people's complexity of moral reasoning fell into the following stages:

I. *Preconventional: Emphasis on external control.*

Stage 1. Punishment and obedience orientation. Right and wrong are decided on whether one obeys authority or whether one gets punished for what one does. Heinz should or should not steal because a person in authority or God says so or because he would be punished by others or God for whatever he did.

Stage 2. Instrumental relativist orientation. Right and wrong are decided upon whether one gets a reward (by others, society, or God) for what one does. Heinz should steal the drug because he wants his wife to live; he should not steal because the druggist has a right to make a profit.

II. *Conventional: Emphasis on pleasing others, maintaining standards.*

Stage 3. Interpersonal concordance or "good boy," "nice girl" orientation. Right and wrong are based on what a "good" person would do under the circumstances; motives and intentions are taken into account in efforts to please others. Heinz should steal because that is what a good and loving husband would do; he should not steal because it is not his fault, it is the druggist who is being selfish and Heinz should not have to do anything illegal.

Stage 4. Social system maintenance; law and order orientation. Right and wrong are based on maintaining the social system and living within reasonable, established rules; showing respect for higher authority and doing one's duty is important. Heinz should steal because it is his responsibility to do everything possible for his wife, with the intention of repaying the druggist. He should not steal because it is wrong to violate the established social principles.

III. *Postconventional: Acknowledgement of conflict and internal choice among alternatives.*

Stage 5. Social contract orientation. Right and wrong are based on agreed-upon social contracts; value the implicit or explicit will of the majority. Stealing the drug is justified in this case because our social contract with society was not designed, or at least cannot adequately handle, situations such as this; this would not be normal criminal behavior. Alternatively, stealing should not be done even in this case because the ends don't justify the means.

Stage 6. Universal ethical principles orientation. Right and wrong are based on internalized standards regardless of conformity or nonconformity with social mores. Stealing is right in order to save life because life is ultimately valuable and property is not. Stealing in this situation is wrong because others may need the drug just as badly as Heinz's wife; their and all lives are equally valuable.

Scoring Moral Reasoning Level   ~~R e s t~~

Kohlberg's method was to transcribe each subject's interview and then have its content analyzed and scored on his six-step scale for amount of thought present at each level. This was exceedingly tedious, so James Rest invented the *Defining Issues Test* (DIT) instead (Rest, 1986). Rest's DIT was composed of Kohlberg's dilemmas followed by a series of twelve statements from which the subject could choose. Each statement reflected one of the levels. In this way the subject would, for example, merely have to read the Heinz story, think and decide about it, and then choose from among a set of answers those that most closely represented his or her rationale for the decision. These answers could later be scored, and percentages of thought at each stage could be calculated. Also, this kind of scoring procedure seems to be sensitive in detecting proportions of thought that lie between or are a mixture of adjacent stages. And this raises the possibility that whether we see these levels of reasoning as being relatively fixed "stages" or more gradual "phases" depends on the scoring technique that we use to measure them. Thus our knowledge is technique-tied (Chapter 3). Similarly, the interpretation of DIT scores should be done carefully by taking into consideration the type of religiousness in the particular sample of subjects, because there is evidence that some DIT items have distinctly religious connotations for conservative religious subjects (Rest et al., 1986; Richards, 1991; Richards & Davison, 1992). Some of this research is pertinent to the question of whether people with different religious orientations (intrinsic, extrinsic, quest [see Chapter 8]) demonstrate different levels of moral reasoning. The DIT made Kohlbergian research a lot easier.

Critique of Kohlberg's Model

Two aspects of Kohlberg's model that are problems, but not catastrophes, should be mentioned. The first is that it has an implicit political bias in favor of Western democratic liberalism. It is not an accident that the "higher" one goes on his scale, the "more developed" one is. The implicit assumption is that more developed equals better. These are obviously value-laden notions that should be made explicit. To illustrate the opposite, if this were Nazi Germany, I have no doubt that Kohlberg's Level 1 would be labeled "more developed" and Level 6 "least developed." The lessons for us are twofold: (1) keep our research as free from such biases as possible, and (2) make explicit those values that are unavoidably inherent in our work.

The second problem, or correction, to Kohlberg's model has to do with a subtle sex bias in the nature of the sequence of stages and the scoring for them. Carol Gilligan (1982) discovered that there are differences in the way men and women think about morality. Men tend to think in terms of abstract principles such as justice, whereas women tend to think in terms of responsibility to particular people. To use only one of Gilligan's illustrations of this difference, consider two Biblical stories. Abraham is willing to sacrifice his son Isaac in order to demonstrate conformity to the principle of absolute faith (Genesis 22:10). In contrast, the woman who came to Solomon confirmed her motherhood by relinquishing the truth that the child was hers, in order to save her child's life (I Kings 3:26). Gilligan, therefore, has offered helpful modifications to a Kohlbergian approach.

The contributions of Piaget and Kohlberg have been enormous in general psychology, with important implications for philosophy, education, and religious studies. Piaget's work mostly concerned children. Kohlberg's lower stages paralleled Piaget's, but Kohlberg's model extended the general idea to include additional stages presumably reaching into adulthood. Their models of moral development have recently prompted several models of religious development to account for changes in religiousness through adolescence and adulthood. Some of these are presented in Chapter 5 in the context of adolescence. It remains for future research to tease out any subtle biases in these models, analogous to the contribution of Gilligan to Kohlberg's approach, as well as to relate them to other attitudes and behaviors.

In sum, there is overall evidence that different levels of cognitive ability and moral reasoning, whether they are stages or phases, are real. If this is true, then the meaning of religion to a child can be understood as paralleling these developmental stages. As the cognitive stages/phases evolve, the depth of the child's understanding of religion evolves also. The meaning of religion becomes more psychologically developed in the process.

Thus far, we have a sense of how children differ from adults and of what sorts of cognitive psychological substrates account for this. We also have an idea of how children develop. Now let's examine how religion is acquired. The dominant research findings and theorizing all point to a stage process.

Stages of Religious Development

By applying psychological principles, we conclude that children's religious behavior is regulated by means of a series of interwoven processes. One of these processes is social learning and imitation, especially imitation of parents but also of religious instructors such as priests, rabbis, and Sunday School teachers. Another key set of processes includes social psychological forces such as group conformity expectations, coupled with the child's personal needs for approval and belonging, plus the power of the parents and secondary reference groups to dispense rewards and punishments. A final key process involves progressing through a sequence of cognitive stages. During each stage, the belief that was initially held in a simple way becomes more complex. This occurs as the child's thinking matures.

The general points are that children seem to pass through a series of developmental stages, and religious development should logically parallel these stages. It seems that over the course of development all types of knowledge, including understanding of religion, become more complex and abstractly comprehended as the stages progress. Various versions of the religious-stage notion have been offered by theorists and researchers in this area. In this section and the next, let's examine them and some relevant research.

Elkind's Stage Theory

One of the most important attempts to account for observed changes over time in childhood religion in terms of changes in general psychological development is a theoretical statement by David Elkind (1970), a follower of Piaget. Elkind's fundamental point is that, because the child's mentality passes through a series of increasingly complex stages, the intellectual needs satisfied by religion change with age. Elkind proposes that there are four types of mental needs that emerge as the child grows older. Each need begins at a stage of child development and lasts throughout life. A corresponding aspect of religion serves to meet each need. The process by which the needs are satisfied involves an implicit cognitive "search."

Elkind's first stage is called the *search for conservation,* and it begins in infancy. It is based on the idea that children lack object permanence. Since very young children apparently do not yet realize that objects exist whether or not they see them, it is inferred that they do not yet have the capacity called conservation—the mental ability to conserve the physical reality of the object across time and space. Elkind says that the capacity to deal with absent objects emerges with a need, the search for conservation, which he says is "a life-long quest for permanence amidst a world of change."

In applying this idea to religion, Elkind says that the young child first assumes that life is permanent. However, children are later surprised to find that it is not, that people do die. When this is realized, the child begins another search for conservation, only this time the search is for the conservation of life. The answer to the conservation of life question is provided by religion. According to Elkind, by accepting the concept of God at any age a person participates in God's immortality, and thereby solves the problem of the conservation of life that began in early childhood.

Elkind's second stage is called the *search for representation* and begins during the preschool years. As children grow older it becomes necessary for them to develop mental representations of their world that they can use to regulate their interaction with it. Two of the most important types of representations are mental images and language. For example, a child will develop the linguistic symbol "boat," which is one type of representation of an actual boat. Like the search for conservation, the search for representation, once it has begun, lasts throughout life. Once the child has accepted God, it becomes necessary to find representations of God. In the case of Judaism, Christianity, and Islam, these are offered by the Scriptures. Within the general representation found in them are other specific images such as "Father," which are more narrowly focused representations.

Elkind's third stage is the *search for relations,* and it begins during middle childhood. Again, it lasts throughout life. It is here that the capacity for more mature forms of reasoning appear. The child begins to use rules of logic and rules of numbers as a means of searching for relationships between things and events in his or her environment. The child at this stage wants to know how things work or how things fit together. In a similar way, children begin to relate themselves to their social world, the people and principles of their world, in an effort to discover the relationships in it and how they fit into it. Carrying this theme to religion, the youth who accepts God and the Scriptural representation must now have a way of relating to God. This is accomplished through worship, whether public or private. Through the medium of worship the person can talk in a personal way with God, see his or her own role as contrasted to God's role, and gain direction from God. In this way people discover their relationship to God. For Elkind, once someone has accepted God and the Scriptural representation, the question of putting oneself in relation to God is inevitable.

Elkind's final stage is the *search for comprehension.* During adolescence a child goes beyond the mere grasping of relationships, and develops the ability to theorize. The youth begins to speculate as to the underlying reasons for relationships. Elkind calls this the capacity for theory construction, which corresponds to the search for comprehension. At this point people begin to try to fully understand and explain their world. They may want to explain why people, including themselves, behave the way they do. This search for comprehension can be baffling since so many things in life seem unexplainable. In Elkind's view, here again religion offers a solution. In religion, according to Elkind, we find the explanations for things that otherwise defy our comprehension. Once a person has accepted God, the Scriptural representation, and a relationship of worship, the search for comprehension is resolved by theology. In summary, Elkind proposes that the phases in the development of religion from infancy to adolescence correspond to the emergence of the four cognitive needs, and that at each stage one aspect of religion meets the need and makes the religious system in the mind of the individual one step more complex.

2. Research on Religious Stages

The results of several research studies of religious thinking are generally consistent with a stage model. In one early study that attempted to discover religious development stages, Harms (1944) asked several thousand children covering the full childhood age range to draw their idea of God. He also discussed this with them and thus obtained verbal (written or spoken) statements about what they thought God was like. He concluded that there were three stages:

1. Ages 3 to 6 years were called the "fairy-tale stage." At this stage religion, as reflected in ideas about God, seemed to be to the child at the same level as stories about giants, talking animals, ghosts, angels with wings, and Santa Claus. It appeared difficult for a child at this stage to tell the difference between fantasy and reality. A further, practical complication is that adults sometimes tell the child that an actual fantasy is a reality (as is commonly the case in the United States with Santa Claus), so that the difficulty in distinguishing fantasy from reality becomes even greater.
2. The second stage was between 7 and 12, and was called the "realistic stage." Here the child tended to concretize religious concepts. God and angels were seen as real persons. They were superhuman, but influenced events on earth, like the gods of ancient Greece. Religious symbols began to acquire meaning. The children's drawings included institutional symbols such as the Cross, Star of David, drawings of churches, etc. At this stage, children begin to differentiate obvious fantasy. For example, they begin to realize that Santa Claus is a fantasy and, if they were previously taught that Santa Claus is reality and now reverse this conception, they may begin the same mental reversal with the God concept as well.
3. Ages 13 to 18 were called the "individualistic stage." This stage was characterized by the greatest diversity, and was broken down into three categories. One group held conventional religious ideas and basically adhered to the mainline religion of their group. A second group was more mystical. Their drawings contained fewer of the traditional religious symbols and more of the abstract expressions such as a sunset or light in the clouds. A third group expressed religion through symbols of religions and cults that they had imagined and/or learned something about but which they never had experienced—such as religions of foreign or primitive cultures or ancient religions.

Ronald Goldman (1964) later conducted landmark research on religious development. He used an interview method in which children were asked questions relating to religious pictures and Bible stories. Ten boys and ten girls at each age from 6 to 16 were interviewed (a total of 200 white, Protestant British children). Like Harms, Goldman concluded that there were three stages of religious development. Goldman's stages parallel Harms' very closely, but are couched in distinctively Piagetian terms. His first stage (up to 7-8 years) was called "preoperational intuitive thought." It was characterized by unsystematic and fragmentary religious thinking, illustrated by lack of understanding of religious material due to not being able to consider all the evidence involved in a religious story. For example, when asked "Why was Moses afraid to look at God?" (Exodus 3:6), the answer is of the form "Because God had a funny face" (p. 52). The second stage (ages 7–8 to 13–14) was labeled "concrete operational thought" (obviously Piagetian again), and was typified by the children focusing on specific details of pictures and stories. When asked why Moses was afraid to look at God, children at this stage referred to aspects of the story itself but in a concrete way: "Because it was a ball of fire. He thought it might burn him," or "It was a bright light and to look at it might blind him" (p. 56). Goldman's third stage (ages 13–14 and up) was called "formal (abstract) operational thought." Goldman's interviews with this age group contained evidence of hypothetical and abstract religious thought. For example, Moses was said to be afraid to look at God because "God is holy and the world is sinful," or because "The awesomeness and almightiness of God would make Moses feel like a worm in comparison" (p. 60).

Goldman's research caused a bit of controversy because it seemed to have implications for how children should be taught religion. That is, the results might be interpreted to mean that inculcating young children with a literal interpretation of the Bible could, in the long run, be counter-productive. Children's minds were constructed so that (so the argument went) they were prone to accept literalism only up to a certain point. When, through the natural course of development, their minds moved to higher levels of functioning, they would be inclined to reject the literal teaching of their past. Two (uncertain) consequences might follow: the youth might then either retain the beliefs but in a nonliteral way, or the youth might reject them. And both of these outcomes would be seen as negative by those who insist on a literal approach as the only true one. Hyde (1990) reports that Goldman even received "abusive, anonymous letters" by some who were critical of his conclusions.

After Goldman's work, several key studies emerged. One series of studies by Pealting (1974, 1977) included the creation of the *Thinking About the Bible* (TAB) test. This instrument was created in a fashion roughly analogous to the way Rest created the DIT after Kohlberg's work. Like Kohlberg's method, Goldman's method involved "semi-clinical" interviews that yielded much verbal material that had to be content analyzed. Pealting took the stories Goldman used and wrote four questions for each one. Each question had four response options. Of the four response options (of which the subject had to choose the most and the least acceptable), one represented each of the following levels of religious thinking: very concrete, concrete, abstract, very abstract. The answers for the two concrete categories were combined, and the answers for the two abstract categories were combined. This yielded two scores, one for abstract and one for concrete religious thinking.

When Pealting (1974) used this technique, he got results that were in general similar to those of Goldman. The TAB was given to 1,994 students in

Episcopalian schools, from grades four to twelve. There was a linear increase in abstract thinking scores across the grade levels, as would be expected based on Goldman's results. There was some (I believe unclear) question of whether the data showed plateaus in strict accordance with a stage model, or whether they showed a gradual incline in abstract religious thinking. This difference is probably due to the difference between the two techniques, Goldman's interview method and Pealting's scaling method.

The overall trend of subsequent research tended to corroborate Goldman's and Pealting's findings, although there were some differences in whether the subjects were Episcopalian, Lutheran, Methodists, Catholics, or Jews (Hoge & Petrillo, 1978; Nye & Carlson, 1984; Pealting & Laabs, 1975; Pealing, Laabs, & Newton, 1975). Indeed, the general direction of the results was sufficiently robust to be replicated in Finland by Kalevi Tamminen (1991) with youth from ages 9–20. Figure 4.2 presents Tamminen's findings for the trend in the scores

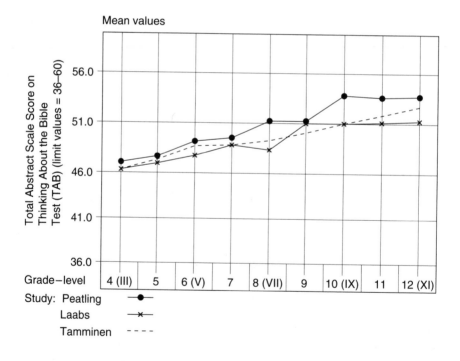

FIGURE 4.2   Total Abstract Scale Score on the Thinking about the Bible Test (TAB) across the grade levels for the studies by Pealting, Laabs, and Tamminen. Abstract scale scores can range from 36–60.

on the abstract scale of the TAB, along with the findings by Pealting and Pealting and Labbs. I find this cross-cultural replication remarkable.

Religious Stages in Prayer

Long, Elkind, and Spilka (1967) studied religious developmental stages by asking children about their understanding of prayer. They asked 160 boys and girls, aged 5–12, questions such as, Do you pray? Does your family pray? Do all boys and girls pray? Do dogs and cats pray? What is prayer? Can you pray for more than one thing? What must you do if your prayer is answered? If it is not? Where do prayers come from? Where do prayers go? They also asked children to respond to the following incomplete statements: "I usually pray when . . ." "Sometimes I pray for . . ." "When I pray I feel . . ." "When I see someone praying I . . ."

It should be no surprise to discover that their results suggest that religious development, as traced via children's statements about prayer, appears to evolve across three stages: (1) Global, undifferentiated stage (ages 5–7). Here the child's understanding of prayer is very rudimentary and vague: "A prayer is about God, rabbits, dogs and fairies and deer, and Santa Claus and turkey and pheasants, and Jesus and Mary and Mary's little baby." "A prayer is God bless people who want to say God bless. Now I lay me down to sleep" (p. 104). (2) Concrete, differentiated stage (7–9 years). Here prayer is understood as uttering verbal requests, as distinct from expressing a deeper thought or feeling that in older children will underlie it. (3) Abstract, differentiated stage (ages 11–12). Here prayer behavior becomes an external expression of an internal activity that, in essence, is conversation with God. Concrete requests become proportionally less prevalent. Prayer becomes sharing of intimacies— a way to communicate with God.

Although there are differences between Long et al.'s research and the recent work of Tamminen (1991) (e.g., at what stage the shift from petitionary prayer to nonpetitionary prayer takes place—such differences can be attributed to cultural factors), the overall theme that emerges from the new findings is similar. For example, Tamminen found that from Grade 3 to Grade 9 (American Grades 4–10) there was a slight decrease from 30 percent to 24 percent in the proportion of answers to the question "I think prayer is . . ." that were concrete in nature, such as asking something from God. Conversely, across that same age range there was an increase from 19 percent to 40 percent in the proportion of answers that were more abstract, such as conversation with God or general reliance on God. Similar trends resulted when the youngsters were asked "Has God answered your prayers in some way or other? . . . If so, please write about the occasion(s)." From Finnish Grades 3–9 there was a decrease from 22 percent to 10 percent in the proportion of concrete answers ("help in illness") and an increase in the more abstract answers ("the spiritual effect of prayer"). Extending the findings, in response to being questioned about the effect of prayer, the youngest (7 to 10-year-olds) mostly saw God as acting directly, whereas the children aged 11–12 were more likely to see God as acting indirectly, e.g., through medication or circumstances. Overall, the general pattern of the above set of findings suggests that we can attribute them to basic psychological processes, and the individual differences among findings of various studies suggest that they can be attributed to unique features of the religious subgroup being studied or to cultural variations.

Perceptions of God and Retardation

Finally, research from an area novel to the psychology of religion adds to our picture of the cognitive developmental component of religious development. It comes from a study of the concept of God in a sample of people with mental retardation. Rodney Bassett (Bassett et al., 1994) measured perceptions of God among persons with three levels of retardation: mild, moderate, and severe/profound. The rationale followed straightforwardly from our knowledge of what mental retardation is, i.e., by definition a lack of mental development.[3] One would expect that those with the least degree of retardation would be most likely to show evidence of abstract thinking when asked to select from among a set of pictures those that reminded them of God. Bassett's subjects were shown 15 pictures (e.g., king on a throne, bearded man, angel, mother holding baby, heart, Bible, crosses on a hill) and were free to select as many or as few as they wished. The data revealed that for the severe/profound group, all of the pictures that reminded the subjects of God were scenes that involved people. In contrast, subjects in the mild group were likely to select an even mix of pictures that included symbols and people. The implication is that the less the retardation, the more the person is able to include symbolization in his or her God concept. Such findings are consistent with a cognitive developmental model.

Conclusions

Several conclusions can be drawn from this review of religious development. First, the concept of stages of religious development has been a repeated finding of research studies (Fleck, Ballard, & Reilly, 1975; Hyde, 1990). The replication of the stage finding across several studies is evidence for its validity. Second, the similarity among the findings—what the stages are like—is also apparent. It appears that children's religion develops from the vague to the concrete to the abstract, with each stage becoming more sophisticated conceptually. Third the finding that these obtained stages of religious development all closely parallel the general stages of cognitive development as illustrated in the work of Piaget and Kohlberg suggests that, at least as far as current psychological theorizing is concerned, the obtained religious stages have a general psychological-developmental substrate. It appears that religious development can be accounted for by stages of general psychological development, plus our understanding of the limits of childhood experience, and family and social modeling influences with their associated selective exposure to religious ideas, teachings, and practices.

The Meaning of Childhood Commitments

A penetrating question emerges here: What is the meaning of childhood commitments? Many people claim to have made their religious commitment at relatively young ages—10, 8, 6. I have even heard of people claiming to have done so at 4 years old. (Some of these are reported to have occurred at home with parents, while others occurred at church services.) The question here is, "How valid are such childhood commitments?" Or, in what sense can they be considered valid? Given the limited life experience and cognitive capability of young children, one wonders whether it is possible for a young child to make a meaningful decision to adopt a belief. My own view at the time of this writing is that childhood commitments cannot be properly understood apart from the psychological level of the child. That is, psychologically speaking, they are valid within the child's developmental context. It seems clear that the psychological meaning of a child's religiousness is not the same as that of an adult. As the child grows, he or she goes along with the religious beliefs and practices of the family, essentially without serious question or doubt, until adolescence. It is during adolescence that new cognitive abilities and social forces spark the real religious conflict and period of decision making.

Projects and Questions

1. Study the extent to which children strain for consistency between religious belief and behavior. Is this related to age? (Observational and laboratory methods could be used.)

2. When do children have religious experiences? Devise a way of measuring religious experience in children. Do reported experiences vary by religious group, or other key variables in the child and family? .

3. How do parents interpret the religious statements and actions of their children? Of other children? Would this vary by parent variables, such as sex, belief system, etc.?

4. Is there a developmental sequence to the dimensions of religious commitment (Chapter 1)? to the categories of religious orientation (Chapter 8)?

5. Should religious development be distinguished from religious indoctrination? If so, test to see how the outcomes of these two approaches to religious instruction might differ.

6. Might the value and consequences of doubting vary according to a youth's personality, cognitive style, and the parenting philosophy of his or her family? Is there an association between strength of belief and doubting?

Further Reading

Hyde, K. E. *Religion in childhood and adolescence: A comprehensive review of the research.* Birmingham, AL: Religious Education Press, 1990. —   E D N   c 2 5 5   R 4 5

Oser, F. K., & Scarlett, G. (Eds.). *Religious development in childhood and adolescence* [New Directions for Child Development, #52]. San Francisco, CA: Jossey-Bass, 1991.

Strommen, M. P. *Research on religious development: A comprehensive handbook.* New York: Hawthorne Books, 1971.   E D   B V 1 4 6 4   5 8 7

Tamminen, K. *Religious development in childhood and youth: An empirical study.* Helsinki: Suomen Tiedeakatemia, 1991. (Finnish Academy of Science and Letters, Tiedekirja, Kirkkokatu 14, 00170, Helsinki, Finland.)   —

Notes

1. This argument could be extended to include additional symbols such as pictures, images, and numbers.

2. Male reference to diety is used in original source.

3. The American Association of Mental Retardation (AAMR) and the American Psychiatric Association identify mental retardation as involving significant subaverage intellectual functioning, related limitations in adaptive skills such as communication or self-care, and an onset before age 18 (AAMR, 1992; American Psychiatric Association *Diagnostic and Statistical Manual of Mental Disorders,* 4th edition, 1994).

Religious Development Through the Lifespan: Adolescence and Adulthood

Now that we have seen the classical development models and research, let's extend the argument into the realm of the religion of adolescent people. Let's explore the degree to which adolescents are religious, what form their religiousness may take, what psychological models have been introduced that are pertinent to this age group, and how well the existent data fit the models.

Religion in Adolescence

It makes sense that childhood religion would not satisfy the intellectual and emotional needs of adolescents. Various consequences could result from this: (1) the adolescent could decide that religion is nonsense, or deny its importance, and reject his or her former beliefs; (2) the adolescent could blindly adhere to the religion in order to avoid having to pursue religious issues in a deeper way; (3) he or she could grapple with new questions and doubts, try to think through and evaluate alternatives, perhaps experiment with alternatives, and eventually arrive at a satisfactory decision or conclusion regarding religious issues. Thus, the question emerges "How religious are adolescents?"

Paradoxically, the data seem to indicate that adolescents are both religious and nonreligious. More precisely, there appears to be a high degree of religious involvement, practice, dialogue, and discussion, while at the same time there is more doubt and less acceptance of traditional and/or literal religious teachings.

Global Measures of Religiousness

Evidence from the past that indicates a high degree of religious interest during adolescence includes the following: In a study of late adolescents and young adults, Allport, Gillespie, and Young (1948) found that 68 percent of Harvard men and 82 percent of Radcliffe women answered Yes to the question "Do you feel that you require some form of religious orientation or belief in order to achieve a fully mature philosophy of life?" Over 20 years later, an extensive analysis conducted by CBS News (Yankelovich, 1969) revealed that 71 percent of noncollege youth and 42 percent of college youth agreed with the statement that "Belonging to some organized religion is important in a person's life." More recently, Gallup (1979–1980) reported similar percentages among college-aged youth. Taken together these results suggest that religious interest is prevalent during adolescence across generations.

What about religious practice? A 1971 Harris Poll, conducted on a national sample of 15-to-21-year-old youths, revealed that 58 percent of the high school students and 43 percent of the college students attended church regularly (*Change, Yes—Upheaval, No,* 1971). In addition, a sizable minority were active in nontraditional or Eastern religious practices (Gallup, 1977–78; Stoner &

Parke, 1977). Even though during the turbulent period of the late 1960s national polls indicated that youths were turning away from traditional religious institutions (Wuthnow & Glock, 1973), subsequent trends revealed a return to more traditional religious preferences among youths. The *Survey of College Freshmen* (1974) reported that the percentage of increase for traditional Judaism was from 3.8 to 5.1 percent, for traditional Roman Catholicism from 30.1 to 34.3 percent, and for traditional forms of Protestantism it was from 38.2 to 44.9 percent. In general, religious activity of adolescents is higher than our intuitive guess would predict, based upon the stereotype of the "rebellious" teenager.

The most reliable current data suggest that a similar pattern of religious interest and practice among adolescents exists today. For example, recent Gallup polls show that 95 percent of those aged 13 to 18 believe in "God or a universal spirit" (Gallup & Bezilla, 1992), about the same percent as adults. Approximately three-fourths say that they pray, and almost half report having attended church or synagogue during the past week (Gallup & Jones, 1989). Forty-four percent said it was "very important" for a teenager to learn "religious faith." Other surveys yielded similar results, with the additional finding that there tended to be a decline during the 1980s in the reports of high school seniors who attended weekly services (to 30 percent in 1990) and in those reporting that religion was "very important" or "pretty important" in their lives (to 56 percent in 1990) (Donahue & Benson, 1995). Gallup's data from the 1987 *Gallup Youth Poll* indicated that 80 percent answered "Very" or "Fairly" to the question "How important are your religious beliefs?" These percentages translate into millions of teenagers.

We are fortunate today to have results from two large-scale surveys. One entitled *Youth in Protestant Churches* (Roehlkepartain & Benson, 1993) sampled 2,365 youths in grades 7 to 12 from five U.S. denominations: Christian Church, Evangelical Lutheran Church, United Methodist, Presbyterian, and United Church of Christ. Data were collected in 1988 and 1989. The results showed that only 4 percent said that their faith was not important in their lives. Seventy-seven percent indicated a commitment to Christ. These findings suggest some level of religious interest among adolescents, but they apply best to U.S. Protestants. What about the rest of the population?

During the 1989–90 school year, Search Institute conducted another large survey of over 46,000 youths in public schools in 111 cities in 25 states, *The Troubled Journey* (Benson, 1993; Donahue & Benson, 1995). The students were from grades 6 to 12. Although not a perfect microcosm of all U.S. youth, this sample is certainly a reasonable representation of youth in the medium-sized communities from which the subjects came. The results show that about half of the youths indicate that religion is important to them and that they attend services. This overall result should be qualified, however, by taking into account the age span involved. Both the importance measure and the attendance measure show an inverse relationship with age. For example, for the importance measure, the percentages dropped from 54 percent for the sixth graders to 46 percent for the twelfth graders. This replicates a similar trend between religiousness and age found in previous smaller studies (Benson, Donahue, & Erickson, 1989).

A few studies reveal differences in religious interest or activity for specialized subgroups. Gender apparently is an important factor. Females have been found to attend religious services more regularly than males and to consistently score higher on measures of prayer and the centrality of one's beliefs (Argyle & Beit-Hallahmi, 1975; Benson, 1991; Benson et al., 1989; DeBord, 1969; Dutt, 1965; Garrity 1961; Moberg, 1971). College-aged students profess less religious belief than high-school-aged students (Parker, 1971). The more educated generally attend church more frequently than the less educated (Hassenger, 1967). Youths who have come from religious families are themselves more involved with religion. Those who attend parochial schools tend to show higher degrees of religious behavior and more faith and church commitment during adolescence than those who attend nonparochial schools (Benson et al., 1989).

2. *Doubt*

In addition to the religious interest, practice, and experimentation of adolescence, there appears to be a high degree of religious doubt and questioning. Generally, the degree of belief decreases with age. It has been found, for example, that among college students there was typically a trend toward a less literal interpretation of religion, with less acceptance of the functions of religion, in the direction of more liberalism. Youths are typically found to interpret things less literally as they grow older (Adelson, Green & O'Neil, 1969; Allport et al., 1948; Hites, 1965; Piaget, 1972).

In one early study (Kuhlen & Arnold, 1944) of over 500 adolescents aged 12, 15, and 18, changes in religious beliefs with age were assessed. The findings are representative of the studies in this area at that time. In general, the findings reflect less tendency to "believe" and increased tendency to "wonder about" specific religious statements as youths approach young adulthood. For example, at 12 years of age, 94 percent agreed with the statement "I know there is a God" whereas only 19 percent of the 18-year-olds agreed with it. Those who "wonder about" that same statement rose from 2 to 16 percent. Equivalent trends were apparent for statements such as "There is a heaven" and "Prayers are answered." Even stronger trends in the direction of less "belief" emerged in regard to a literal interpretation of the Bible. At age 12, 79 percent believed the statement "Every word in the Bible is true"; by age 18 only 34 percent believed it.

Similar trends reflecting decrease in literalness and an increase in doubt are found in current studies in the United States and abroad. In the United

States, research on Catholic high schools compared ninth grade versus twelfth grade students on several measures. The twelfth graders scored higher on religious doubt and lower on measures of intrinsic (see Chapter 8) and comforting religion (Benson, Yeager et al., 1986).

In Finland, Tamminen's (1991) extensive interviews included questions designed to tap Glock's five dimensions of religious commitment (Chapter 1). One of the basic questions asked the 938 youths about their belief in God's existence and care: "What is your opinion about God's existence?" The five possible answer categories in order were "[God] [d]oes exist and takes care of us," "Does exist but does not affect everyday life, "I cannot say," "Does hardly exist," and "Does not exist." This scale of answer options reflects a dimension ranging from belief to doubt. Tamminen's results are shown in Figure 5.1. The vertical axis represents the cumulative percent of respondents who chose the

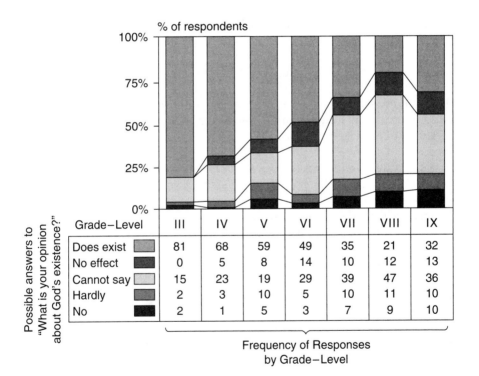

FIGURE 5.1   **Change in belief in God's existence across grade levels**

Source: Tamminen, K. *Religious Development in Childhood and Youth: An Empirical Study.* Helsinki: Suomen Tiedeakatemia, p. 41, 1991. By permission of the Finnish Academy of Science and Letters, Tiedekirja, Kirkkokatu 14, 00170, Helsinki, Finland.

answer options; the horizontal axis represents grade level (Finnish grades 3–9, ages 9–16). The proportion of youngsters in each grade who chose each answer option is represented by the different shaded areas. The graph depicts two clear trends: From grades 3 through 9, the percent of youth who most strongly say God does exist decreases significantly; concurrently, the percent of youth who cannot say increases dramatically.

Secret Doubt and Hidden Observers

In addition to doubts to which people will admit in questionnaire and interview studies such as those above, people also have secret doubts which they have never admitted to another person. These are more difficult to study. But Canadian psychologist Bob Altemeyer (1988) demonstrated an excellent way to do so. The students in his General Psychology class heard a lecture concerning the "Hidden Observer" phenomenon in hypnosis. The metaphorical "Hidden Observer" is a presumed unconscious part of the person's mind that is aware of what is really happening during a hypnotic session, even though the hypnotized person appears to be unaware of it. For example, your arm may be in a bucket of ice water and should hurt very much, but your hypnotized self feels no conscious pain (due to hypnotic suggestion to feel no pain). However, the Hidden Observer is aware that it hurts and can admit such if asked. With this as a background, Altemeyer later gave these instructions to his students as part of an anonymous "Secret Survey":

> *You may recall the lecture on hypnosis dealing with Hilgard's research on the "Hidden Observer." Suppose there is a Hidden Observer in you, which knows your every thought and deed, but which only speaks when it is safe to do so, and when directly spoken to. This question is for your Hidden Observer: Does this person (that is, you) have doubts that (s)he was created by an Almighty God who will judge each person and take some into heaven for eternity while casting others into hell forever?*

The students had to choose one of the following answers:

_____ *Yes, (s)he has secret doubts which (s)he has kept strictly to herself/himself that this is really true.*

_____ *Yes, (s)he has such doubts, but others (such as parents and friends) know (s)he has these doubts.*

_____ *No, (s)he totally believes this, and has* no *doubts whatsoever.*

_____ *Yes, in fact (s)he openly says (s)he does not believe there is a God or an afterlife, but (s)he has some secret worries there might be.*

_____ *Yes, in fact (s)he openly says (s)he does not believe there is a God or an afterlife, and (s)he has no doubts about this whatsoever.*

Altemeyer presents data for 200 subjects, one-half high in authoritarianism and one-half low in authoritarianism. One-fourth (50) of them said that the Hidden Observer indicated "secret doubts which (s)he has kept strictly to herself/himself." For the authoritarians, who are also more likely to firmly hold conservative religious beliefs, the Hidden Observer expressed secret doubts, ones never shared with another person, at a rate of approximately one-third. I find this most revealing.

It appears that, on the surface at least, adolescents are inconsistent. They appear to be religious, yet express disbelief. How can this apparent inconsistency be understood? Various factors would seem to interact to shed light on this question. Perhaps a basic point is to realize that the religious doubt expressed by the typical adolescent is not so much a denial of a specific teaching as it is an expression of a more general tendency to question and wonder about things. Adolescents do not appear to be bent on showing that what they have been taught is wrong. Rather, they seem to question what they have been taught (and question alternatives, also). Questions about specific doctrines are probably not the critical issues for most adolescents, but the general mode of knowing—how one knows what is true or false—probably is. It is really the whole underlying process of knowing, and one's own ability to know, that is in question. Questions and doubts about religious issues are only a reflection of this general trend during this period of life.

One implication of this last point is that there may be great value and variety in doubting. Hunsberger, McKenzie, Pratt, & Pancer (1993), for example, listed eight varieties of religious doubt, such as that based on shortcomings of organized religion or on an apparent clash between science and religion, and created clever ways to research them empirically. They were able to detect a positive correlation between self-reported religious doubt and greater complexity of thought about such doubts. Not until one has probed deeper, raised the critical questions, examined the evidence, and thought the issues through to their logical limits is one prepared to make intelligent decisions for or against some belief system. It is only through facing the critical issues with honest doubt and questioning that one can move from a child's religious mentality to a more mature orientation to what one believes. For us, the question is "What are the psychological processes by which religious development occurs in adolescence and adulthood?" It should be no surprise that psychologists have created some stage models to give us a clue. It is time to look at them.

Models of Lifespan Religious Development

The data summarized above provide a static, descriptive sketch of adolescent religiousness at different ages. In order to understand the dynamics behind it, we need a theoretical model to integrate it into a whole picture. Such a theory would have to account for the changes in various religiousness measures that are apparent in the data. We do not yet have one ideal theory of religious development that does this. But suppose we did. What would it look like? According to Swiss psychologist K. Helmut Reich (1992, p. 151), it would have at least the following properties:

> 1. *It would need to refer to psychical (intellectual, emotional, volitional) processes that take place within the organism, including those aspects of such processes referred to as meaning-making.*
>
> 2. *It would need to characterize development as a gradual coordination of individual psyche and biophysical, sociocultural and perceived spiritual reality, and to explicate the relationships between the internal and the external forces in the course of development.*
>
> 3. *It would need to address the social contexts in which development occurs and the ways in which those contexts relate to individual religious development.*
>
> 4. *It would need to account for the universal features of religious development as well as for individual differences.*
>
> 5. *It would need to specify mechanisms by means of which developmental change occurs, and to explain the workings of factors which favor or hinder religious development.*

Meeting all of the above criteria in one theory is a tall order. Yet, several good theories have recently been offered to account for different aspects of lifespan religious development. Let's examine three of them: a model of the development of religious judgment, a model of generic stages of faith, and a model based on a sequence of motives and needs. Each one tries to answer different questions about the process. Can they be integrated into one theory? After a brief look at each model we shall compare and contrast them.

Development of Religious Judgment: The Double Helix Model

Swiss psychologist and religious educationist Fritz Oser and psychologist Paul Gmünder (1991; Oser, 1991) have offered the developmental model of religious judgment that is summarized in Figure 5.2. The stages are seen as invariant and hierarchical as in the cases of Piaget and Kohlberg. By religious judgment they mean "reasoning that relates reality as experienced to something beyond reality and that serves to provide meaning and direction beyond learned content" (Oser, 1991, p. 6). They say that such judgments can occur in any context but are "especially likely in times of crisis." The rationale is that

FIGURE 5.2 Oser & Gmünder's Stages of Religious Judgment

Stages of Religious Judgment	
Stage	Description
Stage 1	Orientation of religious heteronomy (*deus ex machina*). God (the Ultimate Being) is understood as active, intervening unexpectedly in the world. The human being is conceived as reactive; he or she is guided because the Ultimate Being is provided with power, with the possibility to make things happen.
Stage 2	Orientation of *do et des,* 'give so that you may receive.' God (the Ultimate Being) is still viewed as being always external and as an all-powerful being who may either punish or reward. However, the Ultimate Being can be influenced by good deeds, promises, and vows. The human being can exert a prophylactic influence (restricted autonomy, first form of rationalization).
Stage 3	Orientation of ego autonomy and one sided self-responsibility (deism). The influence of the Ultimate Being is consciously reduced. Transcendence and immanence are separated from one another. The human being is solipsistically autonomous, responsible for his or her own life and for secular matters. The Ultimate Being, if its existence is accepted, has its own domain of hidden responsibility.
Stage 4	Mediated autonomy and salvation plan. God (the Ultimate Being) is mediated with the immanence, as a cipher of the "self" per se. Multiple forms of religiosity are apparent, all accepting a divine plan that brings things to a good end. Social engagement becomes a religious form of life.
Stage 5	Orientation to religious intersubjectivity and autonomy, universal and unconditional religiosity. The individual's religious reasoning displays a complete and equilibrated coordination of the seven polar dimensions. Religion is more a working model than a security concept. The person feels that he or she has always been unconditionally related to the Ultimate Being; *unio mystica, boddhi,* and similar impressions.

Source: Oser, Fritz K. (1991). The Development of Religious Judgment, Table 1, p. 10. In F. K. Oser and W. G. Scarlett (eds.), *Religious Development in Childhood and Adolescence.* New Directions for Child Development, no. 52. Copyright 1991, Jossey-Bass Inc., Publishers.

crises require responses and decisions, and these can easily become tests of one's purported commitment to some higher principle, God, or Ultimate Being. Consider the following crisis situation, called the Paul Dilemma. This is one of three such dilemmas that their subjects must hear during an interview and respond to.

Paul Dilemma

Paul, a young physician, has recently passed his board exams. He has asked his girlfriend to marry him. Before the wedding he goes on a trip to England paid for by his parents as a reward for having successfully completed his education. Paul embarks on his journey. Shortly after take-off, the plane's captain announces that one engine is malfunctioning and that the other one is working unreliably. The plane is losing altitude. Emergency procedures are initiated immediately: Oxygen masks and life preservers are being handed out. At first, the passengers are crying and yelling. Then, there is a deadly silence. The plane races toward the ground at a great speed. Paul's entire life flashes past his eyes. He knows it's all over. In this situation, he remembers God and begins to pray. He promises that, if he was somehow saved, he would invest his life in helping people in the Third World. He would also renounce the marriage to his girlfriend, should she refuse to accompany him. He promises to forgo a high income and social status. The plane crashes in a field—yet, through a miracle, Paul survives! Upon his return home, he is offered an excellent position at a private clinic. Because of his qualifications, he has been selected from among ninety applicants. However, Paul recalls the promise he made to God. Now, he does not know what to do. (Oser & Gmünder, 1991, pp. 102–103.)*

If we apply the concept of "story grammar" from cognitive psychology (Ashcraft, 1989) to an analysis of the Paul Dilemma we can see the following deep structure in the story line: (1) Paul's happy life, (2) the crisis, (3) his reaction to the crisis, (4) his promise, (5) Paul is saved, (6) the dilemma of whether to keep his promise, (7) the decision point. In order to measure the developmental level of their subject's judgment in Paul's situation, Oser and Gmünder (1991, pp. 103–104) ask them an extensive series of questions. Some of them are

- Should Paul keep his promise? Why or why not?
- Do you believe that one has duties to God at all?
- What is your response to this statement: "It is God's will that he should go to the Third World (i.e., that he keep his promise)."
- What does this demand mean for Paul?
- Are persons entitled to claim their personal freedom over against the claims of a religious community? Why or why not?
- Let us assume . . . Paul does not keep his promise. . . . Shortly afterward, Paul gets into a serious car accident for which he is at fault. Does this

**Source:* F. K. Oser and P. Gmünder, *Religious Judgement: A Developmental Perspective* © 1991, published by Religious Education Press, Birmingham, Alabama, 1991, pp. 102–103.

accident have any connection to the fact that Paul did not keep his promise to God?

Religious judgments such as that asked of Paul are seen as requiring a balancing act in response to the tension between two (or more) competing values. Such tension involves disequilibrium and requires the person to solve the problem in order to arrive at a state of balance. According to Oser (1991) this tension exists along seven bipolar dimensions that are part of the essence of producing a religious judgment. These are (1) the feeling of either freedom *versus* dependence on God or the Ultimate Being, (2) thinking that God's interaction with the world is either transcendent *versus* immanent, that God either does things on earth directly or does not, (3) the feeling of hope *versus* absurdity, (4) the functional transparency *versus* opacity of God's will, that God either gives people a clear "sign" versus God's will being a mystery, (5) the feeling of either faith *versus* fear in the situation, (6) focusing on only the holy *versus* the profane aspects of the issue or circumstance, (7) seeing things as involving only the eternal *versus* the ephemeral. According to Oser, these tensions are intimately involved in situations like the Paul Dilemma. Such dilemmas can be seen through the eyes of any combination of the seven polar opposites.

Through analysis of the subjects' responses to the dilemmas, Oser and Gmünder realized that at the lower stages of religious judgment, one thought in terms of only one or the other of each polar dimension, e.g., one had either faith or fear but not both, saw values in decisions as either eternal or temporal but not both. At the higher stages, however, there was the tendency to think in terms of both ends of the spectrum at the same time. Paul's situation was both hopeful and absurd, Paul should have both faith and fear, God is both immanent in the situation and transcendent from it. For Oser and Gmünder, it is how a person coordinates these polar opposites that constitutes the deep structure of his or her religious judgments. And it is the development of this deep structure through the process of differentiation and integration and transition from one plateau to the next that is described by the stages of religious judgment in Figure 5.2. They diagram this model as a "Double Helix" with contrary loops going up in ever-expanding spirals, with successively larger plateaus at alternate spiral intersections, representing both differentiation as the stages go up the hierarchy and reintegration at each successive plateau.

Do these stages appear across the age span in the way that Oser and Gmünder suppose? Figure 5.3 describes the percent of responses from 112 Swiss subjects, male and female, from ages 8–9 to 20–25 that are in stages 1–4. The dramatic decrease in stage 2 judgments and the corresponding increase in stage 3 judgments across the age span is apparent, and stage 4 judgments do not appear to an appreciable degree until the late teen-young adult years.

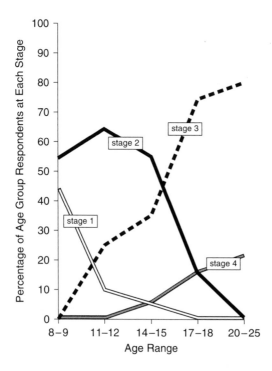

FIGURE 5.3 Changes in stages of religious judgment across the age span

Source: Oser, F. K. (1991). The development of religious judgment. In Oser, F. K., & Scarlett, W. G. (Eds.), *Religious Development in Childhood and Adolescence*, p. 14, San Francisco: Jossey-Bass. Used by permission of Religious Education Press.

Such correspondence between their ideas about the stages and the data showing how subjects' judgments change across the age span suggests that Oser and Gmünder may be on the right track, at least up to young adulthood— a point addressed again later. Their theory is concerned with only a cognitive task, however—that of making religious judgments. We are aware that religion involves more than the cognitive dimension and that not all faith is religious faith, so we must proceed to examine a model whose author intends it to reach beyond cognition and to nonreligious faith.

Stages of Faith Development

James Fowler (1981, 1986, 1991) created a model of faith development that attempts to cast a wide net and to account for all forms of faith, including nonreligious faith. His is an attempt to capture the essence of faith development in a generic sense, devoid of the meanings that it might have when said in the language of a particular religious tradition. He says that from the time we are born we must create some kind of order out of the chaos of the world and in so doing we find or compose a system of meaning in which we live. In this context "faith is our way of discerning and committing ourselves to centers of value and power that exert ordering force in our lives. Faith . . . grasps the ultimate conditions of our existence, unifying them into a comprehensive image in light of which we shape our responses and initiatives, our actions (1981, pp. 24–25)." Faith is relational because the self is bound to others by their mutual two-way loyalty and their joint loyalty to a "center of superordinate value" (CSV). A CSV may be the principles of liberty that are at the heart of a free democracy, the vows one makes at marriage, or the principles of excellence in the professions. In religions, the "ultimate environment" of faith is provided by the supreme CSV under which all subordinate faith relationships exist. In Jewish and Christian terms this is God (Fowler, 1986).

Note that whatever serves this faith function appears also to serve a religious function even without religious content or substance (Chapter 1), and, according to Fowler's model, the development of faith in terms that are not typically religious follows the same path as does identifiably religious faith development. This model is a direct intellectual descendent of Kohlberg's moral development model combined with the neo-Freudian psychosocial model of Erik Erikson (1963). According to Fowler, faith development proceeds in the following order.

Primal, Undifferentiated Faith.   This is a pre-stage in which the lifelong impact of a basic trust and loyalty relationship with the caregiver is laid down. As a result of proper nurturing from ages 0–2 years, the foundations of hope and courage although rudimentary are established. If this stage is deficient, then the rudiments of mistrust and lack of faith are laid down. The establishment of basic trust offsets the anxiety of separation during infancy.

1. *Intuitive-Projective Faith.* The onset of thought, language, and the ability to symbolize prompts the transition to the first real stage of faith. It rests upon the child's tendency for imagination and the development of episodic thought patterns. Children's fantasies fill stories with meaning and enable the child to retain the moods, examples, and stories of adults. In this stage, the child is confronted with new material without a background of established, fixed experiences or images with which to deal with them. The child therefore develops his or her own preoperational logic and emotional attachments and fears. The child constructs rich ideas, yet there is the danger of too much exploitation of them based on fear, in order to enforce taboos or make children conform. This corresponds to Piaget's preoperational stage and to Kohlberg's punishment and obedience stage, and occurs approximately between the ages of 3 and 7.

2. *Mythic-Literal Faith.* In this stage, the development of the capacity for concrete operations enables the child to make more ordinary sense and meaning out of experience. Lessons and images are taken literally and there is more coherence within the child's logico-emotive system. There is less reliance on intuition and truth is based on external criteria (as in the story of Henry, noted in Chapter 4, who broke 15 cups). Moral rules are literal, and symbols are concrete in meaning. This corresponds to Piaget's concrete operational stage and Kohlberg's instrumental stage. Age range: 7–11.

3. *Synthetic-Conventional Faith.* Here the sphere of facets of one's life broadens greatly and includes family, friends, society, media influences, and perhaps work and religion. Because such an array of factors demanding our attention and allegiance can cause confusion, we need a coherent orientation as an overall guide. Because of this "faith must synthesize values and information," and as a consequence must be the basis for who you are, your identity. You show the beginnings of being able to take the other's point of view. This stage corresponds to adolescence and is conformist in the sense that one conforms to mutually held values and perspectives that are not yet independently assessed or chosen. Ideology formation occurs as one begins to combine values and beliefs. This requires Piaget's early formal operational level and corresponds to Kohlberg's interpersonal concordance stage. Age range: 12 and later; adults may remain at this stage.

4. *Inductive-Reflective Faith.* The movement to stage 4, which might occur during late adolescence, involves the confrontation of unavoidable tensions. And it is how one negotiates these that determines movement to the next stage. The confrontations might be, for example, between being an individual versus being a member of a group, the tendency toward subjectivity versus the need for objectivity, believing in relativism versus the possibility that there is an absolute. An outgrowth of the struggle is that the self forms its own identity and adopts its own outlook or world view, acknowledged as separate from those of others. This process involves critical reflection on self and outlook and results in "demythologizing" of faith. It requires Piaget's full formal operations and corresponds to Kohlberg's fourth social system maintenance orientation. Age of onset: late adolescence to 30s or 40s.

5. *Conjunctive Faith.* The transition to conjunctive faith occurs as one discovers polar tensions in the self and "paradox in the nature of truth." Such tensions move one to find a way to unify the opposites both in mind and experientially. In order to do this, the mind develops a "second naiveté," which is an "epistemological humility." Truths are no longer seen in an either/or fashion but as relative. It is not essential that one side be right and one wrong, even in religion. Instead one is free to experience truth in paradox and experience the blend of opposites whether this be in personal, social class, ethnic, or religious ways. For Fowler, this stage requires an extension of Piaget's formal operations into dialectical thinking, and corresponds to the end of

Kohlberg's social contract stage and the beginning of the stage of universal ethical principles. Age of onset: before mid-life if at all.

6. *Universalizing Faith.* Few people reach this stage. One may move toward it due to the discrepancy between what life is and what unity with the Ultimate leads one to make it. Such persons are said to experience a oneness with an "ultimate environment" and have a sense of the inclusiveness of "all being." They see beyond human categories and believe that they live with a power that "unifies and transforms" the world. Drawing on this, they contribute to humanity by trying to transform the human community and may be punished for so trying. There is no corresponding stage in Piaget's system; it may correspond roughly with an additional stage beyond Kohlberg's system.

An empirical assessment of Fowler's system is difficult to make. One could criticize his model for being stated in extremely abstract, almost obtuse language. The parallel between his model and the moral developmental models that came before his is obvious, but because of the abstractness and globality of his ideas there has been little effort to develop empirical measures of his stages (as was done, for example, with Rest's DIT measure for the Kohlberg stages). The one attempt by Barnes, Doyle, and Johnson (1989) may be a beginning.

Fowler's own content analyses of 359 semi-clinical interviews showed that the relation between chronological age and stages of faith were roughly as expected up to early adulthood. For children in ages 0–6, 88 percent were found to be in stage 1 and 12 percent were transitioning between stages 1 and 2. For the 7–12 age group, just over 72 percent were at stage 2, and just over 17 percent were transitioning between stages 2 and 3, and approximately 10 percent were still at stage 1. In the 13–20 age group, 50 percent were at stage 3 and 28.6 percent were transitioning between stages 3 and 4. For subjects aged 21–30, 40 percent were in stage 4, 33.3 percent were at stages 3–4 transitional, and smaller percentages were at surrounding stages.

At higher ages, the reliability of Fowler's stages, as reflected in his data, is not clear. For those aged 31–40 there was a reversal, with 37.5 percent "back" at stage 3, and there was an increase in those transitioning between stages 4 and 5 and at stage 5. The subjects aged 41–50 had the largest percentage at stage 4 (56.2 percent) and only 9.4 percent at stage 3. Beyond that age, there continued a variable pattern of percentages with subjects' responses ranging from stages 2–5, with one exception: in the entire sample there was one subject scored at stage 6, and this person was over 60.

Fowler's data show minor differences between males and females in stages of faith, but his reported differences do not seem important. Whether these would appear more or disappear if different measuring techniques were used in unknown. There has not yet been a critique and correction of Fowler's model based on possible sex bias in the wording of the stages, as was done by Gilligan with Kohlberg's model.

The degree of validity that we ought to assign to Fowler's system is difficult to assess. There seems to be an intuitive sense to it, but because of its diffuse terminology and few tools created to measure it, there have been few scientific hypotheses derived from it and few empirical tests of it. Such tasks await future research.

3. *Sequence of Motives: Religion as Used, Lived, and a Quest*

Meadow and Kahoe (1984) have offered a model of religious development that differs from those of Oser and Gmünder and Fowler in an important way: It stems from a motivational-attitudinal research base in social psychology. According to Kahoe and Meadow, religious development moves along a path described by the counterclockwise circular line in Figure 5.4. A person goes from an extrinsic faith to an observance-oriented faith to an intrinsic faith to an autonomous faith. Let's explain what each of these is.

As shall be seen in detail in Chapter 8, an extrinsic motivational orientation is one in which you do something in exchange for something else. For example, you can perform a religious practice in order to get a nonreligious reinforce-

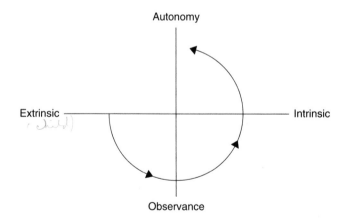

FIGURE 5.4 Kahoe and Meadow's developmental model of religious orientation

Source: M. J. Meadow and R. D. Kahoe, *Psychology of Religion: Religion in Individual Lives,* p. 321 © 1984 by Harper & Row. Or, Kahoe, R. D., & Meadow, M. J. (1981). A developmental perspective on religious orientation dimensions. *Journal of Religion and Health, 20,* 8–17.

ment for doing so. In contrast, an intrinsic motive is one that leads you to do something "for it's own sake;" the act is inherently reinforcing, it motivates itself. Religion can be performed with both extrinsic and intrinsic motives.

In Meadow and Kahoe's model, a child first learns to perform religious acts from extrinsic motivation. Children are not born religious; they learn it by modeling what adults do and by being rewarded for doing so. It is only at a later time, after they have been taught and have internalized the teaching that their religion ought to be selflessly lived, not manipulated for selfish ends, that they develop an internalized, intrinsic religious motivation.

Between the extrinsic and intrinsic stages is religion-as-observance, or institutional religion. It is through the participation in religious activities in organizations such as churches that a child learns to perform rituals and to conform to group standards of religious practice, doctrine, and affective expression. Religious truth is derived from authority. Thus, what is begun as religious behavior performed under an ordinary system of external reinforcement control becomes a set of group-tied beliefs and actions that are regulated by principles of social control. This is the transition from extrinsic to observance religiousness. According to this model, after one separates from an observance type of religiousness and develops an internalized (intrinsic) commitment to one's faith, one is ready to become truly independent and religiously autonomous—the final stage. In an intrinsic faith, one still has a commitment to a fixed belief (although that commitment is internalized), whereas an autonomous faith is said to be more reflective and questioning about it.

For all of the practical, common-sense insight that this model offers, there are two major obstacles to accepting it. The first obstacle has to do with the nature of the intrinsic and extrinsic constructs and the tools used to measure them. There has been an extensive line of research with the Intrinsic-Extrinsic Religious Orientation Scale (Allport & Ross, 1967), but the meaning of this measuring tool has come into question and other conceptualizations of religious constructs have been suggested (Kirkpatrick & Hood, 1990).

The second obstacle concerns the sequence of stages and the transitions between them. It is not exactly clear why, for example, a person must go from being at an extrinsic stage through an observance stage to arrive at the intrinsic stage. Although it is easy to imagine someone going through this sequence, I do not see the theoretical rationale that requires it, nor do I see the necessary mechanisms of transition. Why can't a person go directly from extrinsic to intrinsic, and bypass observance? Why can't someone skip both the extrinsic and observance stages, and through a religious conversion as an adult become immediately intrinsic? Indeed, some psychologists of religion have posed extensive arguments that someone can be both extrinsic and intrinsic at the same time (Pargament, 1992) or both intrinsic and autonomous, committed and questioning, at the same time (Batson, Schoenrade, & Ventis, 1993).

Little research of a strictly developmental nature on intrinsic-extrinsic religiousness has been done. This is partly due to the lack of measuring tools appropriate for use with children. Fortunately, one new scale has been created that allows for the study of intrinsic-extrinsic religiousness with children, and the existence of this tool should make the study of such religious orientations in children easier (Gorsuch & Venable, 1983).

4. *Are Stage Models Valid? An Assessment*

Upon surface exposure to the above stage models of religiousness, you might be tempted to conclude that they are all partially valid with each one merely focusing on a particular facet of the developmental process and that they could explain it all if correctly put together. In fact, it would be easy to construct a chart that appears to integrate the models by listing them along the vertical axis and listing the stages along the horizontal axis. Then at each intersection within the matrix you would write the particular facet of religious development that is addressed by that theory at that stage.

Unfortunately, such a conclusion is not warranted at this stage in the development of this line of research because there are serious questions about whether even the combined theories come close to meeting the criteria for a truly developmental theory or the criteria for the ideal theory mentioned above by Reich. Would any one of the models or even a combination of them correctly and fully account for the factors that favor or hinder religious development, explain those features of religiousness that are common among people and those that are unique to individuals, and integrate intellectual, emotional, and behavioral processes in religiousness? These are big psychological questions. We can focus on a few aspects of them and point to some research possibilities.

First, is there is a psychological process that is common to the sorts of changes described by the models? Helmut Reich (1991) has proposed that one aspect of cognitive development, the step-by-step increase in the ability to reason in complementary terms, not either/or terms, "fits into" the models of Oser and Gmünder and Fowler. Reich describes a five-stage model of such reasoning. This appears in Figure 5.5. At the lower stages one thinks in terms such as "Either A or B is true, but not both." At intermediate stages the possibility of A and B is allowed. At the highest stages both A and B are allowed or required, and they might be related by means of a generalized overarching theory that integrates or supplants them. As a way to illustrate this sequence as applied to the models of Oser and Fowler, Reich points to the increased tendency of polar opposites to be integrated with each successive stage: both transcendence and immanence, fear and faith, union of faith relations around a center of superordinate value (CSV), God as both omnipotent and self-limiting.

FIGURE 5.5 Reich's developmental model of complementarity reasoning

Level	Description
1	Explanation A and explanation B are considered separately; spontaneous judgment "true" or "false" (emphasis on alternatives, not on complementarity). Usually single-track choice of A *or* B, occasionally of both without offering a detailed justification and depending on chance, knowledge, or socialization.
2	The possibility that A *and* B may both be right is considered. A may be right, B may be right, both may be right, possibly with very different weighting factors.
3	The necessity of an explanation with the help of A as well as of B is examined. Whereas neither A nor B is generally considered correct individually, both are needed (partially).
4	Conscious connecting of A and B, explicit indication of their relation. Neither A nor B is correct (alone). The relation between A and B is analyzed (for instance "B permits the use of A" or "B cannot exist without A"). The situation-specificity of the relative contribution of A and B to the total explanation is at least intimated.
5	Construction of a generalized overarching theory (or at least synopsis), including (reconstructed/supplemented parts of) A and B and possibly an additional C. The complex mutual relationship of A and B (and C) as well as the situation-specificity of their explanatory weight is understood and incorporated into the overarching theory. Any resulting shift of meaning in the terms used is explained.

Source: Reich, K. Helmut. The Role of Complementarity Reasoning in Religious Development. Table 1, p. 83. In F. K. Oser and W. G. Scarlett (eds.), *Religious Development in Childhood and Adolescence.* New Directions for Child Development, No. 52. Copyright 1991, Jossey-Bass, Inc., Publishers.

Reich reports one set of data collected from 37 subjects aged 7–19. The findings, based on analysis of interviews, showed a positive correlation between scores on level of complementarity reasoning and Piaget's stages. Extending this line of research to include other stage models remains for the future. Especially needed are data that test for the hypothesized relationships between level of complementarity reasoning and religious developmental levels presumed to unfold across the full adult age span. No such studies have been done. Also, Reich's model does not seem to have a strict application to Meadow and Kahoe's view and he did not offer such. Although not conclusive, Reich's notions are an interesting beginning and suggest where future work can be done.

Second, do the models have a clear invariant, stepwise hierarchy? The answer to this question is basic to any theory that wants to call itself "developmental." For example, people are supposed to go through Piaget's or Kohlberg's stages in the sequence in which they were written. No skipping stages, although they may overlap when people are transitioning between stages. Related to this is that it is still not decided whether the stages in question should be considered "hard" or "soft," i.e., whether the course of religious development is described by a step function or a smooth function, stages or phases. The available data seem consistent with the studies of children's prayer and the God concept discussed earlier and suggest that the proposed sequence of stages may occur up to about young adulthood, but I do not see sufficient evidence for the validity of those stages as a necessary chronological sequence throughout adulthood. For example, Fowler's data suggest that adults may indeed be religious in different ways but do not demonstrate that they necessarily go through this sequence in order to get where they are. Similarly, there is little hard evidence from the other approaches for an essential sequence of religious stages during adulthood.

Third, there are two aspects of our research methods that must be addressed before the above issues can be settled. The first is that we need reliable and valid ways of measuring religious development in adulthood. The second is that we need longitudinal research in which data are collected from the same set of subjects at several times across a long span of years. The data that we now have, collected with cross-sectional methods in which measurements are taken all at the same time from subjects of different ages, let us know that different people of different ages differ in their styles of religiousness. But they do not let us know by what psychological process the older people got where they are, or whether they individually went through a prescribed sequence of steps. If we conducted longitudinal research we would be more likely to answer the critical question of whether the proposed stages are truly invariant. As the research now stands, the answer to this question lies ahead.

Fourth, the need for research on religious development in a cross-cultural context is apparent. Even if the above stage models were known to be valid in the Judaic and Christian contexts in which they were invented, we would need to extend the research to include religion in non-Western contexts in order to explore the applicability of such models there.

Psychological Processes Prompting Adolescent Religious Development

Paradox

Each of the above models includes the notion that at some point along the road during religious development the adolescent faces paradoxes that confront his or her current manner of religious thinking. Such confrontations include disequilibrium and tension that feed the more generic adolescent religious paradox of simultaneously being interested in religion while still doubting or questioning it. However, this inconsistency should be properly understood as one instance of a general paradox orientation of the adolescent years. These paradoxes include, for example, the need for the youth to be independent from parents while still being dependent upon them, to be conservative regarding sexual behavior yet exploratory, to believe in God yet tend to discount the supernatural, and to believe in a superior moral principle yet lean toward moral relativism. It would appear that the same basic questions that plague many adults throughout life begin to have their influence during adolescence.

Seen in this light, religion in the life of the adolescent can be understood as part of a general coping pattern in which the youth is attempting to deal with life's conflicting needs and demands. Cole and Hall (1970) have pointed out that religion is particularly useful in helping to meet at least three needs of adolescents: the first need is that of morality and reduction of guilt feelings. Through prayer, confession, and talks with ministers or church youth group sponsors, the youth may experience feelings of forgiveness, reduced tension, and enhanced adjustment. The second need is security. Religious belief and activity can provide security in that the youth feels attached to a great external power who has overcome death (hence there is reduced fear of death). Also, there is security in the sense that the youth belongs to and is accepted by a group. The third need is for a sound philosophy of life. The youth may gain a sense of direction and momentum for living as well as a rationale for right and wrong and a priority of life values through his or her religion. Other facets of adolescent life are no doubt involved in this overall coping mechanism in addition to religion.

Overall, it seems clear in the light of the research data and the stage models, that childhood religion will not satisfy adolescent needs. Consequently, religion during adolescence must be properly understood within the context of the complex series of life transitions occurring during that period. Because adolescence begins the period of independent decision making, it is no surprise that youth begin to make their own decisions in the religious area just as they must do in other areas (such as vocation, marriage, sexual behavior, military service, etc.). At least three types of psychological processes interact not only to allow or set the stage for the religious quest, but in some ways to actually encourage it. These are cognitive, social, and personal factors.

Cognitive Factors

The cognitive factors refer to the youth's more complex mental abilities as elaborated in Chapter 4. During adolescence, the youth moves into the stage of formal operational thought. It is then that adolescents are mentally able to conceptualize at the abstract level necessary to think through the basic religious issues.

Social Factors

During childhood, two main social factors, family and church, work to mold the child in varying degrees toward (or against, in the case of a nonreligious family) religion. During adolescence, on the other hand, new social factors enter the picture and confront the old. The first new influence is peers. Although peers influence younger children, they are an especially potent influence during adolescence. Religious youth acquire nonreligious friends whose beliefs and practices regarding recreational, sexual, or other morally loaded activities may directly challenge their own. The extent of the influence can be great, all the way from challenging a specific practice (e.g., you should not dance) to challenging the foundations of any prohibition (e.g., all morals are relative). Because youth attempt to regulate their behavior in part by means of a social comparison process in which others are looked to as guides for belief and behavior, the challenging example set by peers can force the youth to reassess his or her own point of view. Even if the peers do not place direct pressure on the youth to do this (e.g., as if they were to tease, debate, or flaunt their "freedom"), their mere presence as a locus of comparison prompts the self-reevaluation to some degree.

The second critical social influence is school. At home, the youth may have been taught religious explanations for events—that is, to account for phenomena in terms of God language, to make supernatural attributions. But then in school, the emphasis is on naturalistic explanations. The heavy emphasis that schools place on science, objectivity, and a scientific way of accounting for and interpreting phenomena may in the youth's mind tend to discredit the value of religious accounts. It is not that science by nature or science teachers necessarily try to show religion to be false. Rather, it is that the emphasis on the scientific way of looking at things could appear, by implication (although not by logical necessity), to make a religious world view seem irrelevant.

It is possible, of course, that active teaching against a religious way of thinking may occur in a particular school, or that active teaching against a scientific way of thinking may occur in a particular church. Instances of these are probably rare, however, and ought to by far be the exception rather than the rule. Whenever it does occur, it would be a function of either of two factors: (1) the teacher or preacher is airing his or her personal biases, or (2) the teacher or preacher still mistakenly thinks in terms of the either/or philosophy (i.e., religion *versus* science)—which was shown in Chapter 3 to be not only unnecessary but also a logical error. The general point is that the mere existence of a scientific approach serves to prompt legitimate questioning and analysis of religious foundations.

Personal Factors

The personal factors may be summarized in terms of the concepts of individuation and identity. *Individuation* refers to the process of becoming separate; *identity* refers to the process of developing a stable self-definition.

When the fetus is still in its mother's womb, it is in a very real sense one with its mother. It has no sense of a separate existence or separate identity, no sense of individuation as a unique human being. Even in infancy, the sense of one's separate existence is rudimentary at best (Fromm, 1941). But as children grow, they gradually learn that they are separate human beings with a unique existence. This process of individuation is discovered and developed gradually over a long period of time. By the time of adolescence, the process of individuation has impressed upon the youth that he or she is unique, has a separate existence, and therefore has a unique identity. The only problem is that adolescents often have difficulty in figuring out just who this separate identity is.

Several psychological consequences occur because of this individuating process. Perhaps the most basic is that the youth must now arrive at his or her own self-definition. What Erik Erikson (1963) has called the *identity crisis* occurs. Rice has noted that adolescents confronted with the quest for religious identity ask questions such as "Who am I? Why am I here? What is the purpose of life? What can I believe? What can I value? How should I live?" (1975, p. 309). The identity crisis is not only a religious quest. It is part of a whole constellation of dimensions that cut across many facets of life (Hoffman, 1970, 1971). The crisis of identity prompts religious as well as other questions.

A corollary to this is that adolescents begin to develop a sense of separateness and responsibility. They come to realize, perhaps only intuitively or unconsciously, that they are separate people subject to the same fundamental existential aloneness as every other person is. Along with this, however, comes the sense of individual responsibility for facing life and the dilemmas it poses.

It is the interaction of these factors—the adolescent's cognitive ability, the social context of peers and school as part of an expanding world, and the natural inducement toward individuation and building a separate identity—that both prompts the adolescent religious quest and enables the young person to move through it. The cognitive abilities enable the youth to think about the issues in a mature enough way; the social environment provides the necessary challenge and is a source of new information; and the individuation-identity process provides the personal impetus for arriving at one's own satisfactory resolution of the issues. It is through this process that questions that are fundamentally religious in nature get asked. And it is the process of maturing through this phase that enables the youth to develop into an independent decision maker in regard to religious and other issues.

Religion and Spirituality in Adulthood and Old Age

Just because, by the time of young adulthood, someone may have settled into a form of religiousness or nonreligiousness with which he or she is comfortable

Participating in religious activities may meet some needs unique to people as they get older. What personal, social, cognitive, or physical needs might be met in part by performing activities such as those illustrated above?

does not mean that the person's spiritual life is settled once and for all, completely static (or ecstatic) thereafter. There may be changes in both the context and function of one's spiritual side of life. Such changes may be prompted by the sorts of life issues faced as part of the natural progression of years. In later life, many people are beset with a number of physical difficulties such as both acute and chronic health problems that sometimes result in a loss of mobility. They also may experience increased problems with vision and audition. Financial problems can increase due to forced retirement, widow-hood, or the loss of job. Emotional grief occurs following the loss of a spouse, sibling, friends, or even an adult child. These are normal occurrences. Most poignant to me is that the older a person gets, the more his or her perception of life and its possibilities changes from a future-oriented vision to a past-oriented observation. A young person looks forward to a future life; there is not much to look back to. In contrast, an old person looks forward unavoidably to narrowing time and closer death; the only large space of life that is available to look at is that which has already happened. It has been argued that such decrements in functioning during mid-life and aging and the facing of death actually create the opportunity for spiritual *ascent* (Bianchi, 1982). It makes sense that people's way of dealing with religious or spiritual issues would be involved with how they deal with old age issues such as the above.

Psychologists in the future will face questions about the interface between the religious or spiritual concerns of people and the other facets of their lives with ever-increasing frequency, because of the sheer number of old people that will be alive over the next quarter century and the high percentage of them that will either be involved in religion or have spiritual concerns. The reason we will see high numbers of aged people is the post-World War II baby boom. Using projections from U.S. Census statistics as an example, as the "Boomers" go through the population, the number of people who are older than 65 years will increase from approximately 12.7 percent to 20 percent of the population over the next 35 years (McFadden, 1995). In addition, the aged population will itself have an older average age as a consequence of medical advances that help people live longer. Professionals in psychology and allied disciplines will have to serve the needs of such persons, and those needs will involve religious and spiritual issues. In order to do this, we will need to know how important religion is to people during the middle adult and aged years, its trajectory over the adult span of years, and its contribution to positive and negative outcomes such as mental and physical health.

How Religious Are Adults?

We can learn about the degree to which adults regard religion as important by examining three types of data. The first type is raw percentages based on surveys of adults, and it is not necessarily reported by age breakdown. The second is cross-sectional "age-trajectory" data because it is reported as a function of the ages of the subjects. In principle, we would also have much of the third type, longitudinal data, but only a little of that is available. Let's look at a representative sample of all three types of information.

Baseline Data on Religion and Spirituality

Baseline statistical information gives us nonspecific but interesting information about religiousness and spirituality in adults. Gallup Poll data report that 88 percent say they pray to God. In a 1987 poll, 76 percent answered "completely" or "mostly" that "prayer is an important part of my daily life" (Gallup & Jones, 1989). This is the same percentage of older Americans (over 65 years) that says that religion is very important in their lives; and an additional 16 percent say it is fairly important (Gallup, 1994). The number of people who pray is extremely high even among those who are "unchurched" (77 percent) and is almost universal (97 percent) among the "churched." One-third of the population reads the Bible weekly or more. The above statistics show a high degree of religious interest.

Data on religious behavior help round out and qualify our picture of religion in adults. For example, older people tend to watch more religious television than younger people. For people aged 18–29 years, 39 percent watch it; for those aged 30–49 years, 47 percent watch it; and for those aged 50 and older, 58 percent watch it. In contrast, although the base rate of attendance at institutional religious services is high, there is (except for people over 50) an increased tendency for people to be *absent* from church or synagogue as they approach mid-life. Thirty-three percent of the people aged 18–24 indicated that there had been a two-year period during which they did not attend church or synagogue; 44 percent of those aged 25–29 indicated the same as did 47 percent of those aged 30–49. This percentage declined after age 50 to 39 percent (Gallup & Jones, 1989).

Examination of trends in data such as the above indicates that people do not necessarily express their religious motivation to an equal degree through each of the dimensions of religious commitment. Taking the population as a whole, there is a gap between degrees of religious interest people have and the amount of formal religious participation or other religious behaviors that they perform. And this raises the possibility that in addition to the substantial number of people who are religious in a traditional sense, there may also be a large number who focus on spirituality in nontraditional, nonreligious ways. For those reasons, Susan McFadden has argued that studies of spirituality should be added to studies of religiousness in gerontological research. Spirituality involves people's tendency toward transcendence, of relating to things that are beyond them. This may or may not be expressed through religion, but it is motivated by the human need for meaning and purpose (Frankl, 1963) and it can include a sense of connectedness or integration (McFadden, 1995, in press). This ought to be related to how people cope.

Additional studies give possible clues to how religious and spiritual issues are part of adults' lives. For example, one study of 836 older adults (average age, 73) found moderate positive correlations between a measure of morale and intrinsic religiosity and religious activity (Koenig, Kvale, & Ferrel, 1988). In another study of 100 older adults, the subjects' spontaneous reports of emotion-regulating coping strategies to stressful situations were recorded. Of the 556 coping behaviors reported for 289 stressful experiences, religion was the most frequently mentioned item—97 times. Overall, these studies raise the possibility that religion and spirituality are involved in mental and physical health and in coping in a variety of ways (Koenig, Smiley, & Gonzales, 1988; Koenig, 1990; Levin, 1994; McFadden, in press), but they do not tell us much about the process of religious development. The relationship between religiousness and health and coping will be explored more fully in Chapter 9.

Age-Trajectory Data
Both cross-sectional and longitudinal data allow us to plot the trajectory of various religiousness measures across the age span. The age ranges studied in the various studies range from the college years to the whole of adult life.

Focusing only on the college years, Canadian psychologist Bruce Hunsberger tested the conventional wisdom of the stereotype that college education makes students lose their beliefs. He surveyed freshmen and seniors in two studies (one cross-sectional, one longitudinal) and found that there was little evidence that his subjects became more liberal by going to college. The questions posed to the students concerned such things as doubt of one's beliefs, agreement with those beliefs one had been taught, their importance, etc.; little change appeared on these measures. The only consistent finding was that the seniors reported less church attendance than the freshmen (Hunsberger, 1978).

How stable are people's religious views over a lifetime? Fortunately, some findings relevant to this question have been offered by a longitudinal study by Jack Shand (1990). The sample is somewhat "select," but the findings are interesting. In 1942, a set of 154 students at Amherst College (all white male) filled out questionnaires asking for their views on a variety of topics such as the existence of God, the soul, life after death, purgatory, the literalness of Bible stories, the right to question church authority, etc. These same people were contacted again in 1964 and in 1984 and completed the same questionnaire. This is a rarity: a 40-year follow-up study of religious beliefs and attitudes. The results showed that over the 40-year period there was not much overall change in the group as a whole in most religious attitudes.

In fact, Shand comments that the interesting thing about these findings is the stability of religiousness after 40 years. Keep in mind that in this age group of subjects we would have men who grew up in the Great Depression of the 1930s, fought in World War II, were more susceptible to marital breakdown and mobility in living than their parents' generation, and lived through the cultural upheaval of the 1960s. Shand was surprised that there was such continuity of religion in the face of such far-reaching cultural movements. There were a few specialized results. There was a slight increase (9–15%) in those who disbelieved in a God of any kind. There was also some individual reversals—some who were believers in 1942 were disbelievers in 1984, and some who were not believers in 1942 became believers by 1984. Such changes were the exception, however, and tended to balance each other out. Shand acknowledges the uniqueness of his particular sample of subjects, but because his concern was with religious change (not static differences between religious groups), he points out that religious change was not affected by the subject's religion (e.g., Catholic or Protestant) nor by undergraduate grade point average or major.

One of the most important recent programs of research attempting to answer questions about the age-trajectory of religion was reported by Peter Benson (1991). It is massive in scope. The data came from a stratified random sample of 561 congregations from five denominations: Christian Church (Disciples of Christ), Evangelical Lutheran, Presbyterian, United Church of

Christ, and United Methodist. The subjects included 3,500 adults and 2,000 adolescents. They filled out a detailed survey that contained 110 questions about all aspects of religion. Due to the large number of subjects, the data can be reported as a function of age across the whole span from 13–15 to 80+ years.

Such data are rarely available. They are not truly developmental because they do not represent repeated measures taken from the same people across a long time span, but they do give us information about age changes in religion for different people who are now inside the churches.

The first question posed by Benson was simple: Are there age-related changes in religiousness? The answer turns out to be yes, but it depends on what aspect of religiousness is measured. Figure 5.6 describes his data on four measures. Mean scores could range from 1 to 7. It can be seen that for the top three measures (religious importance, frequency of private prayer, and frequency of Bible reading), the mean scores for each age group continue to go up (except for the single, slight peak in Bible reading for those in their 20s). In contrast, the one item that measures activity that requires people to go out of their houses (church involvement) shows an incline from age 20–29 to age 70–79 but then drops off at age 80+, probably due to functional health decline.

The second question was whether there was a change in the substance or form of religiousness. In order to measure this, a *Faith Maturity Scale* was developed (Benson, Donahue, & Erickson, 1993) that was designed to reflect both a "vertical" and a "horizontal" form of religiousness in two subscales. The total score reflects their fusion and the degree to which one would be said to have an integrated faith. The degree of faith maturity scored as percent of integrated faith for males and females appears in Figure 5.7. It can be seen that there is a significant upward trend toward greater integration of faith across age groups.

Given that I think the above represents marvelous, hard-to-get data sets, I must nevertheless be cautious when interpreting them. The main reason for this is that they come only from people who are in churches. The subjects by definition are already interested in and involved in religion. A consequence of this is that because they are already committed, they are psychologically obligated to show an increasing love for it, a "development" of it, so long as they choose to remain in it. It would be difficult to not demonstrate such an increase and, at the same time, maintain a sense of cognitive consistency with one's own public behavior. If not that, then it would at least be difficult to answer questions in a way that didn't indicate increased importance of the faith. Once the commitment is made it must be sustained, and saying that your religion increased in importance the longer you stay with it is one way to do so. Overall, as Benson said, the conclusions do not represent the population as a whole, which would also include those not in churches. Therefore, these findings can be thought of as approximating the trends in the United States

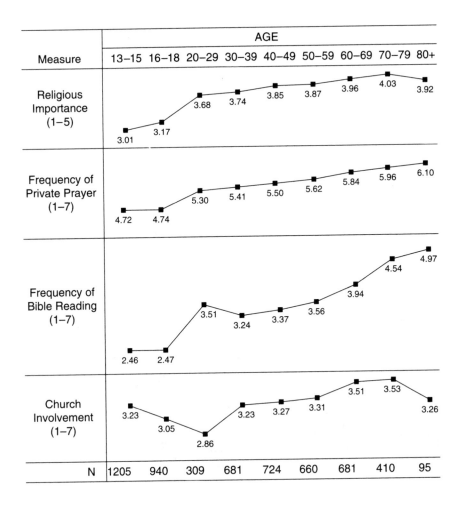

FIGURE 5.6 Change in measures of religiousness across the age span, based on church samples

Source: P. L. Benson, "Patterns of Religious Development in Adolescence and Adulthood," published in the *Psychology of Religion Newsletter* © Spring 1992 (Vol. 17 No. 2), pp. 2–9. Used by permission of the author.

only to the degree that the American population as a whole is involved in churches.

A brief sketch of additional findings raises interesting questions about religious stability. The uncertainty of the stability of a person's religiousness is raised by a study of 713 people in Sweden aged 16–55 years (Hamberg, 1991).

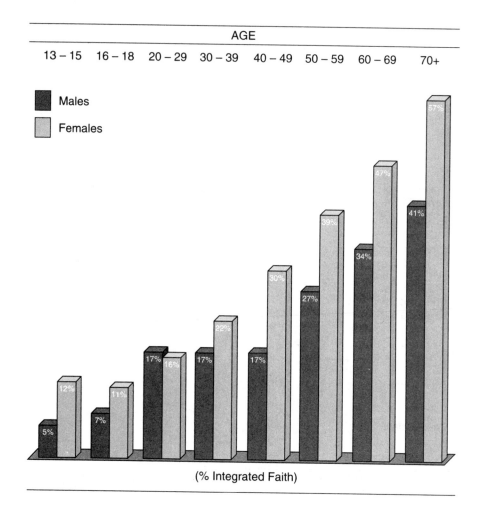

| | | | AGE | | | | |
| 13 – 15 | 16 – 18 | 20 – 29 | 30 – 39 | 40 – 49 | 50 – 59 | 60 – 69 | 70+ |

■ Males

☐ Females

(% Integrated Faith)

FIGURE 5.7   Changes in scores on the faith maturity index as a function of age and gender, based on churched samples

Source: P. L. Benson, "Patterns of Religious Development in Adolescence and Adulthood," published in the *Psychology of Religion Newsletter* © Spring 1992 (Vol. 17 No. 2), pp. 2–9. Used by permission of the author.

The same subjects answered questions in 1955 and again in 1970 about their religious beliefs (God, Heaven, Hell), activities (prayer, attendance at services), and religious interest. Two conceptual models about the trajectory of religiousness across that age span were posed. In the "traditional model" we would expect a slight decrease in young adulthood followed by an increase throughout the rest of one's life. In the "stability model" religiousness remains mostly unchanged throughout adult life. Hamberg says that her findings suggest a "modified stability model." There were general cultural changes in Sweden from 1955 to 1970 that were evident in the data that produced a decline in religiousness, but being middle-aged seemed to insulate people from such changes. That is, there was an overall cultural decline in religiousness; but people in the mid-life years were more likely to remain religiously stable.

Regardless of the methodology of a study or the particular measure used, there does seem to be a consistent, stable difference between men and women in religiousness. Women are more religious than men; and this difference is stable across the age span. For example, Benson (1991) reported that both the mean scores for importance of religion and for frequency of personal prayer were higher for women than for men for all age groups from 13–15 to 70+. Similarly, women scored higher than men on the *Faith Maturity Index* for seven out of eight age brackets (Figure 5.7). The same general trend consistently appears for various other measures of religiousness with the middle adult and aged populations (Argyle & Beit-Hallahmi, 1975; Gallup & Jones, 1989; Koenig, Kvale, & Ferrel, 1988; Levin, Taylor, & Chatters, 1994). We do not yet know whether these differences between men and women are the consequence of different developmental processes. But this consistent pattern might suggest, in Benson's terms, "that the male walk through the middle adult years deflects attention away from things spiritual or away from a sense of connection to energies, passions, and commitments beyond the sphere of self (p. 7)."

The cross-sectional research by Benson suggests that for people who are already within a particular faith tradition, the importance of religion tends to increase with age. However, other research suggests that once people have become aged they do not necessarily turn to religion (Markides, 1983), and the longitudinal study by Shand showed that specific beliefs are fairly stable for his sample of the same individuals over a long time span. In addition, the Swedish study (Hamberg, 1991) highlights the point that there are cross-cultural contexts and historical time periods that must be taken into account when trying to decide how far to generalize a conclusion about the age-trajectory of religion. Finally, one longitudinal study suggested that as people age, their active participation in religion declines (this may be due to decreased physical ability and mobility), but their religious attitudes remain stable and become increasingly important to overall adjustment with age (Blazer & Palmore, 1976).

Spirituality and Functional Religious Development

Does spirituality develop? If you think that religion continues to develop throughout adulthood and aging, you are also likely to assume that the meaning of religion changes with age even though the content remains the same. Is this so? One possibility, for example, is that intrinsic and extrinsic forms of religion are combined into a more mature type of spirituality (McFadden, in press; Pargament et al., 1987, 1992) in which the means or pathway (intrinsic) serves the end (extrinsic) of arriving at a destination of significance. A more elaborate global model of spiritual development has been sketched by Daniel Helminiak (1987) and is an intellectual relative of the stage models discussed earlier in this and the preceding chapter. In it, spirituality functions differently at each successive stage. No empirical data yet exist to test the model, and no measuring tools are yet available for it. McFadden (in press) has well reminded us that spirituality, like religion, is multifaceted and that the systematic theoretical and empirical work to tease it apart lies ahead. It may be that for some people an earlier religious development evolves into a more global type of spirituality, or, alternatively, that spirituality develops in parallel rather than in tandem to religiousness. For now, these are fascinating unsolved puzzles.

If religion and spirituality develop, they do so in ways that are functional. Questions about the functionality of religion are big ones because they are related to many different psychological processes. For purposes of psychological understanding, we cannot learn anything—how one became religious (slow development or quick conversion), whether such acquisition of religion was due to an individual search or to group influence, the degree to which the person has a high degree of phenomenal religious experience, the relation between one's religion and one's morally relevant attitudes and behavior, and the relation between one's religion and mental and physical health—without knowledge of how religion is functional. Such issues involve dynamic processes and relationships among variables across time. It is on truly developmental questions that such a great deal of research is needed, and an invitation to the field must ecourage it. It will be helpful for you to keep the developmental perspective in the back of your mind as we examine both positive and negative psychological functions of religion in the next few chapters and interpret that material in a developmental context to the degree that it makes sense.

In sum, examining the course of religious development reveals at least two basic things. First, over the course of development religion is constantly changing, yet it is the same. That is, as a child grows he or she may be involved in the same religion, but the meaning of that religion to the person may change in dramatic ways from, for example, ages 5 to 50. It should be understood that an expression of belief, a vocalized prayer, or a religious practice may look the same to the outside observer but may be performed for quite different reasons at different ages—because the social and psychological factors that mediate these expressions evolve with age.

Second, the development of religiousness represents part of the life of someone who is in the process of religious change. As such, it can be thought of as a very slow type of belief evolution. In contrast, religious conversion is normally understood to be a much shorter process, which is nevertheless most prevalent during adolescence. Therefore, the developmental process can be fruitfully used to understand either the gradual unfolding of one's approach to religiousness, or as a process that can set the stage for conversion. The next chapter focuses our attention on issues directly related to the religious conversion process.

Projects and Questions

1. Design and execute a research project that tests a hypothesis concerning the processes and dynamics involved in changes in religiousness across time.

2. Are the standards by which humanistic or cognitive psychologists gauge growth in spirituality the same as or different from those of the believers themselves? If they are the same, explain the basis for this similarity. If they are different, explain how and why. Devise ways to empirically test this.

3. Design and execute a research project to test whether the process of doubt increases, decreases, or has no effect on the process of religious development.

4. Does the model by Fowler have any built-in biases analogous to those in Kohlberg's model?

5. Conduct an interview study of parents and grandparents focusing on their religious histories. What questions could be posed in order to tap developmental processes?

6. Study Erik Erikson's developmental theory and its usage in models of religious growth. How is it related to the models presented in Chapters 4 and 5?

Further Readings

Fowler, J. (1981). *Stages of faith: The psychology of human development and the quest for meaning.* New York: Harper & Row. See also Fowler (1980) and Fowler (1986).

Kimble, M. A., McFadden, S. H., Ellor, J. W. & Seeber, J. J. (Eds.). (1995). *Aging, spirituality, and religion: A handbook.* Minneapolis: Fortress Press. A comprehensive resource reviewing research on the relation between aging, spirituality, and religion; also discuss application.

Oser, F., & Gmünder, P. (1991). *Religious judgement: A developmental perspective.* Religious Education Press, Birmingham, AL. A presentation of the theory and research on Oser and Gmünder's stage model of religious judgment.   *see* BL 625.5

See also the Further Readings for Chapter 4.   R45 /99!

6

conversion

Religious Conversion

(adolescence & young adult)

Projects and Activities

Further Reading

Religious conversion is among the most profound and perplexing of events that can occur in the life of a human being. A person's life may be changed forever because of it. Many people are experiencing it today, and the recent past has been a time of publicized conversions to and reactions against new messiahs and gurus. People have been adopting not only traditional religions such as Protestantism and Catholicism, but also new religious movements (NRMs) such as the Children of God, Divine Light Mission, Moon's Unification Church, Scientology, and others (Barker, 1989; Beckford, 1985; Robbins, 1988; Stoner & Parke, 1977).

It may seem to be a paradox that such a phenomenon as religious conversion would be occurring today. It's puzzling because our age is secular in many ways. More than ever before, standards of acceptable behavior are perceived to rest upon a philosophical foundation of moral relativism. Such a philosophy naturally eats away at religious foundations. Yet, concurrent with this trend, or possibly as a reaction against it, we are witnessing a religious awakening. Not all of it looks like a religious awakening in the nineteenth century meaning of the term; but without doubt some drastic changes are taking place in the minds and actions of many people as far as religious matters are concerned. Look again at the instances of religious belief and behavior at the beginning of Chapter 1; then select those which are conversions and try to explain the "why?" and "how?" of them. We want to understand what happened in the lives of Paul, Augustine, Moses, Malcom X, the young man or woman who follows the NRM, and countless others. What does conversion do for, or to, people? What psychological mechanisms operate to make religious changes happen? What psychological factors make people resistant to religious persuasion influences? In this chapter we think through the psychological issues that are embedded in these questions.

This discussion concerns the general process of conversion to both traditional religions and NRMs. I shall refer primarily to "NRMs" with secondary use of the term "cult." NRM is the more descriptive term and is preferred in scientific scholarship. "Cult" is a more automatically pejorative term applied in more popular writings to groups seen by their critics to have some procedural properties that may be perceived as undesirable. These shall be discussed below. Both traditional religions and NRMs may share certain properties to a greater or lesser degree, just as both can meet some human needs.

Let us begin by differentiating between various areas of life which undergo conversion and various modes of the conversion process. For example, Thouless (1971) distinguished between intellectual, moral, and social conversions. Intellectual conversions are changes in the belief component of the religious attitude; moral conversions are changes in the motivation toward morally relevant behavior; social conversions are changes in one's actions toward the social environment. This three-type characterization illustrates that the facets of conversion can be differentiated along the important life domains of belief, motivation, and action, paralleling part of Glock's dimensions of religious commitment (Chapter 1). Thouless points out that changes in these facets are not mutually exclusive; changes in one area typically accompany changes in others. Nevertheless, separating these facets of change is useful in psychological analysis.

One other distinction must be made that is at the heart of our consideration of conversion models and that is pivotal in the history of the literature on this topic. This distinction is between conversion being understood as an active versus a passive process, at both the individual and the group level of analysis. In the active view, the individual exercises free agency in seeking and choosing to convert. Through one's own volition one adopts a personal belief or joins a different religious group, whether it is culturally accepted or deviant from the norm, Eastern or Western. In the passive view, one's change in belief or religious group is determined for the individual by either psychological processes (e.g., mental or emotional needs) or social forces (e.g., interpersonal manipulation, group pressure) that are more or less irresistible (Richardson, 1985a, 1989).

So, which is correct? Do people actively, voluntarily choose to acquire new beliefs and to join religious groups or are they manipulated and recruited into them as a way of exploiting human psychological needs?

It is a mistake to think that conversions are fundamentally all the same. In fact, a conversion may not be a single event at all, but a process. The final outcome is a result of a complex interaction of personal and social forces; and the relative weight of each in determining the conversion in a particular case depends upon the combined dispositions of the person and the processes of the group. You will see that this issue is in the middle of psychological and legal debate and that it will stretch our minds in search of a resolution.

Prevalence and Definition of Conversion

Popular Opinion

Both a difficulty and a challenge in discussing religious conversion is that the phrase carries many connotations. One person hears the term and immediately experiences a sense of joy at the presumed salvation of a soul, while another concludes that the convert was "brainwashed." Some may think that the convert made a rational choice to change beliefs; others may presume that an emotional explosion occurred in the believer's life. Some feel that the changed person will inevitably become "just another hypocrite in the church"; others see renewed hope for more consistent morality and human compassion. Some professional psychologists view religious conversion as psychologically integrative and conducive to mental health, whereas others almost automatically conclude it is a sign of mental illness or at least gullibility (cf. Ellis, 1977).

Certainly, not all of these views can be simultaneously correct. Or can they? As we shall see, the answer is not a simple "either/or" proposition. Rather, it is a matter of when these views hold, and for whom, for what types of religious changes, to what belief systems, and by means of what processes. These differences of opinion highlight the confusion and disagreement that surrounds the topic of religious conversion.

The Prevalence of Conversion

How much religious conversion is occurring? Looking at the popular media, one gets the impression that it has mushroomed. These apparent societal trends can be assessed with more precision by examining recent statistical information.

The Princeton Religion Research Center has polled the religious attitudes of Americans. In their 1989 Comprehensive Report, the following provocative headlines, which summarize the trends apparent in the polling data, appear:

- Seventy-one percent have experienced change in faith.
- Spiritual "awakening" touches one-third of Americans.
- Born-again experience pervades.

Perhaps more revealing than the above general statements are the statistics presented in Table 6.1, also reported by Gallup, which are based on representative samples of over 1,500 Americans. Statistical projections based upon these figures give us a clue as to how prevalent various types of conversion experiences are. The figure of 38 percent of Americans claiming to have had a born-again experience projects to over 50 million people, aged 18 and over. Among Protestants, this figure is 52 percent, and among Catholics it is 21 percent (Gallup & Jones, 1989). Whether we think that Gallup's percentages reflect "genuine" personal conversions, the indications are clear that religious changes of some type are occurring in the lives of many people.

Data on experiential religions and mystical experiences are equally revealing. The figure of 31 percent reporting religious or mystical experiences projects to about 47 million people. The potency or vividness of these experi-

TABLE 6.1   Sample of Religious Belief and Practice as Evidenced by Gallup Poll

Question	Percent in national sample answering "yes"
Would you say that you have been "born again" or have had a "born again" experience—that is, a turning point in your life when you committed yourself to Christ?	38%
Would you say that you have ever had a religious or mystical experience—that is, a moment of sudden religious insight or awakening?	31%
"Other-worldly" feeling	10%
Natural spiritual awakening	5%
Healing experience	5%
Visions, voices, dreams	4%
Turning to God in crisis	2%
Can't describe	5%
Which, if any, of these are you involved in or do you practice?	
Yoga	3%
Transcendental Meditation	4%
Eastern religions	1%
The charismatic movement	2%
Faith healing	7%
Mysticism	2%
Have you ever been aware of, or influenced by, a presence of a power—whether you call it God or not—which is different from your everyday self?	
Total	43%
Men	38%
Women	47%
Descriptions of Spiritual Presence (selections based on those reporting)	
Presence of God	21%
Indescribable feeling	11%
Like ESP, intuition	5%
A light	2%

Adapted from Gallup and Jones, 1989; Gallup, 1977–78. Sample sizes range from approximately 1,500 to 2,600 adults nationwide. © The Princeton Religion Research Center.

ences is noted by the finding that "most are able to recreate details of the experience; some even remember the exact date of the occurrence" (Gallup, 1977–78, p. 53). Since the focus of that survey was on "religious experiences of a *sudden or dramatic nature*" (conversions?), the percentage probably would have been higher if the question had been broadened to include religious experiences of a more general nature.

A similar point could be argued with regard to the data for experiential religions. Approximately 10 million are involved in faith healing, 6 million in Transcendental Meditation (a derivative of Hinduism), about 4 million in Yoga, 3 million in the charismatic renewal movement, 3 million in mysticism, and 1 million in Eastern religions. Since it is unlikely that in the United States this many people would have been raised from childhood into these various religions, and since the popularity of these is relatively recent, chances are that most of the people involved in them came to adopt the experiential religions on their own.

Similar statistics for NRMs are harder to obtain. When discussing specific NRMs, instead of religious movements in general, we can focus on only a few by way of example. In the mid 1970s, it was estimated that there were more than 1,300 "cults," totaling more than 5 million members, active in North America alone (*Spiritual Community Guide for North America*, 1975–76). Among the more prominent of these were Reverend Sun Myung Moon's Unification Church, Church of Scientology, Satanism, Children of God, Divine Light Mission, and The Way International. By the 1980s it was suggested by anticultists that there were 3,000–5,000 "destructive cults" operating in the United States, even though "no evidence of the existence of such a large number of religious groups, either cultic or otherwise, has been produced (Melton, 1986, p. 5)." Most of the NRMs are small and will never affect a significant number of people. Some, such as the Holy Spirit Association for the Unification of World Christianity (Moon's Unification Church), started with very few core members and grew into large, powerful organizations (Barker, 1984; Sontag, 1977). Other quasireligious groups started with fervor but died, sometimes due to their violent actions and involvement with the law—as with the case of the Manson Family (Bugliosi, 1974; Galanter, 1989). Yet, it is clear that some groups use religious persuasion tactics that can affect particular people in dramatic ways.

The accuracy of the statistics for such groups is variable. For most, we must rely on rough estimates based on either the opinion of an expert or a claim made by people within the group. Therefore, we must interpret the statistics for NRMs cautiously and regard them only as rough estimates of the number of people who have converted to them.

The Definition Issue

In psychological circles there has not been consensus on the most basic problem—that of defining religious conversion. This issue appears in two forms. First, should we reserve the term only for those changes in religious belief that happen all at once, very quickly; for example, the classical sudden conversion experience as most graphically illustrated in the conversion of Paul (The Acts of the Apostles, Chapter 9)? Or do changes in belief that come about by means of a slower, more gradual process also deserve the right to be called conversion? Some researchers reserve the term *conversion* only for the sudden type of experience (Stanley, 1964). These researchers would agree that other people can possess the same belief system as the convert, but the other believers would not be called converts, because they arrived at the belief by means of a slower process, such as gradually thinking through the issues, or being trained in the belief from childhood. However, many people who would label themselves converts cannot easily fit their experience into the sudden stereotype. Because of this, other psychologists consider conversion to be any process by which a person comes to hold a religious belief. They separate conversions into subtypes, including both sudden and gradual processes (Scobie, 1973).

Conversion means change. The same meaning is attached to the concept by chemists, as, for example, when they talk about converting water into steam by boiling it. In this case, something is done to a substance of one form that causes it to be transformed into some new form. So it is with religious conversion. Something happens to people that changes them or transforms them from adherents of one group to another, one belief to another, one cause or cosmology to another. As is the case with the transformation of water into steam, religious conversion may take variable amounts of time. Various psychological explanations of conversion allow from an instant to a lifetime for the forces of religious conversion to complete their work. Thus, though the process of change may be different, the fact of change is, by definition, part of the reality of conversion. It is more fruitful, therefore, if we adopt the broader scheme for defining conversion while allowing for the existence of subtypes.

A second version of the definition of conversion issue concerns whether the change must be religious in particular, or whether any profound change, religious or otherwise, can be considered conversion. Though the term generally connotes change in the religious sense, occasionally we hear of such things as political conversions. For example, former Black Panther Eldridge Cleaver said that he turned around at the political level first, with his religious conversion following afterwards (Cleaver, 1978). A strong case can also be made that some changes that occur through the process of psychotherapy have the nature of conversion (Hobbs, 1962) and that the processes involved in psychotherapy and new religions have several features in common, including their appeal to similar people, sharing the same "deep structure," and functioning to bolster the person's self-concept (Kilbourne & Richardson, 1984).

In our discussion, though we recognize that other conversions occur, we are concerned with conversion in the religious connotation of the term; that is, conversion to an organized set of beliefs that provide a superordinate framework for the individual's life. We recognize that political and therapeutic doctrines can serve this religious function for some people. To the extent that this is true in a particular case, our analysis of religious conversion can be validly applied.

Conversion Types

Sudden and Gradual Conversion

Conversion types have been broken down into two basic categories, sudden and gradual conversion. A third type of belief acquisition, religious socialization, has also been studied in relation to sudden and gradual conversion. Each type takes a different amount of time. Each type has also attracted a different psychological explanation.

Sudden Conversion

The most dramatic of the conversion types is the sudden conversion. Here the conversion occurs all at once, in a short time frame. At one point in time the person is a nonconvert (or preconvert) giving little thought to religious matters. Then very quickly, he or she changes and comes to adopt a new belief. Sudden converts are thought to experience conversion both with and without the prompting provided by evangelistic efforts. For example, one may experience sudden conversion as a result of evangelistic prompting such as in a Billy Graham crusade, or without such prompting. The sudden conversion of the apostle Paul has been interpreted as an example of the latter type in which he was the passive responder in the transaction and the active agent of change was something other than Paul the person (Richardson, 1985a, 1989; Thouless, 1971).[1] In either case, the key feature of the sudden conversion is the short time span in which it occurs.

Psychological explanations of sudden conversion have invoked the concepts of conflict, frustration, and the unconscious. It has been proposed that some people are predisposed to sudden conversion because interpersonal conflicts and frustrations (e.g., feelings of personal inadequacy, lack of self-worth, guilt over a misdeed) have been repressed (Scobie, 1975). These repressed feelings then build up in the unconscious like steam in a pressure cooker. Eventually they must be released. For the sudden convert they are released all at once when the person makes a commitment to God. At that point the conflicts and frustrations come to the surface and are resolved through the conversion. Because the repressed feelings are negative, sudden conversion is said to have a highly emotional quality. The role of the evangelist is to provide the solution to the repressed frustrations. The evangelist presents the releasing cue, or trigger, that sparks the conversion. This type of explanation has a distinctly psychoanalytic flavor, since it involves the concepts of repression and the unconscious, which are classical Freudian concepts.

Gradual Conversion

Between the extremes of sudden conversion and lifelong religious socialization is gradual conversion. We can think of gradual conversion as a process of growth of belief over an intermediate period of time. The time span may extend from a few days to several months or years. During this period the person reassesses aspects of his or her life and begins to consider a religious world view as a viable alternative. A gradual convert may ask some of life's basic questions and weigh religious and other answers to those questions. There may be a series of intellectual objections to religious doctrines which must be thought through. Gradually the person resolves those issues and moves from a point of rejecting a belief to a point of accepting it.

Psychological explanations of gradual conversion imply a more intellectual type of process than either sudden conversion or religious socialization. Theoretically, gradual converts may experience conflict and frustration, but these are not repressed as they are in sudden conversion. Rather, the person makes conscious efforts to resolve them. This implies a more active process. The conflicts might be between personal, societal, and religious values; or the frustration might be due to a discrepancy between the person's actual and desired levels of performance in the moral or intellectual sphere. Also, gradual converts may have a cognitive need to answer basic questions and search for meaning in life. When these needs or search for meaning are not met, frustration may be felt. Gradually, however, these needs are met as the person thinks through and accepts the faith.

Religious Socialization

The extreme opposite of sudden conversion is lifelong religious socialization (sometimes misnamed "unconscious conversion"). It is not conversion but represents belief for which the person cannot remember a time of not believing the faith. People in this category feel that they have always believed. There is no dramatic turning point of acquiring a new religion as there was with the sudden convert. It is called socialization because it occurs in the natural course of development from early childhood onward. The person grows up with the faith and does not recall making a conscious decision for it.

Believers who fit this category have typically been raised in religious homes, or have otherwise been under the long-term influence of religious people. Theoretically, those socialized into their religion would not necessarily be troubled by the repressed conflict and frustration of the sudden convert. The dominant psychological explanation for religious socialization relies upon the concept of social learning (Scobie, 1975). The person learns to accept the beliefs that he or she has been trained to accept during upbringing. While growing up, two learning procedures have influenced the child's acceptance of the beliefs. These are reinforcement and modeling processes. The youth is reinforced for actions and statements which indicate acceptance of the beliefs, and consequently learns to accept them. The youth also imitates the model set by religious parents and thus acquires their beliefs and religious practices.

It is debatable whether such a slow acquisition process should be called "conversion." The utility of this category for research purposes is that it serves as a baseline control group of religious people who have beliefs but who have not acquired them by means of a conversion or change process of which they are aware. Thus, comparisons can be made between believers of the sudden and gradual conversion types and those in the baseline religious socialization category.

Comparison of Conversion Types

Differences emerge when we compare the ideas presumed to underlie these types of conversion experiences along key dimensions. First, there are differences in the relative importance of intellectual, emotional, and learned factors. Intellectual factors seem to be most important in gradual conversion; emotional factors are given the greatest importance in sudden conversion; the social learning process is given greatest importance in religious socialization. (See Table 6.2 for a summary comparison of the three types of belief acquisition.)

Second, by implication at least two of the three types of believers differ in their degree of personal stability. The personality of the sudden convert would presumably be the most volatile due to a high emotionality. The personality of the gradual convert, on the other hand, would presumably be less so due to a tendency to calculate decisions.

Third, according to Scobie (1975) the three types would differ in amount of religious activity, interest, or belief, especially during the process of conversion itself. He suggests that the three types of believers all stabilize at about the same level of religious involvement later in life, but that they differ in degree of involvement during the conversion phase. The sudden converts rise very quickly to a high peak of activity, higher than any other group, but they do not remain there. The gradual converts also increase in activity but do not reach the same height as the sudden converts. Both of these reach levels that are higher than the socialized believers, however, who show a gradual decline through young adulthood.

This model has yet to be tested in the precise form stated by Scobie, but Barker and Currie (1985) have provided a variation of it. In their study, all of the 93 subjects were "born-again" Evangelical Christians in Canada, but half of them were *converts* who "joined the Evangelical Church from outside that tradition" and half of them were *alternators* who were "raised within the Evangelical Church tradition" but also experienced a "re-birth" as an expected part of religious development. Results showed that converts reported a greater identity change than alternators, but that on most measures of religious

TABLE 6.2 Summary of types of belief acquisition

Type	Time span	Supposed important factors	Explanation of psychological process
Sudden conversion	Very brief	Emotions	Conflict and frustration repressed into unconscious; released upon conversion
Gradual conversion	Varies from a few days to several months or a few years	Intellectual, cognitive	Conscious conflict or frustration; cognitive need for answers and meaning of life; needs met after thinking through objections to belief system
Religious socialization	Entire life	Learned beliefs and behaviors	Social learning: reinforcement and modeling

commitment (religion now having an influence on one's life, church attendance, time spent in private prayer, time spent reading religious material, giving money to the church) the two groups scored about the same. Church involvement was higher among alternators, a result that makes sense given the socialization into the church that is part of the background of such persons. This last finding suggests that the social context in which the believer is placed is important in determining religious participation, and notions of social context are central to conversion process models.

Conversion Process Models

The explanations offered for the above conversion types all focus on psychological factors. Unconscious conflict, social learning, and cognitive needs and decision making are all processes presumed to operate fundamentally at a psychological level. However, a shift in focus has evolved in the more recent process models of conversion that is due to the addition of an emphasis on social forces in interaction with personal factors. Some of the elements of the newer models come from the observation of NRMs and some come from psychological analyses of conversion to a traditional Western religion, but these elements can also be usefully applied to other groups as well. In this expanded approach, the distinction between sudden and gradual conversion, though important, becomes less of a central point. Instead, this distinction becomes incorporated into broader, more inclusive descriptions of the overall process of how the religious change happens. In the approaches summarized below, some elements see the person as an active seeker of personal transformation, and others see the person as a passive subject. I will argue for the notion of the interaction of the active and passive roles of the person.

Lofland and Stark's Step Model of Conversion

We now come to the question of how people might become converts to a new group. The specific processes that determine the conversion may vary, due to key differences between specific groups (e.g., different processes may operate in large groups than in small ones). Nevertheless, the best known early model of conversion to an NRM comes from the sociological work of Lofland and Stark (1965) and Lofland (1977b). This model was derived by an in-depth participant observation study of what is widely assumed to have been the beginnings of the Unification Church of the Reverend Sun Myung Moon. According to their model, there are seven steps involved in the complete process of conversion to the group. These steps are categorized into background or predisposing factors and situational factors. The extent to which this model applies widely to conversions to NRMs or traditional religions has yet to be detailed through research (Richardson, 1978; Snow & Phillips, 1980), but it is likely that research will show its elements to be selectively generalizable.

Background or predisposing factors: First, the person must experience enduring, acutely felt tensions. A tension can be thought of as being analogous to a deprivation. It is a gap (or a perceived gap) between the actual and the desired or ideal state of affairs. Examples of such tensions include unrealized desire for wealth or status, frustrated sexual or interpersonal relations, guilt over past misdeeds, and an unsatisfied desire for religious status. In each of these types of tension the person wants circumstances to be different from what they are and is therefore motivated to pursue change through some problem-solving strategy.

Second, the potential convert must adopt a religious strategy instead of some other strategy (e.g., a political one) as a means of solving the problem and reducing the tension. Theoretically, if someone experienced the same tensions but adopted a political problem-solving perspective rather than a religious one, he or she would become a political activist rather than a religious convert.

Third, when a person in tension adopts a religious problem-solving perspective but does not have his or her needs met by conventional religious institutions, the person is led to define himself or herself as a religious seeker. The outcome is a person in quest of unusual religious answers.

The above three factors are regarded as personal conditions that predispose a person to become a convert to an NRM when the situation is right. But certain situational factors must also be present in order for the potential conversion to be realized. The remaining four factors fall into this category.

Situational factors: Fourth, the potential convert must be at some turning point in life and must encounter the religious movement at this point. People in the movement would in turn be recruiting new members. In the group of converts that Lofland and Stark studied, each one had come to a point in life when one phase of life's activity was ending and another was about to begin. For example, one woman's academic career had been disrupted; another woman had recently moved to a new town; a man was terminating his studies; another woman no longer had a child to care for. It is at these turning points that a person is most open to the proselytizing influence of recruiters. Therefore, when a person's turning point occurs concurrently with an initial introduction to the group, that person is more likely to become a follower than if the contact occurs at some other time.

Fifth, when the new convert initially enters the group, strong affective bonds are formed between the newcomer and other group members. The new convert may report feeling a sense of closeness or oneness. These strong emotional ties serve to link group members closely together with a sense of unity.

Sixth, concurrently, the new convert's attachments to people or things outside the group begin to diminish. They could be absent from the start, or they may be neutralized by the development of strong ties to other group members. In either case, the lack of ties with friends and family outside the group tends to solidify the ties with those inside the group.

Seventh, according to Lofland and Stark, in order for a person to become a "total convert" (i.e., a "deployable agent" who will go out and recruit new members) there must be intensive interaction between the new convert and the rest of the members. A "total convert" is one who puts one's life at the disposal of the group. This may mean very frequent, even daily or hourly, contact with other members. Such interaction further cements the convert's commitment to the movement, weakens extra-group ties still further, and increases his or her own availability for recruitment activities.

Motives Are Important: Glock's Expansion of Sect-Church Theory

In an updated analysis of his step-model of conversion, Lofland (1977a) points out that the model is in some ways so broad that aspects of it may apply to a variety of types of groups. Similarly, different process models may prevail for groups different from the small, intense group he studied.

One factor critical in determining the type of group to which someone converts is the person's motive—what kind of tension is felt. Theoretically, the kind of group inducement to which a person may be susceptible would depend upon the type of tension, or deprivation, from which the person desires to escape. Glock (1964; also Glock & Stark, 1965) has offered a theory that enables us to conceptualize how different motives would lend one toward converting to a particular type of group. His model is an expansion of early sect-church theory.

Sect-church theory has traditionally been an important influence in sociological thinking about the origin and development of religious groups. As used in a sociological framework, "church" refers to the church only as a social organization or institution. According to the sect-church view, the church is part of the "establishment." It is an integral part of the society in which it exists. It may be restrained, formalistic, procedural, and ritualistic in its services, and may compromise its principles in order to get along well with other facets of society. Also, according to this view the church would have a primarily inherited membership, that is, its members are likely to have been raised in it and likely to raise their offspring in it.

The sect is the polar opposite of the church. The sect is in tension with the church and with other facets of "main-line" society. The sect would likely consist of people who have converted to the sect movement from the church. It would be smaller than the church and may have as its goal the changing of the larger structure against which it is reacting. Sect members would be less concerned with the formalities of services and might be less willing to compromise their position.

Theoretically, sects emerge when some people in the church feel that it has compromised too much. When this occurs they break off from the main group and form a group of their own. Although the sect begins small as a reaction against the church, it gradually becomes church-like as it grows. That is, as the small sect grows into a large church, it must begin to concern itself with the same formalism, self-perpetuation, organization, and interaction with society as any other church. Thus as the sect makes the slow transition to a highly church-like character, it becomes a breeding ground for new sects.

Important to our discussion of motives for conversion to a group is the assertion that sect members come primarily from the lower socioeconomic classes.[2] The main deprivation-induced motive is economic. It is thought that both religious protest and social protest underlie the formation of a sect. Glock notes that there are weaknesses in the sect-church theory, especially in its simple form presented above. First, some religious groups look more like churches than sects at their very beginning. Second, not all sects grow out of churches. For some sects and NRMs, there is no obvious parent church to be identified. Most important for Glock, there are other types of deprivation besides economic ones that can give rise to religious movements.

Glock uses the term *deprivation* to refer to "any and all of the ways that an individual or group may be, or feel disadvantaged in comparison either to other individuals or groups, or to an internalized set of standards" (Glock & Stark, 1965, p. 246). Two points need to be brought out in this definition. First, feelings of deprivation may result when one compares oneself to another and discovers that the other is "higher" or better off. In different social-psychological language, we would say that feelings of deprivation result when people engage in a social comparison process and detect a negative gap between their own level and the standard set by the comparison group. Second, the standard of comparison can be one's own internal standard. Thus, when a person's level falls below his or her own personal standard, feelings of deprivation may result. Deprivations then function as motives that induce people to change their situation, belief, group, or behavior.

Glock lists five types of deprivation, each of which he says is related to a certain type of religious group movement. The five types are economic, social, organismic, ethical, and psychic deprivation.

1. Economic deprivation refers to the differential distribution across society of money and goods. Those who perceive themselves as having less than they should, especially compared to similar others, are said to feel economically deprived. Note that it is not necessarily the absolute amount of goods that a person has that is important, but the amount one has relative to others or to one's own expectations.
2. Social deprivation refers to the perception of uneven distribution of socially valued attributes such as age, race, and intelligence. For example, in American society, it is somehow "better" to be young, white, and smart than it is to be old, black, and dumb. Society tends to reward the "right" combinations of such attributes with prestige, status, or opportunities.
3. Organismic deprivation refers to feeling disadvantaged due to physical or mental illness, or other disabling traits such as blindness or deafness. Obviously, people with such traits are deprived of certain rewards obtainable by other people.
4. Ethical deprivation refers to the perception of conflicts between society's ideal values and the performance of individuals or groups in light of those values. That is, people may compromise higher values for more self-serving ends. Or the individual may see the society as falling below the ideal standard.
5. Psychic deprivation refers to an unmet cognitive need for satisfactory purpose and meaning. When such needs are not met by existing value systems, deprivation may be felt and movement toward adopting a different value system may begin.

Glock proposes that each type of deprivation is closely linked to the development of one type of religious group. As summarized in Table 6.3,

TABLE 6.3   Origins, forms, and development of religious groups

Type of deprivation	Form of religious group	Success expectations
1. Economic	Sect	Extinction or transformation
2. Social	Church	Retain original form
3. Organismic	Healing movement	Becomes cultlike or is destroyed by medical discoveries
4. Ethical	Reform movements	Early extinction due to success, opposition or becoming irrelevant
5. Psychic	Cult	Total success resulting in extinction through transformation, or failure due to extreme opposition

Source: Glock, C. Y., & Stark, R. *Religion and society in tension.* Chicago: Rand McNally, 1965. Copyright © by Charles Y. Glock. Reprinted with permission.

Glock's model is an extension of the simple version of sect-church theory. Economic deprivation motivates sect development, as stated by the earlier sect-church theory. But the other relationships are extensions and special cases of the basic theme of deprivation leading to group development.

Social deprivation motivates the development of a separate church organization. People who are socially deprived and who belong to an established church are not having their social needs for such things as status, recognition, and opportunity met. Given these conditions, such people may reorganize into a new church more suited to the satisfaction of their own social needs. But rather than take on a new form, as a sect would, the new church movement retains the original form. There is no need to change forms because the new group has as its goal full functioning in society, rather than the transformation of society as in the case of the sect.

Organismic deprivation leads to the development of a religious healing movement, according to Glock. The participants hope that through miraculous healing, their organismic deprivations can be overcome. Such movements would presumably become unnecessary if medical discoveries were made that solve the organismic difficulties. Theoretically, if a healing movement endures, it could become cultlike.

Ethical deprivations are thought to underlie the development of reform movements. The ethical reformer is out to correct what he or she sees as too much moral compromising. If the reform movement succeeds in its early phases, then it is no longer necessary and hence dies. But it may also die for other reasons. For example, the opposition may be great enough to stop it. Or society, and hence the perceived compromises, may change in ways that make the reform movement irrelevant.

Finally, psychic deprivations are thought to foster the development of religious cults. The participants adopt the new religious system in order to replace the old ideology, which was unsatisfactory. In Glock's system, a cult may fail due to extreme opposition. It may also achieve total success, in which case it permeates the entire society and thereby becomes extinct as a distinct cult.

The above presentation of deprivations as precursors to movement toward specialized religious groups is a conceptual analysis. Research is needed to test the limits of the model. Perhaps religions arise not only out of deprivation, but also out of healthiness and the desire to share the abundance of what one has experienced. Nevertheless, it seems clear that motives are important. In Glock's system, a particular type of deprivation-induced motive leads one toward conversion to a particular type of religious group. By fusing Lofland's step processes of conversion with Glock's conceptual breakdown of types of deprivation and religious group, we can hypothesize that the right combination of predisposing and situational forces coupled with a person with a particular need encountering a group that promises to meet that need creates exceptionally strong forces for that person to convert to that group.

The above models of overall process of conversion are conceptually rich and sweeping in scope. I find them to be valuable heuristics because they enable me to think about the multiple, varied factors that must be taken into account when I try to understand profound changes such as the religious transformation of someone's life. They keep me aware that not all conversions are the same and that no single factor is causal in them all. However, it is necessary to further explore some implications of the models in order to assess the degree to which aspects of them fit various cases. For example, must all converts follow the steps in Lofland's model? He did not intend us to think so, and some reviewers suggest that although the model is inclusive of the key variables, in its full form it is most directly applicable to conversion to groups whose organization and demands are similar to the one he studied (Greil & Rudy, 1984). Elements of the model apply somewhat selectively to other conversions. Must converts to one or another NRM, sect, or Catholic or Protestant church fit somewhere in Glock's deprivation schema? The universal application of a psychological model is seldom warranted. We are wise, therefore, to refine our thinking by examining additional material that helps clarify part of the conversion process.

The Relief Effect and Group Process

The hypothesis of a *relief effect* has been offered by Marc Galanter (1989) to account for the "biologically grounded motivation, or instinctive drive" by which a person joins and stays in a "charismatic religious group" (various NRMs). This hypothesis is tied to the question of the motives and emotional deprivations for religious seekership in combination with the ability of the group to satisfy those needs. He says, "When people become involved in a charismatic group, an inverse relationship exists between their feelings of emotional distress and the degree to which they are affiliated with that group (Galanter, 1989, p. 88)." This means that for such persons, their feeling of being at peace depends on their relationship to the group; and this can vary depending on the frequency, quality, or intimacy of contact with it. For example, Galanter reports that a committed member of Alcoholics Anonymous may typically report feelings of unease after missing a number of meetings.

Among the implications of the relief effect are that the closer one's ties with the group, the greater will be the degree of relief from neurotic distress. Also implied is that the magnitude of relief felt is associated with the belief that this is the only path to Truth, the only source from which relief can be obtained. Consistent with the relief hypothesis, Galanter reports finding that in people who were participating in a Unification Church workshop, those experiencing the greatest personal distress were the most likely to join. Similarly, in a group of people who had remained members of the Divine Light Mission for two years, a decrease in feelings of being nervous and tense was associated with an increase in feelings of cohesiveness toward the group. Overall, it is proposed that the interaction between personal motivations such as the need for "relief" and group factors such as a sense of cohesiveness and shared belief fosters conversion to and maintenance in the group (Barker, 1984; Galanter, 1989).

The Conversion-as-Creativity Analogy

In general terms, the attempt to understand the personal factors that are part of conversion includes the desire to know the mental, cognitive processes involved in the change. Surely, religious converts experience some modification of the way they see the world: "Before I was blind, but now I see"; "Before my belief in God life seemed utterly absurd, but now I see that it is full of meaning and purpose." Daniel Batson et al. (1993) have proposed that the mental processes that are involved in religious conversion are like those that are part of the creative process.

The analogy between conversion and creativity is based first on the notion that our perception of reality is embodied in a cognitive structure of the order of the world. Batson points out that the creative process involves "improvement" (I would say "alteration") of one's cognitive organization. The four steps in the creative process are (1) preparation, in which the person faces a dilemma or problem to be solved with the existing cognitive structure, (2) incubation, when one is unable to solve the problem and stops an active attempt to do so, (3) illumination, insight based on new cognitive reorganization in which the problem is seen in a new way, (4) verification, elaborating and then testing the idea to see how well it works.

According to Batson, a similar sequence of steps is involved in religious experience and personal transformation. He labels these (1) existential crisis, in which a person grapples with basic issues of the meaning of his or her life, (2) self-surrender, trying and failing to resolve those issues within the framework of one's current life perspective or world view, (3) new vision, in which the issues are resolved by being seen through the eyes of the new belief system, (4) new life, resulting in a change in behavior and a new way of negotiating one's way through life.

Religious conversion, understood in this way, is thought to constitute a stepwise tension reduction process for which the outcome is personal transformation rooted in a new cognitive structure created in order to resolve an existential crisis. To me, this sounds close to saying that conversion involves the adoption of a better fitting life schema with the sense of satisfaction and closure that would accompany it (Brown & Cateano, 1992). Some problems with this view, however, are that it is not yet clear whether religion should be considered a schema (Paloutzian & Smith, 1995), and I know of no evidence that religious conversions must be precipitated by an existential crisis. The conversion-creativity parallel is a useful working model because it helps us see some personal aspects of the conversion process that we might otherwise miss. I think of it as a good and helpful analogy (which is how Batson et al. meant it) for what is going on inside the convert's head but not, of course, as a fact. Tests for the robustness of the analogy would make a nice contribution to a future research agenda for the psychology of conversion.

A Systemic Stage Model

Is it possible to consolidate the various bits and pieces of research and theory that describe the conversion process into one coherent, integrated picture? Lewis Rambo (1993) has written the most inclusive attempt at this so far. He calls his approach a "systemic stage model" in contrast to a "sequential stage model" because, in his view, the order of the stages is not universal nor invariant, as it typically is in developmental theory. Rather, the stages might be thought of as simultaneous facets. Each "stage" is used to organize part of the "cluster of theme patterns, and processes operative in religious change" (p. 195). The overall process of conversion occurs across time, but the "stages" occur concurrently and in varying degrees, each in continual interaction with the others. This complex description of the conversion process is summarized in Figure 6.1.

The meaning of each stage in Figure 6.1 (context, crisis, quest, encounter, interaction, commitment, consequences) is apparent by Rambo's carefully selected labels for each stage plus an examination of the types of experiences,

FIGURE 6.1 Rambo's systemic stage model of religious conversion

Stage 1 Context	Stage 2 Crisis	Stage 3 Quest	Stage 4 Encounter
Macrocontext	Nature of crisis	Response style	Advocate
• Systems of access and control	• Intensity	• Active	• Secular attributes
	• Duration	• Passive	• Theory of conversion
Microcontent	• Scope		
• Degree of integration and conflict	• Source: internal/ external	Structural availability	• Inducements to conversion
		• Emotional	
	Catalysts for conversion	• Intellectual	
Contours of context	• Mystical experiences	• Religious	Advocate's strategy
• Culture	• Near-death experience		• Strategic style
• Social		Motivational structures	Diffuse
• Personal	• Illness and healing	• Experience pleasure and avoid pain	Concentrated
• Religious Valence of dimension	• Is that all there is?		• Modes of contact
	• Desire for transcendence	• Conceptual system	Public/ private
	• Altered states of consciousness	• Enhance self-esteem	Personal/ impersonal
Contextual influences	• Protean selfhood	• Establish and maintain relationships	
• Resistance and rejection	• Pathology		Benefits of conversion
• Enclaves	• Apostasy	• Power	• System of meaning
• Paths of conversion	• Externally stimulated crises	• Transcendence	• Emotional gratification
• Congruence			• Techniques for living
• Types of conversion			• Leadership
Traditional transition			• Power
Institutional transition			
Affiliation			Advocate and Convert
Intensification			• Initial response
Apostasy			• Resistance
• Motifs of conversion			• Diffusion of innovation
Intellectual			• Differential motivation and experiences
Mystical			
Experimental			
Affectional			
Revivalism			Missionary adaptations
Coercive			
			Convert adaptations
Normative: proscriptions and prescriptions			

Stage 5 Interaction	Stage 6 Commitment	Stage 7 Consequences
Encapsulation Sphere of Change • Physical • Social • Ideological	Decision making Rituals • Separation • Transition • Incorporation	Personal bias in assessment Nature of consequences • Affective
Relationships • Kinship • Friendship • Leadership • Disciple/teacher	Surrender • Desire • Conflict • "Giving In": relief and liberation • Sustaining surrender	• Intellectual • Ethical • Religious • Social/political Sociocultural and historical consequences of conversion
Rituals— choreography of the soul • Deconstruction • Reconstruction	Testimony: biographical reconstruction integrating personal and community story	Religious landscapes Unintended sociocultural consequences • Nationalism
Rhetoric—systems of interpretation • Attribution • Modes of understanding	Motivational reformulation • Multiple • Malleable • Interactive • Cumulative	• Preservation of the vernacular • Secularization
Roles—reciprocal expectations and conduct • Self and God • Self and others		Psychological consequences • Progression • Regression • Stasis Stories of conversion Theological consequences

Source: Rambo, L. R. *Understanding Religious Conversion,* pp. 168–169. © New Haven, CT: Yale University Press, 1993.

circumstances, events, or behaviors listed under each one. Rambo sees these elements as "interactive and cumulative over time (p. 17)." To illustrate: Like all human activity, conversion must occur in some context (from macro to micro in level of analysis), and this context may change radically or evolve slowly during a person's life. A context may, however, also precipitate a crisis or a quest, or serve as the person's refuge from one. Perhaps feeding these, but perhaps also serving as that which satisfies them, are encounters with advocates for or against conversion, the proposed benefits to be gained from it, and the sort of interaction the person has with the individuals or groups involved, their systems of meaning, and attributions and expectations about self and God. These interactions and encounters can of course modify the crisis, quest, and context as well as be outgrowths of them. Both responding to and adding to each of the above are the person's commitment (both public and private acts declaring such, plus the internal sense of motivation and surrender that may accompany it) and the consequences (psychological, behavioral, and social) of it. The complexity of this model is apparent when one tries to picture the intricate web of possibilities for how its elements can be knit together.

From his model, Rambo draws an interesting conclusion: It may be impossible to discover what a "pure" conversion is; "conversion is malleable." For him, this means that the debates about "either/or" assertions about conversion are inadequate; "debates about whether conversion is sudden or gradual, partial or total, internal or external, and the like, can be resolved by acknowledging a spectrum of possibilities (p. 170)." The research hypotheses that can potentially be derived from it are many.

Choice and the Cause of Conversion

Of the many points that can be drawn from the above overviews of aspects of the conversion process, I wish to focus on one that I consider fundamental: the question of choice.

The traditional views, based on categories such as sudden and gradual, differ from the more recent process models. Although both models include psychological and social factors, the older religious conversion models emphasize the psychological process operating in the individual. The question is "What factors work inside the person to stimulate an interest in religion?" Questions of this sort led to the breakdown of psychological processes for different conversion types. In contrast, the broader process models add a heavy emphasis on social and situational forces. The question in its extreme form is, "How do religions gain control over their members?" These different emphases reflect the differences in the fundamental style of the disciplines from which they emerged, psychology and sociology, respectively. The interactionist view is that any conversion is due to a combination of personal and social forces. This distinction highlights the question of when social and psychological determinants end and personal choice begins. To what extent is your changing to a new belief or group a result of your own choice rather than a result of forces beyond your control? Active conversion requires choosing the change for oneself, independent of other psychological or social forces. This point of view raises questions about the usefulness of tactics, whether used by advocates of an old religion or a new one, that step over the bounds and violate the fundamental freedom of choice.

Psychological Issues in Conversion (chap 9)

Religion as Crutch: The Psychopathology Issue

One issue that persists concerns the relationship between psychological disturbance and religious conversion. Put more bluntly, this issue comes in the following two forms:

A. Must you be crazy to convert?
B. Does conversion make you crazy?

If you have strong religious beliefs you will naturally tend to reject information which you think might involve negative connotations toward your conversion experience or belief system. For example, when a researcher reports findings which suggest that converts score higher on an hysteria scale (Spellman, Baskett, & Byrne, 1971), you feel a little irritated and maybe defensive because the psychologist appears to be "putting down" your faith. Analogously, someone with antireligious biases who hears evidence of positive consequences of religious conversion may feel equally threatened. Either way, our personal biases interfere with and color our interpretation of data.

These underlying biases even color our definition of the concept. Conversion has been defined by some as a personally integrative process. This implies that a person has to be "disintegrated" (i.e., psychologically disturbed) before being a candidate for conversion. This kind of reasoning does not help us to understand conversion because it includes the answer to the psychopathology question in the very definition of conversion. Definitions do not answer research questions.

One thing that complicates our view of the psychopathology issue, however, is that some converts say things that fit perfectly with proposition "A" above. The person who reports having suffered from intense existential anxiety and found fulfillment through religious belief, or the one who boasts of having suffered from pathological guilt (in contrast to healthy, growth-inducing guilt) that was removed via conversion, are examples of this. Personal difficulty is a factor in some conversions.

Recent studies of converts support this idea. In one study, 71 percent of the members of the NRM Divine Light Mission reported the presence of symptoms on a Psychological Distress Scale (e.g., anxiety, depression, suicidal ideation, anomie, hearing voices, emotional maladaption) "right before joining" the group (Galanter, 1989). This study is not definitive, however, because it is based only on current NRM members' memories of their pre-NRM experience. The study had no control group and no pre-NRM scores on the distress scale. A report by a participant observer in a San Francisco Satanic church described members as having life histories high in anxiety, sadomasochism, and neuroticism (Moody, 1974). A well-designed study of converts to four different religions (Jewish, Catholic, Baha'i, and Hare Krishna) found that compared to nonconverts, converts had more childhood trauma, unhappier adolescence, and more personal stress during the two years preceding conversion (Ullman, 1982).

Variable findings have emerged on this issue from other studies of conversion to traditional religions. Spellman et al. (1971) found that sudden converts scored higher than others on the hysteria scale of the Minnesota Multiphasic Personality Inventory (MMPI), an extensive personality inventory designed to measure clinical disorders. Sudden converts generally score higher on measures of authoritarianism (Adorno, Frenkel-Brunswik, Levinson, & Sanford, 1950) and dogmatism (Rokeach, 1960). Other reviewers (Kildahl, 1965; Tisdale, 1980) report that these relationships are equivocal. In general, there appears to be some relation between conversion and pathology, but the relationships are slight and depend upon other factors. The research question posed by this is "Under what conditions are particular states of mental health and pathology relevant for conversion?"

The Role of Emotions

This issue concerns the role that feelings play in the conversion process. People often describe their conversions in very experiential language. Some religious groups, including traditional churches and NRMs, place great emphasis on emotion-inducing ritual and public display of intense feelings through crying, shouting, or fainting. Sometimes the impression is given that this is the one mark of genuine conversion. So in one sense, the question of emotions simply asks whether conversion includes a conscious awareness of intense feelings as a necessary part of the process.

In a different sense, the role-of-emotions issue is an extension of the psychopathology issue. That is, psychological disturbance has been classically understood to involve "emotional problems." It is inferred by some that emotional disturbance leads one toward conversion, and conversion experience is evidence that emotional factors were involved.

Psychological theory is pertinent to this question. For example, a psycho-analytic view stresses the role of unconscious emotional conflict. These unconscious conflicts incubate until they are resolved at the moment of sudden conversion. In contrast, the cognitive need theory of conversion deemphasizes feelings, unconscious or conscious, and places its emphasis on the strain toward perceived pattern, purpose, and wholeness of life. Scobie (1975) summarizes the current views by proposing that emotional factors are more important in sudden conversion, and that cognitive factors are more important in gradual conversion.

3. The Convertible-Type Issue

Is there a special type of personality that we should refer to as the "preconvert"? Is there something peculiar about converts' character structure that makes them especially prone to experience dramatic religious changes? If so, is this a sign of personal strength or personal weakness on their part? (Note that if you accept the reality of the hypothetical "convertible personality," your presuppositions about it shed light back on your opinions about the psychopathology issue.)

Though no one has conclusively demonstrated the existence of a convertible type, at a common-sense level the idea is hard to dismiss. We know that many people can be bombarded with the same message or propaganda, yet only some of them convert. The inference follows that because they receive similar messages in similar circumstances, the reason some convert and others don't must be due to their personality differences.

A special version of this issue concerns the relation between personality and the tendency to gravitate toward certain species of doctrine. For example, do people who convert to a Satanic church possess a unique character structure (basically neurotic, with sexual and hostile motives) that makes them especially open to the teachings and practices of Satanism? Or, are all preconverts fundamentally the same, the only difference being the doctrine or group they happen to adopt due to chance circumstances?

Various hypotheses have been offered to account for the so-called preconvert. The writings of Adler (1930) and Hoffer (1951) suggest that the preconvert has a need to gain access to some great power. This need is satisfied via conversion, through which one gains access to the Almighty. According to this view the need for power is a sign of inner weakness. Trying to overcome this weakness is what motivates a person toward conversion.

Other variations of this theme include the ideas that preconverts suffer from over-dependency, repressed hatred for authority, and existential anxiety. The first two are derivatives of Freudian reasoning; the latter is derived from Frankl's (1963, 1975) ideas. These needs are occasionally said to be unconscious, so that the preconvert is not aware of being a preconvert. There is also some evidence that sudden converts are more suggestible and hypnotizable than others (Burtt & Falkenburg, 1941; Gibbons & de Jarnette, 1972).

The Ripe-Age Issue

A look at the religious groups of our day, both traditional and NRM, gives one the impression that religious conversion is primarily for the young. In traditional churches, for example, heavy emphasis is placed on youth programs designed to either create or rekindle a commitment to the faith. Many readers will be familiar with youth camps, outreach programs, or missionary endeavors designed to do this. The NRMs also believe in the importance of adolescence. The vast majority of people who have joined groups such as the Unification Church and Hare Krishna did so in their teens and early twenties. Proselytizers from these groups know that high school and college campuses are among the most fruitful places for recruiting new members.

Professional opinion is in general agreement with the above observation. Several classic studies reported that the mean age for conversion was in the mid-teens (Argyle & Beit-Hallahmi, 1975). Erik Erikson (1963) proposed that the "identity crisis" occurs during teenage years. Religious conversion is one way to resolve major aspects of such a crisis.

The ripe-age issue interacts with the issues already outlined. If conversion is more likely during adolescence, this could be due to certain personal crises (such as crises of identity, searching for purpose, or emotional changes) that occur during that period. In essence, the mere fact of being adolescent could lead one toward being a preconvert. This may also be due to social psychological factors; for example, youth may have difficulty resisting social pressure imposed upon them by religious groups. However, adolescents are also developing their own capacity for making independent decisions about life. Increased convertibility can therefore occur due to youth realistically evaluating alternatives and making their own choices.

Is this stereotype of conversion as an adolescent reaction valid? Perhaps so, but the stereotype could be a result of other factors. For example, many studies use college students or young adults as subjects. With such samples, statistical loading will necessarily push the mean age down. Also, it is during adolescence and young adulthood that many of life's major decisions are made. Decisions about college, marriage, lifestyle, vocation, and military service are routine during this time of life. It is appropriate for decisions about religion to be made at this time also. Therefore, if religious choices are more likely to be made during adolescence, it could be due to the same processes that mediate other adolescent decisions.

Adolescence is not the only possible ripe age for conversion. The ideas of Jung (1933) and Erikson (1963) suggest that the middle years represent a second phase of religious interest. These authors propose that during middle age people begin to strive for more inner understanding and personal integrity. This in turn sets the stage for asking religious questions, which facilitates conversion. Some research supports this view, reporting the mean age of conversion for some churches to be in the early to mid forties (Scroggs & Douglas, 1976).

Conversion as Attitude Change

It has been argued that faith is an attitude. There is a degree of correspondence between the social psychological concept of attitude and the religious concept of faith (Hill & Bassett, 1992). Attitudes contain elements of thought, feeling, and action tendencies toward the attitude object. For example, if you have a positive attitude toward your church, you possess favorable information about it, you feel positively about it, and your behavior reflects its teachings. These three components of attitude—cognitive, affective, and behavioral—are thought to strain for consistency among themselves. *// Cantwell - Smith*

In an analogous fashion, Lewis (1974) says that faith has a cognitive element (certain knowledge about what is believed), an affective element (positive evaluation and attitude of the heart), and a behavioral element (commitment and expected behavioral outcomes). True faith, he argues, involves all three elements.

This idea concerns us for the following reason: Conversion can be defined as the acquisition of a faith. If faith is an attitude, then conversion is attitude change. The practical implication is that evangelistic efforts can draw upon attitude change principles as a reservoir of tactics. It also follows that everything that social psychologists have come to know about attitudes, including their functions and dynamics, applies to changes in religious belief.

It is important to differentiate between saying that faith is analogous to attitude and saying that faith is *nothing but* an attitude. The former allows for the useful application of attitude change theory to conversion phenomena, while acknowledging that such application may be incomplete. The latter presumes that attitude concepts are the only ones relevant to understanding conversion. Much understanding can be gained by exploiting the attitude analogy, but it is simplistic to assume that conversion is nothing but attitude change. Additional things could be involved. In an analogous way, it is illuminating to draw the parallels between the five dimensions of religious commitment and the concept of attitude (i.e., the belief and knowledge dimensions are cognitive in emphasis; the experience dimension corresponds to the affective component of attitude; practice and effects correspond to the behavioral component of attitude), but such correspondence does not rule out the possibility that other, nonattitude concepts also apply to religion.

If we adopt the faith-attitude analogy, we should add that knowing the functions attitudes serve in an individual's personality would give us a clue to how conversion would likely occur for that person. Katz (1960) showed how attitudes can serve four functions: an attitude can be held because it is ego defensive (i.e., it reduces anxiety), represents one's knowledge, expresses one's values, or adjusts to practical contingencies. Which of these four functions is served by a person's religious attitude would be an indication of the person's psychological motive for conversion. Finally, the function served by the attitude reflects back on the pathology and emotions issues. For example, if faith is held for ego-defensive reasons, then we can infer that high anxiety or unconscious conflict is part of what motivated the person toward religious belief.

Some Recent Social Issues

Two Meanings of "Cult"

Much public attention is periodically given to cults. But the term *cult* is popularly used in two senses and covers a wide range of groups. The first sense in which it is used by some refers to doctrinal belief, that is, any religion whose teachings deviate from the doctrines of orthodox Christian belief is said to be cultic. The emphasis is on what the belief is, not on how the belief is held or what the group's procedures are. By this usage the Church of Jesus Christ of the Latter Day Saints (Mormon) would constitute a cult rather than a church regardless of its status in light of, for example, sect-church theory.

The second meaning of the term, surrounded by frequent controversy, connotes a "destructive cult" and refers to a number of religious groups that are charged by their critics (the "anticultists") to seek to control and radically alter the personalities of their members (Melton, 1986). No abstract definition in this sense is given, but the groups' critics do write lists of characteristics, sometimes more than a dozen, that are said to be found among them. The following factors are often included in such lists.

1. *Charismatic leader.* Life in the group is said to center around a single person who has absolute authority. He or she is the final decision maker whose pronouncements on both policy and ideology are binding upon the followers.

2. *Regulation.* Followers may be taught that complete submission to the will of the leader is necessary. The leader's authority can extend into areas of life that are normally regarded as private, such as sexual behavior, marriage, or freedom of speech and movement.

3. *Separation.* Converts and potential converts may be physically and emotionally separated from tangible or identifiable influences from former life, including family, friends, school, and employment.

4. *Control of resources.* Pressure may be placed upon followers to devote all of their resources to the "Master's" cause. This may include their money, time, vocational or educational skills, etc. In some cases, absolute abandonment of one's resources may be a requirement.

5. *Control of information.* In some groups, the content of the doctrine is not revealed to potential converts until they are "ready," i.e., until they have been with the group for some time and have made some concessions to it.

A note of caution: just because a religious group possesses one of the above factors does not mean the group is a cult. Religious groups vary in how much they display features such as the above. For example, some such features can be identified in monastic orders within mainstream traditions that are not described as being destructive. Also, some churches that hold traditional Christian doctrines are charged by prople who have left them to do many of the same things that "cults" have been accused of (Enroth, 1992). The degree to which a group should be regarded as cultic in this particular connotation of the term is a matter of repeated debate (Barker, 1995).

"Snapping" and Brainwashing

An issue that grows out of the faith-as-attitude issue and charges such as the above concerns the responsibility for conversion. On the one hand, people commonly believe that for you to truly accept a belief system, you must choose the belief for yourself. Your mind cannot be taken over; the belief cannot be forced upon you against your will. If you appear to hold a belief but have never really chosen that belief, people would think that the belief was imposed upon you from the outside. In the latter case, you never truly converted.

On the other hand, some religious groups, traditional and recent, are accused of using power and pressure tactics that raise impressions of brainwashing and thought control (Barker, 1989; Conway & Siegelman 1978; Robbins, 1988; Stoner & Parke, 1977). In response, people begin to fear that a person can be converted against his or her will—kidnapped, permanently altered psychologically, and deployed as an automaton-like recruiter for new susceptible victims (see Figure 6.2); in a word, brainwashed.

A variety of popularized views have been offered as to the possible basis of socially induced conversion. These views differ in the proposed psychological substrate for belief acquisition, but they share the core assumption that conversion is something imposed upon people by social and environmental forces. Sargant's (1957) *Battle for the Mind: A Physiology of Conversion and Brainwashing* represents an older version of this idea. Conway and Siegelman's (1978) *Snapping: America's Epidemic of Sudden Personality Change* is a recent variation of this theme.

Conway and Siegelman (1978), arguing from the point of view of information science, propose that conversion occurs because of information overload. They say that there are hypothetical repositories of information in the brain called holograms. According to this view, conversion occurs when the present holographic state is weakened by repetitive bombardments of conversion propaganda. At the point when information overload is reached, a

Interview with Psychiatrist Who Has Treated Unification Church Members and Ex-members

It is relatively easy to learn to control almost completely the behavior and the thinking, the attitude, the mind, and the destiny of another person. . . .

Their attitude is nonhumanistic, that is to say that the individual and his special world view is not important. There is no particular, real concern for the idiosyncratic, individualistic qualities of the other human being. . . .

The first thing the parents see is when the kids come, they are not the same. They don't quite look at them, the language is different, they don't talk in as complicated vocabulary, they are humorless, basically humorless. . . . From that time on the individual is in the state of thought control. You might say also that I think the emotional and intellectual growth stops at that point. What I am describing is a rapid and catastrophic change of mental states, of mental functioning. On the way in and out of this kind of state there is a high vulnerability to breakdown. . . .

FIGURE 6.2   Interview with a psychiatrist who has treated Unification Church members and ex-members

Source: Sontag, F. *Sun Myung Moon and the Unification Church,* pp. 60–61. Copyright © 1977 by Abindgon Press.

transformation occurs in the hologram and the person "snaps." The "snap" moment is analogous to a catastrophe in natural phenomena. For example, before a wave falls on an ocean's beach, opposing forces (i.e., water moving toward the land and water flowing back toward the ocean) cross each other. As they do this a complex threshold of opposing force is reached. At that point the catastrophe occurs and is visible as a "sudden, drastic breaking of a wave." Thus Conway and Siegelman argue that conversion is a catastrophic transformation of information storage in the brain.

Sargant (1957) proposed that conversion occurs when normal brain function is suspended or distorted through fatigue, confusion, or emotional arousal. Sargant was a psychiatrist familiar with Pavlov's (1927) famous conditioning experiments with dogs. Pavlov observed that dogs are more easily conditioned to perform new responses to conditioned stimuli when they are physically tired, confused, or in conflict situations (such as being trained to respond and not respond to the same stimulus). Analogously, Sargant proposed that when the human brain is tired it is less able to resist new information. When it is in conflict or highly stressed (e.g., emotional), it acquires the new belief (much as Pavlov's dog learned the new response) in order to escape from the conflict.

The central (but now we know, too simplistic) research and conceptual issue here is whether people or situations determine religious choices. What is the relative strength of personal versus social and environmental forces in determining religious belief and behavior? The answer is found in a complex interaction of many such factors. These two simple but popularized notions about what conversion is (a freely chosen response; or something that happens to someone, imposed by outside forces) are the "pure" prototypes of the active, individually motivated conversion, and the passive, socially induced conversion, respectively. And, as is apparent from the discussion of conversion processes earlier in this chapter, this simplistic dichotomy is inadequate to account for the complexity of conversion phenomena.

Immunity and Resistance

Because conversion appeals are designed to persuade, they can be difficult to resist. The question, therefore, arises about the extent to which individuals are immune to conversion appeals. What makes some people more resistant than others to attempts at religious persuasion, and how can people be trained to resist such attempts?

Resistance means to be able to stand firm against your foes rather than be overrun by them. But even the strongest among us occasionally weakens. With reference to conversion, if you are going to believe something, you would prefer to choose it on your own rather than have someone else impose it upon you. The "illusion of immunity" is the belief that one has extra strong powers to resist this influence. It is a paradox that believing you are not susceptible to social pressures can make you more vulnerable to such influence. We are less likely to pay attention to social forces if we think they do not affect us. And when we pay less attention, we have less resistance.

Is "resistance" needed against all conversion appeals? Methods of religious persuasion fall along a dimension from those that rely heavily on social pressure to those that do not. Communicators who do not use social pressure try to persuade others in an open and straightforward manner. The content of the proposed doctrine is made salient, together with the individual's capacity to freely accept or reject it by means of personal choice, without social pressure. In contrast, those who use social pressure reduce the right or power of the individual to freely accept or reject the belief. Such tactics dehumanize potential converts by treating them as objects to be manipulated and violating their capacity for choice. It should be clear, then, that resistance is needed only against pressure appeals. With the straightforward approach there is nothing to resist because the person's freedom to choose is not being violated.

If there is one clear lesson from the past 40 years of research in social psychology, it is this: We are all subject to social influence of some type, whether we are aware of it or not, sometimes far more than we would guess. Keeping this in mind, imagine that people representing a religious belief and group with which you were not familiar tried to convert you. How well do you think you would resist their message and procedures?

Figure 6.3 contains an account of one person's successful resistance. As you read this account, project yourself into the situation and think about how you might have reacted.[3] Also, try to identify specific features of the conversion methods used by the group. Describe how these might affect a willing

---

Being a Personal Account of My Near Conversion to the Moon Cult*

The next day Larry picked me up. His friendly smile helped me to forget some of my fears. When he asked me why I wanted to go to the farm I told him I was always interested in sources of positive energy. I was a little suspicious about his friendliness and figured that he would put less pressure on me if I played along. He nodded and smiled as I talked about what I felt about man's future and what must be done. He agreed very strongly with what I said and told me everyone in "the family," as he called the rest of the church was interested in the same thing. He frequently looked me right in the eyes and smiled as he talked. It seemed like he was sincere and I began to feel confident that I wouldn't be held against my will.

. . . The first thing we did on the bus was a "choo-choo." All the brothers and sisters joined hands and chanted with increasing intensity, "choo-choo-choo Choo-Choo-Choo, CHOO-CHOO-CHOO! YEA! YEA! POWW!!!" The act made us a group, as though in some strange way we had all experienced something important together. The power of the choo-choo frightened me, but it made me feel more comfortable and there was something very relaxing about building up the energy and releasing it . . .

After about six hours of sleep . . . everyone rocketed out of their sleeping bags and into their clothes, shaking hands and asking, "How are you, brother?" "Great! Just Great!" was everyone's response.... We all went out to the field and began singing; hand in hand or with arms around each other we formed a great circle. "Is everybody happy?" cried David, one of the leaders. Yesss!!" screamed the crowd wildly. I believed it and let it flow into me. I felt that if I was in control of myself, there was no reason not to enjoy all this good energy. With all the love flowing around I just wanted to be part of it and help spread it. . . .

After the exercises, discussion groups of 13 were formed. David said it was to enhance appreciation of the seminar but I couldn't help thinking it was designed to increase the pressure to adopt the family's ideas. . . . Kristina (the

---

FIGURE 6.3   Being a personal account of my near conversion to the Moon cult

FIGURE 6.3 *Continued*

---

discussion leader) then asked us, one by one, to discuss our life's goals and direction. All the family members talked about how they hadn't known what they wanted . . . or how to be happy until they joined the family They now had to grow spiritually in this little piece of heaven. I always wanted to take time out from my worldly pursuits to examine what I really wanted to do in life. . . . If only I could believe they weren't being brainwashed I'd stay. . . .

It was then time for dodgeball. . . . We formed two teams and each team got in a large, tight, arm-in-arm circle. We were the Righteous Rockets and were to chant "Blast with love!". . . . We were told that chanting was the most important part. . . . The other team was chanting "Roar with love!" I couldn't understand what was making everyone so fanatical and wild-eyed. I still tried to get involved because I didn't want to stick out. . . . When they gave me slaps on the back, I chanted louder and tried harder. It was great! I chanted for the rest of the games, one and a half hours. It began to ring in my ears. It was release, it was energy, it was power! We were all leaping up and down and throwing our fists with the chant. I lost myself and became part of the group. . . .

We then met in groups and Kristina asked if we had any questions. I told them of my disagreement with [a guest lecturer], and their faces immediately dropped. . . . They seemed disappointed and very concerned. "You have to suspend your views like we all did," said Annie. "They were formed in the evil of the outer world. . . ." They looked so concerned that I knew I wouldn't get anywhere. I told them I saw their point and would keep an open mind. They all lit up with love again and I was again accepted. . . .

On the way to dinner I saw Larry and Kristina. "Who founded your movement?" I asked. They said it was Oni. "What about Sun Moon?" I asked. They denied any connections whatsoever with him. I told them I heard that he bought them their land but they said it was donated by local farmers. Then I knew they were lying. I felt lucky to have known the truth about them before I went. . . .

After dinner Kristina and I walked hand in hand to the Chicken Palace. She said we were going to the initiation of the new members. Everyone inside was cheering and screaming, jumping up and down with linked arms, higher and higher, praising the Heavenly Father. I watched nervously as the tempo quickened and the noise became louder. Was I strong enough to keep from being caught up in it all?

. . . I felt a sense of loss, not for myself, but for all those who were *losing their individuality.* It was frightening. I gathered my things and silently walked out. . . .

*This is an account of a participant observation study done by a student at Stanford University. Adapted from Zimbardo et al. 1977.

Source: Zimbardo, P. G., Ebbesen, E. B., & Maslach, C. *Influencing attitudes and changing behavior* (2nd ed.). Copyright © McGraw Hill Book Company, New York: New York City. Reprinted with permission.

and an unsuspecting recruit and assess the degree to which the subject's freedom of choice is violated, if at all. Finally, identify the process by which this person walked away unconverted.

How was this young man able to resist? The principles of social psychology highlight three factors contributing to his response: (1) he was aware of his lack of immunity; he knew the power of social influence and was on guard against it; (2) he had prior information about the doctrine of the group; (3) he was able to retain a type of perceptual detachment, a capacity for self-observation, which kept his own power to choose salient in his mind. These three factors not only help clarify our understanding of the conversion process; they also help us resist unchosen influences in our own lives.

Deprogramming

The issue of deprogramming is a compound version of the previous two issues. First, can someone be deprogrammed, or "unconverted," through pressure methods? The tactics involved in the stereotype of deprogramming procedures seem to assume so. The techniques may involve such things as kidnapping the person from the group to which he or she has been converted, intensive indoctrination, emotional attacks, religious teaching (in the to-be-converted-back-to beliefs), and possible physical mistreatment. Such procedures can be successful. But on occasion an apparently deprogrammed person escapes and returns to the group.

Second, to what degree and by what means can someone resist deprogramming, and what are its effects? Where does the role of the person's own choice fit in, since freedom of religion is a right in most countries? One would presumably resist deprogramming in the same way one would resist any persuasion influence. Paradoxically, however, this would seem difficult for someone who has been changed through those very methods. The case of a 19-year-old young woman who belonged to the Church of Armageddon illustrates this problem. She was abducted by deprogrammer Ted Patrick (1976) and subjected to 102 hours of intensive reindoctrination, an effort thought to be successful. But she then escaped and went back to the Church of Armageddon. How could this occur? Systematic research on the psychological factors involved in the process of deprogramming and its effects is needed. People who have involuntarily left their group tend to report negative feelings about them (Singer, 1979; Wright, 1987). There is some evidence that voluntarily departing from an NRM does not always leave a negative aftermath. Wright (1984, 1987) interviewed 45 "voluntary defectors" and found that 30 said they felt "wiser for the experience," with 7 reporting feeling angry, duped, or brainwashed, and 8 reporting "other."

This leads to an important methodological point: Those whose data document the negative effects of a religion (typically an NRM or a fundamentalist Christian group) tend to study people who have left, sometimes involuntarily. In contrast, those whose data portray positive effects of a religion, pointing to mental health benefits, tend to study people still participating in the religion. This difference in results, based on different methodologies, has fostered fierce debate among professionals, but this should not be surprising. For reasons of cognitive consistency, people who remain in a religion are more psychologically obligated to praise it, whereas people who are no longer participants in that religion (by means of any process) are more psychologically free to dislike it. Also, it may be true that some people are psychologically harmed by participating in a religious group. Such claims have been made by people who have left NRMs as well as those who have "fallen away" from fundamentalist Christian churches. It is clear that a religious body is not functional for someone who has found it sufficiently unsatisfying to leave it. In contrast, however, it is apparent that not all such participation is nonfunctional, because some participants voluntarily stay in their group because it is functional for them—as is the case with some NRMs as well as those who choose to continue in traditional "mainline" religions. Therefore, when future studies are conducted with more complete research designs including representative subject samples and proper control groups, and, wherever possible, pre/post longitudinal measures of subjects taken before, during, and after their participation in a particular religion, then those conclusions that appear opposite or puzzling will fit together into a larger, coherent framework.

As is evident from the above review of the issues, there has been considerable discussion of the psychological basis for religious change and conversion. Clear resolution of the issues has yet to be done. The next step is for us to focus on the nature of religious experience itself, in the next chapter.

Projects and Questions

1. Test the conversion process models. Do people behave the way that the models predict? Do political activists and religious adherents have similar tensions in their backgrounds?

2. Each conversion type has its own explanation. Theoretically, gradual conversion is more cognitively based. Design an experiment to test whether gradual converts have a greater cognitive need to closure than sudden converts or people socialized into their beliefs.

3. Explore whether different conversion types lead to differences in behaviors that indicate a distinct change in life, e.g., breaking all of one's old "worldly" CDs following religious conversion.

4. Religious defection can be considered as a type of deconversion. Do the conversion type categories carry over to de-conversion? If personal and social factors help maintain conversion, what factors lead someone to become unreligious?

5. Do different ways of becoming religious produce different degrees or types of religious activity with age? In what ways might this depend upon the conversion process involved as well as developmental stage?

6. To what degree can the conversion models and types discussed in this chapter be extended to religions other than those in the Jewish and Christian tradition? What research possibilities spring from this extension?

7. Do the two ways in which the term "cult" is popularly used have any relationship to the distinction between functional and substantive ways of trying to define religion that were discussed in Chapter 1?

8. In what ways are various traditional religions and new religious movements alike and different in the content of their belief systems and the functional properties of how they work as groups and in the lives of individuals?

9. Using the research methodologies discussed in Chapter 3, design two projects using different methods to test whether a prediction found in research on creativity is also found in conversion.

Further Reading

Barker, E. (1984). *The making of a Moonie: Choice or brainwashing?* Oxford: Blackwell.

Barker, E. (1989). *New religious movements: A practical introduction.* London: Her Majesty's Stationery Office.

Galanter, M. (1989). *Cults: Faith, healing, and coercion.* New York: Oxford University Press. *M a . BP 603 C35*

Malony, H. N., & Southard, S. (Eds.). (1992). *Handbook of religious conversion.* Birmingham, AL: Religious Education Press.

Melton, J. G. (1986). *Encyclopedic Handbook of Cults in America.* New York: Garland Publishing.

Rambo, L. R. (1993). *Understanding religious conversion.* New Haven, CT: Yale University Press. *L u BL 639 R 35*

Notes

1. Depending on one's theological point of view, the conversion of Paul (Acts, Ch. 9) could also be considered an instance of a prompted conversion, i.e., prompted directly by Jesus' voice.

2. These generalizations from the theory were more applicable in times past. For example, sect conversions are not necessarily from lower social classes today.

3. Before you say, "I would have told those . . .", remember this: you were not there. You did not face the immediate situation as our young man did. Keep aware that your predicted or desired response to social pressure is not necessarily the same as your actual performance.

7

Experience
(adult)

Religion and Experience

There are two fundamental aspects to a human's life. One of them is intensely individual and private: your own experience. The other is necessarily public: your actions upon which you are judged. Your experiences are available in their pure form only to you; no one else can see them. Your actions, on the other hand, are observable in the public arena and it is those, including your verbal behavior with which you describe your subjective experiences, that others use to decide whether you are crazy or sane, criminal or innocent, religiously genuine or a fake. This chapter is concerned with the first aspect, the relation between religion and experience in the individual. The next chapter concerns religion and action.

Relations between Religion and Experience

Experience: The Bottom Line

In a basic sense, your experience of life is the basis for whatever you consider reality for you. An elementary philosophical analysis reveals that at the end of our logic and our data, what we "know" is what is going on inside our own heads, even though what is going on in our heads includes information from the body that includes feelings. Descartes' classic "I think, therefore, I am" is based on the fundamental notion that at the end of one's efforts to know whether there is any "objective" truth outside oneself, there is, at last and at least, awareness of oneself being aware. Each of us as an individual lives with whatever experience of which we are aware, religious or not.

To illustrate how basic this is, suppose you were defined to be "crazy" by clinical psychologists or psychiatrists because you said that you experienced strange visions: you saw a pink elephant on the wall, saw many other such animals and odd sights, and heard their voices talking to you. Other people do not see or hear these but you do; you are certain of it. Who is to say whether what you see and hear is "really there?" Might it be possible that a pink elephant is indeed there and that you have veridical perceptions, but the other people (who do not see it) do not? Technically, this is possible. However, if you claimed to see a pink elephant and nobody else could see it (whether or not it was "really" there), you are likely to be diagnosed as having a mental disorder because the others say your perception is abnormal. Simply put, your mental status is diagnosed in part by your purported experiences. Each of us navigates through our reality based on our experiences, but nobody can see them but us. For reasons such as this, religious experiences are at once the most important and core aspects to religiousness and the most difficult and ephemeral to study. However, it is well known that the experiences that follow a religious commitment and the mystical or altered states of consciousness that are part of some people's religious lives can be potent.

To extend the above illustration specifically to the area of religion, supposed a friend said to you: "I see God." Because in most theologies God is supposed to be invisible, you might at first not take your friend's remark seriously. But suppose he or she persists in the claim, stating unreservedly that he or she saw God. Further, suppose your friend said that God's audible voice told him or her to drop out of college and pursue life as a poor servant in a poverty stricken country in which foreigners have a high rate of attracting infectious diseases. How do you interpret your friend's claim of a vision and conversation with God? The dilemma you are faced with is logically identical to the above case of seeing the pink elephant. Sometimes people who have claimed too loudly to have seen God and heard God's audible voice have been diagnosed as having mental diseases (Chapter 9).

How prevalent are religious experiences? Some statistical summaries of telephone surveys appear in Table 6.1, at the beginning of the last chapter. In addition, Greeley (1974) reports that mystical experiences are reported to have occurred in the lives of up to 35 percent of Americans.

One source of data comes from the National Opinion Research Center (NORC). The NORC General Social Survey (1988) asked people how often they had different experiences. Among the experiences to which the subjects could respond were: "Felt as though you were really in touch with someone who had died" and "Felt as though you were very close to a powerful, spiritual force that seemed to lift you out of yourself." Thirty-nine percent of the people said that they felt contact with the dead. Thirty-two percent claimed to have felt a powerful, spiritual force that seemed to lift them out of themselves. These percentages approximate those of Greeley, which were collected earlier and by a different method. Importantly, people who were strongly religious were more likely to have felt a spiritual force than people who were not very religious, and Protestants were more likely to claim such an experience than Catholics, Jews, or those whose religion was "none."

Similarly, Gallup and Newport (1990) asked the question "Have you ever been aware of, or influenced by, a presence or a power—whether you call it God or not—which is different from your everyday self?" Sixty percent of those who are very religious report feeling the presence of such a power, whereas 39 percent of the not very religious report that experience. These different percentages mean that either religious and nonreligious people have such experiences at different rates, or that they both have experiences but that the religious subjects interpret them in religious terms and the nonreligious people do not. This issue is addressed later in this chapter.

In academic psychology, the study of religious experience is among the oldest topics in the discipline. Indeed, both the theoretical and interpretive work of William James (1902) and the statistical study by Edwin Starbuck (1899) were efforts to understand the causes and consequences of religious experience (Chapter 2). And as Glock would remind us, experience is one of the dimensions of religiousness of which we must take account.

2. *Ordinary and Extraordinary Experience*

What forms do religious experiences come in? They differ along a number of dimensions including the degree to which they are ordinary versus unusual, frequent versus infrequent, prebelief versus postbelief, mystical versus earthly, and so on.

An account of ordinary religious experience is provided by Michael Donahue for Roman Catholics (Donahue, 1995). He says that, for example, even with all the diversity within the Catholic Church, a Catholic is a Catholic. It is what one is. Thus, within the boundaries of Catholicism people may express a wide range of opinion over issues such as whether women should be priests, birth control, abortion, and church hierarchy, but there is neverthe-less an impression of community. This sense of community is strong enough so that, he says, "when Protestants have disputes over belief or practice, their tendency is to schism; Catholics, apparently, prefer to stay together and fight." They are bound together by certain defining features of the Catholic experi-ence, such as the Eucharist, a unique line of authority and church hierarchy, the Mass, and a profound and unique history. Other experiences that might be seen in the ordinary or "common sense" category are the experience of the presence of God during prayer (Brown, 1994), the different images of God and similar experiences one has during different phases of development (Tammi-nen, 1991, 1994; Tamminen & Nurmi, 1995), the "fortress mentality" of being sure that your approach is the only correct one and that the believers must therefore be separate and insulated from the world (Hammond & Hunter, 1984), the sense of awe that accompanies thinking about God as infinite, and the feeling of meaning and sense of values that may come from a religious commitment (Paloutzian, 1981).

More unusual, extraordinary experiences are hard to define. They have an ineffable quality, sometimes termed noetic, and tend to be potent and memo-rable. They are described as having an immediacy and mystical quality that is not reducible. They are said to be numinous (providing an awesome and fascinating sense of the presence of the holy) and nonrepresentational, in the sense that whatever is seen in them is not understood to be a mental picture or visual representation of something in the outside world. They do not require a validity check with the outside world. They are, instead, their own source of validity. They may be paradoxical in the sense that whatever is experienced in them does not have to follow the rules of ordinary logic.

What are the causes and the consequences of experiences of the ordinary and the extraordinary type, and what do they do for or to those people who have them? In trying to answer this, I find it valuable to keep in mind that there are several ways in which religion and experience may be related to each other. First, religiousness may lead to experience, either to a unique, singular experience or in a more general way of experiencing life. In other words, precisely because someone is (or becomes) religious, he or she may experience life in a different way. In fact, a promise of a different experience of life is offered by most religions: "I am come that they might have life, and that they might have it more abundantly (John 10:10)." In this case, a new experience functions as a confirmation of one's faith. Second, one or more experiences may lead to religion or to changes in the way one approaches the task of being religious. For example, profound sorrow over a negative life event (e.g., the death of a daughter) may prompt the parents to seek a conscious awareness of a supreme being in search of an answer to the question, Why? In this case, the negative life experience functions as a stimulus to personal faith. Third, the relation between religion and experience can be one of reciprocal determinism; each causes the other in an interactive manner. Here the experience is both a mediator of one's personal faith, an avenue for its expression, as well as an event to be interpreted through the eyes of that faith. Fourth, one's personal faith and experience may both be mutually determined by some other factor. For example, upon seeing the birth of one's child, a person may both express a devotion to God and feel a sense of awe attributed to God.

Therefore, I find it useful to talk about the relation between religion and experience, rather than about "religious experience." It remains for us to explore the research concerning the kinds of life experiences that flow from religiousness, the nature of religious experience, and the theory and research on how they occur and are interpreted.

Experiential Responses to Religion

Religion as experienced, or the human experiential needs met by religion, are illustrated in the above discussion of Donahue's description of ordinary life within Catholicism. Similar points can be made regarding the experience of religion in other groups and in everyday life. For example, much of the experience that is a consequence of religiousness occurs in connection with groups. They have the ability to satisfy true psychological needs of people, such as needs for belonging, love, support, and interpersonal closeness and attachment. Being part of a group can and does satisfy such needs. Furthermore, participation in a group in which people feel needed fosters their sense of belonging, making the group and its activities more important to them. For example, Wicker (1969a, 1971) studied Methodist congregations and found that people in smaller churches (approximately 300 members), in which there would be more need for their participation, felt a greater sense of belonging to the group and valued the church's activities more than people in larger churches (approximately 1,600 members). In his studies of youth turning to Eastern religions, Cox (1977) reports that one of the most common motives of the participants was a desire to experience simple friendship and belonging.

l. *Phenomenological Descriptions of Becoming Religious*

A phenomenological approach is in part an attempt to gain a complete verbal account of the conscious experience under study. Oates (1973) has offered several phenomenological descriptions of how religious conversion is experienced by the individual. Each of these, he says, adds to our total picture of that experience. The "word-pictures" of the experience which he lists include rapid growth, the unification of a divided self, a change of direction, and an act of surrender.

a. *Rapid Growth*

The description of conversion as rapid growth suggests a speeding up of a natural process by some intervening event that would greatly increase the rate of normal development. An analogy from the field of biology is that we can accelerate the rate of growth of plants by artificially controlling such things as light, temperature, humidity, and nutrients. Or in the case of education, we can increase a person's competence in a field through classroom instruction whereas it might take the person much longer to master the subject on his or her own. Thought of in this way, conversion means that a person "matures quickly." It is partly due to this characterization that many people have considered conversion to be primarily an adolescent phenomenon. If a newly religious youth claims to have "found himself," the assumption is that he would have "found himself" later in time anyway. Accepting a new religion merely made it occur sooner.

b. *Unification of a Divided Self*

Another way that conversion is described is that it unifies, or makes into one, a previously divided self. Before accepting the new faith, various parts of the personality are thought to be in conflict with each other. Integration of the personality into a consistent whole is lacking. There are divided loyalties, as in the case of teenagers who desire to be loyal to both parents and peers. The teenager may experience this conflict of loyalties as a lack of personal integration, a lack of a sense of unity. Related to this, the youth may not have a single direction or center of life. However, the religious commitment leads to an experience of acquiring a central focus for life. With the basic commitment of life settled, the person may experience the sense of unity that was absent before. The conflicts between divided loyalties may become minimized because these loyalties are now subservient to the higher commitment to God as the superordinate, overriding, guiding principle of life.

A Change of Direction

People who accept a religion sometimes describe it as a change of direction. The analogy is of a person traveling on a road, deciding that it is the wrong road, and changing directions in order to go down the right road. Thought of in this way, religious change means becoming dissatisfied with one's direction, and turning around and heading toward God. Oates points out that some Biblical terms for conversion experience literally mean a "wheeling about," a U-turn in life.

An Act of Surrender

Accepting a faith is also described as an act of surrender. The picture is one of "giving in" after having put up a fight. This may involve a sense of relief now that the person knows the "fight" is over. This picture connotes a sense of release and relief. It includes being submissive to the divine will rather than one's own, implicit confession or acknowledgment of one's prior opposition, and risking and giving up one's own self in identifying with God or some other object of worship.

The above descriptions of religiousness are illustrations of the types of accounts that emerge using the phenomenological method. They are useful as post-hoc attempts to describe a past experience, and they may also be descriptions of the person's current "religion-as-experienced". In other words, the person may now feel unified, surrendered, complete, and on the right path. But such descriptive accounts, nevertheless, are always one step away from the actual experience. Perhaps a half-step closer is direct narrative accounts of current religious life by people who attribute their experience to their personal faith. Examine the following brief excerpts from two people's way of describing their religious experience of life (James, 1902):

   a. I have the sense of a presence, strong, and at the same time soothing, which hovers over me. Sometimes it seems to enwrap me with sustaining arms.
   b. God surrounds me like the physical atmosphere. He is closer to me than my own breath. In him literally I live and move and have my being.

Somehow the summary descriptions miss the excitement and vividness, the subjective reality, of the first hand experience. Nevertheless, having these first hand accounts and the summary word-pictures of the experience of religion enables us to develop a more complete conceptualization of the experience than would otherwise be possible. Then, empirical and quantitative methods allow us to explore different types of questions about it.

2. Conversion, Values, and Purpose in Life

One of the most important things religious people say about how their life feels after coming to belief is that the experience gave them a sense of meaning or purpose in life. Changes in the relative value placed on life's alternatives are also commonly reported. The development of tests to measure purpose in life and values has made the study of their relationships to conversion, religious orientation, and other processes feasible. Before discussing research on purpose in life as it relates to religiousness and specific values, it is necessary to describe the Purpose in Life Test and the Value Survey.

a. Measuring Purpose in Life

The concept of "purpose in life" or "meaning in life" is a nebulous one. It is difficult to describe with any degree of precision. We intuitively understand statements such as "my life has no meaning" or "life is full of meaning, " but it is difficult to be objective about what is meant by them. The concept of meaning connotes significance and importance. Thus, the idea of a "life full of meaning" includes the notion that life is significant for something, that there is an important reason for it, and that there is a purpose behind it.

One wonders whether psychologists can objectively measure such a nebulous concept. Crumbaugh and Maholick (1969) developed a Purpose in Life Test based upon the concepts of existential psychiatrist Viktor Frankl (1963). According to this test, a life full of meaning is one which seems exciting, worthwhile, and satisfying. A person with a high sense of meaning has relatively clear goals, sees reasons for existence, sees himself or herself as responsible, is prepared to die, and perceives life as a mission. A person with a low sense of meaning is just the opposite. Low purpose in life is said to represent a frustrated "will to meaning" (Frankl, 1963, 1975). The psychological state associated with this is called existential anxiety or an existential vacuum.

The Purpose in Life Test consists of twenty items, each scored from 1 to 7; the total scores can range from a low of 20 to a high of 140. The higher the score, the greater the sense of meaning. The lower the score, the greater the existential vacuum. Crumbaugh (1968) reports that psychiatric populations, including alcoholics, outpatient and hospitalized neurotics, schizophrenics and other psychotics, tend to score in the 90's and 80's on the Purpose in Life Test. Groups of college undergraduates tend to average between 100 and 109. An average score above 113 or so is considered to be relatively high, while a score of 120 is very high on this test.

b. The Value Survey

Milton Rokeach (1973) developed the Value Survey in order to assess the relative importance of different values as guiding principles in people's lives.

It consists of two parts: a list of 18 terminal values, and a list of 18 instrumental values. Rokeach conceives of the terminal values as end states toward which people strive. The instrumental values are thought of as the means to those end states.

Below are 18 terminal values of the Value Survey. You can take this survey by rank ordering the values according to their degree of importance to you as guiding principles in your life. Before you rank order the values, look over the entire list. Then place a "1" by the value that is most important in your own life, a "2" by the one that is next most important, and so on, down to 18 by the value that is the least important.

A comfortable life (a prosperous life) _____
An exciting life (a stimulating active life) _____
A sense of accomplishment (lasting contribution) _____
A world at peace (free of war and conflict) _____
A world of beauty (beauty of nature and the arts) _____
Equality (brotherhood, equal opportunity for all) _____
Family security (taking care of loved ones) _____
Freedom (independence, free choice) _____
Happiness (contentedness) _____
Inner harmony (freedom from inner conflict) _____
Mature love (sexual and spiritual intimacy) _____
National security (protection from attack) _____
Pleasure (an enjoyable, leisurely life) _____
Salvation (saved, eternal life) _____
Self-respect (self-esteem) _____
Social recognition (respect, admiration) _____
True friendship (close companionship) _____
Wisdom (a mature understanding of life) _____

Purpose in Life as Related to Values

How do people's value preferences relate to their sense of purpose in life? Do people who consider certain values more important have a greater sense of meaning in life than others? I have asked my students to guess which values would predict high purpose in life. Their responses have frequently included the values of a sense of accomplishment, freedom, mature love, and inner harmony as good predictors of high purpose.

Crandall and Rasmussen (1975) gave college students the Purpose in Life Test and the Value Survey and then assessed the relationship between purpose in life and the rank order of each terminal value. They discovered that of the 18 terminal values, only four of them were significantly related to purpose in life. These were the values of pleasure, excitement, comfort, and salvation. Only one of these was positively related to sense of purpose. People who ranked salvation high tended to have higher scores on the Purpose in Life Test than people who ranked it low. The other three values, pleasure, excitement, and comfort, all were negatively related to sense of purpose. People who ranked them high tended to have low purpose in life scores, and people who ranked them low had higher purpose in life scores.

These findings offer a commentary on a materialistic philosophy of life. Taken as a cluster, the values of pleasure, excitement, and comfort can be thought of as materialistic values. The values of comfort and excitement are ranked first and second by Americans (Rokeach, 1973) and can be considered part of the mainline American values, since part of the structure of the American economy rests upon production, distribution of goods, and striving for enjoyment, leisure, stimulation, activity, and prosperity. People who strive directly for these things apparently miss a sense of meaning that comes with more transcendental or spiritual values.

These data relate to the topic of how religion predicts personal experience insofar as a high rank ordering of the value of salvation may be one indicator of a religious conversion. People who place high value on salvation probably have experienced religious conversion of some type. Rokeach (1973) reports that salvation is a distinctly Christian value. Other groups, religious and nonreligious, rank it nearly last. In unpublished research (Paloutzian, 1976) the Value Survey was given to a group of known converts and a group of known nonconverts. As predicted, the converts ranked salvation very high, and the nonconverts ranked it very low. Taken together, these results support the hypothesis that people who experience religious conversion have a greater sense of meaning in life than people who do not experience conversion (Paloutzian, Jackson, & Crandall, 1978; Soderstrom & Wright, 1977).

The Experience of Purpose in Life

A question that stems from the association between valuing salvation, conversion, and purpose in life concerns what happens over time following the initial religious commitment. Does the new believer's sense of meaning change immediately or is the change gradual? Does accepting a new belief lead to a stable or to a fluctuating sense of purpose?

I was able to conduct a natural experiment pertinent to the above questions (Paloutzian, 1981). Purpose in Life scores and Value Survey data were collected from Christian believers who had made their religious commitment only five days earlier. Scores were also obtained from two groups of nonbelievers plus people who had become believers within the previous one month, six months, and six months or longer. The results showing purpose in life as a function of time from the initial commitment are summarized in Figure 7.1.

The data indicate that purpose in life changes over time following conversion. For the nonreligious groups, those answering "no" to being a believer averaged 101.4; the "not sure" group averaged 107.8. For the believer groups,

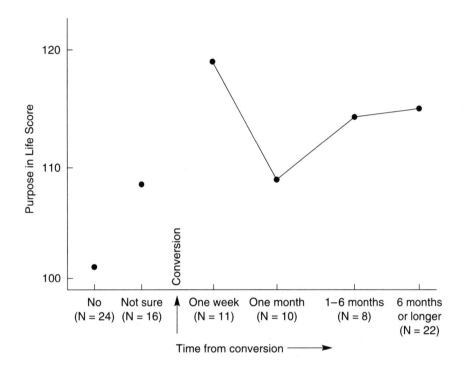

FIGURE 7.1 Purpose in life scores as a function of time from conversion (N = number of subjects in that group)

Source: Paloutzian, R. F. (1981). Purpose in life and value changes following conversion. *Journal of Personality and Social Psychology, 41,* 1153–1160. Copyright © 1981 by the American Psychological Association. Used with permission.

the mean purpose in life scores are: for the one-week group, a sharp rise up to 118.8; for the one-month group, a sharp decline down to 108.6; for the one-to-six-month group, a gradual incline back up to 114.9; and for the six-months-and-longer group, a leveling off at 114.7. Data analysis indicated that the obtained pattern of results is nonchance, as assessed by standard statistical tests. Therefore, we conclude that the graph reflects a trend that probably exists in the population.

Additional analyses of the data revealed that, when lumped together into one large group, the believers scored significantly higher on purpose in life than the nonbelievers. Also, the one-to-six-month and six-month-and-longer believer groups had significantly higher scores than the nonbeliever group. In general, the conclusion is that the sense of meaning in life is unstable following conversion. It tends to fluctuate by going up, then down, and then back up.

Results for the value data indicated that, when values were simply rated according to the degree to which they were guiding principles in people's lives, all 36 values (18 terminal values and 18 instrumental values) were positively associated with sense of meaning. This makes intuitive sense. I would expect people who value things more to sense a greater degree of purpose. When analyzed according to the relative weight assigned to different values, however, certain values received relatively more weight than others for people high versus low in purpose in life. The only terminal value given more relative weight (i.e., ranked significantly higher) by subjects who were high in purpose in life was the value of salvation. In contrast, the four values that were given more relative weight by people who were low in purpose in life were the terminal values of comfort, happiness, freedom, and love. As the importance placed on these latter values went up, the sense of meaning went down. On the whole, these findings replicate those of Crandall and Rasmussen (1975) and indicate that a pleasure oriented lifestyle does not accord with a concern for meaning. The results suggest that the religious believers in this study, who are more likely to espouse a transcendental value such as salvation, gain a heightened sense of purpose as a byproduct.

Additional results showed that believers and nonbelievers differed in other ways. Most important was fear of death. Believers showed a marked decrease in fear of death over the first six months following conversion. This finding is consistent with previous research (Kalish, 1963).

At this point let us question the generality of the relationship between being committed to a religious faith and experiencing purpose in life. Would the effects obtained in this study of conversion to traditional religion also be found in conversion to NRMs? Interviews of Unification Church converts indicate that at least some new members feel that their lives have taken on new purpose (Barker, 1984; Sontag, 1977). One wonders whether different ways of being religious, or belief in diverse religions, produce similar effects in perceived meaning. Does it have to be commitment to a life-encompassing religious system or world view, or will any major change (e.g., getting married) have the same psychological effects? Empirical research from other religious groups on these questions has yet to be done.

Finally, what social psychological processes might be operative to account for the findings that religiously committed persons score higher on measures of meaning? One explanation for this relationship assumes that the life of the religious individual is in fact more purposeful than that of his or her nonreligious counterpart. Another explanation, a uniquely psychological one, draws upon the notion that religiousness is like an attitude (Hill, 1994; Hill & Bassett, 1992). Attitudes are said to consist of three components: cognitive, affective or evaluative, and behavioral. These three elements strain for consistency among themselves, and the person's cognitive system tries to avoid any dissonance that might result from inconsistency. One implication of this is that if a person performs a behavior (especially publicly) or makes a public commitment to believe something, afterwards that person is not too psychologically free to do or believe the opposite. It is not easy, on psychological grounds, to reverse what one has done because the strain for a person to continue to be consistent with oneself, to move forward on the path one has already chosen, is strong. Rather, the person must find psychological ways to confirm the decision, and an excellent way to do so is to feel a sense of purpose as a consequence. That would be psychically easy and would feel very self-assuring. This notion, based on cognitive dissonance theory, is an intellectual predecessor to attribution theory (discussed below), which is one idea used to explain how people assign religious meaning to unusual states of consciousness.

Religious and Mystical Experience

It was noted at the beginning of this chapter that vivid, unusual religious experiences are part of the lives of many religious people. Our present task is to try to understand the nature of such experiences, the theories available to explain them, why they are interpreted the way they are, and the circumstances that make them more likely.

The Common Core Thesis and the Problem of Language

The most basic question is whether the experiences that people have are the same or different from each other. Compare the following verbatim account of religious experience with that in Figure 7.2 and decide whether you think that they are, in their essence, the same.

> *After being awakened one night, one man said, "I then turned . . . to go to sleep again, and immediately felt a consciousness of a presence in the room, and singular to state, it was not the consciousness of a live person, but of a spiritual presence. . . . I do not know how to better describe my sensations than by simply stating that I felt a consciousness of a spiritual presence . . . I felt . . . a strong feeling of superstitious dread, as if something strange and fearful were about to happen" (James, 1902).*

People describe their religious or mystical experience in different terms, either in language unique to their religion or in nonreligious language if they claim none. The common core thesis is the idea that the central essence of such experiences is the same, and that their different descriptions are due to the particular interpretations imposed on them through the various religious

The highest experiences that I have had of God's presence have been rare and brief—flashes of consciousness which have compelled me to exclaim with surprise—God is here!—or conditions of exaltation and insight, less intense, and only gradually passing away. I have severely questioned the worth of these moments. To no person have I named them, lest I should be building my life and work on mere phantasies of the brain. But I find that, after every questioning and test, they stand out today as the most real experiences of my life, and experiences which have explained and justified and unified all past experiences and present growth.

FIGURE 7.2   Sample Item from the Religious Experience Episodes Measure

Source: From Hood, 1970, and the REEM. Reprinted by permission.

traditions. Thus, for example, a sensation of being at one with the universe upon seeing a sunset and the vision of an angel share the same core properties but are given different meanings, one religious and one not, due to the interpretive set of the person. A variant of this idea is that the differences in reports of experiences are due to the language the person has available to describe an otherwise indescribable experience. Because a person can use only the words available to him or her, a religious believer will "filter" the experience through a religious lens and see it in those terms, whereas a nonreligious person will do the same thing but through the medium of nonreligious language. Do the available theories of religious experience shed any light on issues such as these?

The other thesis, complementary to the common core thesis, is the constructivist thesis. This is the notion that for an experience to occur at all it must be mediated by language or learning of some kind. No "pure" experience exists that is not constructed by the language or concepts which create it and through which it is seen (Proudfoot, 1985). In extreme form this would mean that the language, tradition, and concepts through which an experience is interpreted themselves constitute the experience, because an experience has to be described by some kind of language in order to be recognized. On the face of it, it appears that the constructivist thesis is in conflict with the common core thesis. Is it? A sketch of the theories of religious experience and a survey of some of the factors that facilitate it may help us find out.

2. *Theories of Religious Experience*

Each of the three theories presented below is concerned with a successively wider question about the psychological mechanisms of religious experience.

The notion that one's cognitive schemas determine how an experience is perceived focuses on the most immediate cause of the experience, the mental structures that are already inside the mind of the experiencing person. The view that is next widest in scope of explanation is attribution theory; in order to explain how an experience is perceived one looks outside the person to the social context. Even more global in its domain of explanation is attachment theory; the questions for which it seems to be suited are the more general patterns or tendencies to experience religion a certain way. The theories seem complementary; each one focuses on a different question about the nature of religious experience.

Religion-as-Schema

An important, recent way of explaining what mental processes are involved in religious experience invokes the concept of schema from cognitive psychology and social cognition (McCallister, 1995; McIntosh, 1995). A schema is a cognitive structure of knowledge that is organized and based on past experience. It is through a schema that events are interpreted, that their meaning and significance are assessed in light of pre-existing knowledge. For example, the schemas of an Orthodox Jew and a Christian are undoubtedly different regarding the meaning of some Messianic passages in the Hebrew Bible, and they therefore interpret the claim of Jesus as Messiah quite differently.

Different types of schemas can be identified and applied to religion and the interpretation of religious experience. A schematic *knowledge structure* exists for the organization of information. A *script* is a schema containing procedural knowledge, the sequence of steps for doing something such as how to order a meal at a restaurant. A *story grammar* refers to the basic or "deep" structure underlying the description of a human event. *Plans* are schemas that are generalized abstracted rules for how to approach solving a problem.

As applied to religion, it would be too sweeping a use of the schema concept to call religion-in-general a schema (Paloutzian & Smith, 1995); but examples of specific religious knowledge structures would include a Mormon schema, an Orthodox Jewish schema, an Evangelical Christian schema, and a Roman Catholic schema. Each of these contains its own body of information, traditions, some unique sacred writings, and interpretations that are organized into a schema and that are the filter through which other information or events are interpreted. In other words, each of these religions has its own organization of knowledge which serves as the basis for interpretation of the world.

Each religion also has different scripts. For example, the procedures for what to do at a Catholic Mass differ from the script for the ritual hand washing at a Sabbath evening meal. Each religion also has a different story grammar that underlies its own main story of how God deals with people. The deep structure of the story line of the Evangelicals with their singular emphasis on the resurrection of Jesus differs from the deep structure of the story line of the

Catholics with their emphasis on the Tradition of the Church. Finally, the notion of schema as plans, or generalized approaches to problem solving, would differ for different religions. For example, they may differ in the extent to which they encourage people to look first for a "vertical" versus a "horizontal" resource for solving the problem. The schema of those whose religion teaches faith healing might prompt them only to pray to God and to avoid medical intervention, with the belief that the disorder will, of necessity, be cured. In contrast, the schemas of other people may prompt them to first seek the advice of a Western medical practitioner.

A provocative research hypothesis derived from the notion that there are religious schemas is that it ought to be possible to "demonstrate cognitive differences between different religious groups" (McCallister, 1995). In general, schemas are those mental structures that guide our interpretation of events, our approach to the solution of problems, that enable us to follow the rules that we have learned in order to negotiate through ordinary human activities and to relate our own personal life experiences to those of others.

The schema concept can be usefully applied to the understanding of religious experience. For example, suppose someone experiences an ecstatic or mystical state of consciousness. It is obviously going to be framed by the person's schema and must be seen within and through it. If you say that you have had a vision of God, the meaning of that vision can make sense only within the context of the schema that was activated when the vision occurred. Schemas are said to be activated within milliseconds, automatically (Fiske & Taylor, 1991). Thus, when a vision occurs, your mind immediately activates the mental structure most relevant to your making sense of it, and it is given meaning within that. In this way, a general sense of awe is assigned a God-related meaning by someone with a devout Christian or Jewish schema but is given some other meaning by someone who does not have any particular religious schema.

A key to understanding how schemas operate to affect our religious experiences is that they work instantaneously and involuntarily. Because the influence of schemas is virtually automatic, it could be said that their function is to help you decipher the immediate experience. That is, the role of a schema in religious experience is understood to be close to the "raw data" that constitute the experience. Also, because a schema is something that you carry around inside your head, it is part of you, and therefore the root of the religious interpretation of the experience is within you. It is dispositional. More complicated interpretations or meanings perhaps rely on a more elaborate situational attribution process.

Cognitive-Arousal Theory and the Attribution of Religious Meaning

Closely related to the notion of religious schema but coming to the psychology of religion from social psychology is the cognitive-arousal theory of the

Many people view scenes in nature, such as the sun shining through the trees, and feel a sense of awe and wonder to which they attribute religious or supernatural meaning. What personal and cognitive needs may be met when people make attributions, or inferences, such as this?

attribution of religious meaning to experiences (Hill, 1995; Spilka & McIntosh, 1995; Spilka, Shaver & Kirkpatrick, 1985). The central ingredient here is the idea that the core of different experiences is the same but that they are seen as different according to the social context in which they occur. The experience-as-felt is congruent with the cues in the environment that signal to the person what meaning to ascribe to it. Therefore, the cause of the individual's interpretation of the experience is situational, outside the person in the immediate social environment. It is not attributed to the dispositions of the individual such as personality, needs, or schemas. The general approach to attributing experiences in this way is derived from a classic experiment by Schachter and Singer (1962).

What would you think was happening to you if you suddenly noticed your body showing signs of physiological arousal but you did not know the reason why? The experiment by Schachter and Singer (1962) was concerned with the interaction between cognitive, physiological, and social factors in determining someone's emotional state. The fundamental notion was that if someone were experiencing physiological arousal for which he or she had no explanation, that arousal would be given a label that is congruent with the mood in the person's social environment. In other words, in the presence of unexplained arousal one must look to people nearby, discover what they are experiencing, and label one's own arousal the same way. The key experimental groups in their experiment were given (without their knowledge) an injection of epinephrin, a natural substance associated with the adrenal glands that, when secreted into the bloodstream, activates the body and creates physiological symptoms such as increased heart rate, more frequent and shallow breathing, perspiration, and a general feeling of being aroused. Schachter and Singer claimed to have demonstrated that subjects so injected but told the drug was Suproxin (a fictitious "drug" supposedly affecting vision) reported feeling the mood displayed by people near them. In one condition, experimental confederates in the same room as the subject behaved angrily, and anger was the label given by the epinephrin group to describe their arousal. In another condition, the experimental confederates behaved in a happy mood, and the epinephrin subjects reportedly interpreted their arousal as happiness.

The application of the above cognitive-arousal model to the question of how someone attributes religious meaning to an ecstatic or mystical experience is straightforward. From the cognitive-arousal model, one would say that for some (unexplained) reason a person has an experience. Like the unexplained arousal in the Schachter-Singer experiment, the person's experience must explained. But in this case the explanation includes attributing the experience to a source and seeing meaning in it. In attributional terms, if the experience occurs in an environment in which others say that they had experiences and that God caused them, then the person would also attribute his or her own experience to God. Similarly, if others say that their experiences contain religious content and meaning, then the person is more likely to do the same.

A few cautions about universally accepting a narrow version of the cognitive-arousal model of religious experience based on the Schachter-Singer experiment must be offered. First, although there is evidence that the social context partly determines whether a person will make a religious attribution, that the person in a church will more likely have a religious experience than someone doing most other things (Spilka & McIntosh, 1995), the results of the Schachter-Singer experiment do not apply uniformly to all religious experiences. This is because the Schachter-Singer experiment is actually a study of *mis*attribution. The real cause of the arousal was an injection of a hormone, and the subjects were said to label their feelings congruent with the mood of others nearby them only because they did not know the true source of their feelings. But in the case of religious or mystical experiences, one's religion may in fact cause one's experience, and the question of misattribution may be moot, at least in some instances. Second, not all religious experiences occur in a social environment. As shall be discussed below, some profound experiences occur in isolation, or prompted by music, drugs, or other nonsocial factors. Third, there are some methodological difficulties with the original Schachter-Singer experiment which suggest that unexplained arousal is not experienced as emotionally neutral. Marshall and Zimbardo (1979) and Maslach (1979) also induced unexplained arousal, by injection and by hypnosis, and found that it was experienced as aversive and fearful, not neutral. This latter finding seems close to what clinical psychologists would call free floating anxiety, which would make a person afraid that they were "losing control." By extrapolation and application to the case of religion, perhaps if unexplained arousal is felt as negative rather than neutral, maybe unexplained experience is aversive and difficult to infuse with religious meaning. This issue is not resolved. In fact, it is not clear what a "pure" experience is.

Overall, even given the above cautions about a simple application of the cognitive-arousal theory, the general attributional approach is nevertheless among the most powerful approaches available for understanding the perceived causes of religious experience, and it helps account for a wide range of phenomena. People do make religious inferences and they attribute religious meaning to some events and experiences (Hill, 1995; Spilka & McIntosh, 1995; Spilka, Shaver, & Kirkpatrick, 1985).

Attachment Theory

Attachment theory was discussed in Chapter 4 in the context of the role of the family in the religious development of children. It also has an important application to our understanding of the bases of religious experience. The mechanisms through which one's needs direct religious experience are determined by the configuration of needs in the attachment system operating during childhood and the mental models developed as a consequence of this. These subsequently have a regulating influence on behavior and experience.

The kind of religious experience to which attachment theory is applied is less of the ecstatic or mystical nature. Rather, it is used more to understand the emotional needs served by one's religiousness. For example, Lee Kirkpatrick (1995) points out that the phenomenology of attachment includes an affectional bond; "to be attached is to love and to feel loved." Loving God and being loved by God are, it is noted, powerful expressions of a core religious experience for many people. Similarly, Kirkpatrick notes that central ingredients of an attachment bond are the experience of seeking comfort and security and using the source of security as a secure base. And these are some of the experiential properties of religion, seeing one's God as a source of comfort and security and turning to one's God during times of need. The root of these tendencies and experiences, it is said, are laid down in the attachment system during the course of development. Various experiences of adult religiousness can then be interpreted as expressions of this system. According to Kirkpatrick, this would include such things as the feeling of nearness to God, asking God for help in times of stress or danger (e.g., "there are no atheists in foxholes"), likening one's religious conversion as "falling in love" with God, and glosso-lalia or "speaking in tongues" as a childlike form of attachment behavior directed toward God.

d. Brain-Mind

All of our discussion about people having extraordinary conscious experi-ences assumes that such events are occurring somewhere within the human brain. This requires a comment regarding the physiological level of analysis as a type of explanation. Although we cannot see conscious experiences that may indeed be occurring in the brain, we can see and record the behavior of the brain in the form of neural and electrochemical activity. The question emerges, then, as to whether conscious experience is the cause or the conse-quence of brain activity. In other words, is a conscious experience a result of neural firing, or, in contrast, is it mental activity that makes the brain behave in a certain way? Which comes first, if either?

Some of the most important advanced theory about brain function sug-gests that the brain-mind is a unity and that conscious experience is a meta-organ (Sperry, 1983). This is in contrast to the philosophical position of dualism, that mind and brain are two separate entities. The new view is that brain and mind are interactive in the following way. Mind, or mental proc-esses, including consciousness, is regarded as an emergent property of brain function. That is to say, coming out of the neurochemical activity are a variety of factors which have proved to be adaptive, and one of those is conscious awareness of mental experience. However, this very conscious awareness of mental experience has the ability to regulate brain activity. It controls the very thing that created it.

An analogy to this notion of the emergent interaction view of mind-brain can be drawn from the social psychology of group leadership. When a group forms to accomplish a goal, a leader will evolve from among the group members. This is called emergent leadership. However, this leader then has the ability to control the behavior of the group. This means that the group created the leader, but the leader, in turn, influences the very entity from which it came. In a similar way, modern brain scientists are now proposing the idea that mind emerges from brain, and, in turn, influences the behavior of the brain.

As related to religious experience, this means that, at a physiological level of analysis, ecstatic or mystical experiences would be said to be a consequence of brain mechanisms. Persinger (1987), for example, has tried to locate core religious experience in transient patterns of electrical activity in the temporal lobe. In addition, however, it would also be said that mystical states influence people's brain activity, and through that medium affect their lives. Also, it may be possible someday to recast the notions that come from religion-as-schema, attribution theory, and attachment theory in physiological terms. This remains a large, integrative task for the future.

In combination, the above sketch of theories might suggest that religious experience would be facilitated by having the schema of a particular religious tradition, by being in the presence of others who are having religious experiences or being in a religious environment that would foster religious attributions, and by having an attachment system that motivates the meeting of such needs through a religious medium. Such would be the processes, theoretically speaking, that would increase religious experience. But what does research along more practical lines say?

⟨_What Facilitates Religious Experience?

Practically speaking, there are two classes of variables that seem to facilitate religious experience. One class includes general factors that increase the probability of religious experience due to such things as developmental level (See Chapter 4; Tamminen, 1991; Tamminen & Nurmi, 1995), socialization, attachment needs, and religious orientation (Chapter 8). The other class includes certain environmental or physiological states, or the interaction between the two, that may facilitate or perhaps trigger experience (Hood, 1995a). The list includes the effects of isolation, drugs, groups, preparatory set, setting such as church or being in nature, ritual, music, sensory deprivation, sex, prayer, physical exercise, and expectations. A brief sampling of a few studies will illustrate how some of the research into these two classes of variables is done.

⟨_Religious Orientation and Subjective Experience
Part of Allport's concept of intrinsicness is the notion that intrinsics find "experiential meaning" in their faith. Some of the items on the intrinsic subscale ask about one's inner experiences as opposed to opinions or behaviors. Examples: "Quite often I have been keenly aware of the presence of God or the Divine Being"; "The prayers I say when I am alone carry as much meaning and personal emotion as those said by me during services." Because extrinsics have not internalized the religion, we would not expect them to have similar inner experiences. They would have less of a religious schema and be less prone to make religious attributions. This reasoning leads to the prediction that intrinsically religious persons would be more likely to report having had religious experiences than extrinsically religious persons.

In order to test this prediction, Ralph Hood (1970) developed an instrument called the Religious Experience Episodes Measure (REEM). The REEM was made up of a series of fifteen descriptions of profound religious experiences taken from William James' *The Varieties of Religious Experience* (1902). After reading the description, the subject would indicate on a five-point rating scale the degree to which he or she had a similar experience. Responses could range from "I have had absolutely no experience like this" to "I have had an experience almost identical to this." A higher score on the REEM represents a greater amount of religious experience of the type measured by the REEM (see Figure 7.2).

Hood compared the mean REEM scores for each type of religious orientation in a group of introductory psychology students. Four groups were studied: intrinsics, extrinsics, indiscriminately proreligious persons, and indiscriminately antireligious or nonreligious persons (which he expected would score the lowest on the REEM measure). The results are presented in Figure 7.3. The intrinsics reported the greatest amount of religious experience as measured by the REEM, and the nonreligious subjects reported the least. The extrinsics and indiscriminately proreligious subjects each reported a slight amount of religious experience. They differed from each other only by a chance amount, but both were substantially lower than the intrinsics. The prediction

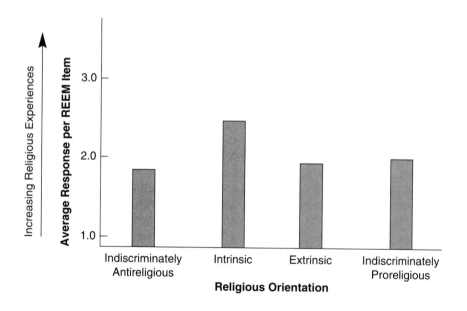

FIGURE 7.3 Average responses per REEM item by religious orientation

Source: Hood, R. W., Jr. (1970). Religious orientation and the report of religious experience. *Journal for the Scientific Study of Religion, 9,* 285–291. Copyright © 1970 by the Society for the Scientific Study of Religion. Used by permission.

that people with an intrinsic religious orientation would have the greatest amount of religious experience is supported by Hood's study.

Situational Facilitators

Studies of situational factors affecting religious or mystical experience tend to be designed to test whether a particular experience occurs and whether it is interpreted with religious meaning. For example, a few experiments have tested the hypothesis that taking psychedelic drugs increases the probability of religious experience. One well known investigation by Pahnke (1970) was described in Chapter 3. To briefly recap: the subjects were at a Good Friday service and half of them received psilocybin and half of them did not. Those who received the drug were more likely to report having had experiences of various kinds and interpreting them in religious terms.

Another intriguing line of research has explored whether being in isolation would facilitate religious experiences. For example, Hood and Morris (1981) placed subjects in water, floating slightly submerged in isolation tanks. They found that whether the subject reported a religious or mystical experience in this sensory deprived environment depended upon the preparatory mental set given to them. Those who were given instructions that suggested that they should try to imagine cartoon figures (a nonreligious mental set) were less likely to report having a religious experience while in the isolation tank than those who were instructed to imagine religious figures. This effect was maximized in intrinsics, an effect perhaps similar to that attained during prayer (Hood, Morris, & Watson, 1989). In general, those whose preparatory instructions hinted that such sensations might have religious meaning were more likely to interpret them in religious ways. Such findings do not imply that a person will have a religious experience merely by being isolated. But they do imply that factors that facilitate experiences (isolation or otherwise) may lead to them and that they can be interpreted religiously if that is what the person expects.

Paradoxically, the opposite of isolation may also facilitate religious experience. It is well known that being in groups can increase the likelihood that people would engage in behavior that they would otherwise avoid. A key concept that comes from social psychology to help explain this is called *deindividuation*. Factors which facilitate such a state include being submerged in a group, not being held responsible for one's own actions, being anonymous and unidentifiable, and having an altered temporal perspective such as an expanded present time sense in which the ability of past learning and future commitments are less able to regulate present behavior. Under these circumstances, someone may behave in deregulated and extravagant ways. It has been speculated that glossolalic speech (see Chapter 9) is facilitated by being deindividuated in a group (Malony & Lovekin, 1985).

Projects and Questions

1. Design a longitudinal study to trace the time-course of various experiences (e.g., purpose in life, fear of death) and behaviors following conversion.

2. Do different phenomenologies of becoming religious lead to different experiential and behavioral effects?

3. Why and when do people make religious attributions? How might you test your ideas about this?

4. What might the theories of religious experience say about whether you can have a religious experience without the language to identify it? Is there a way to test this?

5. This chapter has stated that when one has a vision, a schema is activated. But why is that schema important? Why is that schema granted more meaning and importance than others that could have been invoked?

Further Reading

Hood, Jr., R. W. (Ed.). (1995). *Handbook of Religious Experience*. Birmingham, AL: Religious Education Press. An excellent collection of chapters discussing religious experience from a variety of religious and psychological perspectives. The psychological chapters contain fine presentatins of research and theory.

8

Social [Social]
(adult)

Religious Orientation, Attitudes, and Behavior

> I believe that I am acting in accordance with the will
> of the Almighty Creator: By defending myself against
> the Jew, I am fighting for the work of the Lord.
> —ADOLF HITLER, MEIN KAMPF.

Whatever the mechanisms by which people come to accept a religion, other people will tend to evaluate a person's religious claims by examining the effects of that religion on the believer's life. People in Western societies tend to be pragmatic. We tend to evaluate something as good if it produces the results we think it should, and we think it bad if it doesn't. William James (1902) argued along these lines when he said that a person's religion should be judged by its fruits rather than its roots. As was noted in Chapter 1, examples of both positive and negative fruits of religion are readily available. Unfortunately, there is no simple yes or no answer to the question of whether religion has beneficial or harmful effects. Which type of effects result from someone's religion depends upon the role the religion serves in the person's life. It probably also depends upon the content of the religious teaching itself.

Religion and Morally Relevant Attitudes

People have different styles to their faith. Social psychologists use the term *religious orientation* in characterizing these different faith styles. The concept of religious orientation was developed by Allport (1950, 1954, 1959, 1966) and the closely related work of Allen and Spilka (1967). It refers to one's approach to the faith—what it means in the life of the individual. Some people who attend church, for example, appear to have a mature religious life. They live lives consistent with the moral prescriptions of their religion, without hypocrisy. Others who attend church appear less mature. They may attend church for self-serving ends and are occasionally accused of being hypocrites. Although the distinction as stated here is extreme, it does have some correspondence to what social psychologists refer to as the intrinsic (or committed) versus extrinsic (or consensual) religious orientation. Allport's way of summarizing the distinction between intrinsic and extrinsic orientations to faith is to say that the intrinsic person *lives* the faith, whereas the extrinsic person *uses* it. Let us explore this simple distinction for a while and then, after exploring whether religion predicts morally relevant attitudes and behavior, see why it is, unfortunately, much too simple.

This chapter centers on these two concepts. In the first section we define the intrinsic and extrinsic concepts and discuss the possible psychological differences between intrinsic and extrinsic people. It also outlines the relationship between religious orientation and racial prejudice and presents research relating religious orientation to purpose in life, subjective religious experience, and behavior. Finally, it also reviews the current status of the intrinsic and extrinsic constructs and presents some current research on religion as a quest and on right-wing authoritarianism that may force a re-evaluation of this whole area of work.

Living One's Religion versus Using It

The Intrinsic Orientation

The idea of an intrinsically motivated faith carries with it the notion that the reasons for one's faith lie within rather than outside the person. That is, the motives are personal and internalized. An analogy to the psychological concept of intrinsicness is the biological concept of digestion. When you consume food, it is digested and becomes part of your body, part of the same biological system that took it in in the first place. It becomes internalized, intrinsic to your system, part of the very fabric of it. In a similar way, a religious faith may be internalized and thus become part of the fabric of your personality. For the intrinsically committed person, the faith becomes the master motive in life. Other needs, whether economic or social, may exist but are regarded as subservient to the faith. For example, if there were some conflict between the intrinsic religious motive and an economic or sexual motive, the economic or sexual motive would have to yield to the religious one. The intrinsic person would be less likely to compromise the faith in mixed-motive situations. This is why it is said that intrinsics live their religion.

What kinds of things do intrinsic people say of themselves? A sample of items from Allport and Ross's (1967) Intrinsic-Extrinsic Religious Orientation Scale (Robinson & Shaver, 1973) will give us a clue. Intrinsically motivated people tend to agree with the statements such as: "I try hard to carry my religion over into all my other dealings in life"; "My religious beliefs are what lie behind my whole approach to life"; "The prayers I say when I am alone carry as much meaning and personal emotion as those said by me during services."

Notice an important theme that runs through these items: The notion that one's religion has trans-situational effects; that it influences the person in important ways that extend beyond the boundaries of formal church services. Intrinsics also tend to say that they have "been keenly aware of the presence of God," that they attend church as frequently as possible, and that they read literature about their faith frequently. In the context of most religions, this cluster of statements seems to reflect what we would expect from someone with a true, mature commitment.

Intrinsics tend to disagree with statements that suggest a utilitarian motive for adhering to the faith. For example, one might disagree with a statement such as "What religion offers me most is comfort when sorrows and misfortune strike." The person might agree that religion does offer such comfort but might object to the notion that comfort is what it offers most. The intrinsic would also object to the self-serving theme running through the statement. It implies that one is religious strictly so that one can get something out of it, in this case, comfort. Intrinsics also tend to disagree with statements that compartmentalize religion "for Sunday only," such as "Although I am a religious person I refuse to let religious considerations influence my everyday affairs." Finally, items that imply a "social club" religion are rejected. Statements such as "A primary reason for my interest in religion is that my church is a congenial social activity" tend not to apply very well to intrinsics.

b. The Extrinsic Orientation

Our picture of the person with an extrinsic religious orientation is the reverse of our picture of the intrinsic. Rather than internalizing the faith, the extrinsic tends to use it for his or her own self-interest. He or she is involved in religion for some sort of payoff, gain, or motives that lie outside of the religion itself. In Skinnerian terminology we would say that the extrinsic participates in religion because some sort of tangible reinforcement is contingent upon such participation. Theoretically, if the reinforcement were no longer given in exchange for participation, the person would give up the religion. An extreme example of extrinsic religion would be an insurance salesperson who attends church regularly in order to make contacts with potential customers. He or she may believe nothing of what is preached at church and not be the least bit interested but may still attend as a way of increasing sales. There are many less extreme examples of extrinsicness, of course. But in general, people with the extrinsic orientation are inclined to use religion for their own ends. The full creed is not adopted but only those parts of it that suit the person's own purposes.

Extrinsics tend to agree with statements that imply a compartmentalized "Sunday only" religion and a "social club" religion and that emphasize the personal benefits of being religious. Some statements of each type, respectively, are "Occasionally I find it necessary to compromise my religious beliefs in order to protect my social and economic well-being," "Religion helps to keep my life balanced and steady in exactly the same way as my citizenship, friendships, and other memberships do," "The primary purpose of prayer is to gain relief and protection." The distinction between those statements that emphasize religion's social benefits and those that emphasize religion's personal beneits was at first not highlighted but has subsequently been identified as meaninful (Kirkpatrick, 1989), a point addressed later. As you would predict, extrinsics tend to disagree with the statements with which the intrinsics agree.

c. I versus E, or I and E?

By now you may be picturing intrinsicness (I) and extrinsicness (E) as falling along a bipolar dimension with I and E as the two polar opposites. At least this is how the researchers who originally developed the intrinsic-extrinsic scale thought of it. They assumed that people would answer the questions consistently in one direction, intrinsic or extrinsic. They thought that if people agreed with the intrinsically worded questions, then they would disagree with the extrinsically worded items, and vice versa.

Actually, however, the Religious Orientation Scale is not one bipolar scale with half of the items simply worded in opposite directions. It is really made up of two unipolar subscales. One is designed to measure intrinsicness, and a separate one is designed to measure extrinsicness. The bi-dimensional nature of the scale is illustrated in Figure 8.1. People can score low or high on each measure.

The original researchers may have thought they were dealing with a single bipolar I-E dimension. But they later discovered that they were actually dealing with two separate dimensions of religiosity. This discovery was brought about by a continuing annoying inconsistency in their data. About one-third of their subjects would not answer the 21 items in a consistent intrinsic or extrinsic way. Rather than agreeing with one type of item and disagreeing with the other type, these subjects agreed with both sets of items at the same time. This may seem paradoxical, but about one-third of the people simultaneously agreed with both the extrinsic, self-serving, social type of religion and the intrinsic, selfless, personal commitment type of religion. They agreed with opposite items indiscriminately, apparently without regard to the content or meaning of the item. Thus, the researchers labeled these subjects

1. Unidimensional conception of I-E:

Intrinsic ⬅————➡ **Extrinsic**

2. Bidimensional conception of I-E:

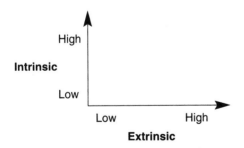

FIGURE 8.1 **The two-dimensional nature of the intrinsic and extrinsic variables**

"indiscriminately proreligious." Other researchers who used scoring procedures slightly different from Allport's noted that some subjects disagreed with both types of items (Hood 1970). These latter subjects were labeled "indiscriminately antireligious."

The Four Possible Types

Figure 8.2 illustrates the fourfold relationship between the intrinsic and extrinsic items on the Religious Orientation Scale. As you can see, since a person can either agree or disagree with items on both subscales, the result is a 2×2 matrix containing four possibilities. Someone who agrees with intrinsic statements and disagrees with extrinsic statements is classified as a pure intrinsic. Someone who agrees with statements of both types is classified as indiscriminately proreligious. A person who disagrees with all items is classified as nonreligious or indiscriminately antireligious.

What proportion of people fall into each of these categories? In most of the research done within the context of religious denominations or organizations on the intrinsic-extrinsic and similar constructs (Allport & Ross, 1967; Allen & Spilka, 1967; Feagin 1964), overall about one-third of the respondents fall into each of the intrinsic, extrinsic, and indiscriminately proreligious categories. But, because the research was done in churches, the investigators were not able to study people in the antireligious category, so these proportions may not be accurate for the population as a whole. There is more recent evidence, however, that the nonreligious type does exist but is not found in

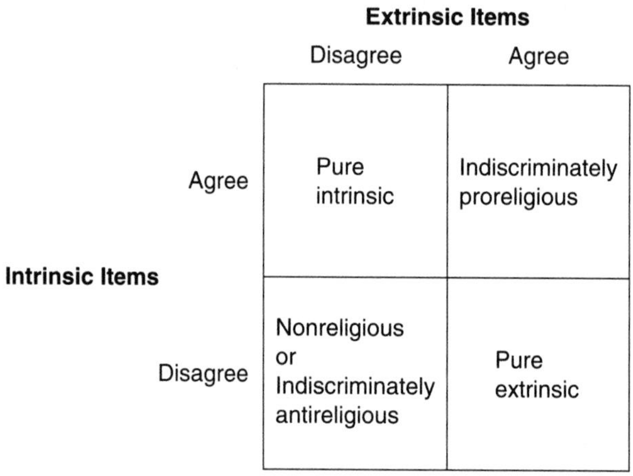

FIGURE 8.2 Matrix illustrating four intrinsic-extrinsic combinations

churches (Hood, 1978). Finally, there is an absence of research studies using the intrinsic-extrinsic variables on anything other than "mainline" nominally Christian groups. It remains to be seen how people of other sects or religions score on the I-E Scale, or whether the concepts of intrinsicness or extrinsicness should even be applied to them.

Importance of I-E Concept

The development of the intrinsic and extrinsic concepts constitutes a turning point in the psychological study of religion. Prior to the 1960s, there were few rigorous studies in this field, but during the 1960s more sophisticated research was undertaken. It was during this period that the major developments in the I-E research occurred.

One possible reason why the I-E research became important is that the concepts are ones to which most people, including psychological researchers, can relate. We can probably all think of people who we think fit the descriptions of intrinsic, committed, and sincere as well as people who are extrinsic, self-serving, and socially motivated. We might even see aspects of each of these characteristics within ourselves. Even though there are important difficulties with the I-E Scale (for example, it reflects an individualistic bias; it is in fact possible for a person to be an intrinsic, yet still like church for social reasons—a point highlighted later by Pargament, 1992), and although it has some mathematical properties that call its precision into question, the I-E concepts still, upon first look, seem to make sense. Note finally how our values "load" our interpretations of the raw findings. Most people see intrinsic as being implicitly better than extrinsic (Dittes, 1971a).

The Extrinsic and Indiscriminate Mentalities

We now come to the question, "Why are these religious types the way they are?" Just what is it that underlies the intrinsic, extrinsic, and indiscriminate mentalities? We can characterize the intrinsic as having reached some degree of personal maturity and integrity. Intrinsics have developed the capacity to make a complete commitment of themselves to their faith with no strings attached and to make decisions independently (Gorsuch & Aleshire, 1974).

Gordon Allport (1966) suggested that the extrinsic has certain personal needs that are partially met through the utilitarian religious orientation. These could be needs for self-aggrandizement, building up one's own ego, security, comfort, status, and social support or recognition. When a person with such needs participates in religion and those needs are met, he or she continues to return to religion as a way of serving these ends.

The explanation of the indiscriminately proreligious mentality invokes the concept of "closed cognitive style" or "undifferentiated thinking" (Allport & Ross, 1967; Rokeach 1960). This concept refers to a style of thinking that is dogmatic: unable or unwilling to make fine discriminations. A person with this type of cognitive style is unable to differentiate between carrying one's religion into all other dealings in life and compromising one's religion in order to protect social and economic well-being. Such an individual does not see the difference between saying that religion is important because it answers questions about the meaning of life, and saying that it does not really matter what one believes so long as one lives a moral life. All these statements fall into one lump category: "All religion is good." Because the indiscriminately proreligious person either cannot or will not make such discriminations, all questions are answered with a blanket affirmation—"Yes"—without regard to the content of the item. Hood (1978) refines this analysis by proposing that the indiscriminately proreligious have not successfully integrated either an intrinsic or extrinsic orientation. The consequence is that they are overly sensitive to both kinds of questions.

Hood further proposed that the indiscriminately antireligious category represents people who are a mirror image of the indiscriminately proreligious category. The "anti" people are said to be "overly sensitive to the suppression or repression of religious attitudes and experiences" (Hood, 1978, p. 420).

2. *Religious Orientation and Prejudice*

a. *Religion's Grand Paradox*

The story behind the development of the Religious Orientation Scale is found in a paradoxical relationship between church attendance and racial prejudice. Studies in the 1940s and 1950s showed repeatedly that, in general, people who go to church score higher on measures of racial and ethnic prejudice than people who do not go to church (Allport & Kramer, 1946; Gorsuch & Aleshire 1974). Additional research appeared to show that the more religious people were, the more prejudiced they were likely to be (Adorno, Frenkel-Brunswik, Levinson, & Sanford, 1950; Glock & Stark, 1966). Allport called this finding a Grand Paradox because racial prejudice is so contrary to clear religious teaching on compassion, humanitarianism, and love for other people. Why is it, he asked, that the very people who are presumably receiving the religious teaching about love for others are at the same time those who are the most intolerant in racial matters? Common sense would dictate just the opposite relationship—those who receive the religious input should be less prejudiced. These relationships are illustrated in Figure 8.3. An extension of this paradox is the fact that religion has been used to justify both the most inhumane bigotry and the battle for civil rights.

A person who had a preliminary bias against religion might find the relationship between church going and prejudice gratifying, for it would seem to confirm an already negative opinion of religion. Such a person might feel that, at last, here was the last word to be spoken against organized religion.

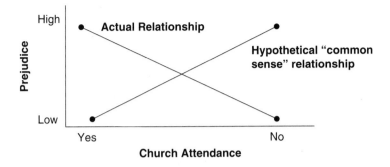

FIGURE 8.3   Hypothetical common-sense relationship and
actual relationship between churchgoing
and prejudice

But this was not the attitude of most of those researching this topic. They were perplexed by the relationship and wanted to explore it more deeply in order to discover why it existed and whether it held true for all religious people.

The Curvilinear Relationship between Churchgoing and Prejudice

As it turned out, the relationship between churchgoing and prejudice was not as simple as the earlier findings suggested. Two different types of churchgoers were discovered. It was not the case that all churchgoers were more prejudiced; only some of them were. Whereas some were the highest in prejudice of all groups, other churchgoers were much lower in prejudice. The latter were typically about the same in prejudice as nonchurchgoers (Allport & Ross, 1967; Gorsuch, 1976; Gorsuch & Aleshire, 1974; Spilka & Reynolds, 1965).

It was now apparent that both the high and low extremes in prejudice were represented in organized churches. The next question asked was whether the high and low prejudice persons differed in their church attendance patterns. Was one group more consistent in attendance than the other? Did one group seem to engage in "social religion" without being truly devout?

As far as the variable of church attendance is concerned, the low prejudice persons were the most devout of all. They were the most consistent and frequent in attendance, going not only to weekend services but also to other services throughout the week. The high prejudice persons, on the other hand, had a different pattern of church attendance. They were usually inconsistent attenders who went to church less frequently than the low prejudice church-goers. Their "hit-and-miss" type of church attendance pattern was thought to represent a less devout, more casual religious orientation. Gorsuch and Aleshire (1974) note that of the 25 studies whose findings address this issue,

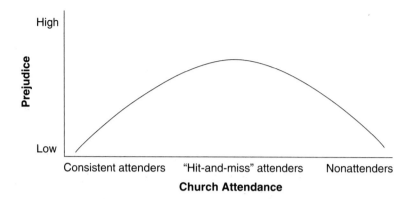

FIGURE 8.4   Curvilinear relationship between church
attendance and prejudice

20 yielded results indicating that the marginal or hit-and-miss church member
is more prejudiced than either the nonattender or the consistent, nuclear
church member. Figure 8.4 illustrates this revised, curvilinear relationship
between church attendance and prejudice.

As can be seen, the earlier group that was just lumped together as
"churchgoers" is now broken down into two separate groups, the consistent
attenders and the hit-and-miss attenders. The latter are the racially intolerant
group. This illustrates that it is a mistake to lump all church attenders or all
types of religion together into a single category, as if all religious people were
the same or all religious orientations were the same. They are not. It is
important that we learn to differentiate between levels of religious variables,
such as frequency of church attendance and type of religious motivation.
When we begin to make these discriminations we may begin to make seeming
paradoxes more understandable.

I-E and Prejudice

In addition to church attendance being shown to have some relationship to
prejudice, it was discovered that intrinsicness and extrinsicness were also
related to prejudice. Allport and Ross (1967) gave the Religious Orientation
Scale to 309 subjects from six mainline denominations (Catholic, Lutheran,
Nazarene, Presbyterian, Methodist, Baptist). Each subject was then categorized as either intrinsic, extrinsic, or indiscriminately proreligious. He also
gave them several questionnaire measures of prejudice, including anti-black,
anti-Jewish, and anti-other sentiment. What he wanted to find out, of course,
was whether intrinsicness and extrinsicness would be related to prejudice.

His data showed that they were. As you might now predict, the intrinsics were the lowest in prejudice of all groups. The extrinsics were high on the prejudice measures. Interestingly, the most prejudiced group of all was the indiscriminately proreligious.

We can combine this relation between religious orientation and prejudice with the previous one between church attendance and prejudice. When we do this we can deduce that intrinsics tend to be consistent, frequent church attenders, whereas the extrinsics and indiscriminately proreligious people tend to be the "hit-and-miss" casual attenders. And this is the way it turns out (Gorsuch & Aleshire, 1974).

Personal Needs, Cognitive Style, and the Religion-Prejudice Relationship

How can we understand the psychological nature of the religious orientation-prejudice relationship? What factors predispose a person to be both extrinsic and racially intolerant? What are the psychological factors that connect racial intolerance to being indiscriminately proreligious? And how are these different from those that link intrinsicness and low prejudice?

It was pointed out that the extrinsic may have personal needs for security, comfort, status, and so forth, that are served by religion. According to Allport, these are the same sorts of needs prejudicial attitudes can also serve. Just as you can get security, comfort, status, or ego building from religious affiliation, you can get these same things by seeing yourself "above" others. Prejudice offers the individual security and comfort (because the outgroup cannot compete economically), as well as status (by "knowing" that one is superior to the outgroup) and social support (from one's own group to help maintain the prejudice). Hence, the relationship between extrinsicness and racial intolerance is due to their common utilitarian life orientation. As Allport and Ross (1967) have suggested, "A life that is dependent on the supports of extrinsic religion is likely to be dependent on the supports of prejudice."

It was also pointed out in the first section that indiscriminately proreligious persons have an undifferentiated mode of thinking—they tend to see things in blanket categories. It turns out that this mode of thinking is part of the very essence of racial prejudice. A prejudice is a negative prejudgment based upon a stereotyped overgeneralization to the whole group. In the case of races, African-American people are seen as one large group rather than many separate individuals who happen to be African-American. Attributes that are assigned to one (e.g., being oversexed, musical, athletic, dumb) are haphazardly assigned to all. Therefore, the connection between being indiscriminately proreligious and prejudiced comes from a common bond in an undifferentiated way of thinking and perceiving the world: all religion is good; all minorities are bad. This "blanket category" type of thinking is referred to as *closed cognitive style*.

The pure intrinsic neither subjugates religion or minorities to personal needs, nor lumps all religion or all minorities together into undifferentiated categories. On the contrary, all other needs and treatment of people are subordinate to the religious commitment. There is a clear necessity to distinguish between the positive and negative effects of religion. It might be said that the intrinsic has been able to escape the trappings of casual religion. It might also be said that intrinsics, like their nonreligious counterparts, have developed a capacity for independent decision making in regard to religious and racial matters.

3. *Religious Orientation and Subjective Experience*

Although the intrinsic and extrinsic concepts emerged from the study of the religion-prejudice relationship, researchers have recently begun to ask whether other variables are related to one's religious orientation. Two such variables are the sense of purpose in life and subjective experience. In this section we shall briefly explore one study relating I-E to purpose in life. One study relating I-E to subjective experience was reviewed in Chapter 7.

a. *I-E and Purpose in Life*

If it is true that, for intrinsics, religion is the "master motive in life, "that it floods the whole life with motivation and meaning," but that for extrinsics, religion is only instrumental in satisfying other needs, then we would expect intrinsics to have a greater sense of meaning in life than extrinsics. In order to explore possible relationships between religious orientation and purpose in life, Bolt (1975) had some of his students complete both the Religious Orientation Scale and the Purpose in Life Test (PIL; see Chapter 7). The subjects included 22 intrinsics, 20 extrinsics, and 10 indiscriminate types. The intrinsics averaged 115.6 on the PIL test; the extrinsics averaged 102.3. The difference between these two mean scores is statistically significant—a nonchance difference. We can conclude that it represents a difference in the sense of meaning that actually exists between intrinsics and extrinsics. Other researchers have also found a positive relation between intrinsicness and PIL scores (Crandall & Rasmussen, 1975; Soderstrom & Wright, 1977; Paloutzian, Jackson, & Crandall, 1978).

One perplexing aspect of Bolt's data is the finding that the indiscriminate group scored almost as high (113.7) as the intrinsic group. How do we interpret this finding? Do the indiscriminately proreligious people actually have the same high sense of meaning in life as the intrinsics? Not necessarily. I think that the high PIL score for the indiscriminate group can be explained by their undifferentiated, "blanket" cognitive style. We already know from the way that they answer the I-E Scale that they tend to answer "yes" to everything without regard for the content of the items. It is likely that their PIL scores represent another instance of this same thing. They probably went down the list of twenty items and affirmed them all without critical regard for item content. I tentatively conclude that Bolt's intrinsic subjects scored high on the PIL test because they actually have a greater experience of meaning, but that his indiscriminate subjects scored high because of the way that they happen to answer questions. Further research could reveal whether the high PIL score for the indiscriminately proreligious group occurred because of their cognitive style or because they are overly sensitized to meaning of life issues as a consequence of a more fundamental lack in that area.

Tentative Conclusions about the Intrinsic-Extrinsic Constructs

Psychologists of religion have found the concepts of intrinsicness and extrinsicness very intriguing. The insights that come with I-E research have done much to advance our understanding of various types of religious people. Although we might all be able to identify an intrinsic or an extrinsic person at the level of surface observation, our knowledge of the intrinsic-extrinsic concepts and research helps us to a deeper understanding of the motivational role of religion in their lives. We now have more insight into the needs and thinking styles of different types of religious individuals, and hence more insight into the role of our faith in our own lives. Such insight enables us to make changes in our own orientation if we want.

One of the major contributions in the body of I-E research has been the refinement of the religion-prejudice relationship, the Grand Paradox. I-E research has demonstrated that the relationship is not as simple as "Religion leads to prejudice." The type of religious orientation and the needs and cognitive styles of the religious individual must always be taken into account. The data tentatively indicate that a mature, intrinsic orientation to one's faith does not foster racial intolerance, but rather works against it.

There are two separate trends in I-E research. The first is devoted to discovering how a variety of variables relate to religious orientation. In addition to the questions we have explored in this chapter, researchers are asking whether the findings in regard to racial prejudice also hold for sexual prejudice, whether certain types of converts (e.g., sudden versus gradual) are more intrinsic or extrinsic than another type, as well as other religion-related questions that may tap the I-E variables.

A similar aspect of this trend is for researchers to assess what personality variables are associated with intrinsicness and extrinsicness. Several thought-provoking findings have emerged. For example, it has been found that intrinsicness is associated with a sense of responsibility, a sense of internal locus of control over oneself, and higher grade point average in college (Kahoe, 1974). In contrast, extrinsicness is associated with dogmatic thinking, a higher degree of authoritarianism and intolerance of ambiguity, a lower sense of responsibility, lower internal locus of control, and lower grade point average (Kahoe, 1974). More recent studies (Wiebe & Fleck, 1980) found that intrinsics had a "greater concern for moral standards, conscientiousness, discipline responsibility, and consistency than those who are extrinsically religious or nonreligious. Intrinsically religious subjects also appeared to be more sensitive, dependent, empathetic and open to their emotions" (pp. 185-186). This same study also reported that extrinsics were more self-indulgent, undependable, flexible, self-reliant, skeptical, pragmatic, and innovative, and were less sentimental. Finally, religious orientation is associated with social interest (concern for others' welfare). Crandall (1980) and Paloutzian et al. (1978) report that intrinsics score higher on the Social Interest Scale (Crandall, 1975) than extrinsics. These two different personality patterns generally fit our intuitive assessment of what intrinsicness and extrinsicness would represent. Note that both orientations are associated with some traits typically thought of as positive and negative, but that most of the traits associated with intrinsicness carry a good connotation and most of the traits associated with extrinsicness carry a bad connotation.

Analogous research is being done in order to test for possible links between religious activity and physiological processes. For example, frequency of church attendance (which we now know is related to religious orientation) has been recently discovered to be related to blood pressure level. Graham et al. (1978) found that frequent church attenders (one or more times a week) had a consistent pattern of lower systolic and diastolic blood pressure than infrequent attenders (less than once a week). This difference was not due to extraneous variables such as age, obesity, cigarette smoking, or socioeconomic status. The overall question for future research raised by such findings concerns the possible links between religious orientation and physical health.

The second trend in I-E research is to move beyond the construct of religious orientation. Proponents of this second view argue that although the I-E construct has been a major contribution, it has basically served its purpose (Dittes, 1971b). They say that what is now needed is another major breakthrough of similar magnitude. The last section of this chapter describes two possibilities. The argument continues that intrinsicness and extrinsicness may not be particular to the religious life of the individual. Rather than being only a religious construct, it may actually be a generalized orientation to all of life—a personality variable—of which religion is only a part (Hunt & King, 1971). If this is so, then an extrinsically religious person would have the same extrinsic orientation to all the other parts of life—including job, love life, family, and school life. The same things would be said of the other orientations also. Therefore, the holders of this view would want to develop an instrument analogous to the Religious Orientation Scale, but one that would assess intrinsicness and extrinsicness toward life in general rather than toward religion only.

Finally, the question frequently arises as to whether the Intrinsic-Extrinsic Religious Orientation Scale is biased. After all, it is pointed out, all the research with that test has been conducted in a Judaic and Christian context, either in churches or American universities. Furthermore, the wording of some of its items has a conservative bias that makes it inappropriate for use with liberal Christian groups (Strickland & Weddell, 1972; Thompson, 1974). Do these points limit the implications of the results? The answer is yes. At present it would be best to limit our generalizing of religious orientation research to a Western religious context.

There is a great need for parallel research to be conducted in Eastern and middle-Eastern religious contexts. This would tell us whether the intrinsic and extrinsic concepts have any meaning in other religions. In order to explore this, you could not merely translate the Religious Orientation Scale into a foreign language in which the religion of interest (e.g., Buddhism) happens to be communicated because a simple translation of the scale may not communicate the same psychological meaning in the foreign culture (although it might be literally correct). Instead, you would need to translate the scale in terms of psychological meaning. Then you could begin to explore whether the I-E concepts have analogues in other religions.

The intrinsic and extrinsic concepts and the Religious Orientation Scale make so much intuitive sense that one is tempted to believe in them. But a warning is in order: Don't be "sold" on them too easily. Daniel Batson and Kenneth Pargament have each recently published some research that might force a reinterpretation of this line of work and that yields new scales sensitive to yet another religious orientation. Batson's work concerns whether intrinsics behave in nondiscriminatory ways, even though they express nonprejudiced attitudes. Pargament's work focuses on human religious motivation as an intrinsic-extrinsic unity. We will examine their work after sketching research on the relation between religion and social behavior.

Religion and Social Behavior

Our discussion up to now has been, in a sense, only half complete. It focused only on the question of whether religious orientation was related to morally relevant attitudes. But a question of perhaps greater importance is whether religious variables predict morally relevant action. The final test of the value of a belief, it may be argued, is in its effects on what people do, not on what they think they would do. Therefore, let us review some of the relevant studies regarding how religious variables might predict helping, harming, and other morally relevant actions.

1. The Good Samaritan Experiment: Evidence for Situational Factors in Helping

Social psychologists are concerned with the disposition-versus-situation issue: To what degree is your behavior a result of traits within your personality rather than the result of environmental forces controlling you? This issue was translated into a creative experiment by John Darley and Daniel Batson (1973). Their experiment was designed to test whether thinking religious thoughts would facilitate helping a victim in a "Good Samaritan" situation or whether situational influences would have a more potent effect on helping behavior. Upon reading the parable of the Good Samaritan one wonders why the priest and the Levite failed to help. Would not they be the ones who would have had religion on their minds and therefore be more likely to help someone in need?

Rationale

Darley and Batson began by inquiring what might be going on in the minds of the priest, Levite, and Samaritan. They reasoned that both the priest and the Levite would be more likely to be thinking religious thoughts. They were, after all, part of the official religion of that time. Samaritans, on the other hand, were religious and social outcasts. Therefore, it is assumed that they would be less likely to be thinking religious thoughts.

Whatever the Samaritan was thinking about, the parable tells us that it is he who helped. From these factors, Darley and Batson raised the question of whether having one's mind occupied by religious thoughts increases one's likelihood of helping someone in an emergency. In their study, they tested the hypothesis that people who have their minds occupied with the Good Samaritan parable would differ from people who are thinking about something else in the degree to which they offered help to a victim in need.

They also tested a second hypothesis derived from the parable. They reasoned that the priest and the Levite, both being in socially prominent positions, would probably be in a hurry. One might speculate that they were in a rush to get to their appointments on time, or otherwise had to keep up with a busy schedule. The Samaritan, being less important, would have fewer important people to meet, fewer items on his schedule that required his speedy arrival, and therefore would be in less of a hurry than the priest and the Levite. The second main hypothesis that Darley and Batson tested was that people who are in a rush are less likely to offer help than people who are not in a rush.

The Study

In order to test their ideas, Darley and Batson set up a Good Samaritan situation on the campus of Princeton University. The subjects, who were students at Princeton Theological Seminary, were sent from one building to another through a particular alleyway. In this alleyway they encountered a "victim" (actually a confederate of the researchers) who apparently was in need of medical aid. As described in the report, "When the subject passed through the alley, the victim was sitting slumped in a doorway, head down, eyes closed, not moving. As the subject went by, the victim coughed twice and groaned, keeping his head down." Darley and Batson wanted to find out whether seminary students given different experimental treatments (having different things on their minds and a different degree of rush) would help to different degrees.

Subjects' thinking was manipulated by asking half of the subjects to go to the second building and give a talk on the parable of the Good Samaritan. The other half of the subjects were asked to give a talk on the jobs in which seminary students would be most effective.

The degree of rush that the subjects were in was also manipulated via the "cover story." Some of the subjects were told that they had to hurry to get to the second building on time. Others were told that there was no reason to rush. Between these extremes, a middle group was given instructions that indicated that only moderate speed was necessary in order to arrive at the second building on time.

Results

Of the 40 seminarians who were subjects, 16 (40 percent) offered some type of aid to the victim. Twenty-four (60 percent) did not offer help. When these overall findings are broken down into subcategories according to their treatment conditions, interesting findings emerge. On the degree-of-rush variable, 63 percent of the subjects in the low-rush condition offered help, 45 percent in the medium-rush condition offered help, and only 10 percent in the high-rush condition offered help. This pattern of results, shown in Figure 8.5, was statistically significant and did not depend upon whether the subject was thinking about the parable. The conclusion is that being in a rush lowers your tendency to help a victim.

Their first question, regarding whether helping behavior would be significantly related to religious thought content, yielded equivocal results. Although subjects who had to give a talk on the Good Samaritan parable were more likely to offer aid (53%) than subjects who had to talk about jobs for seminary students (29%), the trend was not strong enough to be considered nonchance. Darley and Batson concluded that "a person going to speak on the parable of the Good Samaritan is not significantly more likely to stop to help a person by the side of the road than is a person going to talk about possible occupations for seminary graduates."[1]

Interpretation of the Good Samaritan experiment must be done carefully. The experimental arrangement and results do not lead to a straightforward conclusion that having the Good Samaritan parable on one's mind is useless

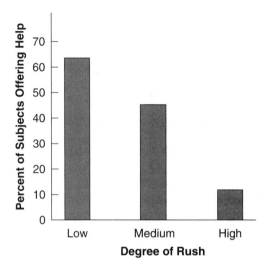

FIGURE 8.5 Percent of subjects in each rush condition who offered help in the Good Smaritan experiment

Source: Darley, J. M., & Batson, C. D. (1973). "From Jerusalem to Jericho": A study of situational and dispositional variables in helping behavior. *Journal of Personal and Social Psychology, 27,* 100–108. Copyright © American Psychological Association. Used with permission.

in facilitating helping behavior. The subjects were, after all, helping the experi-menter by going to the other building to present the talk. The procedures were set up not as a help versus no-help situation, but rather as a conflict between helping situations (i.e., helping the victim versus helping the experimenter). Nevertheless, the potency of the degree-of-rush variable is clear evidence in support of situational factors influencing helping behavior.

The Rescuers: Evidence for Personal Factors in Helping

Two facets of the Good Samaritan situation and the Darley-Batson research warrant further mention. First, the emergency requiring aid was in both cases a medical emergency in which there was relatively little danger, time loss, or risk to the helper involved. This being so, one wonders about nonmedical emergencies and emergencies that take a great deal of time or that place the

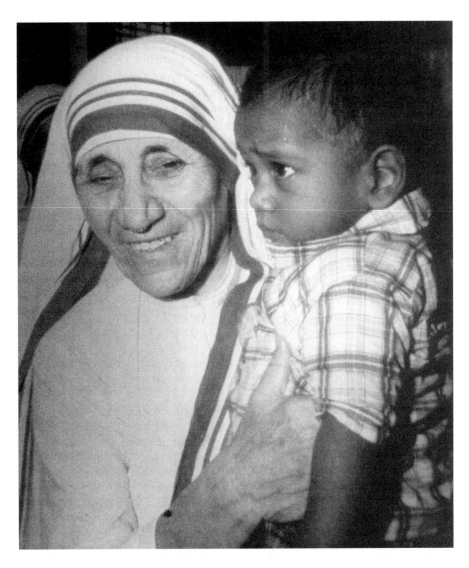

Mother Teresa of Calcutta, India, has become known throughout the world for her life of compassion and service to others. Some have theorized that such a life grows out of an intrinsically motivated faith (Chapter 8) and a high level of religious development (Chapters 4 and 5).

helper in danger. In this latter case, is a person equally likely to lend aid although high personal risk is involved? Second is the issue of which personality traits, if any, constitute the profile of a Good Samaritan.

A report from Perry London (1970) regarding some Christians who hid Jews from the Nazis during World War II provides some information pertinent to these issues. Hiding Jews from Nazis is obviously very different from helping someone who needs medical aid. The former may be very dangerous for oneself and one's family, may consume all of one's personal and monetary resources, and may require months or years to accomplish successfully. The latter is far less dangerous, costs relatively little, and takes only a short time. London's research was designed to discover any common factors in the lives of persons who took the dangerous step of hiding Jews.

London sought out and interviewed 27 "rescuers" who had emigrated from Europe to the United States since 1945. The interviews were designed to get information on such things as their reasons for helping the Jews, their backgrounds, degree of sociability, personal opinions and qualities, etc. Although more precise data would be desirable, such data are rarely available.

London presents a cluster of three traits that seem to be common among the rescuers. These three qualities were

1. A spirit of adventurousness. The rescuers seemed willing to take risks and pursue challenge. This is not to be confused with foolhardiness, however.
2. Social marginality. The rescuers had a sense of being on the margin of society rather than being in the mainstream.
3. Moral identification with parents. Rescuers had a close and moralistic upbringing from parents who were themselves morally committed.

The verbal statements of the rescuers reflected a strict sense of right and wrong. One Dutch rescuer, who described himself as mildly anti-Semitic, when asked why he hid Jews, said simply that it was a Christian's duty. Another of London's rescuers' recollections illustrates the type of moral upbringing common to the rescuers:

> You inherit something from your parents, from the grandparents. My mother said to me when we were small, and even when we were bigger, she said to me . . ." Regardless of what you do with your life, be honest. When it comes to the day you have to make a decision, make the right one. It could be a hard one. But even the hard ones should be the right ones" (p. 247).

According to London, this person "went on to talk about his mother in glowing terms, about how she told him how to live, how she had taught him morals, and how she had exemplified morality for him" (p. 247). Whether these same qualities are present in people who offer help in medical emergencies of the Darley-Batson type is a question to be answered by future research. In general, it appears that personal factors are important in helping behavior, and that these are rooted in one's moral upbringing (Huston & Korte, 1976).

A larger study of 406 rescuers and 126 nonrescuers (Oliner & Oliner, 1988) emphasized that parental modeling of caring behavior was the distinguishing feature of the rescuers.

Religion and Negative Behavior

Factors that Facilitate Harming

If religion is related to helping behavior, it would seem that it would also be related to hurting behavior—one's tendency or willingness to inflict harm on another person. Different models of human nature suggest many factors that may increase the likelihood of one person harming another. These factors include frustration (e.g., I punch you in the nose because you stole my girlfriend), learning (I punch you in the nose because I have previously gotten what I wanted by nose-punching behavior), and social pressure (I punch noses because everyone else in my gang does so, and group policy dictates that I must do what they do).

Important to the psychology of religion is a behavioral study within the third category, social pressure. The study is concerned with a special case of social pressure—obedience to an authority figure who orders one person to inflict harm on another.

Social pressure is used in order to get a person to comply with some command, state an opinion, or perform some act. The classic case of social pressure inducing compliance is conformity. Conformity pressures, which are a special case of social pressure in general, come from a group and converge upon the individual to make the person comply. The concept of social pressure is, of course, one type of situational determinant of behavior.

Obedience to authority is another instance of the social pressure concept. It is not the same as conformity, however. Conformity pressures stem from a group, whereas obedience pressures stem from a single individual. In the case of obedience, the influence is still situational and social, but the power of control is localized in a single authority figure. Another distinction between obedience and conformity is that they may require different types of responses from the complying person. In conformity the response may be verbal, a statement of opinion or judgment; or it could be behavioral, requiring the actual performance of that act. But in the case of obedience, overt behavior is required. One does not obey by holding an opinion. Obedience implies that one does what one is told.

Religion and Obedience to Hurtful Commands

David Bock and Neil Warren (1972) designed an experiment to explore the relation between religious beliefs and the tendency to obey an authority who gave destructive orders. They were trying to find out whether religious moderates would show different degrees of obedience to orders to harm another person than would subjects at the highly religious and nonreligious extremes.

Bock and Warren hypothesized that the religious moderates would be the most likely to disobey an authority who gave orders to inflict harm. They also predicted that both persons who are deeply committed to their religious faith and nonreligious people would be obedient. Their reasoning was based on the notion that institutional religion emphasizes people's responsibility to obey legitimate authority, even though religious teaching places a primary emphasis on people's responsibility to treat a fellow human being with respect and care. Bock and Warren thought that believers in the United States have often placed primary emphasis on obedience, relegating compassion to second place. Thus they predicted that the most committed religious persons would be the ones most likely to follow orders unquestioningly. They also reasoned that people at the nonreligious extreme have their own value structure that serves as their authority. Therefore, they hypothesized that the nonreligious subjects would obey in a way similar to most committed religious groups.

On the other hand, Bock and Warren thought the religious moderates have their values more in balance. Although moderates see obedience to authority as important, they balance this with a concern for human welfare. The prediction was that religious moderates would disobey harmful orders sooner than either of the religious extremes.

The procedures for measuring the degree of destructive obedience were made famous by Stanley Milgram (1963, 1965). Briefly, two people arrive at a laboratory in order to participate in an experiment on learning. Upon arrival one of them is "randomly" selected to be a "teacher," the other is selected to be the "learner." In fact, the learner is always a confederate of the experimenter and the actual subject always is assigned the role of teacher. The learner's task is to learn a list of word pairs. The teacher's job is to read one of the words of each pair, see whether the learner responds with the matching word, and punish the learner with an electric shock for each wrong answer. The learner is strapped into the "electric chair" in which the electric shocks are received. The teacher sits before a row of 30 shock switches, beginning at 15 volts and going up to 450 volts in 15-volt increments. Each time the learner gives a wrong answer, the teacher is to increase the level of shock one switch. By design, the learner gives many wrong answers. After a few "shocks" he begins to grunt and complain of the pain. After a few more, he complains of a bad heart and screams, yelling that he wants to quit. Finally he becomes completely silent. (Note: Nobody ever really receives shocks in this research.)

The dilemma for the subject (teacher) begins when the learner begins to complain of the pain. The teacher wants to stop giving shocks, but the experimenter is issuing orders to continue. The experimenter says, against the teacher's protest "You must go on; you have no other choice; the experiment requires that you continue." The purpose of these procedures is, of course, to see how far along the series of shock switches people will go.

Because Bock and Warren wanted to see whether religious beliefs would affect degree of destructive obedience, they gave their subjects two religion scales. One was the Inventory of Religious Belief (Brown & Lowe, 1951). This test is designed to discriminate religious stances from believer to nonbeliever. The other was the Religious Attitude Inventory (Broen, 1955) designed to measure degree of doctrinal orthodoxy or "fundamentalism-humanism." By using these instruments, they were able to classify the subjects as strong believers, nonbelievers, or moderates.

The results were the exact opposite of what Bock and Warren expected. The religious moderates were the most obedient, while the strong believers were more cautious and resistant in their obedience (see Figure 8.6). Bock and Warren explain these findings by drawing a parallel between their subject categories and those of Allport and Ross (1967). Bock and Warren propose that (1) their own strong believer category corresponds to Allport's intrinsics, who are the most frequent church attenders; (2) their moderates correspond to

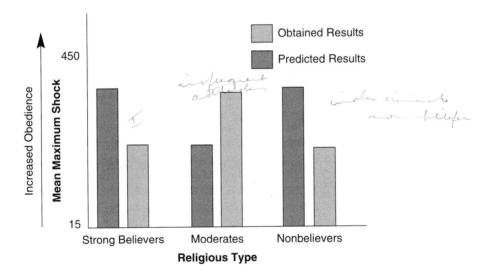

FIGURE 8.6 **Degree of obedience in delivering electric shocks for strong believers, nonbelievers, and religious moderates**

Source: Bock, D. C., & Warren, N. C. (1972). Religious belief as a factor in obedience to destructive commands. *Review of Religious Research, 13,* 185–191. Copyright © Religious Research Association, Washington, D.C.

Allport's infrequent attenders; (3) their nonbelievers correspond to the indiscriminately antireligious category in the intrinsic-extrinsic classification. Therefore, just as intrinsics (frequent churchgoers, strong believers) are the least prejudiced, they are also the least obedient to orders to harm others. And just as infrequent churchgoers (moderates) are the most prejudiced, they are also the most likely to obey orders to harm others.

The task of explaining the psychological processes that underlie these results can be approached in at least two ways. One way is to resort to the intrinsic and extrinsic motivational concepts. The behavior of Bock and Warren's subjects would be interpreted as an outward manifestation consistent with internal motive orientations. Another interpretation is proposed by Gorsuch and Aleshire (1974) and Gorsuch (1976). Their interpretation is that the extrinsic/prejudiced/obedient people regulate their lives by conventional American values, which emphasize the supremacy of authority and conformity to norms. The intrinsic/tolerant/disobedient people and the nonreligious/tolerant/disobedient people have a greater capacity for independent decision making. Intrinsics are able to regulate their lives for reasons that transcend the values of conventional society.

Does Religion Predict Behavior?

The Good Samaritan experiment and the obedience experiment are important for a variety of reasons. One reason is that they are studies of behavior. Most studies in the psychology of religion are questionnaire studies, which of necessity are about attitudes, feelings, opinions, or remembered past behavior (see Chapter 3). It has been argued (Hunsberger, 1991; Warren, 1976) that experiments designed to study overt behavior are what is needed to advance the field. But it has also been argued that the widespread use of experiments in the psychology of religion is an "impossible dream" due to the nature of the topic (see Batson, 1977). The Good Samaritan and obedience studies demonstrate that quality experiments with behavioral dependent variables can be done on psychology of religion questions.

These two studies are also important because they highlight the difference between attitudes and behavior. It is a well known finding in social psychology that people's attitudes do not necessarily predict their behavior (Wicker, 1969b). In popular language, this means that people often say one thing but do another. When asked to predict their hypothetical behavior in the situations in these two experiments, most people predict that they would help the victim and not obey the orders to give electric shock. However, people often do what they think they would not do (Milgram, 1965). This gap between predicted and actual behavior and between attitudes and actions implies that it is not enough for us to know only how religious variables are related to attitudes. We must also learn how religion predicts actions.

Another reason for the importance of these two studies is that they yielded apparently opposite findings regarding whether religious factors are important in predicting what people will do. The Good Samaritan experiment seemed to show that one religious variable (thinking about the parable) did not significantly affect helping behavior, whereas the obedience experiment showed that a different religious variable (strength of belief) did significantly predict blind obedience to pain-inflicting orders. Hence, it becomes necessary to examine this question in more detail. In what sense does religion predict significant human behavior in the real world? This question will re-appear in Chapter 9 in connection with the research on whether religion predicts health related behavior such as being in a mental hospital or alcohol or drug use.

The research on this question, although not generally developed with the conceptual sophistication of the religious orientation research, does yield pertinent results. A review of the literature by Gorsuch (1976) revealed over 20 studies in which religion predicted behaviors in the areas of race relations, sexual behavior, and use of illicit drugs. In contrast, there are only a few studies in which the results are equivocal or opposite to what one might expect. Some of the findings seem intuitively obvious, given knowledge of the doctrinal position of the religious group. For example, Quakers are more likely to have anti-war attitudes than are those of other religions (Connors, Leonard, & Burnham, 1968), and they are also more likely to have participated in anti-war demonstrations. Similarly, Catholics generally have greater opposition to abortion than others do, and people who are active in a religious faith are less likely to have extramarital sexual activities than people who are inactive in any religion (Kinsey, Pomeroy, & Martin, 1948; Kinsey, Pomeroy, Martin, & Gebhard, 1953).

Regarding the use of illicit drugs, Gorsuch (1976) found that the results of 22 out of 24 studies reviewed support the idea that the more religious people are, the less likely it is that they will be involved in the use of illicit drugs. Gorsuch's (1995) more recent review of the research also concludes that religion predicts a lower level of substance and alcohol abuse. An illustrative study on this topic (Blum, Braunstein, & Stone, 1969) found that in a sample of 200 San Francisco adults, 82 percent of those who used no illicit drugs had recently attended church, whereas 38 percent of those who used illicit drugs recently attended church.

Some studies suggest that a liberal versus conservative conceptualization of the religious variable, in addition to the variable of religious activity or attendance rate, is important. For example, Ebaugh and Haney (1978) found that, overall, people who attend church more than once a week were less likely to approve of abortion, compared with people who attend church only several times a year or less. But this difference is far more pronounced for conservative churches. Approximately half of the infrequent attenders in both liberal and conservative churches score highest on approval of abortion. However, among the most frequent attenders, 46 percent of those in liberal churches have high abortion approval scores, compared with 11 percent for frequent attenders in conservative churches. In other words, for those who are active in their religion, being liberal or conservative makes an important difference in approval of abortion.

Analogous findings exist regarding political leanings. People who are liberal in politics tend to be more liberal in religion (Hadden, 1963; Johnson, 1966).

Studies of the relation between religion and positive social behavior are equivocal. In a classic study of cheating in children (Hartshorne & May, 1928), no difference was found in the amount of cheating between those who were regular church attenders and those who were not. Analogous results have been found with college students (Garfield et al., 1967; Goldsen et al., 1960). In one study of this question (Smith, Wheeler, & Diener, 1975), college students were classified into four different types of religious belief (Jesus people, moderately religious, nonreligious, and atheist) by means of their responses to several questionnaire items. They were then given an opportunity to cheat (by correcting their own course examination) and to perform an altruistic act (by volunteering to help in a program with retarded children). Results showed that there were no significant differences among the four groups in rate or extent of cheating nor in the willingness to help with the children. Using a similar research design, Paloutzian and Wilhelm (1983) found that within Smith et al.'s two religious groups, religious orientation did predict behavior. High intrinsics were significantly less likely to cheat.

Overall, the studies seem to indicate that religious variables can be important predictors for some significant human behaviors. But they are not necessarily so, as is the case with honesty and cheating behavior. To interpret these differences properly will take additional careful analysis. Perhaps those religious people who have become socially transcendent have come to the point where they make important decisions independently and consistent with their religious values. For them, religion should predict behavior. For those for whom religion does not predict behavior, it may be either that they have simply not developed such transcendence and independence or that they are motivated to appear good (i. e., socially desirable) as opposed to behave well (Crandall & Gozali, 1969; Ritzema, 1979). New research can resolve these issues.

Re-evaluating I-E Research: Quest and Fundamentalism

The above sketch of the intrinsic-extrinsic research and the religion-behavior relationships appears complete and systematic enough for us to conclude (prematurely) that it reflects the truth. Perhaps there really are intrinsic and extrinsic orientations that are related to attitudes and social behaviors in predictable ways, with different psychological processes mediating them. One is also unavoidably tempted to conclude that the intrinsic and extrinsic scales are good ways to measure these "positive" and "negative" types of religious sentiments. The problem with all of the above, however, is that it may not be so. Researchers have questioned just what is being measured by Allport's Religious Orientation Scale. Some suggest that the scale is valid for only a limited portion of the religious population because its items are sensitive to conservative intrinsicness. Others argue that aspects of religiousness such as religion-as-quest or fundamentalism are more powerful lines of research and that I-E has outlived its usefulness.

Social Desirability and the Quest Measure

One problem with the I-E scale, highlighted by Batson, Naifeh and Pate (1978), is that the score does not necessarily reflect a person's true attitudes. High intrinsic scores could result because subjects gave answers they felt to be socially desirable. In essence, when completing certain items subjects may tend to "fake good." As an example, if you are a religious person it appears to place you in a better light if you agree with the statement that you "try hard to carry my religion over into all my other dealings in life" than if you disagree with it. No one likes to appear to claim a religion but not to live it.

Social psychologists have developed a Social Desirability Scale (Crowne & Marlowe, 1964) designed to measure people's tendency to describe themselves in favorable terms. It is made up of items that, if a person agreed with them all (and disagreed with the negatively worded items), would present the person as too good to be true. Examples of items are "I have never intensely disliked anyone," "Before voting, I thoroughly investigate the qualifications of all candidates," "I never hesitate to go out of my way to help someone in trouble," "No matter who I'm talking to, I'm always a good listener." All of us could attribute a few such statements to ourselves without "faking good." But to attribute an excessive number of such statements to oneself and at the same time be objectively accurate is highly unlikely. People are simply not that good.

Batson et al. (1978) found that the Intrinsic Religious Orientation Scale and the Social Desirability Scale correlated +.36. Those who were intrinsics also had some tendency to present a good appearance. The implications of this result are threefold. First, the commonly used intrinsic scale may not be as pure a measure of devout religion as was once believed. The intrinsic scale may partly measure people's tendency to make themselves look good. Analogous points have been made by Argyle and Beit-Hallahmi (1975) and Ritzema (1979). Second, the previous work on religious orientation can now be re-evaluated in light of the possibility of social desirability artifact in the measuring instruments used in that earlier work. Just as it is possible for someone to agree with intrinsic religious statements in order to present a positive image, one can also disagree with prejudiced statements for the same psychological reason. Third, if Batson et al.'s conclusions are correct, it is necessary to develop an unconfounded measure of religious orientation that also predicts prosocial behavior.

Batson (1976) attempted to develop an unconfounded measure. It has been called religion-as-quest, as opposed to extrinsic (religion-as-means) and intrinsic (religion-as-end). Batson and his colleagues describe the quest orientation as that "in which religion is an open-ended process of pursuing ultimate questions more than ultimate answers" (1978, p. 40). The Quest measure has evolved through different variations, but the basic attribute that it is designed to measure is "an approach that involves honestly facing existential questions in all their complexity, while at the same time resisting clear-cut, pat answers. An individual who approaches religion in this way recognizes that he or she does not know, and probably will never know, the final truth . . ." (Batson, Schoenrade, & Ventis, 1993, p. 166). Sample items from the Quest measure are "It might be said that I value my religious doubts and uncertainties," "I have been driven to ask religious questions out of a growing awareness of the tensions in my world and in my relation to my world," "My religious development has emerged out of my growing sense of personal identity," "God wasn't very important for me until I began to ask questions about the meaning of my own life," "Questions are far more central to my religious experience than are answers." Batson et al. report that the correlation between the Quest measure (Q) and social desirability is almost zero.

How does the Quest measure compare with the Intrinsic scale in predicting prejudiced attitudes and behavior? Batson et al. report that both measures predict less prejudiced attitudes (as assessed by anti-black statements on questionnaires) but that only the Quest measure predicts lower levels of discrimination by white subjects in behavioral tests (an opportunity to interact with a black person during an interview).

Many intriguing questions have been explored using Batson's I-E-Q model (see Batson et al., 1993, for comprehensive review). One of the first focused on the style of helping behavior displayed by the person in the Good Samaritan experiment discussed earlier. He found that people who happened to come across the sick person by the side of the alley differed in the type of help they offered the victim. People who were high in quest were more likely to help only to the degree stated by the victim. When the sick person said "Thank you, I'm fine" the subject went on his or her way. In contrast, people who had high intrinsic scores tended to help more than was desired by the victim, sometimes insisting on helping "too much," even after the victim said he felt well.

A more recent issue that has come up in I-E-Q research concerns level of mental complexity of people who are high in intrinsic, extrinsic, or quest religious orientations. In order to explore this question, Sapp and Jones (1986) gave subjects the religious orientation measures and the Defining Issues Test (DIT) by Rest (1986), discussed in Chapter 4. Their rationale was that higher scores on Kohlberg's scale of moral reasoning were based on higher levels of mental complexity. The results showed that subjects high in the quest orientation were slightly higher in complexity than those who were low in quest but that there was little relation between either intrinsicness or extrinsicness and mental complexity.

An issue surrounding this research question has to do with whether someone who arrives at a religious belief does so by a cognitively simple process. Presumably, intrinsics believe they have arrived at an answer. By definition, they are no longer questioning and, therefore, no longer need to engage in the mentally complex operations of those high in quest. On the other hand, the pattern of results is that those engaging in the quest may indeed have complex minds, but that does not mean that those who have arrived at what they believe to be an answer for them have done so by means of a cognitively simple process.

Has I-E Outlived Its Usefulness?

Early critiques revealed that both Batson's Quest measure and Allport's Religious Orientation Scale have interpretive problems. Batson's Quest measure can be interpreted in at least three ways: (1) as a measure of true intrinsicness, unconfounded with social desirability; (2) as a measure that taps the truly independent tendencies of socially transcendent people who are also committed to social values (Gorsuch, 1976); and (3) as a measure of religious orientation that is sensitive to the liberal aspects of Christianity. Allport's scale has been criticized on the grounds of having a conservative bias. Research suggests that Allport's scale may be inappropriate for use with progressive Catholics (Thompson, 1974) and liberal groups such as Unitarians (Strickland & Weddell, 1972) on the grounds that what is intrinsic for these latter groups may not be what is assessed by Allport's scale.

If Batson's Quest measure taps features intrinsic to liberal religion, whereas Allport's scale taps intrinsic expression of conservative religion, then the possibility is raised that a liberal-conservative distinction is important in a fashion similar to the intrinsic-extrinsic distinction. These two dimensions can be crossed, creating a fourfold classification: intrinsic liberal, intrinsic conservative, extrinsic liberal, extrinsic conservative. The classification system assumes that what one is intrinsic about is as important as the quality of intrinsicness itself. Future research would need to assess the usefulness of such a classification system in predicting attitudinal and behavioral outcomes.

More recent scholarship could result in a major turning point for intrinsic-extrinsic research. The criticism includes the backdrop that the I-E distinction is a too-simplistic good-versus-bad formulation of religion. The criticisms are methodological, empirical, and conceptual, but these are related to each other.

The methodological critiques derive from the fact that the discovery of intrinsic and extrinsic as independent, uncorrelated dimensions, as opposed to one bipolar dimension, was discovered by accident, somewhat as a nuisance, when some of Allport's original subjects agreed with both I and E items (Kirkpatrick & Hood, 1990). Rather than sticking with his conceptualization, Allport stuck with his measure but simply recategorized some subjects into a third group, the indiscriminately proreligious types. It might be said that his methods were driving his theory. The first outgrowth of this was Batson's introduction of the Quest measure. This was originally construed as measuring an aspect of intrinsicness that Allport's own intrinsic measure failed to tap. It has subsequently been treated as an independent dimension. The second outgrowth of this was dialogue concerning the properties of the I-E measuring instruments themselves. That is, do the items on the extrinsic subscale all cluster together on one factor, or are they clustered in two or more subunits? This issue was explored by Kirkpatrick (1989), and it was found that there are two sub-varieties of questions that comprise extrinsic religiousness. These are the extrinsic personal items and extrinsic social items and they may not be related to other attitudes and behaviors in the same way. In other words, people use their religion to gain personal benefit or for social ends.

A simple reading of this literature would suggest that I and E are each linearly related with prejudice, but in opposite directions. As crudely represented in Figure 8.4, this would be one way to possibly account for the curvilinear relationship between church attendance and prejudice. However, the relationships are more complicated than that. The question of exactly how I and E are correlated with prejudice has now been exhaustively analyzed. Donahue (1985) summarized the findings by stating "I is uncorrelated, rather than negatively correlated, with prejudice across most available measures. E is positively correlated with prejudice, but not nearly so strongly as Allport's writings might have predicted" (p. 405). This means either that the I and E concepts are faulty or that I and E measures that were created do not perform as they should. In the context of these methodological and empirical critiques, it has been suggested that the Allportian fourfold typology be dropped.

The conceptual critique centered on the idea that religion, like any human behavior, is founded on a mixture of means and ends. Intrinsic religiousness is construed as an end in itself, whereas extrinsic religiousness is construed as means to an end. In a careful analysis of this issue and in the process of developing a measure of indiscriminate pro-religiousness, however, Pargament (1992) has cogently argued that this is an artificial distinction that masks what religion is about. That is to say, religion does two things for people; it defines for people both where they should go and how to get there. It defines both the destination (end) and the pathway (means). The implication of this is that the "most mature" way of being religious would be that which combines these two functions in an integrated or whole way. Clearly, this is a radical reconceptualization of the nature of indiscriminate pro-religiousness. In Pargament's conceptualization, it is not necessarily the dogmatic person with the closed cognitive style who would be in this category. Rather, it would be someone who has developed the capacity to strive toward a spiritual destination by means of a spiritual pathway.

Authoritarianism and Fundamentalism

The challenges to the traditional conceptualization of intrinsic and extrinsic by Kirkpatrick and Hood, Donahue, and Pargament raise the possibility that this line of research has fulfilled its potential or outlived its usefulness. If so, then a new idea is needed to enable us to press further in our exploration of the relation between how someone is religious and their racial attitudes and behavior. One idea has recently been re-introduced to this line of inquiry after an absence of many years, and it promises to make a powerful contribution. It is the concept of authoritarianism.

Altemeyer (1988) has recast the classical notion of right-wing authoritarianism and has provided new data about its nature and associations. The original conceptualization of the authoritarian personality (Adorno, Frenkel-Brunswik, Levinson, & Sanford, 1950) was cast in psychoanalytic terms. The high authoritarian, who was also the potential fascist and bigot, was construed to have a weak ego, high levels of repressed aggression, and a need to submit to authority. This was a major line of research during the 1950s, but it waned for approximately 25 years. Altemeyer, however, developed a new tool to measure right-wing authoritarianism (RWA), which has enabled him to assess whether RWAs have social and political attitudes that differ from those of others.

Altemeyer's more recent conceptualization of the RWA syndrome is that it contains three elements. These are authoritarian submission to established leaders, authoritarian aggression perceived as sanctioned by authorities, and conventionalism as a high degree of adherence to societal rules. This set of attributes ought to be measurable, and if that is done well then the scores ought to predict other things. Sample items from the Right-Wing Authoritarianism Scale are "It is always better to trust the judgment of the proper authorities in the government and religion, than to listen to the noisy rabble-rousers in our society who are trying to create doubt in people's minds," "Our country will be destroyed someday if we do not smash the perversions eating away at our moral fiber and traditional beliefs," and "Obedience is the most important virtue children should learn." The instrument contains a total of 30 items of this type.

Altemeyer and Hunsberger (1992) supposed that, given the dogmatic and close-minded orientation of RWAs, authoritarianism ought to correlate with fundamentalism. By fundamentalism, Altemeyer and Hunsberger mean "The belief that there is one set of religious teachings that clearly contains the fundamental, basic, intrinsic, essential, inerrant truth about humanity and deity; that this essential truth is fundamentally opposed by forces of evil which must be vigorously fought; that this truth must be followed today according to the fundamental, unchangeable practices of the past; and that those who believe and follow these fundamental teachings have a special relationship with the deity."

Fundamentalism has in the past been operationally defined by questionnaires containing a series of doctrinally orthodox statements peculiar to a particular religion. For example, questionnaires to measure Christian fundamentalism invariably contain statements about the virgin birth, the literalness of scripture, original sin, the reality of hell, and so on. Defined in this way according to content, it became difficult to distinguish a measure of fundamentalism from a measure of Christian orthodoxy. Also, proceeding in this way would require that a separate fundamentalism measure would have to be created for every religion. Fortunately, Altemeyer and Hunsberger developed a measure of fundamentalism that assesses the dogmatic mind-set rather than the content of belief. For example, people who score high on fundamentalism agree with statements such as "Of all the people on this earth, one group has a special relationship with God because it believes the most in his revealed truths and tries the hardest to follow his laws." They tend to disagree with statements such as "Different religions and philosophies have different versions of the truth, and may be equally right in their own way."

Most important in this way of defining fundamentalism is that it is neutral with respect to content. That is to say, one can believe the above statement and be committed to any number of religious traditions. The statement applies equally well to fundamentalist Christians, fundamentalist Muslims, etc. The genius of this measure is that it allows us to assess some ways in which people who have a similar kind of mind-set exist in different religions.

Are authoritarianism and fundamentalism related to each other? Yes. Altemeyer and Hunsberger report data on Canadian students that the two measures correlate .68 with each other, a high moderate correlation. This means that people who hold their religious beliefs in a dogmatic way are also likely to be authoritarian in the political and economic sphere. They are more likely to hold a philosophy of punishment rather than rehabilitation regarding treatment of criminal offenders, more likely to believe that one should always do what the government says, and more likely to disfavor dissent or questioning. Both RWAs and fundamentalists have been shown to have a negative attitude toward homosexuals, score higher on measures of prejudice, and lower on measures of a quest religious orientation. The future potential for research on this topic looks rich, and time will tell whether intrinsic-extrinsic-quest line of research is eventually replaced by fundamentalism as a primary driver of research (Hunsberger, 1995).

Finally, the dimensions of religiousness explored in this chapter have been studied in relation to questions beyond social attitudes and behavior. Intrinsic, Extrinsic, Quest, and Fundamentalism are among the religious variables that have been explored as possible predictors of personality, health, and well-being.

Projects and Questions

1. Develop an unconfounded and unbiased measure of religious orientation.

2. Develop ways of testing the usefulness and limits of the 2 × 2 (intrinsic liberal, intrinsic conservative, extrinsic liberal, extrinsic conservative) classification system noted at the close of this chapter. Does it predict attitude and behaviors?

3. Design procedures for developing an analogue to the Religious Orientation Scale in another religion and culture.

4. Perhaps a developmental model of religious orientation is needed. Are I-E categories related to cognitive stage models of moral development (Kohlberg) and/or faith development (Fowler)? See Chapters 4 and 5.

5. What is the correspondence, if any, between the concept of intrinsicness as it appears in the psychology of religion and as it appears in general motivational theory?

6. Is the Quest measure primarily a cognitively tuned instrument or does it predict religious experience? Is the Quest measure biased toward liberal expressions of religion and not appropriate for use with conservative groups?

7. Replicate the Good Samaritan experiment with modifications: Remove the confounding in the independent variable manipulation so that the cognitive content for the subject does not involve a conflict between helps, but instead involves application of the Good Samaritan principle to oneself. Conduct additional studies involving helping responses other than to medical emergencies.

8. Find ways of testing whether the indiscriminate categories (proreligious and antireligious) are similar or dissimilar. Do these categories have primarily cognitive or emotional bases?

9. What physical health, other physiological, and behavioral outcomes (e.g., aggressive behavior) might be predictable from an individual's religious orientation? Design studies to test such predictions.

10. Analyze various types of religious literature (e.g., children's books, tracts, devotional books, self-help books, conversion literature) for religious orientation content in order to find out what kind of style of religiosity is reflected in each.

11. Is religious orientation associated with independence in decision making? with transcendence of social norms?

12. Why is there a tendency for readers to interpret intrinsic as good and extrinsic as bad? Might this tendency change over stages of faith development?

13. Do the concepts of religious orientation, authoritarianism, and fundamentalism shed light on different "logics" of religious ethics?

Further Reading

The Journal for the Scientific Study of Religion publishes much religious orientation research. Thumb through volumes from 1970 to the present to find a variety of articles on this topic.   *Ma̅i̅ HM 2 7 1 A4/S4/*

Altemeyer, B. (1988). *Enemies of freedom: Understanding right-wing authoritarianism.* San Francisco: Jossey-Bass. A well written presentation of the development of the authoritarianism concept and its relation to aggression, religion, and other factors.

Batson, C. D., Schoenrade, P. & Ventis, W. L. *Religion and the individual.* New York: Oxford University Press, 1993. Includes an overview of the research on religious orientation.

Dittes, J. E. Religion, prejudice, and personality. In Strommen, M. P. (Ed.). *Research on religious development: A comprehensive handbook.* New York: Hawthorne Books, 1971, Chapter 9, pp. 355–390. A review of the literature up to about 1970.

Notes

1. Greenwald's (1975) Bayesian analysis of these data challenges this conclusion.

9

Health [abnormal]

life span

are 6 IV

Religion, Health, and Well-Being

A scene at a mental hospital:
Doctor to patient: *And who are you?*
Patient replies: *I am Napoleon Bonaparte.*
Doctor to patient: *Who told you that you are Napoleon Bonaparte?*
Patient replies: *God did.*
Another patient, from next room: *I did not!*

Do particular kinds of people tend to be religious? And does religion for these people generally help or hinder their quest for mental health, physical health, and a sense of well-being? In the previous chapter we found an equivocal and not-very-simple answer to the question of whether religion was good or bad for people's social health. In this chapter we take up a parallel issue—whether there is a relation between people's professing a religion and their personal well-being. Is there a religious personality—whether normal or abnormal? The issue of whether religious belief is positively or negatively related to the rest of people's lives is nowhere less clear than when we try to understand how religious belief relates to personality, health, and well-being.

The body of research dealing with the question of how religious belief relates to normal and abnormal personality yields few straightforward conclusions. Theorists disagree. Data from various studies show conflicting trends or no trends. Certain religious beliefs and doctrines do affect people's behavior in a straightforward way (e.g., religious teaching against drinking alcohol produces abstinence among adherents). But whether a particular personality type is prone to be religious is unclear. The relationship of religion to mental health is also unclear, in part due to the relativity of the concept of mental health. Perhaps the best summary point is that most of the relationships hypothesized by theorists and researchers (for example, that religion is associated with health and adjustment, as well as with pathology and inadequacy) are true some of the time for some people. However, none of them holds in general for everyone. Just as the research on religious orientation (Chapter 8) suggests that there is both a positive and a negative way of being religious, a parallel conclusion emerges from the research on religion, health, and well-being. Religion is part of a larger constellation of factors that may be either positively or negatively related to mental health, depending upon the role it plays in the person's total life.

The main barrier to making sense out of this material is the absence of theoretical integration. There is no clear conceptual framework that makes coherent sense out of the available data. The data themselves are not consistent; consequently, no strong and direct conclusions are possible. Therefore, in order to avoid merely presenting a list of findings without conceptual organization, it will be helpful to examine the research in a way that allows each topic to expand, qualify, or complement the previous ones. In the first section of this chapter, concrete evidence for a link between religion and pathology is presented in order to make the issue salient. The second section presents research on how religion relates to normal personality functioning. The third section extends the discussion to include research on how religion relates to abnormal, pathological functioning and mental and physical health.

Impressions of Religion and Psychopathology

There are two basic points that it will be useful to keep in mind while examining the relationship between religion and mental illness. The first point is that mental disorder or milder forms of personal inadequacy sometimes do involve religious content and symbols. That is, religious material is present in some disorders. Whether it is causal or consequential is unclear. The second point is that mental health is itself a relativistic concept—a feature that limits the possibility of ever knowing for sure whether and/or how religion and mental health are related.

Religious Material in Psychic Disturbance

There are a variety of pieces of information which individually can give us the impression that religion and mental illness must somehow be related within the personality. Some of these are dramatic instances of that connection and can be vividly remembered. Taken together, they make an intuitively convincing case that religion and abnormal personality, or psychological disturbance, are connected. But is that impression correct? And does its accuracy depend upon how mental health is defined?

Religious Symbolism in Psychotic Speech

One of the most vivid and intuitively appealing of these demonstrations is the common appearance of religious language and symbols in the speech and behavior of psychotic patients. Reprinted in Figure 9.1 is a letter written to me by one such patient. Examine it carefully and note its religious content and Biblical overtones in addition to its conceptual disorganization. This letter is a typical example of psychotic speech.

Several features of this letter warrant comment. First, it has no basis in reality and was unsolicited. I do not know Prophet _____ , and had never been in nor heard of the town from which this letter was mailed. Nor did I lose my employment. I later learned that there is a mental hospital located in that town. I presume that Prophet _____ is a resident there, because the printed stationery on which the letter was written gave detailed information about visiting hours. I can only guess at how the Prophet learned of me and happened to write to me.

Dear <u>Mr</u> Paloutzian.
  Your pain, at present, can easily turn into a GROWTH process —→
  I define maturity(as)
  I feel that you should correspond with me (as) I'm aware of your loss of employment and ETC. (my "LITTLE ONES" DID THIS—so do write or phone the above number. My/our GOD does not WILL that ANY SHOULD PERISH—I was, for over 5 YRS. AN Atheist—Now, after GOD taught me —→ I'm much; much HAPPIER AND I STILL LOVE PEOPLE, I STILL want them SANE, & I'm still a STUDENT of GENERAL SEMANTICS ——→
  I feel that I should CAUTION you against HARMING yourself—just write or phone me.
  I TRY TO NEVER GET IN A HURRY—
  Would you phone your family and let them KNOW that I'VE written you a letter—I'm cautious in BEING OVERLY frank, much less candid, BUT "<u>FEAR NOT</u>"—.
  I wish you kind Regards and I'd like to add that about 20 YEARS ago, I wanted to become a PSYCHOLOGIST—.

                                                        Prophet, _____

[*On back of last page:*]
  I'm watching a NEW, FINE, T.V. PROGRAM FOR CHILDREN—ENTITLED CLUBHOUSE —→ I urge you to watch "it" as its' quite FINE, EXCELLENT and MOST instructive FOR CHILDREN & so-<u>on</u>—(ETC!)
  as a child —→ I learned—"MERRIE MELODIES"! CARTOONS" BY Above TITLE.
  O! GOD IS LOVE."
  MANY MEANINGS, Above.

FIGURE 9.1   Letter from a psychotic patient

Second, the letter as a whole reflects the disorganized thinking present in some types of disorders. Each statement in the letter, taken by itself, seems coherent. But the overall organization of them, strung out together one after the other, makes nonsense.

Third, and most important for the psychology of religion, is the repeated presence of religious symbols in the series of disconnected thoughts. There are references to Bible verses, hints at having been an atheist but now being taught by God, and a closing that says God is love. Even the writer's title, Prophet, is obviously suggestive of the religious meaning of his self-definition. Hospital files contain many cases in which the patients' symptoms included religious symbolism, as is the case in Rokeach's *The Three Christs of Ypsilanti* (1964). How these religious meanings became part of the cluster of symptoms for this particular patient is anybody's guess. But the fact that they are there leaves a

vivid impression of the possible involvement of religious material in psychological disturbance.

Mental Illness in Religious Leaders

Evidence of psychological disturbance in religious leaders also suggests a link
between religion and disorder. Both depressive and excitatory types of disturbance have been documented. For example, John Bunyan and Saint Augustine
are reported to have suffered from severe melancholia and depression (James,
1902). Most saints or founders of religious movements are reported to have
had "their visions, rapt conditions, guiding impressions and 'openings'"
(James, 1902, p. 467), the assumption being that these experiences represent
such things as hallucinations or other abnormal psychological states. Argyle
and Beit-Hallahmi report that well-known mystics such as Saint Teresa had
"marked symptoms of hysteria" (1975, p. 136). The (faulty) argument based
on isolated cases such as these is that because religion and disorder are
associated in the lives of some religious leaders or innovators, they must also
be related in the lives of ordinary religious followers.

The Strange Behavior of Some Religious Followers

The unusual behavior of some religious followers also adds to the apparent
religion-abnormality connection. Some acts performed by some religious
people seem odd to the average onlooker. And it is all too easy for us to infer
that odd behavior equals abnormal personality. Consider one highly unusual
group, for example. The Satan cult of San Francisco reportedly engaged in
ritualized sexual and aggressive practices that carry strong overtones of
feelings of personal inadequacy among the participants, including high levels
of anxiety, low self-esteem, and aggression (Moody, 1974). When we realize
that the acts are largely sexual and aggressive in nature, that the participants
are often failures in those areas of life that involve sexual and aggressive
drives, and that a frustration of such drives forms the root of pathology in the
most important and influential theory of personality (Freud's psychoanalysis),
the implication is all too suggestive of a necessary connection between religiosity and abnormality.

Or, consider more traditional religious followers. Roman Catholics may
repeatedly confess sin to the priest. Pentecostals engage in the practice of
glossolalia (speaking in tongues) purported by some participants and researchers not to be a known human language but a verbal utterance that makes
no sense linguistically (Malony & Lovekin, 1985; Samarin, 1972). Here is a
transcript of a sample of glossolalic "speech:"

> *ke la la iy ya na now. key la la iy yey na yey now. key la la yey ir now. key la
> la iy ya na key la ya a now. key la key la ho ra ya na yey la la iy ye la ya na
> key la ya a now . . . (Jaquith, 1967, p. 3)*

Such practices may appear to the nonparticipant as bizarre; that is, as abnormal and consequently symptomatic of pathology. The case is bolstered further by the appearance of lack of individual will displayed by some members of new religious movements—those who have purportedly "snapped" and have become totally absorbed by their new religion (Chapter 6). None of these phenomena demands the conclusion that religion is for abnormal people, but it is easy to contemplate that idea when such vivid, isolated accounts are considered.

Opinions of Experts

Expert opinion can also feed the same impression of a link between religion and abnormality. For example, Albert Ellis (1962, 1977) argues forcefully that religion is bad for people. In a debate at the American Psychological Association, he gave a talk entitled "There is no place for the concept of sin in psychotherapy" that illustrates his general point of view as an influential expert (Ellis, 1960). The opinions of experts such as Ellis carry a lot of weight. The problem, however, is that when it comes to pronouncements about human nature, the experts do not always agree. O. H. Mowrer (1960, 1961), who is also an expert, takes the opposite point of view from Ellis. Mowrer's talk in the same debate as Ellis was titled "Some constructive features of the concept of sin" (Mowrer, 1960). Of course, you should always examine the data for yourself, whether the experts agree or disagree. Nevertheless, the serious implication of a link between religion and disorder given by many experts contributes to our impression that such a link must exist.

Is the Conclusion Warranted?

With all of the above information—religious ideas in some psychotic speech, psychological disturbance in some religious leaders, abnormal (statistically, low frequency) behavior in some religious followers, and the negative pronouncements about religion made by some psychological experts—is the conclusion that there is a necessary link between religion and abnormal or disturbed personality warranted? The answer is no. In each case, the nature of the evidence yields little information about the role of religion in the normal personality. The finding that religious symbols appear in the language of some mental patients says nothing about the meaning of those same symbols in the fully functioning personality. That disorder may be present in some religious leaders tells us little about whether it is also present in followers. The unusual behavior of some followers is not necessarily evidence that these individuals are suffering from pathology, or even if they are, that the same linkage exists between religion and disorder for other people. Taken together, the above examples can leave a strong impression of a connection between religion and disorder. However, there is no logical basis demanding that conclusion. Only by adopting the strategy of psychological research can we discover whether and in what ways that conclusion does hold.

2. *Relativity of Mental Health*

One problem inherent in examining relationships between religion and abnormal personality that is more basic than even the above sorts of information concerns the relativity of concepts such as mental health, adjustment, and normality. We need to be able to specify what mental health or normality is before we can know how religion relates to it. But when we ask "What is mental health?" we are left with only a partial answer. One type of answer might be called a reverse-negative: mental health is the absence of mental illness. Professionals generate lists of symptoms (anxiety, disorganized thoughts, obsessive thoughts of suicide, etc.) and say that if these symptoms are absent, then you're O.K. Clearly, this approach tells us what mental health is not but still does not tell us what it is.

Different psychological theories lead to different statements about what a mentally healthy, adjusted, "fully functioning" personality should be like. There is a difference of opinion regarding whether people should feel guilty about misbehavior (illustrated in the Mowrer-Ellis debate), whether we should regulate our actions by our feelings or our minds (humanists versus cognitive theorists), and whether health is conceived of as a congruent set of feelings as opposed to learned responses (humanists versus behaviorists). There is also disagreement about whether specific behaviors should be considered evidence of maladjustment (e.g., whether homosexual behavior is a symptom or not). There is even disagreement about whether it is healthy to have accurate perceptions. In 1958, Marie Jahoda included the quality of perceiving the world accurately in her list of the factors that comprise mental health. This view changed in 1988, however, when Taylor and Brown summarized a large body of data arguing that accurate perceptions of the world tend to be associated with mild depression, whereas mental health tends to be found in people who see the world through positive illusions (Taylor & Brown, 1988). Overall, there appears to be general agreement on how people should *not* be: not guilty to the point of being paralyzed; not denying or defensive about true feelings; not harmful to oneself or others; not obsessive or compulsive to the point of being debilitated. But there is less agreement on how people should be.

A closely related point that further broadens and complicates the issue is that the concept of adjustment (i.e., normal, therefore healthy) is culturally relative. Adjustment to what? Something that is abnormal (maladjusted) in one society may be normal in another. In the former Soviet Union, holding political views that were too far removed from those acceptable to the government could have resulted in your being labeled mentally ill or maladjusted, and placed in a mental hospital—the assumption being that sane people would hold to the government's ideology. The fact that a human activity or idea can be healthy in one culture but sick in another highlights the problem of the relativity of the concept of mental health.

The solution lies in a definition of mental health (or normality or adjustment) that is independent of ideological bias and cultural bounds. There must be an idea of a healthy, whole person that provides the core of a definition which everyone will agree upon as correct and which transcends relativistic norms. We need an absolute standard for health, not a relativistic one. This must be developed before we can fully map out the relation between religion and mental health.

The above problems are characteristic of many fields of science. Scientists observe covariation of variables, develop a primitive-intuitive theory of how they relate, and yet have difficulty stating a clear definition of the key concepts. Having a vague idea of what a concept means makes it difficult to clarify how it relates to others. Such is the case with the concepts of "mental health" or "adjustment." For present purposes it is fruitful to conceive of it as a complex mixture of several variables. These components would include, perhaps, lack of debilitating guilt, having a realistic perception and acceptance of one's limitations and faults, neither the absence of nor an excess of tension, effective coping mechanisms, a satisfying social life, a tendency to see the positive side of things, and an ability to feel a reasonable level of happiness.

Because religion, mental health, and personality are not precise concepts, we cannot expect research on their relationship to yield precise conclusions. Does past research indicate clear relationships among these concepts? The rest of this chapter illustrates that no strong overall relationships have been detected as yet. If such associations exist, more refined research is needed to uncover them. At present, we must be content to examine more narrowly focused research on the association between specific religious variables and specific personality and health variables.

Religion and Normal Personality

Early Childhood Factors

Let us begin by looking for possible roots of a personality-religiosity relationship by examining child-rearing practices. Some research and theory pertinent to whether such a relationship exists was examined in Chapter 4. The roots of adult personality are laid down during childhood, largely due to the disciplinary practices of parents. Therefore, it is reasonable to ask whether the way one was treated as a child correlates either with being religious or with particular styles of religiosity as an adult.

The general findings are that more punitive forms of childhood upbringing are associated with more religiosity during adulthood. Parents who use punishment and emphasize their position of authority over their children tend to produce offspring who are more religious. There are also some differences in parenting style between major religious groups. For example, Catholics tend to use physical punishment more than Protestants, and Jews tend to emphasize independence more than do Catholics and Protestants (Lenski, 1963).

Possible explanations for these relatively minor relationships include the ideas that (1) Religious parents generally produce religious offspring. But religious parents also tend to use more punishment in childrearing. It could be, therefore, that the relationship between being punished as a child and adhering to a religion as an adult exists because it is religious parents who happen to use more punishment. (2) The relationship between punishment and religion could be mediated by social class. The lower social classes tend to use more punishment and also tend to be more religious. (3) The punitive child discipline methods more often found in religious families and lower classes foster the development of the authoritarian personality. This personality type tends to be more religious, but in a rigid way.

Authoritarianism and Dogmatism

An appealing idea to some investigators has been that people who gravitate toward religion also have a rigid, submissive personality. The theory is that the cluster of traits and needs that comprise the authoritarian personality also are those that make one susceptible to religious answers and attracted to religious institutions. Research focusing on these issues has gone through three periods. The first period began with the publication of *The Authoritarian Personality* (Adorno et al., 1950) and used the authoritarianism measure (F-Scale) of the 1950s. The authoritarian personality was conceptualized within a psychoanalytic framework. The second period, overlapping and extending the first, replaced the concept of authoritarianism with Rokeach's (1960) concept of dogmatism. The third period involved a revitalization of the concept of authoritarianism but now seeing it as a consequence of social learning processes and using Altemeyer's (1988) psychometrically better Right-Wing Authoritarianism (RWA) Scale (see Chapter 8).

The authoritarian personality is characterized as rigid, inflexible, strict, and conservative. Authoritarians have a strict sense of morality. Acts are either right or wrong, with few shades of grey in between. Authoritarians have difficulty tolerating ambiguity. They feel uncomfortable in the absence of clear perceptions of stimuli and clear answers to questions. When it comes to ambiguous and difficult questions about life, high authoritarians would want simple and clear answers to these also. Because such answers may be provided by religion, the hypothesis follows that religiosity and authoritarianism would be associated. Authoritarians also would prefer a direct line of authority as a guide for regulating behavior. The hypothesis follows, therefore, that authoritarians would feel secure with the authority structure of many religious institutions. These adult personality traits would have been laid down during a childhood characterized by strict discipline and punishment provided by authoritarian parents. The outcome is, theoretically, a personality style with certain needs for authority, discipline, certainty, and security, which are satisfied through religion.

Is religion related to the authoritarian personality? Yes and no. Generally, research from the first period using the F-Scale to measure authoritarianism seemed to show that the degree of orthodoxy of religious beliefs was associated with the degree of authoritarianism. Glock and Stark (1966), in a large multi-church survey, reported that people who believed more orthodox doctrines also were more anti-Semitic, and anti-Semitism was correlated with authoritarianism (Adorno et al., 1950). But Glock and Stark's important study has been criticized by Dittes (1969) who noted that there were methodological problems in the study that could account for the results. Contrary findings were reported by Stark (1971), who found no relationship between orthodoxy of belief and authoritarianism among Protestants and a negative relationship for Catholics—more orthodox beliefs were associated with less authoritarianism.

A relationship between religious practice and authoritarianism also does not seem to hold up in the data. Stark's (1971) review of the research and his own data support this conclusion. In his study, for liberal and moderate Protestants there was no significant association between authoritarianism and regular church attendance. For conservative Protestants and Roman Catholics, the relationship was negative—lower authoritarianism was associated with more regular church attendance. Additional studies (Kildahl, 1965) have found that authoritarianism was not related to other religious variables such as whether one's conversion experience was gradual or sudden. Brown (1962, cited in Argyle & Beit-Hallahmi, 1975) reported that when religion is measured by mere denominational affiliation, people who claim some affiliation score higher in authoritarianism than those who claim no religion. Overall, the findings suggest that there is little consistent relationship between conventional forms of religiosity and an underlying authoritarian personality as measured by the F-Scale. This finding runs counter to the idea of childhood roots of religious tendencies in a punitive and strict upbringing.

Research stemming from the first period on the authoritarian personality was criticized on methodological and conceptual grounds (Christie & Jahoda, 1954); the outcome of such analyses included proposed alternate concepts. One important critique is that the F-scale (designed to measure authoritarianism) is biased in the direction of the political right wing. The F-scale is said to be sensitive to authoritarianism of the right but not to authoritarianism of the left or to middle-of-the-road authoritarianism. In order to correct for this problem, Rokeach (1960) developed an alternative concept, dogmatism, which is purported to be sensitive to authoritarianism in general, not just of the political right. Rokeach conceived of dogmatism as a closed cognitive style (see Chapter 8), rather than as a symptom of underlying psychodynamics, as was the conception of the original authoritarian personality. According to the dogmatism concept, it would be a closed-minded style of thinking and of perceiving the world, rather than a set of unconscious needs for authority and security, that would lead one toward being religious.

What research efforts there have been to test whether religion and dogmatism are related lend slight but general support to that link—at least within the moderate range of dogmatism studied and for certain types of religiosity. Rokeach (1960) reported that religious persons scored higher than others on the dogmatism scale. He also (1973) reported that those who rank the value of salvation, an obviously religious value, high on his Value Survey (see Chapter 7) score higher on dogmatism than those who rank it low. Paloutzian et al. (1978) reported a moderate but positive correlation between dogmatism and extrinsic religious orientation. Dogmatism was not significantly associated with intrinsic religiosity, however. Similarly, Raschke (1973) found that people high on dogmatism also tended to be high on consensual religiosity. Paloutzian et al. (1978) also found that "born-again" believers were higher in dogmatism than "ethical" believers. Stanley (1964) reported a small correlation of .19 between dogmatism and being a sudden convert, as opposed to a gradual convert. Overall, there appears to be some association between scores on Rokeach's dogmatism scale and religiosity, at least for the extrinsic-consensual form of it. To the extent that extrinsicness can be considered to be a personality trait rather than a specifically religious dimension, these findings hint at a link between personality style and religiosity. But again the link appears weak.

The concept of dogmatism has been applied to the concept of fundamentalism by Kirkpatrick, Hood, and Hartz (1991). They highlight a problem with Rokeach's dogmatism scale and offer a new perspective on it. The problem with Rokeach's scale is that 24 of its 40 items tap beliefs presumed to underlie closed-mindedness (e.g., beliefs about human helplessness, inadequacy of self, paranoia), but do not assess closed-mindedness itself. This confuses the structure of a closed mind with the content of that mind. Kirkpatrick et al. propose rejection of Rokeach's scale and a refocusing on the structural distinction between closed- and open-mindedness. In order to avoid the value-laden nature of Rokeach's terminology, they offer the terms "centralized" and "decentralized" in place of the terms "closed-minded" (or "dogmatic") and "open-minded." In a centralized belief system the beliefs derived from an authority (in religion, this might be one's scripture or leader) are held in an absolute and unquestioning way. In a decentralized belief system the beliefs are held in a more tentative and relative way. The implications of this new look at dogmatism for our questions about religion and personality await good measurement tools and research.

What findings emerge from the third period of research? Altemeyer (1988) has reconceptualized the developmental roots of right-wing authoritarianism (RWA) as stemming from a social learning process and being established during adolescence. This is in contrast to the theorizing about authoritarianism during the 1950s, in which its basis was seen as a cluster of unconscious needs stemming from early childhood. Altemeyer reports that parents were the most often cited sources of his Canadian students' answers to items on the RWA scale. High RWA students were the most likely to say that their own opinions were derived from their parents and their religion, whereas low RWA students more often pointed to their own experiences and to peer influence. Altemeyer reports that subjects who score high on the RWA scale are more likely to adhere tightly to the religion they were taught while growing up, regardless of the particular teachings of that religion. He suggests that being raised with authoritarian religion facilitates the behavior pattern of authoritarian submission.

Overall, authoritarianism and dogmatism are supposed to be linked to many of the same variables in the same direction, but for slightly different reasons. For example, high authoritarians and dogmatics both would be expected to be more suggestible, especially when an authority figure is doing the suggesting and when there is much ambiguity over the issue. But for the authoritarians, the greater suggestibility would be due to a greater need to depend upon a superior authority for guidance, whereas for dogmatics it would be due to a greater closed cognitive style in which information from an authority is held unquestioningly. In either case, the hypothesized link between religiosity and suggestibility needs to be examined.

Suggestibility and Hypnotizability

Authoritarians are supposed to be more dependent and dogmatics are supposed to be more closed minded. Both, however, are hypothesized to be more prepared, either emotionally or cognitively, to believe in whatever they are told. Therefore, if authoritarianism and dogmatism facilitate religiosity, we should expect religious people to be more suggestible. The rationale is that people who are dependent upon authority and/or who have difficulty living with uncertainty could be attracted by religious institutions because their needs for authority and guidance and for unambiguous answers to life would be satisfied. They would also more likely believe the answers provided by religious authority. Out of this theory emerges a picture of an interconnected cluster of attributes: Religiosity is associated with authoritarianism and dogmatism, which are associated with suggestibility.

Four types of suggestibility are referred to by psychologists: (1) Persuasability or social suggestibility refers to the tendency to believe or act upon a persuasive message given by a communicator. (2) Psychomotor suggestibility refers to the tendency to perform a bodily movement upon another's suggestion, even if one is not consciously trying to do so. (3) Hypnotic suggestibility refers to the ability to be hypnotized easily, to follow the hypnotist's directions easily, and to go quickly into deeper stages of hypnosis. (4) The placebo effect refers to the tendency to respond to a fake as if it were the real thing; for example, the ability to respond to a sugar pill (placebo) with reduced pain sensations when it is believed to be a pain-reducing drug. Do these types of suggestibility correlate with religiosity?

The general trend of the research findings indicates that people who are more religious are also more suggestible. However, this general finding must be qualified for various religious subgroups: (1) Fisher (1964) reported that people who value religion more and attend church more often also score higher on a questionnaire measure of acquiescence, implying that they are more likely to believe the statements of a prestige communicator. (2) Brown and Lowe (1951) reported that a group of Protestant Bible students scored high on the Hysteria scale of the Minnesota Multiphasic Personality Inventory (a large personality test designed to measure various types of disorders). Hysterics have a high tendency to translate psychological information (such as verbal statements, or conscious or unconscious emotions) into bodily reactions. Consequently, this is interpreted as evidence that religious conservatives are higher in psychomotor suggestibility. (3) Gibbons and de Jarnette (1972) found that students who report having a greater number of religious experiences also tend to be better hypnotic subjects. They are better able to comply with the hypnotist's suggestions. Sudden conversion, in particular, has been interpreted as similar to hypnotic-induced, trance-like phenomena. (4) Finally, different studies (Gelfand, Gelfand, & Rardin, 1965; Lasagna, Mosteller, Von Felsinger, & Beecher, 1954) have reported that people who attend church more regularly and who value their religion highly are also more likely to respond to a placebo with pain relief. In summary, there is some consistency in these results. The findings suggest that all four types of suggestibility are associated with some form of religiosity.

Interpretations of this moderate association between religiosity and suggestibility are threefold. First, it may be that religious institutions facilitate suggestibility in their adherents through instruction in obedience to authority, coupled with a teaching of humility and giving in to the desires of the other. Second, it may be that people with suggestible personalities (authoritarians and dogmatics) are more likely to become religious—precisely because they are more suggestible. However, if this second possibility were correct, we should expect a stronger connection between authoritarianism/dogmatism and religiosity than was apparent in the previous section. A third possibility is that suggestibility is associated with religiosity due to some third factor that facilitates them both. A frequently suggested candidate for this third factor is intelligence. In other words, personality factors may not be the key factor, but intellectual level may be.

Intelligence and Achievement

Therefore, with the lack of strong relationships between religiosity and authoritarianism/dogmatism and moderate relationships between religiosity and suggestibility, let us approach the question of whether religiosity is related to intelligence and other indices of creative or analytic ability. There are three types of questions here: (1) whether degree of religiosity differs according to IQ (intelligence quotient) score; (2) whether scientific achievement is correlated with degree of religiosity; and (3) whether there are differences among professional groups in strength and type of religious belief and practice.

Studies using intelligence tests show that IQ and religiosity are inversely related to a slight degree (Brown & Lowe, 1951). Analysis of this relationship shows that religious conservatives tend to score lower on IQ tests than religious liberals do. A tentative explanation for this latter relationship is that less intelligent people are less analytic, think less critically, and consequently believe doctrines more easily. People with higher intelligence, on the other hand, would be more likely to hold off belief because their minds would lead them to be more critical. In other words, intelligence level has a greater effect on how a person is religious than on whether that person is religious or not.

An analogous trend is apparent in the relation between religiosity and achievement in scientific fields. In a summary of findings, Argyle and Beit-Hallahmi (1975) report that there is a clear difference in the religious profile of American scientists compared with the general population. The percent of scientists claiming "None" for religious affiliation was 45 percent; the percentage in the general population was only 2.1 percent. Twenty-three percent of the scientists claimed Protestant affiliation, whereas fully 66.3 percent of the general population did so. For Catholics, these figures were 1 percent and 26 percent, respectively. Clearly, greater academic achievement, as evidenced by being a scientist, is associated with less religiosity, if the latter is measured by means of claimed religious affiliation. Also, however, Catholics are the most under-represented religious group among the scientific community relative to their proportion in the general population. Other studies (Leuba, 1934; Clark, 1955) report that more eminent scientists less often believe in God and are more skeptical about religious issues. These findings do not necessarily mean that scientists have no interest in religious questions, although they do not claim religious affiliations. They could mean either that scientists have an anti-religious world view (derived from the either/or philosophy) or that they simply spend so much time doing science that they have little time left to cultivate religious interests.

There are also some revealing differences in religiosity between scientific disciplines. Social scientists, especially psychologists, are more likely than natural scientists to reject religion. Early studies reported that 35 percent of American sociologists claimed "None" for religious preference (as opposed to religious affiliation), and the proportion of psychologists who believed in God was only 24 percent (Leuba, 1934). The more distinguished the psychologist was, the less likely he or she was to believe in God. Henry, Sims, and Spray (1971) report that in a survey of over 1,300 clinical psychologists, 42 percent claim no religious affiliation. Recent studies continue to find that psychologists, as a group, are the least religious of all groups in the academic community (Ragan, Malony, & Beit-Hallahmi, 1980).

Can these differences among professional groups be explained as a result of time pressures peculiar to academicians and scientists? Probably not. Many types of employment occupy much of people's time. Other explanations are more plausible. The difference is more likely to be due to a perceived conflict in world view. It is easy for psychologists and other scientists to perceive an apparent incompatibility between a religious world view and a scientific world view. Some may hold a fundamental belief that science and religion cannot coexist. Another explanation has to do with the scientist's self-identity. Stark (1963), for example, surveyed over 2,800 American graduate students and found that those who attended church less frequently also perceived themselves more as intellectuals. Finally, Argyle and Beit-Hallahmi (1975) suggest that some psychologists in particular may be less religious due to self-selection for unconventionality. Psychology is a young and unconventional field among the academic disciplines, and its creators are bent on finding new ways of accounting for human nature. Those who choose this field may naturally tend toward novel, untried points of view. It may also be that such fields represent a kind of substitute religion for some, or that peer pressure suppresses religious interest. These possibilities need to be tested.

Summary

Can the above survey of findings be integrated? Out of these bits and pieces of data, does there emerge a coherent picture of the religious personality—a distinct entity that is identifiably different from the nonreligious personality? The results are equivocal. The hypothesized relationship between authoritarianism and religiosity (stemming from the first period), even with the ingenious psychoanalytic theoretical underpinnings for that link, is not replicated enough to be considered solid. The hypothesized relationship between religiosity and dogmatism is more stable than the relationship between religiosity and authoritarianism, but even in the case of dogmatism the effects are not dramatic. Also, the relationships hold only with certain forms of religiosity (conventional-extrinsic) rather than with religion in general. The more recent work of Altemeyer on right-wing authoritarianism is beginning to yield a more consistent pattern of results and promises to be a fruitful research area in the future.

However, the relation between religiosity and suggestibility is better established, and the inverse association of religiosity with scientific achievement is most clearly demonstrated. Overall, it appears that little can be said in the form of a general statement that links personality with religiosity. There does not appear to be a religious personality as such.

More specific attributes, however, do appear to be associated with particular indices of religiosity: dogmatism with extrinsic-consensual religiosity; suggestibility with conservative/orthodox beliefs; higher IQ with more liberal religious beliefs; lower academic achievement, especially in the social sciences, with religious affiliation and belief in God. Whether there is one theory that can integrate these trends remains to be seen. The long-term outcome of research on these issues could lead to a conclusion similar to that reached through the research on religious orientation (Chapter 8). There may be positive traits in some people that prepare them for a positive form of religiosity and negative traits in others that cast religion in their lives in a negative light.

A major limitation of the research so far has been its methodological weaknesses. Most studies have been paper-pencil correlational designs that correlate one personality scale with some religious index. The latter have been notably simplistic (e.g., Catholic, Protestant, Jewish; frequency of church attendance; religious affiliation or preference, belief in God—yes or no). A few studies have attempted to scale the religious variables (e.g., fundamentalism–liberalism), but these have been less frequent although more recent. Clearly, some way must be developed to enable us to research these issues in a more refined and precise way.

The issue of a trait–religiosity connection has so far been examined only within the domain of normal personality. In the absence of any single, over-arching relationship, the question remains whether maladjusted or pathological forms of personality have any tie with religiosity. Strong, overarching relationships will again be absent. Nevertheless, let us widen our circle of investigation to include research on the extent to which religiousness is related to abnormality, mental and physical health, and well-being.

Religion, Mental and Physical Health, and Well-Being

Four possibilities exist for the relation between religion and psychological disturbance: (1) people with disturbances become religious as a coping mechanism; (2) religion induces pathology in initially healthy people; (3) certain forms of religiosity are associated with health, while other forms are associated with pathology; (4) religiosity and pathology or maladjustment are unrelated.

Here again the problem of the relativity of the concept of mental health surfaces: health relative to what standard? adjustment to what? It is no small argument that adjusting (or conforming) to a sick society may itself be a sick response. In this discussion, it is best to think of adjustment and health as basically an ability to function effectively within oneself and an ability to live harmoniously with others.

Religion and Mental Health

Anxiety and Inadequacy

Data exist which suggest that religiosity is associated with various types of personal inadequacy. Dittes (1969) reports that religious persons tend to score higher than nonreligious persons on measures of anxiety, and lower on measures of self-esteem. Early research (Rokeach, 1960) reported that people who had stronger religious belief experienced more tension and were more likely to lose sleep at night. The implication is that religious people are both more anxious and have a lower perception of themselves. However, the links of anxiety, low self-esteem, and loss of sleep with religiosity are based on correlational findings; the causal sequence producing these associations is unclear.

The above trends must be qualified for conversion type, doctrinal belief, and religious orientation. Sudden converts are apparently more anxious than gradual converts (Salzman, 1953, 1966), and those who espouse orthodox beliefs are apparently more ego defensive than those who espouse more liberal beliefs. Spilka and Werme (1971) suggest that it is those who score high on extrinsic (consensual) religiosity who also score high on measures of inadequacy and anxiety. Those who score high on intrinsic (committed) religiosity apparently do not. What emerges is a tentative conclusion that it is extrinsic religiosity, not intrinsic religiosity, that attracts people who are anxious. Furthermore, the overall trend in recent work suggests that how someone is religious is more important than whether someone is religious, a point addressed below. That is, in empirical studies, intrinsic religiosity is consistently associated with measures of positive self-esteem and extrinsic religiosity is associated with negative self-esteem (Hood, 1992; Watson, Morris, & Hood, 1987).

Although it is not clear that there is an overall relation between religion and anxiety in the general population, the two may nevertheless occur together in the symptomology of people with common psychological disorders for which anxiety is a basis. For example, in one study of 82 neurotics suffering from obsessions, an analysis of the content of their obsessions resulted in five categories in the following order, from most to least frequent: (a) dirt and contamination, (b) aggression, (c) the orderliness of inanimate objects, (d) sex, and (e) religion (Akhtar et al., 1975).

However, some paradoxes emerge when we compare the results of several studies. One paradox is in the relation between religious orientation, anxiety, and sudden conversion. It is those who have a committed orientation to their faith who are lower in anxiety (Baker & Gorsuch, 1982); and Scobie (1975) argues that it is the sudden converts who are more likely to be devout and committed. Therefore, we should expect sudden converts to have low anxiety. But Salzman (1953,1966) argues that sudden converts are higher in anxiety, which would imply that the committed persons are higher in anxiety. Perhaps one way to resolve this dilemma would be to ask when the anxiety is high and low. Sudden converts may be highly anxious before conversion. But after conversion they may be low in anxiety because of the anxiety-reducing aspect of the conversion experience. After conversion they may be both more intrinsically committed and lower in anxiety. This idea has yet to be formally tested, although it is consistent with the "relief effect" found in Galanter's (1989) observations of converts to new religious movements (Chapter 6). Overall, intrinsic religious orientation tends to be correlated with lower anxiety and extrinsic religious orientation tends to be associated with higher anxiety (Pressman, Lyons, Larson, & Gartner, 1992; Bergin, Masters, & Richards, 1987).

Another paradox is that religiosity is not always associated with anxiety or other measures of inadequacy. Pressman et al.'s (1992) review found no overall relation between religiosity and anxiety measures, and concluded that whether a relationship was found in a particular study depended upon other factors such as public versus private religiosity, with somatic manifestations of anxiety associated with private religiosity. Earlier, Sanua (1969) found no relation except for those who "felt guilty about not living up to expectations of their religious teaching." In an important study, Stark (1971) found that "on all measures of religious commitment, the persons diagnosed as mentally ill (in treatment at an outpatient clinic) are significantly less religiously committed than are persons chosen from the general population." Although being in psychotherapy at a clinic is not the same as scoring high on a questionnaire measure of anxiety, Stark's study is probing the same basic issue as the previously cited studies because patients are especially likely to suffer from intense anxiety and lower self-esteem. It would be interesting to learn whether patients are also more likely to score high on extrinsic religiosity but not intrinsic religiosity.

Stark's (1971) findings include the following: 16 percent of the mentally ill persons said that religion was "not important at all," whereas only 4 percent of the normal population indicated this; 21 percent of the mentally ill "never" attend church; only 5 percent of the normal control subjects never do so; 54 percent of the mentally ill do not belong to a congregation; only 40 percent of the normal population do not. Parallel findings emerged with regard to the relation between orthodox belief and measures of psychic inadequacy (e.g., "I worry a lot," "I often feel quite lonely," "I tend to go to pieces in a crisis"). For all groups (liberal, moderate, and conservative Protestants, and Roman Catholics), being high in orthodox belief was more likely to be associated with low psychic inadequacy than with high psychic inadequacy. The same trends were found when weekly church attendance was used as the measure of religiosity.

The above studies suggest opposite conclusions: religiosity is both associated and not associated with evidence of pathology and personal inadequacy. How can we account for this apparent contradiction? At least three ways of handling these conflicting findings are possible.

First, we could decide that one conclusion is false. Stark (1971), for example, concluded that the theory that says there must be a psychological link between religiosity and various measures of abnormality, even authoritarianism, is simply false. He presents a strong argument, proposing that social scientists find it hard to shake the old idea because of their own built-in prejudices. Being for the most part nonbelievers, they find it hard to believe that any truly normal person could be religious.

Second, as Argyle and Beit-Hallahmi (1975) point out, participation in any public religious practice, such as being involved in church activities, requires a reasonable level of mental health to begin with. People who are highly anxious or are otherwise severely inadequate are unable to function adequately enough in social groups to participate in typical forms of religious practice. Some basic level of mental health is a prerequisite to displaying religious practice in the normal sense.

Third, it may be that both conclusions hold, but for different measures of pathology and religiosity. Perhaps no overall general statement can be made about religion in general being linked with pathology in general. Rather, as Masters and Bergin (1992) argue and as Baker and Gorsuch's (1982) results show, it might be more fruitful for us to think in terms of forms of religiosity (e.g., intrinsic/extrinsic, committed/consensual) and how these forms relate to types of pathology. That is, both hypotheses about the relation between religiosity and mental health versus pathology could be true but only for specialized groups and detectable only upon refined analysis.

"Hard" versus "Soft" Measures of Mental Health

An important review was conducted by Gartner, Larson, and Allen (1991). They reviewed more than 200 studies concerning religious commitment and psychopathology. Importantly, they categorized the studies according to whether the measures of mental health were "soft variables," that is, paper-and-pencil tests designed to measure theoretical constructs, or "hard variables," that is, real-life behaviors that evidence mental health status. For example, a soft variable would be a paper-pencil test of anxiety, an attitudinal measure, or a score on a self-esteem inventory. A hard variable would be using versus not using illicit drugs, alcohol abuse, suicide, or physical health. Their findings are summarized in Figure 9.2. Overall, the studies which seemed to link religious commitment with measures of pathology used the soft measures. In contrast, the studies whose results tended to link religiosity with positive mental health more often had hard variables. The overall trend from this review is consistent with that of Stark, namely, that when people are asked to give answers to questionnaire statements about their feelings, religiousness tends to predict negative scores. But when health is measured by whether somebody is actually a patient or actually commits suicide, religion tends to predict the more positive outcome.

Religious Orientation

Larry Ventis (1995) examined the relation between the intrinsic (religion as end), extrinsic (religion as means), and quest dimensions of religious orientation and various measures of mental health. His analysis showed that no overall statement about the relation between religious orientation and mental health can be made because the direction of the association depends upon the particular measures of health used in each study. This is consistent with the point made early in this chapter that the definition of mental health is relative.

FIGURE 9.2   Summary of the literature relating religious commitment to mental health factors

Religion associated with mental health		
Physical health	Mortality	Suicide
Drug use	Alcohol use	Delinquency
Well-being	Mental health outcome	Depression
Divorce and marital satisfaction		

Ambiguous or complex associations between religion and mental health		
Anxiety	Psychosis	Self-esteem
Sexual disorders	Prejudice	Intelligence/Education

Religion associated with psychopathology	
Authoritarianism	Dogmatism/tolerance of ambiguity/rigidity
Suggestibility/dependence	Self-actualization
Temporal lobe epilepsy	

Source: Gartner, J., Larson, D. B., & Allen, G. D. (1991). Religious commitment and mental health: A review of the empirical literature. *Journal of Psychology and Theology, 19*(1), p. 7. Copyright © Journal of Psychology and Theology and John Gartner.

However, when the data were examined according to each of seven different definitions of mental health, there were some patterns that were apparent. The seven definitions of mental health were (1) absence of illness, (2) appropriate social behavior, (3) freedom from worry and guilt, (4) personal competence and control, (5) self-acceptance and self-actualization, (6) unification and organization of personality, and (7) open-mindedness and flexibility.

The overall trend for religion-as-end was to be negatively associated with all seven conceptions of mental health. Religion-as-means was positively, but not uniformly, associated with the seven definitions. It tended to be associated with absence of illness, appropriate social behavior, freedom from worry and guilt, personal competence and control, and unification and organization of personality, but not self-acceptance and self-actualization and open-mindedness and flexibility. The quest orientation overall showed neutral associations with the definitions, except for one: quest was positively associated with open-mindedness and flexibility.

Competence and Coping

Anxiety per se is a generalized, negative emotion. But anxiety often affects personal adequacy by finding expression in more narrowly focused life domains including negative attitudes about one's self, work, and ability to function. Consequently, we can develop alternative measures of personal adequacy by assessing people's competence in these more specific life domains. Psychosocial competence is one such measure. High psychosocial competence includes positive self-attitudes, work-attitudes, efficacy, and coping skills—all of which would be negatively associated with immobilizing levels of anxiety. The higher our psychosocial competence is, the more we have a sense of personal adequacy, the better we cope, and the less we experience anxiety.

In attempting to do refined analyses of the relation between religiosity and personal adequacy, it may be fruitful to assess psychosocial competence as a function of the interaction of different facets of religiosity. Religious motivation and religious practice (e.g., church attendance) are different facets of religiosity. It could be that it is the consistency between the two facets that is the critical factor in relation to the degree of well-being, rather than a person's level on each facet separately.

An illustrative study was done by Pargament, Steele, and Tyler (1979). They found that intrinsic religious motivation was positively associated with psychosocial competence. But the role of interaction between religious motivation and practice is evident in the next result. Those who scored low in intrinsic religious motivation but were also frequent church attenders were low in competence. It was the incongruity between religious values and behaviors that was the key link with lower levels of efficacy, trust, and ability to plan and cope. The key point here is that one's level of psychosocial competence may not be related directly to one's religious belief or practice, but rather to the degree of consistency between them. This idea needs more refinement and research.

Whether a lower level of competence leads people to be religious may be discovered in part by examining what happens to people as they become progressively disturbed and inadequate. One of the common symptoms of psychological disorder is withdrawal. Highly anxious people tend to withdraw from normal social relations. Their coping skills and sense of efficacy diminishes. They may become isolated, socially and emotionally. Often a vicious circle emerges with more isolation leading to less competence and even greater withdrawal, hence, the relevance of Stark's (1971) findings that mentally ill people are less involved in religion. They are less involved in social activities generally.

Stark's finding does not mean that disturbed persons have no interest in religious activity of any kind or that they are anti-religious. It simply means that due to their disturbance they are not involved in the normal, public forms of religiosity. Such persons may still be intensely involved in other forms of religiosity. For example, Lindenthal, Myers, Pepper, and Stern (1970) have shown that the frequency of private prayer increases with pathology. This finding can be interpreted to mean that, at least for disturbed persons, withdrawal leads only to less public religious display. For some there is increased interest in private religion or at least an interest in prayer as a possible coping mechanism.

What, then, is the relation between religion and coping? Pargament and Park (1995) surveyed a large amount of literature relating religiousness, various measures of mental health and well-being, and coping. Their overall conclusion is contrary to the older stereotype that religion is associated with pathology. It is based on careful examination of several bodies of information that Pargament has summarized as follows: "(1) Religious people faced with stressful life situations do not appraise their crises as less threatening or harmful than their less religious counterparts; (2) Religious items, when included in measures of coping activities, factor into active coping strategies . . . rather than passive ones; (3) Some styles of religious coping . . . are associated with high levels of personal initiative and competence; (4) Various measures of religious involvement and commitment have been tied to an internal rather than an external locus of control; (5) Seemingly passive religious strategies may be, in a paradoxical sense, quite active . . .; (6) Even when defensive religious strategies are used, they may set the stage for more active religious coping to follow" (quoted in Paloutzian, 1994).

Physical Health

The question of whether there is any relation between religion and physical health is as old as the presumed relation between religion and mental health.

A phenomenon, seen in both ancient and modern times, is people turning to their religion in search of a miraculous remedy for physical disease. Above, people come each year to Lourdes, France, in hope of cure.

In ancient scriptures as well as in some contemporary religious books and preaching, sickness is construed as a consequence of sin. Likewise, it is also believed by some that people's physical diseases can be healed by praying, performing a ritual, or calling upon one's God for supernatural intervention. Does religion have a direct causal effect on physiological healing?

Astronomer Carl Sagan (1994) examined this question by analyzing the rate at which people got well from diseases following their efforts to have a miraculous cure. He comments that over the past 136 years approximately 100 million people have traveled to Lourdes, France to be healed from disease. During this time, sixty-four cases of miraculous cures are said to be authenticated by the Roman Catholic Church. This means that the probability of cure is approximately one per million, similar to the odds of winning the lottery or dying in an airplane crash. It may even be that one is better off by not going to Lourdes. For example, Sagan says that the rate of spontaneous remission from cancers is somewhere between one in 10,000 and one in 100,000. The rate of getting well by doing nothing for such cases is higher than the rate of getting well for those who visit Lourdes.

There appears to be little scientific evidence that religious faith has a causal curative effect on purely organic disease. What is clear, however, is that belief in supernatural healing can help to temporarily relieve the feeling of suffering from the symptomology of a physical disease. That is to say, belief in healing can help pain reduction and an improved general perception of well-being.

There are data that indicate a statistical association between various dimensions of religious commitment and specific health variables. For example, Larson et al. (1989) found that people who attended church frequently and viewed their religion as important were more likely to have lower diastolic blood pressure. Koenig, Smiley, and Gonzales (1988) document research indicating that religious practice such as church attendance tends to be associated with lower coronary heart disease and lower mortality rates. Religious belief tends to be associated with more positive outlook in coping with disease. Ellison and Smith (1991) reviewed literature on spiritual well-being and found that a higher degree of spiritual well-being tends to predict hardiness when coping with HIV infection and terminal illness. It is clear that the behaviors performed because of one's religion, as well as the positive outlook on life provided by one's religious beliefs, contribute to physical well-being, but the pathways by which this occurs are indirect.

What might these pathways be? Dull and Skokan (1995) developed a model of the process by which religion may affect physical disease. The first pathway is through health practices due to one's religion. For example, a person's beliefs may dictate exercise, diet, or alcohol avoidance, and such behaviors would facilitate physical health as measured by reduced heart disease, better weight control, and a lower probability of liver disease or death by auto accidents due to alcohol abuse. The second pathway is through the combination of perceiving life events in the context of a larger meaning system and having positive illusions (Taylor & Brown, 1988) or a positive outlook on the world provided by one's religious belief. For example, coping with negative life events may be enhanced by seeing the event as part of God's larger plan or as a stimulus to personal growth, as well as believing that one has control over the events through invoking God's agency. The combination of these would foster an optimistic outlook and promote health-related behaviors. It would also enhance the cognitive control over microscopic physiological processes such as influencing the levels of T-cells and NK-cells in the blood or secretory immunoglobulin-A in the saliva (Ader, 1991), both parts of the psychoneuroimmunologic system. Therefore, the second pathway linking religion to physical health may be through the medium of social cognition. Consistent with this view, McIntosh and Spilka (1990) point out that intrinsic religious orientation is associated with health and that the intrinsics' use of prayer and their belief that they have a collaborative relationship with God provide a general sense of control and a positive outlook, both cognitive processes that may buttress the body's immune system.

Fear of Death

One important concept to examine as part of psychological well-being is the fear of death. Level of death anxiety is a rough index of well-being. For example, it has been shown that people with low fear of death score higher on the Purpose in Life Test (Crumbaugh & Maholick, 1969; Paloutzian, 1981). And high purpose in life is associated with the absence of pathological conditions such as alcoholism, neurosis, and psychosis and various positive measures of well-being (Chamberlain & Zika, 1992; Crumbaugh, 1968). Therefore, less fear of death is associated with a greater sense of purpose and greater well-being.

It was previously noted that anxiety can find expression in localized, focused ways. One of the most prevalent sources and manifestations of anxiety is fear of death. One wonders whether religion, with its many pronouncements and doctrines relating to what happens to people after they die, is related to the degree of death anxiety.

In early research, Kalish (1963) found that the relationship between religiosity and death anxiety followed an inverted "U" curve. Deeply religious people, who attended church most frequently, feared death the least. Irregular church attenders had the highest degree of death anxiety. Nonattenders had an intermediate level of death anxiety. Recent studies show a similar curvilinear pattern, with people with a moderate religious commitment scoring the highest on measures of fear of death and people having either the greatest or no commitment scoring the lowest (Pressman et al., 1992).

Two aspects of these findings should be pointed out. First, they can be interpreted in a straightforward way. People who are sincere believers in a teaching of eternal life would be expected to have less fear of death. Second, the pattern of these findings is parallel to the relation between church attendance (and therefore intrinsic and extrinsic religious orientation) and prejudice discussed in Chapter 8. Again, it is the hit-and-miss attender who appears to be the worst off—the most prejudiced and the most fearful of death. This lends credence to the distinction between a devout and nondevout form of religiosity. It also argues that inconsistencies in results in other areas of the religiosity-personality question may be clarified if in future research religiosity is broken down according to such a typology.

Although this intuitively appealing, devout versus nondevout typology makes sense, new research using multidimensional, refined measures forces a refined conceptualization of the relation between religiosity and death anxiety. Hoelter and Epley (1979) used multiple measures of fear of death and found that only a certain aspect of death anxiety, fear of the unknown, was negatively associated with religiosity. Religiosity was assessed by multiple measures including church attendance, self-perception of religiosity, belief in a supreme being, and orthodoxy of belief. Results showed that different facets of death anxiety, such as fear of being destroyed, fear for significant others, fear of the dying process, or fear of conscious death, were either not related to religiosity, or were slightly, and often positively, related to religiosity measures. It would appear that the religious doctrines regarding heaven and life after death reduce one major component of death anxiety, fear of the unknown, while not affecting some components and even sensitizing people to other components. Again we find that religiosity is related to both positive and negative aspects of well-being.

Spiritual Well-Being and Loneliness

The typical research study reported above involved placing people in a religious category and seeing how they scored on some measure of adequacy or well-being. This approach presumes that well-being is in essence separate from religious life—that well-being facilitates religiosity, that religiosity facilitates well-being, or that personality traits and dynamics produce them both. An alternative conception, however, is that well-being is an integral aspect of religiosity, analogous to physical and social well-being. We can then talk in terms of religious well-being (or lack of it) and existential well-being (and existential anxiety), connoting the experience of the religious and nonreligious aspects of life, respectively.

Paloutzian and Ellison (1982) developed a scale to measure spiritual well-being, made up of religious and existential subscales. These tests of well-being were conceived of as indices of the perceived quality of religious and existential life. Also, in this research loneliness was conceived of as an index of the perceived quality of social relations. Greater loneliness corresponds to less well-being and lower quality of social life.

Several findings have emerged relating spiritual, religious, and existential well-being to a variety of other health and well-being measures. Results showed that people high on religious well-being were also high on existential well-being and low on loneliness. High spiritual well-being was also correlated with higher purpose in life and intrinsic religious orientation and less extrinsic religious orientation. Spiritual well-being is positively correlated with people's ratings of their own health as well as being closer to their ideal body weight, and negatively correlated with blood pressure. It has been found to be positively associated with people's adjustment to hemodialysis, hardiness and hope among AIDS patients, lower anxiety in facing the trauma of being diagnosed with cancer, and self-esteem. Spiritual well-being has been shown negatively related to depression (Chamberlain & Zika, 1992; Bufford, Paloutzian, & Ellison, 1991; Ellison & Smith; 1991; Paloutzian & Ellison, 1991). Our interpretation is that spiritual well-being is an overriding concept of one's perception of the quality of life, of which the religious and existential aspects are components.

Counseling

One of the most practical areas in which the possible relation between religion and mental health is important is in the area of counseling. One's minister or priest is still the first, most likely person to be called if someone has a personal problem. Much counseling occurs in the context of religious ministry, churches, pastoral counseling, and para-professional religious self-help groups. Although individuals who have been helped by religious counselors understandably feel convinced that it was the special blend of religious teaching and counseling method that helped them, the research question is whether this blend is more effective than counseling without religious components. Fortunately, Rebecca Propst (1992) has done systematic investigation of this question. One group of Christian counseling subjects received cognitive-behavioral therapy that included "Christian religious rationales for the procedures," "religious arguments to counter irrational thoughts," and "religious imagery procedures." Another group received the same treatment without the religious material. Both treatments were done by both religious and nonreligious counselors. Overall, for subjects who were themselves religious, the combination of religious material plus the counseling technique was more effective in facilitating therapeutic movement and lowering depression. Interestingly, this effect was slightly better for the therapists who, themselves, were personally nonreligious but who used religious material during the counseling sessions.

What Conclusions Can Be Drawn?

What conclusions can be drawn regarding whether a "religious personality" exists and whether it is of a normal or an abnormal sort? The results repeatedly conflict. The concept of a distinctive type of personality that lends itself to being religious is lacking. None of the associations of religiosity with normal personality dimensions—authoritarianism, dogmatism, even suggestibility—are strong enough to establish firmly the existence of such a typology. Academicians and scientists, especially psychologists, are certainly less religious by any measure than the general population. But this finding is easily explainable by factors other than personality, such as the trends imbedded in one's professional identity and world view.

Furthermore, no consistent trends emerge regarding whether abnormal personality or states of non-well-being are associated with religiosity. Certain forms of religiosity (extrinsic, sudden conversion) appear to be associated with questionnaire measures of anxiety; but actually being a patient in therapy is negatively related to religiosity. Psychosocial competence, which would be negatively associated with anxiety and being a patient, depends on the interaction of the nature of one's religious motivation and the practice of the religion. Finally, religiosity appears to reduce one major aspect of death anxiety while mildly sensitizing people to other facets of it.

It seems clear, therefore, that no overall statement can be made. There are no general effects, only specialized ones. Religious persons, as far as personality and psychological adequacy are concerned, appear to be neither better off nor worse off than other persons. They are only different—slightly better off and worse off, each in specialized ways.

Projects and Questions

1. To what extent is the apparent connection between religiosity and psychological disturbance (illustrated in the first part of this chapter) believed to reflect reality? Does the extent of this belief differ for special groups (e.g., professional groups, religious groups, patients) compared with the general population? If so, what social and psychological processes produce such differences?

2. Do certain religious doctrines themselves attempt to define mental health and pathology? A content analysis of religious documents might be revealing.

3. Test to see whether there is any systematic relation between the type and meaning of religious symbolism in psychotic speech and speech representative of other forms of disorder.

4. Are there differences in the frequency, form, and intensity of religious experiences as a function of personality and level of mental health?

5. Test to see how anxiety, deviant and coping behaviors, and other measures of personal adequacy are affected by conversion. Use a repeated measures design if possible.

6. What changes in religiosity might produce changes in various facets of fear of death? in religious and existential well-being?

7. Test to see in what ways the meaning and content of prayer change as the level of psychological disturbance increases. If such changes are found, what process mediates them? Content analysis of written or transcribed prayers might be a useful technique here.

8. Does the question of whether religiousness is correlated with intelligence have any connection to the models of the development of mental complexity presented in Chapter 4?

Further Reading

Argyle, M., & Beit-Hallahmi, B. *The social psychology of religion.* London: Routledge and Kegan Paul, Ltd., 1975, Chapters 6, 8, and 9 summarize literature in this area.

Paloutzian, R. F., & Kirkpatrick, L. A. (Eds.). (1995). Religious influences on personal and societal well-being. *Journal of Social Issues* (Whole Issue), 51(2). Includes ten articles on the relation between religion and coping, mental health, physical health, alcohol and substance abuse, child abuse, prejudice and authoritarianism, HIV infection, adolescents, and the elderly.

Pargament, K. I., Maton, K. I., & Hess, R. E. (Eds.). (1991). *Religion and prevention in mental health: Research, vision, and action.* New York: Haworth Press. Includes 16 chapters covering the relation between religion and mental health, physical health, coping, and a variety of applied topics.

Schumaker, J. F. (Ed.). (1992). *Religion and mental health.* New York: Oxford University Press. Contains 24 chapters that address many topics concerning the relation between religion and mental health from the vantage point of historical perspectives, affective and cognitive consequences, psychosocial dimensions, and cross-cultural perspectives.

Spilka, B., & Werme, P. H. Religion and mental disorder: a research perspective. In Strommen, M. P. (Ed.), *Research on religious development: A comprehensive handbook.* New York: Hawthorne Books, 1971, Chapter 12, pp. 461–481. A review of the literature up to about 1970.

10

Evaluation and New Directions

General Evaluation
  Areas and Issues
  Cross-Topic Themes
  Method and Theory

Psychology of Religion and General Psychology

This book begins with the question "How does religion operate in people's lives?" In order to answer this question, we have explored many diverse topics. Each one leaves the impression of only tentative, qualified conclusions. Few hard conclusions seem permissible at this stage of the history of the psychology of religion. It is helpful, however, to reexamine the content and see what points can be made. Let us step back and gain a picture of the field as a whole, in order to learn how to move forward.

General Evaluation

Recommendations on how to proceed are an integral part of any general evaluation. What are our areas of evaluation? We are concerned with three different facets of the psychology of religion: specific areas, cross-topic themes, and the need for better research methods and theory.

Areas and Issues

Each area of research offers a set of tentative conclusions. But each one also leaves a series of topically focused issues that remain unsettled.

Religious Development

The analysis of religious development is an example of the application of concepts from general psychology to the psychology of religion. In particular, the cognitive-developmental/social thrust of that analysis is a reflection of the dominant themes in developmental psychology today. The meaning of religious language and symbols is different for children than it is for adults. This difference is due to the child's lower cognitive stage and the child's selective exposure to religious practices and ideas. The real religious challenge occurs when the youth develops adultlike cognitive abilities. Youths then think critically about religious issues and apply their own analyses of those issues to their own lives. Because of this, our interpretation of early childhood religiousness should be made with caution.

However, religious development is far from fully understood. Especially needed is an overall religious developmental framework that will integrate the vast array of data into a systematic whole. Fowler's (1981) recent faith-stage model might be exploited as a possible example of this. Such a model would need to be tested in order to find out whether people at various stages behave as the model predicts. As was seen in our discussion of lifespan religious development, several models exist. Future research can test their compatibility.

Knowledge we have from other areas of the psychology of religion may need to be modified when we take developmental considerations into account. For example: Are the principles we have developed regarding conversion and religious orientation age-specific? Might our understanding of religious orientation and conversion processes change if we see these in a developmental perspective? Research is needed to test these possibilities.

Conversion and Experience

Religious conversions are controversial, and the issues are not easily resolved. Conversion may be considered as change from unbelief to belief. It is useful to allow for the existence of subtypes of conversion, such as sudden and gradual, as well as more narrowly focused conversions, such as changing from negative effects to positive effects while maintaining the same beliefs. Conversion experiences are not necessarily pathological, emotional, or a result of adolescent identity crises, although they can be. Whether the convert should doubt the validity of his or her own conversion experience depends on the degree to which the religious change was a result of personal choice. A conversion is considered to be of the "passive" type to the extent that it is induced by external forces such as group pressure and social manipulation. People are not immune to religious persuasion although resistance to conversion appeals can be gained by learning about both social influence processes and the content of various belief systems. Awareness of these two things enables people to make their own independent choices regarding religious matters.

Different conversion models have emerged in the professional literature. The frequently used early distinction of conversion types includes sudden and gradual categories, sometimes contrasted with religious socialization. Each type corresponds to one theory of conversion. Sudden conversion corresponds to an emotional/psychodynamic theory; gradual conversion corresponds to a cognitive need theory; religious socialization corresponds to a social learning theory. The degree to which these distinctions are psychologically and empirically real, and the degree to which converts of each type function in ways predicted by the corresponding theory, has yet to be researched.

Some new religious movements have been characterized as having an oppressive social structure and a lack of freedom of choice allowed new converts. Others seem to evidence more positive attributes. The conversion models such as that by Lofland and Stark (1965) and by Richardson (1985a, 1989) typically emphasize the interaction between chance life events, personal needs of the convert, and strong social forces within the group. There are a variety of personal and social motives for joining traditional or new religious groups including a feeling of alienation and a need to belong. The concept of the "relief effect" may be useful in stimulating further research into how motives and religiousness are related.

As far as the conversion experience itself is concerned, it seems clear that converts regard it as a positive experience and develop a heightened sense of purpose as a byproduct. Among the many questions yet to be researched are questions about why the heightened sense of purpose is unstable and what other life events produce the same or similar effects.

Several kinds of work are missing in the area of religious conversion and experience. Both topical and methodological improvements are necessary. Topically, we need to know more about the behavioral effects of conversion. The ramifications of the active/passive distinction warrant investigation. Are these two hypothetical types of conversion empirically real? Do they predict different behaviors? To what degree is the conversion-as-creativity analogy a robust one? Are religious experiences truely unique? Methodologically, there are several possibilities for improvement. Most studies of conversion and experience rely on questionnaire methods. Possible improvements could include natural experiments and observational studies on behavior change following conversion or following an experiential manipulation. True experiments are possible, in which hypnosis is used to induce temporary mental states in experimental subjects.

Religious Orientation

Perhaps the most systematic line of research in the psychology of religion has been the work on religious orientation. Intrinsics have less-prejudiced attitudes toward racial minorities than extrinsics. The relation between religious orientation and prejudice corresponds to the relation between church attendance and prejudice, with intrinsics being more frequent attenders and extrinsics more likely to be casual attenders. Opposing theoretical explanations for these relationships, which have yet to be resolved through research, are that intrinsics have a different set of psychological motives from those of extrinsics or that intrinsics have a greater capacity for independent social judgment than extrinsics.

Religious orientation research comes the closest to being truly theoretical. However, even with this topic, many conclusions are problematic. For example, after 25 years of research we are still not sure whether the Religious Orientation Scale is a good measure. Is the underlying psychological dimension it taps attitudinal, motivational, cognitive, or confounded? Or does it simply tap those actions and attitudes prominent in a sincere but conservative religious posture? For what range of religious persons is it valid? One potentially fruitful line of research to add to this area might be based on a liberal/conservative distinction. A most important potential outcome might be the gradual replacement of intrinsic-extrinsic-quest research by the concepts of right-wing authoritarianism and fundamentalism as the primary concepts that drive research. Finally, we need studies of the behavioral consequences of religious orientation and the extensions of the religious orientation concept to nonWestern religious contexts.

Religion, Health, and Well-Being

The search for a religious personality, either normal or abnormal, yields few solid findings. Many of the findings about the relation between religiosity and personality dimensions are either inconsistent (e.g., early research on religiosity and authoritarianism) or are present but weak (e.g., religiosity and intelligence). The strongest finding is that religiosity is negatively associated with achievement in science and academics, especially in the social sciences and particularly psychology. These trends do not require a personality explanation, however.

A major limitation of the studies in this area is their over-reliance on simple measures of religiosity; for example, church attendance or affiliation, or orthodoxy of belief. Recent studies using more refined techniques for measuring the religious variable suggest that religiosity may be associated with personality and mental health in ways not detectable by the simpler methods. Pargament et al.'s (1979) study of the relationship between the interaction of intrinsicness and church attendance (i.e., belief and behavior) and psychosocial competence is an example of the type of study we need in order to improve our approach to this line of research.

Global questions (e.g., Are religious people more authoritarian?) will no longer suffice in the area of religion and personality. More specific, focused questions with refined measurements of variables are needed. Future research need not inquire whether personality or mental health are generally associated with religion. Past research indicates they are not. The more precise question is for whom and under what circumstances these relations are to be expected. A nice illustration of this general approach is by Larry Ventis (1995) who documented how three distinct dimensions of religious orientation (I-E-Q) are associated in different ways with seven different aspects of mental health.

The idea of there being particular personality traits that determine religiousness should be tempered, in light of Mischel's (1968) finding that traits are poor predictors of behavior. A preferred emphasis in future research would be on person x situation interaction in determining religiousness. Also, future research could include attention to the salience of the religious belief; that is, religion could be important in predicting behavior if it is made salient by situational influences.

Cross-Topic Themes

Several ideas have appeared in various places throughout the book. These are highlighted here because they are part of the essential approach of the field.

Psychology and Religion Are Complementary

This is true in three senses. First, we no longer need to think in terms of psychology versus religion as opposing explanations for human behavior. It is not essential to rule out the validity of one area merely because you accept the validity of the other, because they are not mutually exclusive. It is clear from a modern philosophy of science that the "either-or" philosophy is unnecessary. Because a psychological explanation of people's lives does not rule out nor rule in the possible truth-value of a religious account (and vice versa), researchers and practitioners in one field need not perceive the others as a threat. Instead, they are free to draw upon and cross-fertilize the research and experiences of each other.

Second, psychology and religion have at some points arrived at parallel conclusions. The clearest example of this is in the case of committed versus consensual (or intrinsic versus extrinsic) religiousness being parallel to what religion has described as devout versus hypocritical religious commitment. Another example is the distinction between sudden and gradual conversion. Both psychological research and religious teaching seem to document the existence of each. There are probably many areas of inquiry where religious teaching and psychological research do not grant us the luxury of such obvious parallelism. When apparent conflict exists, however, we can exploit it as an opportunity to study further and gain deeper insight into both.

Third, psychology and religion are complementary in practice. For example, we need not think in terms of psychotherapy versus pastoral/spiritual counseling. Although these are two different approaches to dealing with people's problems (the former connoting treatment of disease, the latter connoting evaluation and guidance), they can be used in combination to help people through different aspects of their problems.

b. Religion Is a Multidimensional Variable

This idea has appeared throughout the text in several ways. First and most prominent has been the dimensions of religious commitment. The necessity and utility of separating religion into belief, practice, knowledge, feelings, and effects has been repeatedly illustrated. The usefulness of dividing people into simple religious and nonreligious categories has long since passed. Research has repeatedly shown that more precise knowledge is gained by the more refined, multidimensional conceptualization of the religious variable. This point is most clearly illustrated in studies in which belief-behavior consistency is examined. It must be emphasized that the five-dimensional schema used in this book is not necessarily true or false. Nor is it the only conceptual breakdown for religious material. Like other schemas, it is a useful conceptual tool for breaking down, organizing, and thinking about complex material. I regard it only as a working model.

Second, the distinction between a personal and social level of analysis has been implicit. In order to fully understand the psychological processes operating in people's religious lives, it is necessary to know both what is happening inside people (thoughts, feelings, unconscious processes) and the social forces surrounding them. There are both personal and social motives for religion and personal and social consequences of religion in people's lives.

Religion Is a Value-Laden Topic

We cannot discuss religious topics without two things occurring. First, value-laden issues are impossible to avoid. All science involves value issues of some kind. However, this is especially true in the social sciences and in particular in a field such as the psychology of religion. To illustrate, even though researchers attempt to do empirical studies in an unbiased way, it is nevertheless difficult for most researchers and readers not to evaluate the intrinsic religious orientation as better than the extrinsic orientation (Dittes, 1971a). Similarly, some social scientists may have had a built-in antireligious bias because they assumed that because they do not believe religious teachings, it would not be normal for others to believe them. We also have the view prominent among some social scientists that religious people must be authoritarian (Stark, 1971), whereas the appearance of this association may be the result of a fundamentalist mind set (Altemeyer, 1988; Altemeyer & Hunsberger, 1992). Value dilemmas such as these should be acknowledged and clarified as objectively as possible (Bergin, 1980).

Second, when researching and reading the psychology of religion it is easy to project yourself into the material and make personal evaluations and applications. This is healthy, if not carried to the extreme. By applying newly gained insights into your own life, you can choose to change your own religious posture.

Method and Theory

None of the questions we have raised are answered to our complete satisfaction. Questions asked previously need to be re-researched with refined methods. Replications of prior studies are needed to document the stability of findings. Especially, repeated testing of a hypothesis by using several and better methods is needed to bolster the truth-value of the results of any given study.

One of the greatest challenges to any science is the generation of good theory. This is missing in the psychology of religion. We have theoretical orientations and models of human nature from general psychology that we apply to religious phenomena. We also have mini-theories about particular issues, such as theories of conversion. But there is not yet a comprehensive theory that integrates the whole field into a coherent picture. Future researchers will want to build one.

Psychology of Religion and General Psychology

The psychology of religion has developed a body of solid scholarship in academic psychology. This book, its contemporaries, the increasing volume of published research in this field, and the establishment of its own division within the American Psychological Association are all evidence of this trend as well as stimuli that will increase the trend. High quality empirical research in the psychology of religion is being published. Psychologists have begun to acknowledge that no complete psychological understanding of human beings can be attained without including a knowledge of the psychological aspects of religion. I hope this book has served its purpose in making the field especially inviting to you.

References

The author and publishers want to express their appreciation to the individuals and firms granting reprint permission.

Adelson, J., Green, B., & O'Neil, R. (1969). The growth of the idea of law in adolescence. *Developmental Psychology, 1,* 327–332.

Ader, R., Felton, D. L., & Cohen, N. (1991). *Psychoneuroimmunology,* 2nd ed. San Diego: Academic Press.

Adler, A. (1930). Individual psychology. In C. Murchison (Ed.), *Psychologies of 1930.* Worcester, MA: Clark University Press.

Adorno, T. W., Frenkel-Brunswik, E., Levinson, D. J., & Sanford, R. N. (1950). *The authoritarian personality.* New York: Harper.

Akhtar, S., Wig, N. H., Verma, V. K., Pershod, D., & Verma, S. K. (1975). A phenomenological analysis of symptoms in obsessive-compulsive neurosis. *British Journal of Psychiatry, 127,* 342–348.

Allen, R. O., & Spilka, B. (1967). Committed and consensual religion: A specification of religion-prejudice relationships. *Journal for the Scientific Study of Religion, 6,* 191–206.

Allport, G. W. (1950). *The individual and his religion.* New York: MacMillan.

Allport, G. W. (1954). *The nature of prejudice.* Cambridge, MA: Addison.

Allport, G. W. (1959). Religion and prejudice. *Crane Review, 2,* 1–10.

Allport G. W. (1966). The religious context of prejudice. *Journal for the Scientific Study of Religion, 5,* 447–457.

Allport, G. W., Gillespie. J. M., & Young, J. (1948). The religion of the post-war college student. *Journal of Psychology, 25,* 3–33.

Allport, G. W., & Kramer, B. M. (1946). Some roots of prejudice. *Journal of Psychology, 22,* 9–39.

Allport, G. O., & Ross, J. M. (1967). Personal religious orientation and prejudice. *Journal of Personality and Social Psychology, 5,* 432–443.

Alston, J. P. (1971). Social variables associated with church attendance, 1965 and 1969: Evidence from national polls. *Journal for the Scientific Study of Religion, 10*, 233–236.

Altemeyer, B. (1988). *Enemies of freedom: Understanding right-wing authoritarianism.* San Francisco: Jossey-Bass.

Altemeyer, B., & Hunsberger, B. (1992). Authoritarianism, religious fundamentalism, quest, and prejudice. *The International Journal for the Psychology of Religion, 2*(2), 113–133.

Argyle, M., & Beit-Hallahmi, B. (1975). *The social psychology of religion.* London & Boston: Routledge & Kegan Paul.

Asch, S. E. (1952). *Social psychology.* Englewood Cliffs, NJ: Prentice-Hall.

Ashcraft, M. H. (1989). *Human memory and cognition.* Glenview, IL: Scott, Foresman.

Augustine, St. (397/360). *The Confessions of St. Augustine.* Trans. by J. K. Ryan. Garden City, NY: Doubleday.

Baker, M., & Gorsuch, R. (1982). Trait anxiety and intrinsic-extrinsic religiousness. *Journal for the Scientific Study of Religion, 21*, 119–122.

Bandura, A. (1977). *Social learning theory.* Englewood Cliffs, NJ: Prentice-Hall.

Barker, E. (1984). *The making of a Moonie: Choice or brainwashing?* Oxford: Blackwell.

Barker, E. (1989). *New religious movements: A practical introduction.* London: Her Majesty's Stationery Office.

Barker, E. (1995). The scientific study of religion? You must be joking! *Journal for the Scientific Study of Religion, 34*(3), 287–310.

Barker, I. R., & Currie, R. F. (1985). Do converts always make the most committed Christians? *Journal for the Scientific Study of Religion, 24*(3), 305–313.

Barnes, M., Doyle, D., & Johnson, B. (1989). The formulation of a Fowler Scale: An empirical assessment among Catholics. *Review of Religious Research, 30*(4), 412–420.

Bassett, R. L., Camplin, W., Humphrey, D., Dorr, C., Biggs, S., Distaffen, R., Doxtator, I., Flaherty, M., Hunsberger, P. J., Poage, R., & Thompson, H. (1991). Measuring Christian maturity: A comparison of several scales. *Journal of Psychology and Theology, 19*(1), 84–93.

Bassett, R. L., Perry, K., Repass, R., Silver, E., & Welsh, T. (1994). Perceptions of God among persons with mental retardation: A research note. *Journal of Psychology and Theology, 22*(1), 35–49.

Batson, C. D. (1976). Religion as prosocial: Agent or double agent? *Journal for the Scientific Study of Religion, 15*, 29–45.

Batson, C. D. (1977). Experimentation in psychology of religion: An impossible dream. *Journal for the Scientific Study of Religion, 16*, 413–418

Batson, C. D. (1979). Experimentation in psychology of religion: Living with or in a dream? *Journal for the Scientific Study of Religion, 18*, 90–93.

Batson, C. D. (1986). An agenda item for psychology of religion: Getting respect. *Journal of Psychology and Christianity, 5*(2), 6–11. Also in H. N. Malony (Ed.), *Psychology of religion: Personalities, problems, possibilities* pp. 325–333. Grand Rapids, MI: Baker Book House, 1991.

Batson, C. D., Naifeh, S. J., & Pate, S. (1978). Social desirability, religious orientation, and racial prejudice. *Journal for the Scientific Study of Religion, 17*, 31–41.

Batson, C. D., Schoenrade, P., & Ventis, W. L. (1993). *Religion and the individual.* New York: Oxford University Press.

Batson, C. D., & Ventis, W. L. (1982). *The religious experience: A social-psychological perspective*. New York: Oxford University Press.

Beckford, J. A. (1985). *Cult controversies: The societal response to new religious movements*. London & New York: Tavistock Publications.

Beit-Hallahmi, B. (1974). Psychology of religion 1880–1930: The rise and fall of a psychological movement. *Journal of the History of the Behavioral Sciences, 10*, 84–90.

Beit-Hallahmi, B. (1989). *Prolegomina to the psychological study of religion*. Lewisburg: Bucknell University Press; London and Toronto: Associated University Presses.

Benson, P. L. (1991/1992). *Patterns of religious development in adolescence and adulthood*. Address presented to the American Psychological Association annual meeting, San Francisco, August 17, 1991. Published in *Psychology of Religion Newsletter, 17*(2), pp. 2–9, Spring 1992.

Benson, P. L. (1993). *The troubled journey: A portrait of 6th–12th grade youth*. Minnesota: Search Institute.

Benson, P. L., Donahue, M. J., & Erickson, J. A. (1989). Adolescence and religion: A review of the literature from 1970 to 1986. In M. Lynn & D. Moberg (Eds.), *Research in the Social Scientific Study of Religion, Vol. 1*, (pp. 153–181). Greenwich CT: JAI Press.

Benson, P. L., Donahue, M., & Erickson, J. (1993). The faith-maturity scale: Conceptualization, measurement, and empirical validation. In M. Lynn & D. Moberg (Eds.), *Research in the Social Scientific Study of Religion, Vol. 5*, (pp. 1–26). Greenwich: JAI.

Benson, P. L., Yeager, R. J., Wood, P. K., Guerra, M. J., & Manno, B. V. (1986). *Catholic high schools: Their impact on low-income students*. Washington DC: National Catholic Educational Association.

Bergin, A. E. (1980). Psychotherapy and religious values. *Journal of Consulting and Clinical Psychology, 48*, 95–105.

Bergin, A. E. (1991). Values and religious issues in psychotherapy and mental health. *American Psychologist, 46*(4), 394–403.

Bergin, A. E., Masters, K. S., & Richards, P. S. (1987). Religiousness and mental health reconsidered: A study of an intrinsically religious sample. *Journal of Counseling Psychology, 34*, 197–204.

Bianchi, E. C. (1982). *Aging as a spiritual journey*. New York: Crossroad Publishing Company.

Blazer, D., & Palmore, E. (1976). Religion and aging in a longitudinal panel. *The Gerontologist, 16*, 82–85.

Blum, R. H., Braunstein, L., & Stone, A. (1969). Normal drug use: An exploratory study of patterns and correlations. In J. O. Cole & J. R. Wittenborn (Eds.), *Drug abuse: Social and psychopharmacological aspects*. Springfield, IL: Charles C. Thomas.

Bock, D. C., & Warren, N. C. (1972). Religious belief as a factor in obedience to destructive commands. *Review of Religious Research, 13*, 185–191.

Bolt, M. (1975). Purpose in life and religious orientation. *Journal of Psychology and Theology, 3*, 116–118.

Bowlby, J. (1969). *Attachment and loss, Vol. 1: Attachment*. New York: Basic Books.

Bowlby, J. (1973). *Attachment and loss, Vol. 2: Separation, anxiety, and anger*. New York: Basic Books.

Bowlby, J. (1980). *Attachment and loss, Vol. 3: Loss*. New York: Basic Books.

Broen, W. E., Jr. (1955). Personality correlates of certain religious attitudes. *Journal of Consulting Psychology, 19*, 64. See also J. P. Robinson & P. Shaver (Eds.), *Measures of social psychological attitudes* (Rev. ed.). Ann Arbor, MI: Institute for Social Research, 1973, pp. 671–674.

Brown, L. B. (1962). A study of religious belief. *British Journal of Psychology, 53,* 259–272.

Brown, L. B. (Ed.). (1985). *Advances in the psychology of religion.* Oxford and New York: Pergamon.

Brown, L. B. (1987). *Psychology of religious belief.* London and Orlando: Academic Press.

Brown, L. B. (1994). *The human side of prayer.* Birmingham, AL: Religious Education Press.

Brown, W. S., & Caetano, C. (1992). Conversion, cognition, and neuropsychology. In H. N. Malony & S. Southard (Eds.), *Handbook of religious conversion* (pp. 147–158). Birmingham, AL: Religious Education Press.

Brown, D. G., & Lowe, W. L. (1951). Religious beliefs and personality characteristics of college students. *Journal of Social Psychology, 33,* 103–129.

Bufford, R. K., Paloutzian, R. F., & Ellison, C. W. (1991). Norms for the spiritual well-being scale. *Journal of Psychology and Theology, 19*(1), 56–70.

Bugliosi, V. with Curt Gentry. (1974). *Helter skelter: The true story of the Manson murders.* New York: Norton. Bantam edition, 1975.

Burtt, H. E., & Falkenburg, D. R. (1941). The influence of majority and expert opinion on religious attitudes. *Journal of Social Psychology, 14,* 269–278.

Butman, R. E. (1990). The assessment of religious development: Some possible options. *Journal of Psychology and Christianity, 9*(2), 14–26.

Chamberlain, K., & Zika, S. (1992). Religiosity, meaning in life, and psychological well-being. In J. F. Schumaker (Ed.), *Religion and mental health* (pp. 138–148). New York: Oxford University Press.

Change, Yes-Upheaval, No. (1971). *Life, 70,* 21–30.

Christie, R. C., & Jahoda, M. (Eds.). (1954). *Studies in the scope and method of the authoritarian personality.* New York: Free Press.

Clark, M. H. (1955). A study of some of the factors leading to achievement and creativity with special reference to religious skepticism and belief. *Journal of Social Psychology, 41,* 57–69.

Clayton, R. R. 5-D or 1? (1971). *Journal for the Scientific Study of Religion, 10,* 37–40.

Cleaver, E. (1978). *Soul on fire.* Waco, TX: Word Books.

Cole, L., & Hall, I. N. (1970). *Psychology of adolescence* (7th ed.). New York: Holt.

Coles, R. (1990). *The spiritual life of children.* Boston: Houghton Mifflin.

Connors. J. F., III, Leonard, R. C., & Burnham, K. E. (1968). Religion and opposition to war among college students. *Sociological Analysis, 29,* 211–219.

Conway, F., & Siegelman, J. (1978). *Snapping: America's epidemic of sudden personality change.* Philadelphia & New York: J. B. Lippincott.

Cox, R. H. (1973). *Religious systems and psychotherapy.* Springfield, IL: Charles C. Thomas.

Cox, H. (1977). *Turning east: The promise and peril of the new orientalism.* New York: Simon and Schuster.

Crandall, J. E. (1975). A scale of social interest. *Journal of Individual Psychology, 31,* 187–195.

Crandall, J. E. (1980). Adler's concept of social interest: Theory, measurement, and implications for adjustment. *Journal of Personality and Social Psychology, 39,* 481–495.

Crandall, J. E., & Rasmussen, R. D. (1975). Purpose in life as related to specific values. *Journal of Clinical Psychology, 31,* 483–485.

Crandall, V. C., & Gozali, J. (1969). The social desirability responses of children of four religious-cultural groups. *Child Development, 40,* 751–762.

Crowne, D., & Marlowe, D. (1964). *The approval motive.* New York: Wiley.

Crumbaugh, J. C. (1968). Cross-validation of a Purpose-in-Life test based on Frankl's concepts. *Journal of Individual Psychology, 24,* 74–81.

Crumbaugh, J. C., & Maholick, L. T. (1969). *The purpose in life test.* Munster, IN: Psychometric Affiliates.

Darley, J. M., & Batson, C. D. (1973). From Jerusalem to Jericho: A study of situational and dispositional variables in helping behavior. *Journal of Personal and Social Psychology, 27,* 100–108.

De Bord, L. W. (1969). Adolescent religious participation: An examination of sib-structure and church attendance. *Adolescence, 4,* 557–570.

Deci, E. (1975). *Intrinsic motivation.* New York: Plenum.

Deconchy, J-P. (1991). Religious belief systems: Their ideological representations and practical constraints. *The International Journal for the Psychology of Religion, 1*(1), 5–21.

Dittes, J. E. (1969). Psychology of religion. In G. Lindzey & E. Aronson (Eds.), *The handbook of social psychology* (2nd ed.), Vol. V., (pp. 602–659). Reading, MA: Addison-Wesley.

Dittes, J. E. (1971a). Typing the typologies: Some parallels in the career of church-sect and extrinsic-intrinsic. *Journal for the Scientific Study of Religion, 10,* 375–383.

Dittes, J. (1971b). Religion, prejudice, and personality. In M. P. Strommen (Ed.), *Research on religious development.* New York: Hawthorn.

Donahue, M. J. (1985). Intrinsic and extrinsic religiousness: Review and meta-analysis. *Journal of Personality and Social Psychology, 48,* 400–419.

Donahue, M. J. (1995). Catholicism and religious experience. In R.W. Hood Jr. (Ed.), *Handbook of religious experience.* Birmingham, AL: Religious Education Press.

Donahue, M. J., & Benson, P. L. (1995). Religion and the well-being of adolescents. *Journal of Social Issues, 51*(2), 145–160.

Douglas, W. (1963). Religion. In N. L. Farberow (Ed.), *Taboo topics* (pp. 80–95). New York: Atherton.

Dull, V. T., & Skokan, L. A. (1995). A cognitive model of religion's influence on health. *Journal of Social Issues, 51*(2), 49–64.

Durkheim, E. (1915). *The elementary forms of the religious life.* London: Allen & Unwin.

Dutt, N. K. (1965). Attitudes of the university students toward religion. *Journal of Psychological Research, 9,* 127–130.

Ebaugh, H. R. F., & Haney, C. A. (1978). Church attendance and attitudes toward abortion: Differentials in liberal and conservative churches. *Journal for the Scientific Study of Religion, 17,* 407–413.

Eliade, M. (Ed.). (1987). *The encyclopedia of religion.* New York: Collier MacMillan.

Elkind, D. (1970). The origins of religion in the child. *Review of Religious Research, 12,* 35–42.

Ellis, A. (1960). There is no place for the concept of sin in psychotherapy. *Journal of Counseling Psychology, 7,* 188–192.

Ellis, A. (1962). *Reason and emotion in psychotherapy.* New York: Lyle Stuart.

Ellis, A. (March/April 1977). Religious belief in the United States today. *The Humanist*, 38–41.

Ellison, J. W. (1965). Computers and the testaments. In *Computers for the humanities* (pp. 64–74). New Haven: Yale.

Ellison, C. W., & Smith, J. (1991). Toward an integrative measure of health and well-being. *Journal of Psychology and Theology, 19*(1), 35–48.

Enroth, R. (1992). *Churches that abuse.* Grand Rapids, MI: Zondervan.

Erikson, E. H. (1963). *Childhood and society* (2nd ed., rev. and enlarged). New York: Norton.

Faulkner, J. E., & DeJong, G. F. (1966). Religiosity in 5-D: An empirical analysis. *Social Forces, 45*, 246–254.

Feagin, J. R. (1964). Prejudice and religious types: A focused study of Southern fundamentalists. *Journal for the Scientific Study of Religion, 4*, 3–13.

Festinger, L. (1957). *A theory of cognitive dissonance.* Stamford, CA: Stanford University Press.

Festinger, L., Riecken, H. W., & Schachter, S. (1956). *When prophecy fails.* Minneapolis: University of Minnesota Press.

Fishbein, M. & Ajzen, I. (1975). *Belief, attitude, intention, and behavior: An introduction to theory and research.* Reading, MA: Addison-Wesley.

Fisher, S. (1964). Acquiescence and religiosity. *Psychological Reports, 15*, 784.

Fiske, S. T., & Taylor, S. E. (1991). *Social cognition*, 2nd ed. New York: McGraw-Hill.

Fleck, J. R., Ballard, S. N., & Reilly, J. W. (1975). The development of religious concepts and maturity: A three stage model. *Journal of Psychology and Theology, 3*, 156–163.

Fowler, J. (1980). Moral stages and the development of faith. In B. Munsey (Ed.), *Moral development, moral education, and Kohlberg.* Birmingham, AL: Religious Education Press.

Fowler, J. (1981). *Stages of faith: The psychology of human development and the quest for meaning.* New York: Harper & Row.

Fowler, J. W. (1986). Faith and the structure of meaning. In C. Dykstra & S. Parks, *Faith development and Fowler* (pp. 15–42). Birmingham AL: Religious Education Press.

Fowler, J. W. (1991). Stages in faith consciousness. In F. K. Oser & W. G. Scarlett (Eds.) *Religious development in childhood and adolescence* (pp. 27–45). San Francisco: Jossey-Bass.

Frankl, V. (1955). *The doctor and the soul: An introduction to logotherapy.* New York: Knopf.

Frankl, V. (1963). *Man's search for meaning.* New York: Washington Square Press.

Frankl, V. (1975). *The unconscious god.* New York: Simon & Schuster. (Originally published, 1947.)

Freud, S. (1900/1955). *The interpretation of dreams* (J. Strachey, trans.). New York: Basic Books. (Originally published, 1900.)

Freud, S. (1927/1961). *The future of an illusion* (J. Strachey, trans.). New York: Norton. (Originally published, 1927.)

Fromm, E. (1941). *Escape from freedom.* New York: Holt, Rinehart & Winston.

Fuller, A. R. (1994). *Psychology and religion: Eight points of view.* Lanham, MD: Rowman & Littlefield, Publishers Inc.

Fullerton, J. T., & Hunsberger, B. (1982). A unidimensional measure of Christian orthodoxy. *Journal for the Scientific Study of Religion, 21*, 317–326.

Galanter, M. (1989). *Cults: Faith, healing, and coercion.* New York: Oxford University Press.

Gallup, G. (1987). *Gallup youth poll.* Princeton Religion Research Center.

Gallup, G. (1994). Importance of religion. *PRRC Emerging Trends, 16,* 4.

Gallup, Jr., G. H., & Bezilla, R. (1992). *The religious life of young Americans.* Princeton, NJ: Gallup Institute.

Gallup Opinion Index. (1977–78). *Religion in America 1977–78.* Princeton, NJ: The American Institute of Public Opinion.

Gallup Opinion Index. (1979–80). *Religion in America 1979–80.* Princeton, NJ: The American Institute of Public Opinion.

Gallup, G., & Jones, S. (1989). *One hundred questions and answers: Religion in America.* Princeton, NJ: Princeton Religion Research Center.

Gallup, G., & Newport, F. (1990, June). More Americans now believe in a power outside themselves. *Gallup Poll Monthly,* 33–38.

Garfield, S. J., Cohen, H. A., & Roth, R. M. (1967). A correlative study of cheating in college students. *Journal of Educational Research, 61,* 171–173.

Garrity, F. D. (1961). A study of some secondary modern school pupils' attitudes towards religious education. *Religious Education, 56,* 141–143.

Gartner, J., Larson, D. B., & Allen, G. D. (1991). Religious commitment and mental health: A review of the empirical literature. *Journal of Psychology and Theology, 19*(1), 6–25.

Gelfand, D. M., Gelfand, S., & Rardin, M. W. (1965). Some personality factors associated with placebo responsivity. *Psychological Reports, 17,* 555–562.

Gergen, K. J. (1994). Exploring the postmodern: Perils or potentials? *American Psychologist, 49*(5), 412–416.

Gibbons, D., & De Jarnette, J. (1972). Hypnotic susceptibility and religious experience. *Journal for the Scientific Study of Religion, 11,* 152–156.

Gilligan, C. (1982). *In a different voice: Psychological theory and women's development.* Cambridge, MA: Harvard University Press.

Glock, C. Y. (1962). On the study of religious commitment: Review of recent research bearing on religious character formation. Supplement to *Religious Education* (July-August 1962). New York: Religious Research Association, *42,* 98–110.

Glock, C. Y. (1964). The role of deprivation in the origin and evolution of religious groups. In R. Lee & M. E. Marty (Eds.), *Religion and social conflict.* New York: Oxford University Press.

Glock, C. Y., & Stark, R. (1965). *Religion and society in tension.* Chicago: Rand McNally.

Glock, C. Y., & Stark, R. (1966). *Christian beliefs and anti-semitism.* New York: Harper & Row.

Goldman, R. (1964). *Religious thinking from childhood to adolescence.* London: Routledge and Kegan Paul.

Goldsen, R., Rosenberg, M., Williams, R. M., & Suchman, E. A. (1960). *What college students think.* New York: Van Nostrand.

Gorsuch, R. L. (1976). Religion as a significance predictor of important human behavior. In W. J. Donaldson, Jr. (Ed.), *Research on mental health and religious behavior.* Atlanta: Psychological Studies Institute.

Gorsuch, R. L. (1980). Identifying the religiously committed person. In J.R. Tisdale (Ed.), *Growing edges in the psychology of religion.* Chicago: Nelson-Hall.

Gorsuch, R. L. (1982). Practicality and ethics of experimental research when studying religion. *Journal for the Scientific Study of Religion, 21,* 370–372.

Gorsuch, R. L. (1984). Measurement: The boon and bane of investigating religion. *American Psychologist, 39*(3), 228–236.

Gorsuch, R. L. (1988). Psychology of religion. *Annual Review of Psychology, 39,* 201–221.

Gorsuch, R. L. (1995). Religious aspects of substance abuse and recovery. *Journal of Social Issues, 51*(2), 65–83.

Gorsuch, R. L., & Aleshire, D. (1974). Christian faith and ethnic prejudice: A review and interpretation of research. *Journal for the Scientific Study of Religion, 13,* 281–307.

Gorsuch, R. L., & Smith, C. S. (1983). Attributions of responsibility to God: An interaction of religious beliefs and outcomes. *Journal for the Scientific Study of Religion, 22,* 340–352.

Gorsuch, R. L., & Venable, G. D. (1983). Development of an "age universal" I-E scale. *Journal for the Scientific Study of Religion, 22,* 181–187.

Graham, T. W., Kaplan, B. H., Cornoni-Huntly, J. C., James, S. A., Becker, C., Hames, C. G., & Heyden, S. (1978). Frequency of church attendance and blood pressure elevation. *Journal of Behavioral Medicine, 1,* 37–43.

Greeley, A. M. (1974). *Ecstasy: A way of knowing.* Englewood Cliffs, NJ: Prentice-Hall.

Greenwald, A. (1975). Does the Good Samaritan parable increase helping? A comment on Darley and Batson's no-effect conclusion. *Journal of Personality and Social Psychology, 32*(4), 578–583.

Greil, A. L., & Rudy, D. R. (1984). What have we learned from process models of conversion? An examination of ten studies. *Sociological Focus, 17*(4), 306–323.

Hadden, J. K. (1963). An analysis of some factors associated with religion and political affiliation in a college population. *Journal for the Scientific Study of Religion, 2,* 209–216.

Hamberg, E. M. (1991). Stability and change in religious beliefs, practice, and attitudes: A Swedish panel study. *Journal for the Scientific Study of Religion, 30*(1), 63–80.

Hammond, P. E., & Hunter, J. D. (1984). On maintaining plausibility: The worldview of evangelical college students. *Journal for the Scientific Study of Religion, 23*(3), 221–238.

Hargrove, B. W. (1973). Organizational men on the frontier. *Journal for the Scientific Study of Religion, 12*(4), 461–466.

Harms, E. (1944). The development of religious experience in children. *American Journal of Sociology, 50,* 112–122.

Hartshorne, H., & May, M. A. (1928). *Studies in deceit.* New York: Macmillan.

Hassenger, R. (Ed.). (1967). *The shape of Catholic higher education.* Chicago: University of Chicago Press.

Havens, J. (Ed.). (1968). *Psychology and religion: A contemporary dialogue.* Princeton, NJ: Van Nostrand. © Belmont, CA: Wadsworth.

Hay, D. (1985). Religious experience and its induction. In L. B. Brown (Ed.), *Advances in the psychology of religion* (pp. 135–150). New York and Oxford: Pergamon Press.

Hay, D., & Morisy, A. (1978). Reports of ecstatic, paranormal, or religious experience in Great Britain and the United States: A comparison of trends. *Journal for the Scientific Study of Religion, 17*(3), 255–268.

Heller, D. (1986). *The children's God.* Chicago: University of Chicago Press.

Heller, D. (1987). *Dear God: Children's letters to God.* New York: Doubleday.

Helminiak, D. A. (1987). *Spiritual development: An interdisciplinary study.* Chicago: Loyola University Press.

Henry, W. E., Sims, J. H., & Spray, S. L. (1971). *The fifth profession.* San Francisco: Jossey-Bass.

Hill, P. C. (1994). Toward an attitude process model of religious experience. *Journal for the Scientific Study of Religion, 33*(4), 303–314.

Hill, P. C. (1995). Affective theory and religious experience. In R.W. Hood Jr. (Ed.), *Handbook of religious experience.* Birmingham, AL: Religious Education Press.

Hill, P. C., & Bassett, R. L. (1992). Getting to the heart of the matter: What the social-psychological study of attitudes has to offer psychology of religion. In M. Lynn & D. Moberg (Eds.), *Research in the Social Scientific Study of Religion, 4,* 159–182. Greenwich, CT: JAI Press.

Hites, R. W. (1965). Change in religious attitudes during four years of college. *Journal of Social Psychology, 66,* 51–63.

Hobbs, N. (1962). Sources of gain in psychotherapy. *American Psychologist, 17,* 741–747.

Hoelter, J. W., & Epley, R. J. (1979). Religious correlates of fear of death. *Journal for the Scientific Study of Religion, 18,* 404–411.

Hoffer, E. (1951). *The true believers.* New York: Harper.

Hoffman, M. L. (1970). Conscience, personality and socialization techniques. *Human Development, 13,* 90–126.

Hoffman, M. L. (1971). Identification and conscience development. *Child Development, 42,* 1071–1082.

Hoge, D. R., & Petrillo, G. H. (1978). Development of religious thinking in adolescence: A test of Goldman theories. *Journal for the Scientific Study of Religion, 17*(2), 139–154.

Hood, R. W., Jr. (1970). Religious orientation and the report of religious experience. *Journal for the Scientific Study of Religion, 9,* 285–291.

Hood, R. W., Jr. (1973). Religious orientation and experience of transcendence. *Journal for the Scientific Study of Religion, 12,* 441–448.

Hood, R. W., Jr. (1975). Construction and preliminary validation of a measure of reported mystical experience. *Journal for the Scientific Study of Religion, 14,* 29–41.

Hood, R. W., Jr. (1977). Eliciting mystical states of consciousness with semistructured nature experiences. *Journal for the Scientific Study of Religion, 16,* 155–163.

Hood, R. W., Jr. (1978). The usefulness of the indiscriminately pro and anti categories of religious orientation. *Journal for the Scientific Study of Religion, 17,* 419–431.

Hood, R. W., Jr. (1992). Sin and guilt in faith traditions: Issues for self-esteem. In J. F. Schumaker (Ed.), *Religion and Mental Health* (pp. 110–121). New York: Oxford University Press.

Hood, R. W., Jr. (1995a). The facilitation of religious experience. In R.W. Hood Jr. (Ed.), *Handbook of religious experience.* Birmingham, AL: Religious Education Press.

Hood, R. W., Jr. (Ed.). (1995b). *Handbook of religious experience.* Birmingham, AL: Religious Education Press.

Hood, R. W., Jr., & Kimbrough, D. L. (1995). Serpent-handling holiness sects: Theoretical considerations. *Journal for the Scientific Study of Religion, 34*(3), 311–322.

Hood, R. W., Jr., & Morris, R. J. (1981). Sensory isolation and the differential elicitation of religious imagery in intrinsic and extrinsic persons. *Journal for the Scientific Study of Religion, 20,* 261–273.

Hood, R. W., Jr., & Morris, R. J. (1983). Toward a theory of death transcendence. *Journal for the Scientific Study of Religion, 22,* 353–365.

Hood, R. W., Jr., Morris, R. J., & Watson, P. J. (1989). Prayer experience and religious orientation. *Review of Religious Research, 31,* 39–45.

Hood, R. W., Jr., Spilka, B., Hunsberger, B., & Gorsuch, R. L. (in press). *The psychology of religion: An empirical approach* (2nd ed.). New York: Guilford.

Hunsberger, B. (1978). The religiosity of college students: Stability and change over years at university. *Journal for the Scientific Study of Religion, 17*(2), 159–164.

Hunsberger, B. (1979). Sources of "Psychology of Religion" journal articles: 1950–1974. *Journal for the Scientific Study of Religion, 18,* 82–85.

Hunsberger, B. (1991). Empirical work in the psychology of religion. *Canadian Psychology, 32*(3), 497–504.

Hunsberger, B. (1995). Religion and prejudice: The role of religious fundamentalism, quest, and right-wing authoritarianism. *Journal of Social Issues, 51*(2), 113–129.

Hunsberger, B., McKenzie, B., Pratt, M., & Pancer, S. M. (1993). Religious doubt: A social psychological analysis. In M. Lynn & D. Moberg (Eds.), *Research in the Social Scientific Study of Religion, Vol. 5,* (pp. 27–51.) Greenwich, CT: JAI Press.

Hunt, R.A. (1972). Mythological-symbolic religious commitment: The LAM scales. *Journal for the Scientific Study of Religion, 11,* 42–52.

Hunt, R. A., & King, M. B. (1971). The intrinsic-extrinsic concept: A review and evaluation. *Journal for the Scientific Study of Religion, 10,* 339–356.

Huston, T. N., & Korte, C. (1976). The responsive bystander: Why he helps. In T. Lickona (Ed.), *Moral development and behavior.* New York: Holt, Rinehart & Winston.

Hyde, K. E. (1990). *Religion in childhood and adolescence: A comprehensive review of the research.* Birmingham, AL: Religious Education Press.

Jahoda, M. (1958). *Current concepts of positive mental health.* New York: Basic Books.

Jaquith, J. R. (1967). Toward a typology of formal communicative behaviors: Glossolalia. *Anthropological Linguistics, 9*(8), 1–8.

James, W. (1902). *Varieties of religious experience.* New York: Longmans. (Mentor ed., New American Library, 1958).

Jaynes, J. (1976). *The origin of consciousness in the breakdown of the bicameral mind.* Boston: Houghton Mifflin.

Johnson, B. (1966). Theology and party preference among Protestant clergymen. *American Sociological Review, 31,* 200–208.

Johnson, P. E. (1959). *Psychology of religion* (Rev. ed.). Nashville, TN: Abingdon Press.

Jolo Serpent Handlers. Karen Kramer Film Library, P.O. Box 315, 779 Susquehanna Avenue, Franklin Lakes, NJ 07417, (Film).

Jones, S. L. (1994). A constructive relationship for religion with the science and profession of psychology: Perhaps the boldest model yet. *American Psychologist, 49*(3), 184–199.

Jung, C. G. (1933). *Modern man in search of a soul.* New York: Harcourt, Brace.

Jung, C. G. (1938). *Psychology and religion.* New Haven: Yale University Press.

Kahoe, R. D. (1974). Personality and achievement correlates of intrinsic and extrinsic religious orientations. *Journal of Personality and Social Psychology, 29,* 812–818.

Kahoe, R. D., & Meadow, M. J. (1981). A developmental perspective on religious orientation dimensions. *Journal of Religion and Health, 20,* 8–17.

Kalish, R. A. (1963). Some variables in death attitudes. *Journal of Social Psychology, 59,* 137–145.

Katz, D. (1960). The functional approach to the study of attitudes. *Public Opinion Quarterly, 24,* 163–204.

Kemeny, J. G. (1959). *A philosopher looks at science.* Princeton, NJ: Van Nostrand; © Belmont, CA: Wadsworth.

Kilbourne, B., & Richardson, J. T. (1984). Psychotherapy and new religions in a pluralistic society. *American Psychologist, 39*(3), 237–251.

Kildahl, J. P. (1965). The personalities of sudden religious converts. *Pastoral Psychology, 16,* 37–44.

Kimble, M., McFadden, S. H., Ellor, J. W., & Seeber, J. J. (Eds.). (1995). *Aging, religion, and spirituality: A handbook.* Minneapolis: Fortress Press.

Kinsey, A. C., Pomeroy, W. B., & Martin, C. E. (1948). *Sexual behavior in the human male.* Philadelphia: Saunders.

Kinsey, A. C., Pomeroy, W. B., Martin, C. E., and Gebhard, P. H. (1953). *Sexual behavior in the human female.* Philadelphia: Saunders.

Kirkpatrick, L. A. (1989). A psychometric analysis of the Allport-Ross and Feagin measures of intrinsic-extrinsic religious orientation. In M. Lynn & D. Moberg (Eds.), *Research in the Social Scientific Study of Religion, Vol. 1,* (pp. 1–31). Greenwich, CT: JAI Press.

Kirkpatrick, L. A. (1992). An attachment-theoretical approach to the psychology of religion. *The International Journal for the Psychology of Religion, 2,* 3–28.

Kirkpatrick, L. A. (1995). Attachment theory and religious experience. In R. W. Hood, Jr. (Ed.), *Handbook of religious experience.* Birmingham, AL: Religious Education Press.

Kirkpatrick, L. A., & Hood, Jr., R. W. (1990). Intrisic-extrinsic orientations: Boon or bane? *Journal for the Scientific Study of Religion, 20,* 442–462.

Kirkpatrick, L. A., Hood, R. W., Jr., & Hartz, G. (1991). Fundamentalist religion conceptualized in terms of Rokeach's theory of the open and closed mind: New perspectives on some old ideas. In M. Lynn & D. Moberg (Eds.), *Research in the Social Scientific Study of Religion, Vol. 3,* (pp. 157–179). Greenwich, CT: JAI Press.

Kirkpatrick, L. A., & Shaver, P. (1990). Attachment theory and religion: Childhood attachments, religious beliefs, and conversion. *Journal for the Scientific Study of Religion, 29,* 315–334.

Kirkpatrick, L. A., & Shaver, P. R. (1992). An attachment-theoretical approach to romantic love and religious belief. *Personality and Social Psychology Bulletin, 18*(3), 266–275.

Koenig, H. G. (1990). Research on religion and mental health in later life: A review and commentary. *Journal of Geriatric Psychiatry, 23,* 23–53.

Koenig, H. G., Kvale, J. N., & Ferrel, C. (1988). Religion and well-being in later life. *The Gerontologist, 28*(1), 18–28.

Koenig, H. G., Smiley, M., & Gonzales, J. A. P. (1988). *Religion, health, and aging: A review and theoretical integration.* New York: Greenwood Press.

Kohlberg, L. (1964). Development of moral character and moral ideology. In M. L. Hoffman & L. W. Hoffman (Eds.), *Review of child development research,* Vol. 1. New York: Russell Sage Foundation.

Kohlberg, L. (1969). Stage and sequence: The cognitive-developmental approach to socialization. In D. A. Goslin (Ed.), *Handbook of socialization theory and research.* Chicago: Rand McNally.

Kuhlen, R. G., & Arnold, M. (1944). Age differences in religious beliefs and problems during adolescence. *Journal of Genetic Psychology, 65,* 291–300.

Kupky, O. (1928). *The religious development of adolescents.* New York: Macmillan.

Kwilecki, S. (1990). Religious-moral development: A case study of two Black Baptists. *Journal of the American Academy of Religion, LVIII/3,* 439–468.

Kwilecki, S. (1991). The relationship between religious development and personality development: A case study. In M. Lynn & D. Moberg (Eds.), *Research in the Social Scientific Study of Religion, Vol. 3* (pp. 59–87). Greenwich, CT: JAI Press.

La Barre, W. (1962). *They shall take up serpents: Psychology of the southern snake-handling cult.* Minneapolis: University of Minnesota Press.

Lasagna, L., Mostellar, F., von Felsinger, J. M., & Beecher, H. K. (1954). A study of the placebo response. *American Journal of Medicine, 16,* 770–779.

Larson, D. B., Koenig, B. H., Kaplan, B., Greenburg, R. S., Logue, E., & Tyroler, H. A. (1989). The impact of religion on men's blood pressure. *Journal of Religion and Health, 28,* 265–278.

Larson, C. (1979/November). The Watson-McDougall debate: "The debate of the century." *APA Monitor,* p, 3.

Lehr, E, & Spilka, B. (1989). Religion in the introductory psychology textbook: A comparison of three decades. *Journal for the Scientific Study of Religion, 28*(3), 366–371.

Lenski, G. (1963). *The religious factor* (Rev. ed.). Garden City, New York: Doubleday.

Leuba, J. H. (1896). A study in the psychology of religious phenomena. *American Journal of Psychology, 5,* 309–385.

Leuba, J. H. (1934). Religious beliefs of American scientists. *Harper's, 169,* 297.

Levin, J. S. (Ed.). (1994). *Religion in aging and health.* Thousand Oaks CA: Sage Publications.

Levin, J. S., Taylor, R. J., & Chatters, L. M. (1994). Race and gender differences in religiosity among older adults: Findings from four national surveys. *Journal of Gerontology: Social Sciences, 49,* S137–S145.

Lewis, V. L. (1974). A psychological analysis of faith. *Journal of Psychology and Theology, 2,* 97–103.

Liddon, S.C. (1989). *The dual brain, religion, and the unconscious.* Buffalo, New York: Prometheus Books.

Lindenthal, J. J., Myers, J. K., Pepper, M. P., & Stern, M. S. (1970). Mental status and religious behavior. *Journal for the Scientific Study of Religion, 9,* 143–149.

Lofland, J. (1977a). "Becoming a world-saver" revisited. *American Behavioral Scientist, 20,* 805–818.

Lofland, J. (1977b). *Doomsday cult: A study of conversion, proselytization, and maintenance of faith* (Enlarged ed.). New York: Irvington.

Lofland, J., & Stark, R. (1965). Becoming a world-saver: A theory of conversion to a deviant perspective. *American Sociological Review, 30,* 862–875.

London, P. (1970). The rescuers: Motivational hypotheses about Christians who saved Jews from the Nazis. In J. Macaulay & L. Berkowitz (Eds.), *Altruism and helping behavior.* New York: Academic Press.

Long, D., Elkind, D., & Spilka, B. (1967). The child's conception of prayer. *Journal for the Scientific Study of Religion, 6,* 101–109.

Lynn, M., & Moberg, D. (Eds.). (1989–1994). *Research in the social scientific study of religion* (Vols. 1–6). Greenwich, CT: JAI Press.

MacKay, D. M. (1974). *The clockwork image.* Downers Grove, Ill.: InterVarsity Press.

Malcom X. (1964). *The autobiography of Malcom X,* assisted by Alex Haley. New York: Grove Press.

Malony, H. N. (February, 1980). Psychology "of," "through," "and," "for," and "against" religion—The uses and abuses of the behavioral/social sciences. Paper presented to the California State Psychological Association, Pasadena, CA.

Malony, H. N. (Ed.) (1991). *Psychology of religion: Personalities, problems, possibilities.* Grand Rapids, MI: Baker Book House.

Malony, H. N., & Lovekin, A. A. (1985). *Glossolalia: Behavioral science perspectives on speaking in tongues.* New York: Oxford University Press.

Malony, H. N., & Southard, S. (Eds.) (1992). *Handbook of religious conversion.* Birmingham, AL: Religious Education Press.

Mark, V., & Ervin, F.R. (1970). *Violence and the brain.* New York: Harper & Row.

Markides, K. S. (1983). Aging, religiosity, and adjustment: A longitudinal analysis. *Journal of Gerontology, 38,* 621–625.

Marshall, G. D., & Zimbardo, P. G. (1979). Affective consequences of inadequately explained physiological arousal. *Journal of Personality and Social Psychology, 37,* 970–988.

Maslach, C. (1979). Negative emotional of biasing of unexplained arousal. *Journal of Personality and Social Psychology, 37,* 953–969.

Maslow, A. (1964). *Religions, values, and peak experiences.* New York: Viking. (Also Columbus: Ohio State University Press, 1964.)

Maslow, A. (1970). *Motivation and personality* (2nd ed.). New York: Harper & Row.

Masters, K. S., & Bergin, A. E. (1992). Religious orientation and mental health. In J.F. Schumaker (Ed.), *Religion and mental health,* (pp. 221–232). New York: Oxford.

May, R. (1967). *Psychology and the human dilemma.* Princeton, NJ: Van Nostrand.

McCallister, B. J. (1995). Cognitive theory and religious experience. In R. W. Hood, Jr. (Ed.), *Handbook of religious experience.* Birmingham, AL: Religious Education Press.

McFadden, S. H. (1995). Religion and well-being in aging persons in an aging society. *Journal of Social Issues, 52*(2), 161–175.

McFadden, S. H. (in press). Religion, spirituality, and aging. In J. E. Birren & K. W. Schaie (Eds.), *Handbook of the Psychology of Aging,* 4th ed., San Diego: Academic Press.

McIntosh, D. N. (1995). Religion-as-schema, with implications for the relation between religion and coping. *The International Journal for the Psychology of Religion, 5*(1), 1–16.

McIntosh, D., & Spilka, B. (1990). Religion and physical health: The role of personal faith and control beliefs. In M. Lynn & D. Moberg (Eds.), *Research in the Social Scientific Study of Religion, Vol. 2,* (pp. 167–194). Greenwich, CT: JAI Press.

Meadow, M. J., & Kahoe, R. D. (1984). *Psychology of religion: Religion in individual lives.* New York: Harper & Row.

Melton, J. G. (1986). *Encyclopedic handbook of cults in America.* New York: Garland Publishing.

Melton, J. G. (1993). *Encyclopedia of American religions* (4th ed). Detroit, MI: Gale Research, Inc.

Middlemist, R., Knowles, E., & Matter, C. (1976). Personal space invasions in the lavatory: Suggestive evidence for arousal. *Journal of Personality and Social Psychology, 33,* 541–546.

Milgram, S. (1963). Behavioral study of obedience. *Journal of Abnormal and Social Psychology, 67,* 371–378.

Milgram, S. (1965). Some conditions of obedience and disobedience to authority. *Human Relations, 18,* 57–75.

Mischel, W. (1968). *Personality and assessment.* New York: Wiley.

Moberg, D. O. (1971). Religious practices. In M. P. Strommen (Ed.), *Research on religious development.* New York: Hawthorn Books.

Moody, E. J. (1974). Urban witches. In J. P. Spradley & D. W. McCurdy (Eds.), *Conformity and conflict: Readings in cultural anthropology* (2nd ed.), (pp. 326–336). Boston: Little, Brown & Co.

Morton, A. Q. (Nov. 3, 1963). A computer challenges the church. *The Observer.*

Mowrer, O. H. (1960). Some constructive features of the concept of sin. *Journal of Counseling Psychology, 7,* 185–188.

Mowrer, O. H. (1961). *The crisis in psychiatry and religion.* Princeton. NJ: Van Nostrand.

Narramore, B. (1973). Perspectives on the integration of psychology and theology. *Journal of Psychology and Theology, 1,* 3–18.

Newton, J., & Mann, L. (1980). Crowd size as a factor in the persuasion process: A study of religious crusade meetings. *Journal of Personality and Social Psychology, 39*(5), 874–883.

Nye, W. C., & Carlson, J. S. (1984). The development of the concept of God in children. *Journal of Genetic Psychology, 145,* 137–142.

Oates, W. E. (1973). *The psychology of religion.* Waco, TX: Word Books.

Oliner, S. P., & Oliner, P. M. (1988). *The altruistic personality: Rescuers of Jews in Nazi Europe.* New York: Free Press.

Oser, F. (1991). The development of religious judgment. In F. K. Oser & W. G. Scarlett (Eds.), *Religious development in childhood and adolescence* (pp. 5–25). San Francisco: Jossey-Bass.

Oser, F., & Gmünder, P. (1991). *Religious judgement: A developmental perspective.* Birmingham, AL: Religious Education Press.

Oser, F., & Scarlett, W. G. (Eds.). (1991). *Religious development in childhood and adolescence.* San Francisco: Jossey-Bass.

Otto, R. (1923/1950). *The idea of the holy* (2nd ed.) New York: Oxford University Press (1st ed. 1923). [Translated by John W. Harvey.]

Pahnke, W. N. (1970). Drugs and mysticism. In B. Aaronson & H. Osmond (Eds.), *Psychedelics: The uses and implications of hallucinogenic drugs* (pp. 145–165). New York: Doubleday.

Paloutzian, R. F. (1976). Values and conversion. Unpublished research.

Paloutzian, R. F. (1981). Purpose in life and value changes following conversion. *Journal of Personality and Social Psychology, 41,* 1153–1160.

Paloutzian, R. F. (1983). *Invitation to the psychology of religion.* Glenview, IL: Scott, Foresman.

Paloutzian, R. F. (1986). Psychology of religion as a medium of communication with general psychology. *Journal of Psychology and Christianity, 5,* 62–66. Reprinted in H.

N. Malony (Ed.), *Psychology of religion: Personalities, problems, possibilities* (pp. 491–496). Grand Rapids, MI: Baker Book House, 1991.

Paloutzian, R. F. (1994). Doing psychology of religion in year APA 101. *Psychology of Religion Newsletter, 19*(1), 1–7.

Paloutzian, R. F., & Ellison, C. W. (1982). Loneliness, spiritual well-being, and the quality of life. In L. A. Peplau & D. Perlman (Eds.), *Loneliness: A sourcebook of current theory, research, and therapy.* New York: Wiley-Interscience.

Paloutzian, R. F., & Ellison, C. W. (1991). *Manual for the spiritual well-being scale.* Nyack, New York: Life Advance Inc.

Paloutzian R. F., Jackson, S. L., & Crandall, J. E. (1978). Conversion experience, belief system, and personal and ethical attitudes. *Journal of Psychology and Theology, 6,* 266–275.

Paloutzian, R. F., & Kirkpatrick, L. A. (Eds.). (1995). Religious influences on personal and societal well-being. *Journal of Social Issues* [Whole issue], *51*(2).

Paloutzian, R. F., & Santrock, J. (in press). The psychology of religion. In J. Santrock, *Psychology,* 5th ed. (Chapter REL). Minneapolis, MN: Brown & Benchmark.

Paloutzian, R. F., & Smith, B. S. (1995). The utility of the religion-as-schema model. *The International Journal for the Psychology of Religion, 5,* 17–22.

Paloutzian, R. F., & Wilhelm, R. (1983). *Faith and works: A behavioral study of religion, cheating, and altruism.* Paper presented at the meeting of the American Psychological Association, Anaheim, CA.

Pargament, K. I. (1992). Of means and ends: Religion and the search for significance. *The International Journal for the Psychology of Religion, 2*(4), 201–229.

Pargament, K. I., Brannick, M. T., Adamakos, H., Ensing, D. S., Keleman, M. L., Warren, R. K., Falgout, K., Cook, P., & Myers, J. (1987). Indiscriminate pro-religiousness: Conceptualization and measurement. *Journal for the Scientific Study of Religion, 26*(2), 182–200.

Pargament, K. I., Maton, K. I., & Hess, R. E. (Eds.). (1992). *Religion and prevention in mental health: Research, vision, and action.* New York: Haworth Press.

Pargament, K. I., & Park, C. L. (1995). Merely a defense? The variety of religious means and ends. *Journal of Social Issues, 51*(2), 13–32.

Pargament, K. I., Steele, R. E., & Tyler, F. B. (1979). Religious participation, religious motivation and individual psycho-social competence. *Journal for the Scientific Study of Religion, 18,* 412–419.

Parker, C. A. (1971). Changes in religious beliefs of college students. In M. P. Strommen (Ed.), *Research on religious development: A comprehensive handbook.* New York: Hawthorn Books.

Patrick, T., with Dulack, T. (1976). *Let our children go!* New York: Thomas Congdon Books/E. P. Dutton.

Pavlov, I. P. (1927). *Conditioned reflexes.* (G. V. Anrep, trans.). London: Oxford University Press.

Peatling, J. H. (1974). Cognitive development in pupils in grades 4–12: The incidence of concrete and abstract religious thinking in American children. *Character Potential, 7*(1), 52–61.

Peatling, J. H. (1977). Cognitive development: Religious thinking in children, youth, and adults. *Character Potential, 8*(2), 100–115.

Peatling, J. H., & Laabs, C. W. (1975). Cognitive development of pupils in grades 4–12: A comparative study of Lutheran and Episcopalian children and youth. *Character Potential, 7*(2), 107–115.

Peatling, J. H., Laabs, C. W., & Newton, T. B. (1975). Cognitive development: A three-sample comparison of means on the Peatling Scale of Religious Thinking. *Character Potential, 7*(3), 159–162.

Persinger, M. A. (1987). *Neuropsychological bases of God beliefs.* New York: Praeger.

Piaget, J. (1932). *The moral judgment of the child.* Translated by Marjorie Gabain. New York: Free Press, 1965.

Piaget, J. (1972). Intellectual evolution from adolescence to adulthood. *Human Development, 15*, 1–12.

Piaget, J., & Inhelder, B. (1969). *The psychology of the child.* (H. Weaver, trans.). New York: Basic Books.

Popper, K. R. (1963). *Conjectures and refutations.* London: Routledge and Kegan Paul. New York: Basic Books.

Popper, K. R. (1972). *Objective knowledge: An evolutionary approach.* New York: Oxford University Press.

Pressman, P., Lyons, J. S., Larson, D. B., & Gartner, J. (1992). Religion, anxiety, and fear of death. In J. F. Schumaker (Ed.), *Religion and mental health* (pp. 98–109). New York: Oxford University Press.

Propst, L. R. (1992). Comparative efficacy of religious and non-religious cognitive-behavioral therapy for the treatment of clinical depression in religious individuals. *Journal of Consulting and Clinical Psychology, 60*, 94–103.

Proudfoot, W. (1985). *Religious experience.* Berkeley: University of California Press.

Pruyser, P. W. (1987). Where do we go from here? Scenarios for the psychology of religion. *Journal for the Scientific Study of Religion, 26*(2), 173–181.

Ragan, C., Malony, H. N., & Beit-Hallahmi, B. (1980). Psychologists and religion: Professional factors and personal belief. *Review of Religious Research, 21*, 208–217.

Rambo, L. R. (1993). *Understanding religious conversion.* New Haven, CT: Yale University Press.

Rambo, L. R., & Reh, L. A. (1992). The phenomenology of conversion. In H. N. Malony & S. Southard (Eds.), *Handbook of religious conversion* (pp. 229–258). Birmingham, AL: Religious Education Press.

Raschke, V. (1973). Dogmatism and religiosity, committed and consensual. *Journal for the Scientific Study of Religion, 12*, 339–344.

Reich, K. H. (1991). The role of complementarity reasoning in religious development. In F. K. Oser & W. G. Scarlett (Eds.), *Religious development in childhood and adolescence* (pp. 77–89). San Francisco: Jossey-Bass.

Reich, K. H. (1992). Religious development across the lifespan: Conventional and cognitive developmental approaches. In B. L. Featherman, R. M. Lerner, & M. Perlmutter (Eds.), *Lifespan development and behavior, Vol. 11* (pp. 145–188). Hillsdale, NJ: Erlbaum.

Rest, J. R. (1986). *Manual for the defining issues test* (3rd ed.). Center for the Study of Ethical Development, University of Minnesota, Minneapolis.

Rest, J. R., Thoma, S. J., Moon, Y. L., & Getz, I. R. (1986). Different cultures, sexes, and religions. In J. R. Rest & Robert Barnett (Eds.), *Moral development: Advances in theory and research* (pp. 89–132). New York: Praeger.

Rice, F. P. (1975). *The adolescent: Development, relationships, and culture.* Boston: Allyn.

Richards, P. S. (1991). The relation between conservative religious ideology and principled moral reasoning: A review. *Review of Religious Research, 32*(4), 359–368.

Richards, P. S., & Davison, M. L. (1992). Religious bias in moral development research: A psychometric investigation. *Journal for the Scientific Study of Religion, 31*(4), 467–485.

Richardson, J. T. (1978). *Conversion careers: In and out of new religions.* Beverly Hills, CA: Sage.

Richardson, J. T. (1985a). The active vs. passive convert: Paradigm conflict in conversion/recruitment research. *Journal for the Scientific Study of Religion, 24*(2), 119–236.

Richardson, J. T. (1985b). Psychological and psychiatric studies of new religions. In L. B. Brown (Ed.), *Advances in the psychology of religion* (pp. 209–223). Oxford: Pergamon Press.

Richardson, J. T. (1989). The psychology of induction: A review and interpretation. In M. Galanter (Ed.), *Cults and new religious movements: A report of the American Psychiatric Association* (pp. 211–238). Washington, DC: American Psychiatric Association.

Ritzema, R. J. (1979). Religiosity and altruism: Faith without works? *Journal of Psychology and Theology, 7,* 105–113.

Rizzuto, A-M. (1979). *The birth of the living God: A psychoanalytic study.* Chicago: University of Chicago Press.

Rizzuto, A-M. (1991). Religious development: A psychoanalytic point of view. In F. K. Oser and G. Scarlett (Eds.), *Religious development in childhood and adolescence* [New Directions for Child Development, #52], (pp. 47–60). San Francisco: Jossey-Bass.

Robbins, T. (1988). *Cults, converts, and charisma: The sociology of new religious movements.* Newbury Park, CA: Sage Publications.

Robert Hogan (1979, April). *APA Monitor,* pp. 4–5.

Robinson, J. P., & Shaver, P. R. (Eds.). (1973). *Measures of social psychological attitudes.* Ann Arbor, MI: Institute for Social Research.

Robinson, J. P., Shaver, P. R., & Wrightsman, L. S. (Eds.). (1991). *Measures of personality and social psychological attitudes: Volume 1 in measures of social psychological attitudes series.* San Diego: Academic Press.

Roehlkepartain, E. C., & Benson, P. L. (1993). *Youth in Protestant churches.* Minneapolis, MN: Search Institute.

Rogers, C. (1961). *On becoming a person.* Boston: Houghton Mifflin.

Rokeach, M. (1956). Political and religious dogmatism: A alternative to the authoritarian personality. *Psychological Monographs, 70* (whole no. 425).

Rokeach, M. (1960). *The open and closed mind.* New York: Basic Books.

Rokeach, M. (1964). *The three Christs of Ypsilanti.* New York: Knopf.

Rokeach, M. (1973). *The nature of human values.* New York: Free Press.

Rosenau, T. M. (1992). *Post-modernism and social sciences: Insights, inroads, and intrusions.* Princeton, NJ: Princeton University Press.

Sagan, C. (1994, December 4th). Channelling and faith healing—scam or miracle? *Parade Magazine,* pp. 10–11.

Salzman, L. (1953). The psychology of religious and ideological conversion. *Psychiatry, 16,* 177–187.

Salzman, L. (1966). Types of religious conversion. *Pastoral Psychology, 17,* 8–20.

Samarin, W. J. (1972). *Tongues of men and angels.* New York: Macmillan.

Sanua, V. D. (1969). Religion, mental health, and personality: A review of empirical studies. *American Journal of Psychiatry, 125,* 1203–1213.

Sapp, G. L., & Jones, L. (1986). Religious orientation and moral judgment. *Journal for the Scientific Study of Religion, 25*(2), 208–214.

Sargant, W. (1957). *Battle for the mind: A physiology of conversion and brainwashing.* New York: Harper & Row.

Schachter, S., & Rodin, J. (1974). *Obese humans and rats.* Hillsdale, NJ: Lawrence Earlbaum.

Schachter, S., & Singer, J. E. (1962). Cognitive, social, and physiological determinants of emotional state. *Psychological Review, 69,* 379–399.

Schumaker, J. F. (Ed.). (1992). *Religion and Mental Health.* New York: Oxford University Press.

Scobie, G. E. W. (1973). Types of Christian conversion. *Journal of Behavioral Science, 1,* 265–271.

Scobie, G. E. W. (1975). *Psychology of religion.* New York: Halsted Press, Wiley.

Scroggs, J. R., & Douglas, W. G. T. (1976). Issues in the psychology of religious conversion. *Journal of Religion and Health, 6,* 204–216.

Sethi, S. & Seligman, M. E. P. (1993). Optimism and fundamentalism. *Psychological Science, 4,* 256–259.

Shand, J. D. (1990). A forty-year follow-up of the religious beliefs and attitudes of a sample of Amherst College grads. In M. Lynn & D. Moberg (Eds.), *Research in the Social Scientific Study of Religion,* Vol. 2, (pp. 117–136). Greenwich, CT: JAI Press.

Singer, M. T. (1979, January). Coming out of the cults. *Psychology Today,* 72–82.

Skinner, B. F. (1953). *Science and human behavior.* New York: Macmillan.

Skinner, B. F. (1972). *Beyond freedom and dignity.* New York: Knopf.

Smart, N. (1989). *The world's religions.* Englewood Cliffs, NJ: Prentice Hall.

Smith, M. B. (1994). Selfhood at risk: Postmodern perils and the perils of postmodernism. *American Psychologist, 49*(5), 405–411.

Smith, R. E., Wheeler, G., & Diener, E. (1975). Faith without works: Jesus people, resistance to temptation, and altruism. *Journal of Applied Social Psychology, 5,* 320–330.

Snow, D., & Phillips, C. (1980). The Lofland-Stark conversion model: A critical reassessment. *Social Problems, 27,* 430–447.

Soderstrom, D., & Wright, W. E. (1977). Religious orientation and meaning in life. *Journal of Clinical Psychology, 33,* 65–68.

Sontag, F. (1977). *Sun Myung Moon and the unification church.* Nashville, TN: Abindgon Press.

Spellman, C. M., Baskett, G. D., & Byrne, D. (1971). Manifest anxiety as a contributing factor in religious conversion. *Journal of Counseling and Clinical Psychology, 36,* 245–247.

Sperry, R. (1983). *Science and moral priority: Merging mind, brain, and human values.* New York: Columbia University Press.

Spilka, B., Comp, G., & Goldsmith, W. M. (1981). Faith and behavior: religion in introductory psychology texts of the 1950's and 1970's. *Teaching of Psychology, 8,* 158–160.

Spilka, B., Hood, Jr., R. W., & Gorsuch, R. L. (1985). *The psychology of religion: An empirical approach.* Englewood Cliffs, NJ: Prentice-Hall.

Spilka, B., & McIntosh, D. N. (1995). Attribution theory and religious experience. In R.W. Hood Jr. (Ed.), *Handbook of religious experience.* Birmingham, AL: Religious Education Press.

Spilka, B., & Reynolds, J. (1965). Religion and prejudice: A factor-analytic study. *Review of Religious Research, 6,* 163–168.

Spilka, B., Shaver, P., & Kirkpatrick, L. A. (1985). A general attribution theory for the psychology of religion. *Journal for the Scientific Study of Religion, 24*(1), 1–20.

Spilka, B., & Werme, P. H. (1971). Religion and mental disorder: A research perspective. In M. P. Strommen (Ed.), *Research on religious development.* New York: Hawthorn Books.

Stanley, G. (1964). Personality and attitude correlates of religious conversion. *Journal for the Scientific Study of Religion, 4,* 60–63.

Stanovich, K. E. (1992). *How to think straight about psychology,* 3rd ed. New York: Harper Collins.

Starbuck, E. D. (1897). A study of conversion. *American Journal of Psychology, 8,* 268–309.

Starbuck, E. D. (1899). *The psychology of religion.* London: Walter Scott.

Stark, R. (1963). On the incompatibility of religion and science: A survey of American graduate students. *Journal for the Scientific Study of Religion, 3,* 3–20. (Also in Glock & Stark, 1965.)

Stark, R. (1971). Psychopathology and religious commitment. *Review of Religious Research, 12,* 165–176. (Also in Tisdale, 1980).

Stark, R., & Bainbridge, W. S. (1985). *The future of religion: Secularization, revival, and cult formation.* Berkeley and Los Angeles, University of California Press.

Stark, R., & Glock, C. Y. (1968). *American piety.* Berkeley: University of California Press.

Stoner, C., & Parke, J. (1977). *All God's children: The cult experience—salvation or slavery?* New York: Penguin.

Strickland, B. R., & Weddell, S. C. (1972). Religious orientation, racial prejudice, and dogmatism: A study of Baptists and Unitarians. *Journal for the Scientific Study of Religion, 11,* 395–399.

Strommen, M. P. (Ed.). (1971). *Research on religious development.* New York: Hawthorne.

Survey of College Freshmen. (1974). *Intellect, 102,* 482.

Tamminen, K. (1991). *Religious development in childhood and youth: An empirical study.* Helsinki: Suomen Tiedeakatemia. (Finnish Academy of Science and Letters, Tiedekirja, Kirkkokatu 14, 00170, Helsinki, Finland.)

Tamminen, K. (1994). Religious experiences in childhood and adolescence: A viewpoint of religious development between the ages of 7 and 20. *The International Journal for the Psychology of Religion, 4*(2), 61–85.

Tamminen, K., & Nurmi, K. E. (1995). Developmental theories and religious experience. In R. W. Hood, Jr. (Ed.), *Handbook of religious experience.* Birmingham, AL: Religious Education Press.

Taylor, S. E., & Brown, J. D. (1988). Illusion and well-being: A social psychological perspective on mental health. *Psychological Bulletin, 103*(2), 193–210.

Thompson, A. D. (1974). Open-mindedness and indiscriminate anti-religious orientation. *Journal for the Scientific Study of Religion, 13,* 471–477.

Thouless, R. H. (1971). *An introduction to the psychology of religion* (3rd ed.). London: Cambridge University Press.

Thurstone, L. L., & Chave, E. J. (1929). *The measurement of attitude.* Chicago: University of Chicago Press.

Tillich, P. J. (1952). *The courage to be.* New Haven: Yale University Press.

Tillich, P. J. (1963). *Systematic theology.* Chicago: University of Chicago Press. (See also Tillich, P., *Ultimate concern, Tillich in dialogue.* [D. Brown, Ed.] . New York: Harper, 1965.)

Time (1978, December 4). Nightmare in Jonestown. *112*(23), 16–27.

Time (1987, March 16). Offering the hope of heaven. *129*(11), 69.

Time (1993a, March 15). Cult of death. *141*(11), 36–39.

Time (1993b, May 3). Tragedy in Waco. *141*(18), 26–43.

Tisdale, J. R. (Ed.). (1980). *Growing edges in the psychology of religion.* Chicago: Nelson-Hall.

Today Program. (1992, August 25). New York: National Broadcasting Company.

Ullman, C. (1982). Cognitive and emotional antecedents of religious conversion. *Journal of Personality and Social Psychology, 43,* 183–192.

Vande Kemp, H. (1992). G. Stanley Hall and the Clark school of religious psychology. *American Psychologist, 47*(2), 290–298.

Van Wicklin, J.F. (1990). Conceiving and measuring ways of being religious. *Journal of Psychology and Christianity, 9*(2), 17–40.

Ventis, W. L. (1995). The relationships between religion and mental health. *Journal of Social Issues, 51*(2), 33–48.

Waller, N. G., Kogetin, B. A., Bouchard, Jr., T. J., Lykken, D. T., & Tellegen, A. (1990). Genetic and environmental influences on religious interests, attitudes, and values: A study of twins reared apart and together. *Psychological Science, 1*(2), 138–142.

Warren, N. C. (1976). Empirical studies in the psychology of religion: An assessment of the period 1960–1970. *Journal of Psychology and Theology, 4,* 63–68.

Watson, J. B. (1925). *Behaviorism.* Chicago: University of Chicago Press.

Watson, P. J., Morris, R. J., & Hood, R. W., Jr. (1987). Antireligious humanistic values, guilt, and self-esteem. *Journal for the Scientific Study of Religion, 26,* 535–546.

Weiner, B. (1993). On sin versus sickness: A theory of perceived responsibility and social motivation. *American Psychologist, 48*(9), 957–965

Wicker, A. W. (1969a). Size of church membership and members' support of church behavior-settings. *Journal of Personality and Social Psychology, 13,* 278–288.

Wicker, A. W. (1969b). Attitudes versus actions: The relationship of verbal and overt behavioral responses to attitude objects. *Journal of Social Issues, 25,* 41–78.

Wicker, A. W. (1971). Assimilation of new members in a large and a small church. *Journal of Applied Psychology, 55,* 151–156.

Wiebe, K. F., & Fleck, J. R. (1980). Personality correlates of intrinsic, extrinsic, and nonreligious orientations. *The Journal of Psychology, 105,* 181–187.

Woodberry, J. D. (1992). Conversion in Islam. In H. N. Malony & S. Southard (Eds.), *Handbook of religious conversion* (pp. 22–40). Birmingham, AL: Religious Education Press.

Wright, S. A. (1984). Post-involvement attitudes of voluntary defectors from controversial new religious movements. *Journal for the Scientific Study of Religion, 23*(2), 172–182.

Wright, S. A. (1987). *Leaving cults: The dynamics of defection.* Washington D.C.: Society for the Scientific Study of Religion. [Business office: Pierce Hall, Room 193, Purdue University, West Lafayette, Indiana.]

Wulff, D. M. (1991). *Psychology of religion: Classic and contemporary views.* New York: John Wiley & Sons.

Wuthnow, R., & Glock, C. Y. (1973). Religious loyalty, defection, and experimentation among college youth. *Journal for the Scientific Study of Religion, 12,* 157–180.

Yankelovich, D. (1969). *Generations apart.* New York: Columbia Broadcasting System.

Yeatts, J. R., & Asher, W. (1979). Can we afford not to do true experiments in psychology of religion? A reply to Batson. *Journal for the Scientific Study of Religion, 18,* 86–89.

Yinger, J. M. (1967). Pluralism, religion, and secularism. *Journal for the Scientific Study of Religion, 6,* 17–28.

Yinger, J. M. (1970). *The scientific study of religion.* New York: Macmillan.

Zeligs, R. (1974). *Children's experience with death.* Springfield, IL: Charles C. Thomas.

Zimbardo, P. G., et al. (1973, April 8). The mind is a formidable jailer: A Pirandellian prison. *New York Times Magazine, Sec. 6,* 38–60.

Zimbardo, P. G., Ebbesen, E. B., & Maslach, C. (1977). *Influencing attitudes and changing behavior,* (2nd ed.). Reading, MA: Addison-Wesley.

Author Index

Subject Index

Abortion and religion, 223, 224
Achievement, 246–247
Adolescents
   and conversion, 164
   and cults, 164
   doubt in, 108–111
   religious behavior in, 107–108
   religious development in, 106–111, 124–127
Adults
   religious development in, 127–135
   religious stability, 132–135
   and spirituality, 127–129, 135–137
Age
   as factor in conversion, 164–165
Aging and religiousness, 127–135
Aggression
   and religion, 3, 237
Agnosticism. *See* Doubt
Altered consciousness. *See* Experience; Religious Experience
The American Journal of Religious Psychology and Education, 39
American Psychological Association, 43, 51
Anxiety, 163, 249–251, 253–254, 257
Associations, professional 51
Attachment theory, 49, 86–89, 179, 193–194
Attitude(s)
   authoritarian, 229–230, 241–244
   faith as an, 165–166, 186–187
   prejudiced, 206–210. *See* Religious orientation
   toward religion, 42
Attribution theory, 49, 190–193
Augustine, St., 5, 237
Authoritarianism, 49, 229–230, 241–246
   and fundamentalism, 229
   right-wing, 49, 229–231, 244

Baha'i, 16, 162
Behavior
   in adolescents, 107–108
   in adults, 129–135
   aggressive, 219, 237
   and belief, 20, 89–90, 213–224
   conditioning of, 26

   helping, 216–219
   moral, and religion, 213–219
   negative, 219
   odd, in religious people, 237
   religious, 4–6, 11–12, 16–18, 20, 222–224
   rescuing, 218–219
   sexual, 150, 166, 223, 237
Behaviorism, 26, 56
Belief
   and behavior, 15, 21, 89–90, 213–224
   dimension of religious commitment, 15–16
   liberal vs. conservative, 227
   orthodoxy of, and authoritarianism, 229–230, 241–246
   in supreme being. *See* Gallup Poll data
   versus practice, 15, 21, 89
Beyond Freedom and Dignity, 56
"Blind faith," 14, 15
"Born-again" believers, 142, 143, 243
Brain-mind theory, 194–195
Brainwashing, 16. *See also* Conversion, 167–169
Buddhism, 10
Bunyan, John, 237

Catholicism, 82, 178, 189–190, 237
Causality, 61–62
Charismatic renewal movement, 143
Children. *See also* Development
   conversion of, 103
   needs in, 86–89
   and moral development, 90–95
   family influences, 86–89
   and religion, 89–90, 240–241
   religious development in, 82–90, 95–102
   religious socialization of, 147–149
Children of God, 140, 144
Christianity. *See* specific denominations
Church attendance
   and aggressive behavior, 221
   and anxiety, 251
   and authoritarianism, 242
   and competence and coping, 253
   and fear of death, 257
   and opinion on abortion, 223–224